INDIE FONTS 3

A Compendium of Digital Type from Independent Foundries

Richard Kegler
James Grieshaber
Tamye Riggs
Editors

ROCKPORT

Library of Congress Control Number: 2006928773

ISBN-13: 978-1-59253-313-8
ISBN-10: 1-59253-313-2

Published by:
Rockport Publishers, Inc., a member of
Quayside Publishing Group
100 Cummings Center
Suite 406-L
Beverly, MA 01915-6101
Phone: (978) 282-9590
Fax: (978) 283-2742

10 9 8 7 6 5 4 3 2

Designed in the USA
Printed and bound in China

Contents

Introduction

Even today's casual computer user knows their serifs from their sans but may not care about the controversies surrounding the mysterious origin of Times and the shamelessly inferior imitation of Helvetica that is Arial. The fact remains that all typefaces have some traceable origin, and new ones are designed every year. So the recurring question is— do we really need more fonts? Beyond a basic serif and sans serif and a Comic Sans for the kids, who needs more? The same argument could be made about painting (do we need another portrait?) or, more accurately, about music. New songs may recall older melodies or be intentional riffs (rips), with some occasionally breaking new ground. As in the music industry, the font business has its established major labels and upstart indies. Yves Peters tackles the topic of the need for more indie fonts (and more *Indie Fonts*) in his essay included here.

Fonts are not just cool things that magically appear on computers and the internet. The decision to make a font is a commitment to dedicate time, effort, and personal attachment to a design that will be offered up to the cold, cruel world. The business side of type design is the doppelganger of the independent foundry—but a necessary side if a designer wishes to market his own work. A major business connection between foundry and user is the EULA (End User License Agreement). All software has one, but most people don't read them. In the second essay in this book, Tiffany Wardle makes a case for why the EULA is not so awful to read and can actually help typographers understand the legally allowed uses of fonts.

The previous two volumes of *Indie Fonts* showcased a wide variety of type from independent designers working from small studios. *Indie Fonts 3* features twenty more foundries in an exploration of the diverse styles and personalities found in the world of type today. The types in this book range from solid text faces to whimsical display designs and cheeky dingbats. The featured designers run the gamut from magazine designers and photographers to students of the American Wild West and tiki culture. Each foundry has fonts included on the bonus CD, with a license for use extended to the individual who owns this book.

For those who know that Times and Arial were not designed for use on absolutely everything, there are plenty of type designers who create fonts with subtleties that will enhance and complement a variety of creative work. The trick is finding the perfect font for your project— it's not as easy as seems. Luckily, the three-volume *Indie Fonts* reference library puts thousands of font specimens is at your fingertips. Proceed with enthusiasm and caution.

—The Editors

Foreword:

Eight Is *Not* Enough

By Yves Peters

Late in 2005, I received a pretty unexpected question by email: "Does the world need another volume of *Indie Fonts*?" My gut reaction was, "Hell yeah, of course we can use more *Indie Fonts*!" But once I started thinking this through, it became less obvious. Aren't these books a little redundant? We have FontBook, a veritable bible of digital type that features a large number of independents. Most of the smaller foundries' fonts are available on thewebsites of large online distributors. On top of the web-based exposure, type distributors occasionally send out printed catalogues. So, yes, why is it that, although I'm a *FontBook* devotee, I had to buy both *Indie Fonts* and *Indie Fonts 2* as soon as they came out? And why would we need yet another volume of *Indie Fonts*? What makes these books so appealing, and, in my opinion, so indispensable?

Erik Spiekermann (the sharp-dressed, globetrotting founder of FontShop and MetaDesign) told me fifteen years ago that "the future belongs to the independent foundries." Boy, was he right on the money. After the democratization of the type design process (thanks to the lightning-fast adoption of desktop publishing systems), the grunge boom in typography and design proved to be the equivalent of popular music's punk revolution. Just as punk incited hordes of enthusiasts to pick up electric guitars and start banging away thirty years ago, in the early 1990s, a whole lot of people started designing fonts.

The notion that this arcane craft was reserved for a select few soon gave way to a sense of freedom and unlimited possibilities. During the initial flood of type from "the masses," much of the output was amateurish and derivative. But distinct creative voices rapidly emerged, and a whole new generation of daring type designers was soon establishing its reputation. And the way type was marketed and sold changed: rather than sign on with major foundries and be swallowed up by those face-less behemoths, individual designers used the internet to self-publish and sell directly to the end user, or as a means of associating with smaller independent foundries. Outfits such as Emigre, FontFont, T-26, and GarageFonts led by example, showing the way to dozens of budding foundries.

These days, most innovation in type comes from the independents. It makes perfect sense—the independent type designer is the straight line, the shortest trajectory from creator to user of digital type. There's no marketing department that might influence creative decisions, no sales-people who might misinterpret and misrepresent the designer's inten-tions, and no shareholders whose interests might conflict with the designer's vision. It's the transmission of the love of type in its purest from, like an intravenous injection of the designer's undiluted creative force straight into the arm of the type user. That's what makes the work so exciting and refreshing.

One can draw a parallel with the current situation in the music business. The commercialization of popular music somehow, somewhere, got completely out of hand. Major music companies treat music like a simple commodity. The sole objective of these monolithic conglomerates is to make as large a profit as possible, and the fact that it's through selling music is purely circumstantial. Bands and performers are systematically built and popularized through television programming. Music companies feed the audience formulaic, manufactured pap, catering to the lowest common denominator, and sell the "product" using sex—check out the videos that go with the songs. Rather than attribute the crisis of declining album sales to the practice of illegal downloading, the majors might want to take a long hard look at themselves and the homogenous, disposable music they market.

To find real music, quality music, the *good* stuff, there's nowhere to turn but the independent labels. Innovation and unprocessed talent lives on through the indies as they batter at the towering wall of bland erected by big music. Sometimes they're successful in breaking through; sometimes they're not.

Which brings us back to the independent type foundry. Its greatest strength—its independence—is, at the same time, its biggest weakness. A privately owned and operated retail website has its limits. In his quest to find an (new) audience, the indie font creator doesn't usually have the financial resources needed to advertise adequately. The obvious solution is for the little guy to join forces with a large distributor. This has a major drawback, though: small type collections tend to get lost among the hundreds, sometimes thousands of fonts offered by the majors. Apart from the odd promotion, most indies have a hard time standing out in the crowd. The *Indie Fonts* books enable them to reach a wider audience and still maintain their unique identity.

One of the most important aspects of the *Indie Fonts* series is that the font showings are grouped by foundry. Whereas at the large vendors the font families of a particular foundry are strewn throughout their catalogs and websites, here you can actually get the feel of a library, taste its specific flavor. It's fascinating to see how the different fonts by a single designer or foundry interact with one another and reveal common themes. Much more than with major foundries, this helps them develop a recognizable identity, creating a brand-like quality.

This is exactly what made me notice the Latin sensuality of Feliciano's Spanish revivals, the forward-thinking—but subtly so—collection of Psy/Ops, the stylish class of Typotheque, the futuristic techno of Identikal, the vintage Americana of Parkinson, the oblique modernism of the Test Pilot Collective, the playfulness of Underware…I could go on and on. The first two *Indie Fonts* opened up a whole new world of type delicacies to a large audience, because the format does *all* of the featured foundries justice, allowing them to present themselves in the best possible light, which ultimately benefits the reader/user.

Just as in the two previous volumes, the diversity of the work presented in this catalog is impressive. The fonts range from graffiti with an attitude to exquisite fine typography, from faithful historical revivals via fashionable interpretations of period type to cutting-edge contemporary designs. Offerings range from straightforward PostScript Type 1 and TrueType to feature-rich OpenType fonts whose capabilities border on artificial intelligence. There are established names next to young upstarts, compact libraries with just a handful of fonts alongside extensive collections, and even a type co-op that assembles some of the brightest talents in type design today. All this and more is presented in another lush, beautifully produced tome.

These books do not pretend to be timeless, all-encompassing Bibles of digital type. No, they are fascinating snapshots of the current state of the type industry that show who's actively furthering the craft and making valuable additions to the type canon today. And still, unavoidably, there are people missing—Iñigo Jerez Quintana (Textaxis), whose Quixote won in the serif category of the Type Directors Club TDC2 2006 type design competition, Tim Ahrens (Just Another Foundry), whose peculiar Leipziger Antiqua revival Lapture has everyone talking, Dino Santos (DSType Foundry), whose exquisite Andrade won the *Creative Review* Type Design Awards for Best Revival/Extension family, OurType, which carries the designs of Dutch mainstays Fred Smeijers and Peter Verheul—to name just a few. There are still a lot more out there, and all of these talented designers deserve to have their work in the spotlight.

So, does the world need another volume of *Indie Fonts*? Hell yeah! And three is *definitely* not enough.

Yves Peters is a designer, writer, musician, and type critic. Called a "champion of type design" by indie designer/distributor chester (Thirstype/Village), Peters moderates the type identification forum at Typophile.com with a nerd's eye and a velvet fist. His typographic musings appear semi-regularly on Typographica and Typographer.org, and more often on FontShop Belgium's blog, *Unzipped*. Peters lives in Ghent, Belgium, with his lovely wife and an indeterminate number of children.

Essay:

How I Learned to Stop Worrying and Love the EULA

By Tiffany Wardle

Once upon a time, I might have said that an End User License Agreement (EULA) was just a bunch of legal mumbo-jumbo—no one really cared whether I followed its terms, as long as I paid for the font. Today, I'm singing a different tune. Type designers and foundries *do* care. If I ignore EULAs, it could lead to bad business headaches and legal problems down the road.

Respecting the EULA goes beyond the mechanics of following the terms of a contract—it's a professional courtesy. Just as I expect my clients to understand and adhere to any contracts I might have with them, I, in turn, must do the same with the contract terms I accept when I license fonts.

All EULAs are not created equal. Every foundry has a different EULA, and every EULA has its own terms of use. Before I enter into this sort of agreement (just as with any other contract), I make it a habit to read and understand it.

My own experience has proved that it is possible to make sense of the more important clauses without wanting to poke my eyes out with a pencil from sheer frustration or stop reading out of sheer boredom. Although many EULAs are written by lawyers for lawyers, with a little patience and time, I've learned to grasp the basic concepts within the EULA. For the most part, they've ceased to hinder my creativity. I'd like to share a few key things to keep in mind when you're shopping for fonts and reading EULAs.

The License

When we "buy" a typeface, we are not actually buying fonts—we are purchasing a license to use them. It's common for all rights to be retained by the foundry, and it is up to them to define how we are allowed to use their intellectual property. As confusing and frustrating as it may be, we are expected to understand and follow their definitions of use. A license agreement typically includes a warning that we are entering into a legally binding situation and have been given information about the terms to which we will be held.

There are limitations as to what we are allowed to do with the fonts we license. Without taking the time to understand the EULA, however, breaking its terms is easier than expected. For instance, we might go over the allowed number of users and output devices, or modify a font when the foundry expressly asks us not to. We might embed the font in different file formats for distribution on the web when it's not kosher to do so. These limitations can greatly narrow the ability to use a wonderful typeface design for a given project, but we need to respect the wishes of the font's creator and/or publisher.

Grant of License

For many designers (myself included), the grant of license is one of the clauses to which particular attention should be paid. Grant of license defines how and where the font software can be used. In most EULAs, a license is granted for use on a set number of devices (usually CPUs) and/or by a specific number of users at a single location. For example, if you use offsite freelance or contract designers, you would usually be required to obtain additional licensing if the EULA is location-specific. Even though the license might allow for five users and there are only two at the licensed address, it doesn't mean that you can send the font to three freelancers working away from your site. Before you distribute the font outside your location, it's important to confirm that you're actually allowed to do so.

Embedding

When discussing embedding, most designers first think of something that is part of their everyday workflow—the PDF (Portable Document

Format). The definition of embedding goes way beyond this particular acronym, however, and includes any file format in which font software can be stored. It's such an important point that many EULAs carefully define those instances when we can and cannot embed their fonts, and the conditions under which we can and cannot share those files if embedding is allowed. Other popular embedding formats include, but are not limited to, PowerPoint presentations, Word documents, HTML via linked EOT (embedded OpenType) or PFR (portable font resource), EPS (Encapsulated PostScript) files, Flash files, and printer spool files.

Modification

Many foundries do not allow font modification. The modification of a font by an end user or third party is akin to one of your own works being changed by your client or another designer. I don't often give source files to my clients—I would rather they come to me for changes. Most designers balk at giving up their files and charge additional fees if a client insists on making their own changes or repurposing material. I would hope that the client would see the creator as the person who should perform any modifications or corrections.

Foundries that don't allow modification of their fonts usually won't budge on this point. Even though there is reasonably priced software available that would allow me to make my own modifications, the best way to warrant the continued proper function of fonts is to have the foundry do the work for me. This also gives me the right to call them when I have any kind of problem without having to explain that I made changes to a font without permission.

This is not to say that all foundries are against the modification of their fonts. Some foundries do allow for this, as long as it is for internal use only and is not resold or given away as "your" creation. Be very clear on the EULA terms before modifying your licensed fonts.

Derivative Work

Derivative works are considered to be imitative and taken from another original source or idea. Because we do not own the rights to fonts we license, we don't have the right to create anything derivative from the font software.

With regard to fonts, being derivative usually means making another font by altering an existing font. Even for those foundries that allow this, "new" fonts made using someone else's original font software data are usually not to be resold or otherwise distributed unless the original creator specifies their font software is open source.

Derivative work isn't limited to creating another digital font—it also encompasses using a font to create another product featuring all or part of the character set, such as rubber stamps, stickers, or house numbers, or using a dingbat or image font as focal artwork in a logo or item for resale. The main point is that derivations take the font beyond the scope of use that the creator intended (such as in an ad layout), turning it into a principal "value" element. Rub-on letters or alphabet sticker sheets are essentially the font produced in a different format for resale. The authorized manufacture of these types of products more often than not requires additional licensing.

Conversation

Though it isn't possible to discuss all facets of a given EULA, I cannot stress enough the importance of thinking of foundries as business allies and not as enemies of creativity. Foundries are people too. They *are* in business to make money, and we must keep in mind that their creations assist *us* in making money. Just as we designers may use the law to protect work we've created, foundries are entitled to use the law to protect their interests. After reading a EULA, I contact the foundry if I have any questions. If you do this, you will find people who want to help and will do what they can to enable you to do your work.

As you browse for fonts online and discover your favorite foundries, keep copies of their current EULAs for reference. This will help keep you from making the same mistake that I made recently. I was working on a presentation for a client and found myself using a family of fonts from a foundry that doesn't allow embedding. You'd think that with all of the reading I've done on the subject of EULAs that this wouldn't happen, but it did. I was lucky—I was able to find a replacement font from a different foundry that does allow embedding. I explained the situation to my client (who promptly admitted that they didn't even notice the difference).

Before you sell your client on a design, read the EULAs for any fonts you are considering licensing for your project. In my case, I could have done the wrong thing and ignored the EULA, but that would have put my client and myself at a risk and wouldn't have been fair to the creator of the fonts in question.

The key thing to remember is that you shouldn't be afraid of the EULA. There are thousands of fonts available from many different foundries, and you'll be able to find one that offers the terms you need for your project. Happy hunting!

Tiffany Wardle is a graphic designer, educator, and typographer. In her quest to unlock the mysteries of the EULA, she has helped foundries and end users understand each other better. Wardle is a member of the board of directors of The Society of Typographic Aficionados, the librarian at Typophile.com, and a lover of Dwiggins and soft-serve ice cream. She lives and works in the wild world of advertising outside of Salt Lake City.

Font Style Index

	Serif					
229	Aaux Office Light	229	Altar Fractions ⅛¼⅓½⅜⅝⅞⅙½⅔ ❋ ❧	275	Beaufort Light
229	*Aaux Office Light Italic*	229	**Altar Bold**	275	*Beaufort Light Italic*
229	Aaux Office Regular	258	Amethyst Light	275	Beaufort Regular
229	*Aaux Office Regular Italic*	258	*Amethyst Light Italic*	275	*Beaufort Italic*
229	Aaux Office Medium	258	*Amethyst Light Italic Swash*	275	**Beaufort Medium**
229	*Aaux Office Medium Italic*	258	Amethyst Light SC	275	*Beaufort Medium Italic*
229	**Aaux Office Bold**	258	Amethyst Light Italic SC	275	**Beaufort Bold**
229	***Aaux Office Bold Italic***	258	*Amethyst Light Ital Sw SC*	275	***Beaufort Bold Italic***
111	ACADEMY THIN	258	Amethyst Book	275	**Beaufort Heavy**
111	**ACADEMY**	258	*Amethyst Book Italic*	275	***Beaufort Heavy Italic***
111	**ACADEMY STUNTED**	258	*Amethyst Book Italic Swash*	275	Beaufort Condensed Light
111	ACADEMY OUTLINE	258	Amethyst Book SC	275	*Beaufort Condensed Light Italic*
256	Albertan Light	258	Amethyst Book Italic SC	275	Beaufort Condensed Regular
256	*Albertan Light Italic*	258	*Amethyst Book Italic Sw SC*	275	*Beaufort Condensed Italic*
256	Albertan Light SC	258	Amethyst	275	**Beaufort Condensed Medium**
256	Albertan Light Italic SC	258	*Amethyst Italic*	275	*Beaufort Condensed Medium Italic*
256	Albertan	258	*Amethyst Italic Swash*	275	**Beaufort Condensed Bold**
256	*Albertan Italic*	258	Amethyst SC	275	***Beaufort Condensed Bold Italic***
256	Albertan SC	258	Amethyst Italic SC	275	**Beaufort Condensed Heavy**
256	Albertan Italic SC	258	*Amethyst Italic Swash SC*	275	***Beaufort Condensed Heavy Italic***
256	Albertan Bold	258	**Amethyst Bold**	275	Beaufort Ext Light
256	*Albertan Bold Italic*	258	***Amethyst Bold Italic***	275	*Beaufort Ext Light Italic*
256	Albertan Bold SC	258	***Amethyst Bold Italic Sw***	275	Beaufort Ext Regular
256	Albertan Bold Italic SC	258	**Amethyst Bold SC**	275	*Beaufort Ext Italic*
256	**Albertan Black**	258	**Amethyst Bold Italic SC**	275	**Beaufort Ext Medium**
256	***Albertan Black Italic***	258	***Amethyst Bold Ital Sw SC***	275	*Beaufort Ext Med Ital*
256	ALBERTAN TITLE	274	Artefact Regular	275	**Beaufort Ext Bold**
256	*ALBERTAN TITLE ITALIC*	274	Artefact Bold	275	***Beaufort Ext Bold Ita***
229	Altar Regular	273	Austin Regular	275	**Beaufort Ext Heavy**
229	Altar Small Caps	273	*Austin Italic*	275	***Beaufort Ext Hvy Ita***
229	Altar Petite Caps	273	**Austin Bold**	293	Billy Serif Light
		273	***Austin Bold Italic***	293	**Billy Regular**

310	Teimer Semibold	286	*Walburn Text Italic*		**Sans Serif**
310	*Teimer Semibold Italic*	287	Worldwide Regular	220	Aaux Pro Thin
310	**Teimer Bold**	287	*Worldwide Italic*	220	*Aaux Pro Thin Italic*
310	***Teimer Bold Italic***	287	WORLDWIDE SMALL CAPS	220	AAUX PRO THIN SMALL CAPS
337	That Light	287	**Worldwide Bold**	220	*AAUX PRO THIN SMALL CAPS ITALIC*
337	*That Light Italic*	287	***Worldwide Bold Italic***	220	Aaux Pro Thin OSF
337	That Book	287	**Worldwide Black**	220	*Aaux Pro Thin OSF Italic*
337	*That Book Italic*	287	**Worldwide Ultra**	221	Aaux Pro Light
338	That Medium	287	**Worldwide Bold Condensed**	221	*Aaux Pro Light Italic*
338	*That Medium Italic*	287	Worldwide Headline Regular	221	AAUX PRO LIGHT SMALL CAPS
338	**That Bold**	287	*Worldwide Headline Italic*	221	*AAUX PRO LIGHT SMALL CAPS ITALIO*
338	***That Bold Italic***	287	**Worldwide Headline Bold**	221	Aaux Pro Light OSF
339	THAT IRREGULAR	287	**Worldwide Headline Black**	221	*Aaux Pro Light OSF Italic*
339	That Open			221	Aaux Pro Regular
339	THAT SMALL CAPS			221	*Aaux Pro Regular Italic*
106	Vatican Clement			221	AAUX PRO REGULAR SMALL CAPS
106	*Vatican Gregory*			221	*AAUX PRO REGULAR SMALL CAPS I*
106	Vatican Innocent			221	Aaux Pro Regular OSF
106	Vatican Vrban			221	*Aaux Pro Regular OSF Italic*
395	**Vecta Serif**			222	Aaux Pro Medium
286	Walburn Light			222	*Aaux Pro Medium Italic*
286	Walburn Regular			222	AAUX PRO MEDIUM SMALL CAPS
286	*Walburn Italic*			222	*AAUX PRO MEDIUM SMALL CAPS I:*
286	**Walburn Bold**			222	Aaux Pro Medium OSF
286	***Walburn Bold Italic***			222	*Aaux Pro Medium OSF Italic*
286	**Walburn Black**			222	**Aaux Pro Bold**
286	***Walburn Black Italic***			222	***Aaux Pro Bold Italic***
286	**Walburn Ultra**			222	**AAUX PRO BOLD SMALL CAPS**
286	**WALBURN TOOLED CAPS**			222	***AAUX PRO BOLD SMALL CAPS ITAL***
286	Walburn Text Light			222	**Aaux Pro Bold OSF**
286	*Walburn Text Light Italic*			222	***Aaux Pro Bold OSF Italic***
286	Walburn Text Regular			223	**Aaux Pro Black**

223	Aaux Pro Black Italic
223	AAUX PRO BLACK SMALL CAPS
223	AAUX PRO BLACK SMALL CAPS I1
223	Aaux Pro Black OSF
223	Aaux Pro Black OSF Italic
223	Aaux Pro Ultra
223	Aaux Pro Poster
75	Acton Two
75	Ainsdale Medium
75	Ainsdale Medium Italic
75	Ainsdale Bold
75	Ainsdale Bold Italic
274	Alphaville Thin
274	Alphaville Thin Oblique
274	Alphaville Light
274	Alphaville Light Oblique
274	Alphaville Regular
274	Alphaville Oblique
274	Alphaville Medium
274	Alphaville Medium Oblique
274	Alphaville Bold
274	Alphaville Bold Oblique
232	Ayumi Light
232	Ayumi Light Italic
232	Ayumi Normal
232	Ayumi Normal Italic
232	Ayumi Medium
232	Ayumi Medium Italic
232	Ayumi Bold
232	Ayumi Bold Italic
112	Bank Gothic MD
112	Bank Gothic MD Cond

381	Benjamin Medium
381	Benjamin Bold
381	Benjamin Black
292	Billy Light
292	Billy Regular
292	Billy Bold
149	Bliss Pro ExtraLight
149	Bliss Pro ExtraLight Italic
149	Bliss Pro Light
149	Bliss Pro Light Italic
149	Bliss Pro Regular
149	Bliss Pro Italic
149	Bliss Pro Medium
149	Bliss Pro Medium Italic
149	Bliss Pro Bold
149	Bliss Pro Bold Italic
149	Bliss Pro ExtraBold
149	Bliss Pro ExtraBold Italic
149	Bliss Pro Heavy
149	Bliss Pro Heavy Italic
322	Botanika Lite
322	Botanika Lite Italic
322	BOTANIKA LITE SC
322	Botanika Lite Alt
322	Botanika Lite Bold
322	Botanika Lite Bold Italic
322	BOTANIKA LITE SC BOLD
322	Botanika Lite Alt Bold
322	Botanika Demi
322	Botanika Demi Italic
322	BOTANIKA DEMI SC
322	Botanika Demi Alt

322	Botanika Demi Bold
322	Botanika Demi Bold Italic
322	BOTANIKA DEMI SC BOLD
322	Botanika Demi Alt Bold
322	Botanika Lite Mono
322	Botanika Lite Mono It
322	Botanika Lite Mono Bo
322	Botanika Lite Mono Bo
322	Botanika Demi Mono
322	Botanika Demi Mono It
322	Botanika Demi Mono Bo
322	Botanika Demi Mono Bo
365	Bourgeois Light
365	Bourgeois Light Italic
366	Bourgeois Light Alternate
366	Bourgeois Light Italic Alternate
365	Bourgeois Book
365	Bourgeois Book Italic
366	Bourgeois Book Alternate
366	Bourgeois Book Italic Alt
365	Bourgeois Bold
365	Bourgeois Bold Italic
366	Bourgeois Bold Alternate
366	Bourgeois Bold Italic Alt
365	Bourgeois Ultra
365	Bourgeois Ultra Italic
366	Bourgeois Ultra Alternate
366	Bourgeois Ultra Italic Alt
365	Bourgeois Light Condensed
365	Bourgeois Light Condensed Alternate
366	Bourgeois Light Condensed Alternate
366	Bourgeois Light Condensed Italic Alternate

313	*Dederon Sans Light Italic*	262	*Dokument Cond Medium Italic*	78	***Dynasty Demi Bold Italic***
313	Dederon Sans Regular	262	Dokument Cond Medium SC	78	**Dynasty Bold**
313	*Dederon Sans Italic*	262	*Dokument Cond Medium Ital SC*	78	***Dynasty Bold Italic***
313	Dederon Sans Semibold	262	**Dokument Cond Bold**	78	**Dynasty Heavy**
313	*Dederon Sans Semibold Ita*	262	***Dokument Cond Bold Italic***	78	***Dynasty Heavy Italic***
313	**Dederon Sans Bold**	262	**Dokument Cond Bold SC**	78	English Grotesque Thin
313	***Dederon Sans Bold Italic***	262	***Dokument Cond Bold Italic SC***	78	English Grotesque Light
262	Dokument Light	262	Dokument Extra Cond Light	78	English Grotesque Med
262	*Dokument Light Italic*	262	*Dokument Extra Cond Light Italic*	78	**English Grotesque Bold**
262	Dokument Light SC	262	Dokument Extra Cond Light SC	78	**English Grotesque Ex B**
262	*Dokument Light Italic SC*	262	*Dokument Extra Cond Light Italic SC*	78	**English Grotesque Bk**
262	Dokument	262	Dokument Extra Cond	204	Family Cat
262	*Dokument Italic*	262	*Dokument Extra Cond Italic*	204	Family Cat Bob
262	Dokument SC	262	Dokument Extra Cond SC	204	Family Cat Fat
262	*Dokument Italic SC*	262	*Dokument Extra Cond Italic SC*	204	Family Dog
262	Dokument Medium	262	Dokument Extra Cond Med	204	**Family Dog Fat**
262	*Dokument Medium Italic*	262	*Dokument Extra Cond Med Italic*	278	Figgins Pro Regular
262	Dokument Medium SC	262	Dokument Extra Cond Med SC	278	*Figgins Pro Italic*
262	*Dokument Medium Italic SC*	262	*Dokument Extra Cond Med Italic SC*	278	**Figgins Pro Semibold**
262	**Dokument Bold**	262	Dokument Extra Cond Bold	278	**Figgins Pro Bold**
262	***Dokument Bold Italic***	262	*Dokument Extra Cond Bold Italic*	243	FindReplace Thin
262	**Dokument Bold SC**	262	**Dokument Extra Cond Bold SC**	243	FindReplace Light
262	***Dokument Bold Italic SC***	262	***Dokument Extra Cond Bold Italic SC***	243	FindReplace Regular
262	Dokument Cond Light	78	Dynasty Thin	243	FindReplace Medium
262	*Dokument Cond Light Italic*	78	*Dynasty Thin Italic*	243	**FindReplace Bold**
262	Dokument Cond Light SC	78	Dynasty Extra Light	243	**FindReplace Black**
262	*Dokument Cond Light Italic SC*	78	*Dynasty Extra Light Italic*	318	Fishmonger MT
262	Dokument Cond	78	Dynasty Light	319	*Fishmonger MT Italic*
262	*Dokument Cond Italic*	78	*Dynasty Light Italic*	318	Fishmonger ML
262	Dokument Cond SC	78	Dynasty Medium	319	*Fishmonger ML Italic*
262	*Dokument Cond Italic SC*	78	*Dynasty Medium Italic*	318	Fishmonger MR
262	**Dokument Cond Medium**	78	**Dynasty Demi Bold**	319	*Fishmonger MR Italic*

318	**Fishmonger MS**	318	**Fishmonger EB**	79	*Galicia Light Italic*
319	***Fishmonger MS Italic***	319	***Fishmonger EB Italic***	79	**Galicia Medium**
318	**Fishmonger MB**	318	Fishmonger EET	79	***Galicia Medium Italic***
319	***Fishmonger MB Italic***	319	*Fishmonger EET Italic*	96	**Glendale Gothic**
318	Fishmonger CT	318	Fishmonger EEL	79	Gravel Light
319	*Fishmonger CT Italic*	319	*Fishmonger EEL Italic*	79	*Gravel Light Italic*
318	Fishmonger CL	318	Fishmonger EER	79	Gravel Medium
319	*Fishmonger CL Italic*	319	*Fishmonger EER Italic*	79	*Gravel Medium Italic*
318	Fishmonger CR	318	Fishmonger EES	79	**Gravel Bold**
319	*Fishmonger CR Italic*	319	*Fishmonger EES Italic*	79	***Gravel Bold Italic***
318	Fishmonger CS	318	**Fishmonger EEB**	103	Impersonal Light
319	*Fishmonger CS Italic*	319	***Fishmonger EEB Italic***	103	Impersonal Regular
318	**Fishmonger CB**	281	Fontesque Sans Ultra Light	321	Katarine Light
319	***Fishmonger CB Italic***	281	Fontesque Sans Light	321	*Katarine Light Italic*
318	Fishmonger ECT	281	*Fontesque Sans Light Italic*	321	KATARINE SC LIGHT
319	*Fishmonger ECT Italic*	281	Fontesque Sans Regular	321	KATARINE PC LIGHT
318	Fishmonger ECL	281	*Fontesque Sans Italic*	321	**Katarine Light Bold**
319	*Fishmonger ECL Italic*	281	**Fontesque Sans Bold**	321	***Katarine Light Bold Italic***
318	Fishmonger ECR	281	***Fontesque Sans Bold Italic***	321	**KATARINE SC LIGHT BOLD**
319	*Fishmonger ECR Italic*	281	**Fontesque Sans Extra Bold**	321	**KATARINE PC LIGHT BOLD**
318	**Fishmonger ECS**	117	**FRESHBOT**	321	Katarine Medium
319	***Fishmonger ECS Italic***	348	Galaxie Polaris Light	321	*Katarine Medium Italic*
318	**Fishmonger ECB**	348	*Galaxie Polaris Light Italic*	321	KATARINE SC MEDIUM
319	***Fishmonger ECB Italic***	348	Galaxie Polaris Book	321	KATARINE PC MEDIUM
318	Fishmonger ET	348	*Galaxie Polaris Book Italic*	321	**Katarine Medium Bold**
319	*Fishmonger ET Italic*	348	Galaxie Polaris Medium	321	***Katarine Medium Bold Italic***
318	Fishmonger EL	348	*Galaxie Polaris Medium Italic*	321	**KATARINE SC MEDIUM BOLD**
319	*Fishmonger EL Italic*	348	**Galaxie Polaris Bold**	321	**KATARINE PC MEDIUM BOLD**
318	Fishmonger ER	348	***Galaxie Polaris Bold Italic***	321	Katarine Bold
319	*Fishmonger ER Italic*	348	**Galaxie Polaris Heavy**	321	*Katarine Bold Italic*
318	**Fishmonger ES**	348	***Galaxie Polaris Heavy Italic***	321	KATARINE SC BOLD
319	***Fishmonger ES Italic***	79	Galicia Light	321	KATARINE PC BOLD

321	Katarine Bold Bold	248	*Maple Bold Italic*	387	*Modus Bold Italic*
321	*Katarine Bold Bold Italic*	248	**Maple Black**	388	North Condensed Light
321	KATARINE SC BOLD BOLD	248	*Maple Black Italic*	389	Oslo Light
321	KATARINE PC BOLD BOLD	120	marshmallow	284	PANOPTICA SANS REG
244	Klavika Light	120	*marshmallow italic*	284	PANOPTICA SANS MED
244	*Klavika Light Italic*	120	marshmallow outline	284	PANOPTICA SANS BOLD
244	Klavika Regular	120	*marshmallow super*	284	PANOPTICA OCTAGONAL
244	*Klavika Regular Italic*	356	**Mavis Regular**	83	Paralucent Thin
244	**Klavika Medium**	356	**Mavis Counterpunch**	83	*Paralucent Thin Italic*
244	*Klavika Medium Italic*	48	Maxime Regular	83	Paralucent Extra Light
244	**Klavika Bold**	48	*Maxime Italic*	83	*Paralucent Extra Light Italic*
244	*Klavika Bold Italic*	48	**Maxime Bold**	83	Paralucent Light
242	Lingua Light	48	*Maxime Bold Italic*	83	*Paralucent Light Italic*
242	Lingua Regular	48	Maxime Shadow	83	Paralucent Medium
246	Locator Ultra Light	82	Ministry Thin	83	*Paralucent Medium Italic*
246	*Locator Ultra Light Italic*	82	*Ministry Thin Italic*	83	**Paralucent Demi Bold**
246	Locator Light	82	Ministry Extra Light	83	*Paralucent Demi Bold Italic*
246	*Locator Light Italic*	82	*Ministry Extra Light Italic*	83	**Paralucent Bold**
246	Locator Regular	82	Ministry Light	83	*Paralucent Bold Italic*
246	*Locator Regular Italic*	82	*Ministry Light Italic*	83	**Paralucent Heavy**
246	**Locator Medium**	82	Ministry Medium	83	*Paralucent Heavy Italic*
246	*Locator Medium Italic*	82	*Ministry Medium Italic*	83	Paralucent Condensed Thin
246	**Locator Bold**	82	**Ministry Bold**	83	*Paralucent Condensed Thin Italic*
246	*Locator Bold Italic*	82	*Ministry Bold Italic*	83	Paralucent Condensed Extra Light
246	**Locator Black**	82	**Ministry Extra Bold**	83	*Paralucent Condensed Extra Light Italic*
246	*Locator Black Italic*	82	*Ministry Extra Bold Ital*	83	Paralucent Condensed Light
66	*Majarette*	82	**Ministry Heavy**	83	*Paralucent Condensed Light Italic*
248	Maple Regular	82	*Ministry Heavy Italic*	83	Paralucent Condensed Medium
248	*Maple Regular Italic*	121	Moderna	83	*Paralucent Condensed Medium It*
248	**Maple Medium**	387	Modus Regular	83	**Paralucent Condensed Demi Bold**
248	*Maple Medium Italic*	387	*Modus Italic*	83	*Paralucent Condensed Demi B It*
248	**Maple Bold**	387	Modus Bold	83	**Paralucent Condensed Bold**

113	Calypsico Latino	115	CREAKY	78	Egret Light
76	Cantaloupe	115	CREAKY FRANK	78	Egret Light Flourish
113	CARAMBA!	115	CREAKY TIKI	78	Electrasonic XX-Fine
185	LHF CASABLANCA	115	Croissant	78	Electrasonic X-Fine
114	CAT SCRATCH	77	Custard Regular	78	Electrasonic Fine
114	Caterpillar	77	Custard Condendensed	78	Elektron Light
114	CATNIP	115	CYNCYN REGULAR	78	Elektron Medium
76	Catseye Medium	358	Daily	78	Elektron Bold
76	Catseye Medium Italic	115	DANCEPARTY	78	Elektron Shaded
76	Catseye Bold	116	Dannette	215	Elevator Boy
76	Catseye Bold Italic	116	Dannette Outline	214	Empty Head
76	Catseye Narrow	77	darkside	214	Empty Head 2
76	Catseye Narrow Italic	77	darkside italic	186	LHF English Rose
114	Celsius	77	darkside bright	187	LHF ESOTERIC
76	CHASE	77	DATA 90 REG	278	Eunoia
43	CHITCHY	77	DATA 90 OUT	278	Eunoia Round
114	Cilantro	77	DATA 90 SHA	278	Eunoia Unicase
114	Cinnamon Regular	116	Daydream	278	Eunoia Condensed
171	circlejerk light	77	DAZZLE	278	Eunoia Condensed Round
171	circlejerk bold	77	DAZZLE UNDERPRINT	278	Eunoia Condensed Unicase
115	Circus Dog	367	DELUX	117	Eyeliner
43	CIRCUS KS	367	DELUX DELUX	188	LHF FAIRGROUND
76	Citrus	77	DIECAST	370	False Idol Regular
186	LHF CLASSIC CAPS	116	DiMiTRi SWANK	295	Farmer
367	COMO REGULAR	78	DOOM PLATOON MED	265	Fellowship
367	COMO BLOCK	78	DOOM PLATOON BD	215	Fig Bun
77	CONTOUR REG	116	DOYOURTHING	240	Fig Serif
77	CONTOUR IT	373	DRAYLON	240	Fig Sans
77	CONTOUR OUT	78	drexler	188	LHF FIREHOUSE
77	CONTOUR SHA	368	DRONE NO.666	78	Flak
115	CornDog	368	DRONE NO.90210	78	Flak Nailed
43	COUNTRY FANG	116	EERIE	78	Flak Heavy

78	Flat Spraycard	79	Gran Turismo Outline	118	henparty sans
117	FLASH	79	Gran Turismo Shaded	119	Hot Coffee
203	Fligerish	79	Gran Turismo Ext	67	Hot Fudge
117	FLIMFLAM	79	Gran Turismo Ext I	80	HOUNSLOW SOLID
280	Fontesque Regular	386	Granola	80	HOUNSLOW SOLID ITALIC
280	Fontesque Italic	80	GRIDLOCKER ONE	80	HOUNSLOW OPEN
280	Fontesque Bold	80	GRIDLOCKER TWO	80	HOUNSLOW OPEN IT
280	Fontesque Bold Italic	80	Griffin Black	80	HOUNSLOW SHADOW
280	Fontesque Extra Bold	80	Griffin Italic	80	HOUNSLOW SHADOW IT
79	Foonky Heavy	80	Griffin Dynamo	370	INFIDEL A
79	Foonky Starred	80	Griffin Shaded	370	INFIDEL B
117	Freestyle	118	GRIT	371	INFIDEL C
117	FREEZE	45	Grit Egyptienne Regular	371	INFIDEL D
79	GAME OVER SHADED	45	Grit Egyptienne Italic	170	Influenza
189	LHF GARNER	45	Grit Egyptienne Alt. Regular	80	INTERCEPTOR
118	Gelato Light	45	Grit Egyptienne Alt. Italic	80	INTERCEPTOR ITALIC
118	Gelato Regular	45	Grit Egyptienne Bold	80	INTERCEPTOR NITRO
118	Gelato Bold	45	Grit Egyptienne Bold Italic	80	INTERCEPTOR NITRO I
118	Gemini	45	Grit Egyptienne Alt. Bold	211	Jellygest
118	Gemini 1972	45	Grit Egyptienne Alt. Bold Italic	215	Jilly Bean
118	Gemini Alternate Italic	68	Grumble	129	HO Joker Straight Letter L
118	Gemini Outline	80	GUSTO	129	Ho Joker Straight Letter Lt Smash
79	Gentry Medium	80	GUSTO SOLID	129	Ho Joker Straight Letter Lt Smash
79	Gentry Bold	80	GUSTO HIGHLIGHT	130	HO Joker Straight Letter M
79	Glitterati Light	98	Hadank Regular	130	Ho Joker Straight Letter Md Smash
79	Glitterati Alternates	98	Hadank Engraved	130	Ho Joker Straight Letter Md Smash
99	Golden Ticket Regular	189	LHF Hamilton Ornate	131	HO Joker Straight Letter Bl
99	Golden Ticket Base	211	Happy Heinrich	131	Ho Joker Straight Letter Bld Smash
99	Golden Ticket Fill	228	HEADCOLD REGULAR	131	Ho Joker Straight Letter Bld Smash
99	Golden Ticket Highlight	228	HEADCOLD SHADOW	96	Journalistic
79	Gran Turismo Regular	209	HEFTY GALLOON	209	JUNKFOOL
79	Gran Turismo Italic	118	henparty	47	KANDT TEXT

82	Moonstone	49	Old Paris Nouveau	83	PAYLOAD NARROW OUTLINE
82	Moonstone Starlight	49	Old Paris Nouveau Italic	83	PAYLOAD WIDE
372	MORON REGULAR	49	Old Paris Nouveau Alt	83	PAYLOAD W OUT
372	MORON THICK	49	OLD PARIS NOUVEAU TITLING	213	Peanutbutter Man
283	Morphica Regular	49	OLD PARIS NOUVEAU TITLING Bc	389	Peekaboo
283	Morphica Bold	121	OOZE	122	PINBALL
82	MULGRAVE	191	Lhf Orange Grove	122	PINBALL GALAXY
299	Munter	309	ORGOVAN ROUNDED	122	PINBALL WIZARD
82	MYSTIQUE BLA	309	ORGOVAN BRUSH	70	Pinky
82	MYSTIQUE COS	309	ORGOVAN PUNK	229	Plastek Regular
82	MYSTIQUE FAMY	309	ORGOVAN HAIRY	229	Plastek outline
210	NAGHEAD	309	ORGOVAN FLOWER POWER	229	Plastek Left Shadow
210	NAGHEAD ITALIC	309	ORGOVAN FAT CAP	229	Plastek Right Shadow
210	NAGHEAD TIGHT	83	Outlander nova Light	121	PLASTICBAG
210	NAGHEAD TIGHT ITALIC	83	Outlander nova Lt It	83	Platinum
103	NATE WARD	83	Outlander nova med	83	Platinum Inline
372	NEWSPEAK LIGHT	83	Outlander nova med It	122	PlzPrint
372	NEWSPEAK HEAVY	83	Outlander nova Bold	84	Popgod
279	Nicholas Regular	83	Outlander nova Bd It	269	POSTER PAINT
279	Nicholas Italic	83	Outlander nova Black	210	Powder Punk
279	Nicholas Semibold	83	Outlander nova Bk It	210	Powder Punk Fatty
279	Nicholas Bold	121	Paella Regular	122	POWERSTATION BLOCK
82	Nightclubber	341	Pannartz Book	122	POWERSTATION
82	Nightclubber Zip	284	PANOPTICA DOESBURG	192	LHF PRENTICE
300	NISSWA PLAIN	284	PANOPTICA PIXEL	375	PROTOTYPE PLAIN
300	NISSWA FANCY	213	PARTY NOID	375	PROTOTYPE BOLD
373	NixonScript Medium	374	PATRIOT LIGHT	375	PROZAC LITE
373	NixonScript Bold Italic	374	PATRIOT HEAVY	375	PROZAC MAX
82	Novak Spring	83	PAYLOAD	192	LHF QUADREX
82	Novak Winter	83	PAYLOAD OUTLINE	84	Radiogram
373	NYLON	83	PAYLOAD SPRAY	84	Radiogram Solid
121	ODYSSEUS	83	PAYLOAD NARROW	84	Radiogram Tall

84	Radiogram Solid Tall
123	RANDISIOUS
84	Range Light
84	Range Medium
84	Range Bold
84	Range Extra Bold
84	Range Black
84	Reasonist Medium
84	Reasonist Medium It
167	Replywood Thin
167	Replywood Thin Alt
165	Replywood
166	Replywood Alternat
167	Replywood Bold
167	Replywood Bold Alt
85	ROADKILL
85	ROADKILL HEAVY
51	Rodeo Rope Text
51	Rodeo Rope Superchunk
211	Rosa Love
303	RUBY
303	RUBY HIGHLIGHT
303	RUBY SHINES
123	RUNTRON 1985
123	RUSTLER
123	RUSTLER FANCY
123	RUSTLER RAWHIDE
123	RUSTLER SALOON
139	HS Sable Ghetto Gothic Regular
139	HS Sable Ghetto Gothic Swash Caps A
139	HS Sable Ghetto Gothic Swash Caps B
320	SANDWICH

98	Satinheime Base
98	Satinheime Left
98	Satinheime Right
86	SCROTNIG MEDIUM
86	SCROTNIG MEDIUM IT
86	SCROTNIG HEAVY
86	SCROTNIG HEAVY IT
86	SCROTNIG CONDENSED
86	SCROTNIG CONDENSED IT
123	SEASONED HOSTESS
201	SHAKE YOUR HEAD
159	SHIRE CHESHIRE
159	SHIRE DERBYSHIRE
159	SHIRE SHROPSHIRE
159	SHIRE STAFFORDSHIRE
159	SHIRE WARWICKSHIRE
159	SHIRE WORCESTERSHIRE
376	SHOCK & AWE ENOLA GAY
376	SHOCK & AWE TOMAHAWK
86	Silesia Thin
86	Silesia Light
86	Silesia Medium
86	Silesia Bold
86	Silesia Heavy
86	Silesia Inline
123	SILVERSTEIN
86	Sinclair Biform
86	Sinclair Display
86	SKYLAB REGULAR
86	SKYLAB CAPSULE
86	SKYLAB CODE
87	Slack Casual Medium

87	Slack Casual Medium Italic
87	Slack Casual Bold
87	Slack Casual Bold Italic
211	Slowmotion Girl
224	Sneakers Medium
224	Sneakers Medium Obliqu
224	Sneakers Medium SC
224	Sneakers Medium SC Ob
224	sneakers medium Bif
224	sneakers medium Bif
224	Sneakers Narrow
224	Sneakers Narrow Oblique
224	Sneakers Narrow SC
224	Sneakers Narrow SC Obli
224	sneakers narrow Bifor
224	sneakers narrow Bifor
224	Sneakers Wide
224	Sneakers Wide Obliqu
224	Sneakers Wide SC
224	Sneakers Wide SC Ob
224	sneakers wide Bif
224	sneakers wide Bif
224	Sneakers UltraWi
224	Sneakers UltWide
224	Sneakers UltraW
224	Sneakers UltWid
224	sneakers ultwi
224	sneakers ultwi
228	Sneakers Script Medium
228	Sneakers Script Narrow
228	Sneakers Script Wide
228	Sneakers Script

#	Font	#	Font	#	Font
123	SNICKER	96	Temporal	332	Tubby Swash
124	SNIPLASH	88	TERRAZZO	52	Tuscan Condensed
124	SNIPLASH BOLD	331	Thaw Thin	52	Tuscan Loose
87	SPACECADET	331	Thaw Light	125	TWOBYFOUR
87	SPARROWHAWK	331	Thaw Book	197	LHF TYLER BOLD
70	Spell Bound	331	Thaw Medium	125	typing with Rudolf
124	Sprout	331	Thaw Bold	88	UNTITLED 1
87	Stadia	331	Thaw Black	174	Urban Regiment
87	Stadia Outline	331	Thaw Medium Rough	314	Vafle Classic
376	STATE MACHINE LIGHT	304	Thri Light	314	Vafle Egyptienne
376	STATE MACHINE MEDIUM	304	Thri Regular	314	Vafle Blindy
377	STATE MACHINE DEMI BOL	304	Thri Bold	314	Vafle Shadow
377	STATE MACHINE BOLD	125	THUGLIFE	314	Vafle Stencil
99	STENTORIAN REG	336	TIC TAC TOE	314	Vafle Tape
99	STENTORIAN ENG	335	TIC TAC BACK	88	Valise Montréal
194	LHF STETSON	196	LHF TIMBERLODGE	88	VANILLA
195	LHF STEVENS PERCEPTA	88	Tinderbox	202	Vegacute
87	Straker	196	LHF TONIC	88	Vertex Light
124	STUBBY	125	TOON	88	Vertex Medium
213	Stumbeleina	96	TORONTO GOTHIC	88	Vertex Demi Bold
213	Stumbeleina thin	377	Tourette Normal	88	Vertex Bold
213	Stumbeleina Fat	377	Tourette Extreme	88	Vertex Inline
87	SUBSTATION	96	Transcriptural	125	VERYMERRY
201	SURE SHOT	88	TRANSMAT REGULAR	102	VOGUE
124	Swimsuit Boys	233	Truss UltraLight	197	LHF Wade Grotesque
124	SWIMSUIT BOYS ALT CAPS	233	Truss UltraLight Oblique	125	WELTRON URBAN
124	TABLETRON	233	Truss Light	88	WESTWAY EASTBOUND
201	TABBOYHARDCORE	233	Truss Light Oblique	88	WESTWAY WESTBOUND
209	Talk Seek	233	Truss Bold	89	Wexford Oakley Regular
305	Tarnation	233	Truss Bold Oblique	89	Wexford Oakley Alt
87	TELECAST REGULAR	332	Tubby Book	208	Whimsy
87	Telstar	332	Tubby Italic	53	Woodgrit Thin

53	**Woodgrit Medium**		

53	**Woodgrit Medium**
53	**Woodgrit Heavy**
125	WOODY
89	**WORMWOOD GOTHIC**
208	Xantigo
89	Xenotype
89	Xenotype Shaded
89	**Yellow Perforated**
89	**Yellow Perforated Solid**
89	Yolanda Countess
89	Yolanda Duchess
89	Yolanda Princess
89	z i n g e r
89	z i n g e r i t a l i c
89	ZOND DIKTAT MEDIUM
89	**ZOND DIKTAT BOLD**

	Script
168	Absotone
111	Americratika
61	**Azuki**
225	Baka
225	Baka Too
183	**Lhf Ballpark Script**
112	Belair Light
112	Belair Regular
112	**Belair Shadow**
382	Brown Fox
107	Buchstaben
113	Byrnebook
113	Californian
383	Cannette & Alternates
384	Carnegie with Flourishes
76	CHANTAL LIGHT
76	CHANTAL LIGHT ITALIC
76	CHANTAL MEDIUM
76	CHANTAL MEDIUM ITALIC
76	CHANTAL BOLD
76	CHANTAL BOLD ITALIC
100	Compliments Regular
100	Compliments Upright
77	cottingley
65	Delorita
384	Diplomat
385	Duet 2 with Flourishes
385	Duet Bold with Flourishes
368	Echelon
368	Echelon Alternate
187	Lhf Ephemera Script

369	Expletive Script Light
369	Expletive Script Light Alternate
369	Expletive Script Regular
369	Expletive Script Alternate
370	False Idol Italic
71	**FASHIONISTA**
240	Fig Script
352	**Galaxie Cassiopeia Bold**
44	George Gibson
60	**Gros Marqueur**
282	Handsome Pro Thin
282	Handsome Pro Regular
282	**Handsome Pro Bold**
282	**Handsome Pro Extra Bold**
282	Handsome Pro Classic
282	Handsome Pro Rough
119	Holy Cow
119	Joybug
228	**Juicy Regular**
228	**Juicy Regular Italic**
228	**Juicy Bold**
228	**Juicy Bold Italic**
228	**Juicy Black**
228	**Juicy Black Italic**
219	**Kari Pro Regular**
219	**Kari Pro Regular Italic**
219	**Kari Pro Wide**
219	**Kari Pro Wide Italic**
119	Kinescope
101	Lanier Regular
101	Lanier Small Caps
119	Laundromat

Ornaments

169	Aether		374	Olympukes Light
363	Apocalypso Crosses		374	Olympukes Dark
363	Apocalypso Pictograms		212	Omibez
75	Autofont		83	Pic Format
114	Chickabiddies		62	Pink Martini Icons
115	Cinnamon Sprinkes		177	Psychophante
178	Contamination		85	Roadkill Symbols
116	Derekbats		51	Rodeo Rope Superchunk Dingbats
116	Diva Doodles		51	Rodeo Rope Wranglers
97	Extra Extra		179	Rorschach
280	Fontesque Ornaments		86	Scrotnig Hexes One
280	Fontesque Ornaments Fine		86	Scrotnig Hexes Two
280	Fontesque Ornaments Black		123	Ski-Pop!
281	Fontesque Sans Ornaments		213	Stumbeleina Scribble 1
117	Garanimals		213	Stumbeleina Scribble 1 Black
117	Glee Club		213	Stumbeleina Scribble 2
80	Iconics One		213	Stumbeleina Scribble 2 Black
80	Iconics Two		59	Taroca Extras
80	Iconics Three		87	Telecast Spare Parts
80	Iconics Four		125	The Kids
175	Karmaflage		67	Tis The Season
119	Lindkvist1		212	Tomoli
119	Lindkvist2		212	Tomoli 2
210	Malonia Voigo Xtras		88	Transmat Terminals
81	Mastertext Symbols One		64	Valentines
81	Mastertext Symbols Two		176	Wappenbee
206	Meloneads		89	Why Two Kay
207	Meloneads 2			
81	Menswear			
212	Mutaints			
212	Mutaints Xtra			

Baseline Fonts Design & Type Co.

4421 N Rushwood Court

Bel Aire, KS 67226 USA

(316) 260-5294 Office

(316) 519-9900 Direct

www.baselinefonts.com

www.baselinecreative.com

Nathan Williams, founder of Baseline Fonts, spent most of his time at the University of Kansas Art Museum Library and Print Research Department.

Nathan was consistently a miserable student but was quick to study printing methods, graphic design, and reverse-engineering of undocumented printing methods. While attending the university, he developed an affinity for typography and began creating fonts from historic samples in 1995.

Since then, many originals have also emerged, most notable the collaborative typeface Country Fang, designed by Brian Miller, VP of Gardner Design.

AaBbCcDdEe

AaBbCcDdEeFfGgHhIiJjKkLlMmNnOo
PpQqRrSsTtUuVvWwXxYyZz1234567

YEEHAW!

AaBbCc

AaBbCcDdEeFfGgHhIiJj
KkLlMmNnOoPpQqRrSs

RETRO SENSIBILITY

DdEeFf

AaBbCcDdEeFf

WAGON TRAILS

Atlanta, Georgia

WICHITA KANSAS

AaBbCcDdEeFfGgHhIiJjKkLlN m

NnOoPpQqRrSsTtUuVvWwXxYy

AaBbCcDdEeFfGgHhIiJjKkLlMm

NnOoPpQqRrSsTtUuVvWwXxYy

AaBbCcDdEeFf

80s PXL Thin
Nathan Williams
2005

AaBbCcDdEeFfGgHhIiJjKkLlMmNnOoPpQqRrSsTt
UuVv!@#$%^&*()_+[[:;"'?||00123456789

AaBbCcDdEeFf

80s PXL Bold
Nathan Williams
2005

AaBbCcDdEeFfGgHhIiJjKkLlMmNnOoPpQqRrSsTt
UuVv!@#$%^&*()_+[[:;"'?||00123456789

AaBbCcDdEeFf

80s PXL Outline
Nathan Williams
2005

AaBbCcDdEeFfGgHhIiJjKkLlMmNnOoPpQqRrSsTt
UuVv!@#$%^&*()_+[[:;"'?||00123456789

80s PXL™ Thin and Outline

80s PXL
Nathan Williams
2005

AaBbCcDdEeFfGgHhIiJjKkLlMmNnOoPpQqRrSsTt
UuVv!@#$%^&*()_+[[:;"'?||00123456789

80s PXL™ Bold

Domo arigato, Mr. Roboto_

TURBULENT WATERS AHEAD

Insurrection aboard the ship led

AaBbCcDdEeFfGgHhIiJjKkLl

1234567890!@#$%*{[:';?<

TURBULENT WATERS AHEAD

Insurrection aboard the ship led

AaBbCcDdEeFfGgHhIiJjKkLl

1234567890!@#$%*{[:';?

FOX

THE QUICK BROWN FOX JUMPED OVER THE LAZY DOG

The quick brown fox jumped over the lazy dog

AaBbCcDdEeFfGgHhIiJjKkLlMmNn
OoPpQqRrSsTtUuVv123456789!$(*&

Chitchy

Nathan Williams
2003

Baseline Fonts

ABCDEFGHIJKLM

ABCDEFGHIJKLMNOPQRST
UVWI234567!@#$%&*(){};(I+~

Circus KS

Nathan Williams
2006

Country Fang

Brian Miller & Nathan Williams
2003

IF YOU WANTED SMALL SAMPLES,
YOU WOULD GO ONLINE TO TRY IT.

ABCDEFGHIJKL
MNOPQRSTUVW

AaBbCcDdEeFfG

Scrapbooking fun!

CRAFTERS IMAGINE
LONG WEEKENDS AT
CROPPING PARTIES.

12345

crafters imagine long
weekends at cropping
parties, working on a

HhIiJjKkLlMmNn

George Gibson

Historical type offering to evoke and

Scripted handwriting from parchment

Grit Egyptienne™ Regular

AaBbCcDdEeFfGgHhIiJjKkLlMmNnOoPpQqRrSs

Grit Egyptienne™ Italic

AaBbCcDdEeFfGgHhIiJjKkLlMmNnOoPpQqRrSs

Grit Egyptienne™ Bold

AaBbCcDdEeFfGgHhIiJjKkLlMmNnOoPpQqRrSs

Grit Egyptienne™ Bold Italic

AaBbCcDdEeFfGgHhIiJjKkLlMmNnOoPpQqRrSs

Grit Egyptienne™ Alternate

AaBbCcDdEeFfGgHhIiJjKkLlMmNnOoPpQqRrSs

Grit Egyptienne™ Alternate Italic

AaBbCcDdEeFfGgHhIiJjKkLlMmNnOoPpQqRrSs

Grit Egyptienne™ Alternate Bold

AaBbCcDdEeFfGgHhIiJjKkLlMmNnOoPpQqRrSs

Grit Egyptienne™ Alternate Bold Italic

AaBbCcDdEeFfGgHhIiJjKkLlMmNnOoPpQqRrSs

Grit Primer™ Regular

AaBbCcDdEeFfGgH

Grit Primer™ Italic

AaBbCcDdEeFfGgH

Grit Primer™ Bold

AaBbCcDdEeFfGgH

Grit Primer™ Bold Italic

AaBbCcDdEeFfGgH

Grit Primer™ Titling

AaBbCcDdEeFfGgHh

Grit Primer™ Titling Bold

AaBbCcDdEeFfGgH

Grit Primer™ Swash

ABC

American Original

Grit Primer™ Swash Italic

ABC

Grit Primer provides options for layout, *and enables* QUICK SUBSTITUTION *between a variety of letterforms*

316-260-5294

AABCCDEFGHHIIJKLMN
OPQRSTUV123456189?

Kandt Text

Jim Kandt & Nathan Williams
2004

AABCCPEFGHHIIJKLMN
OPQRSTUV123456189?

Kandt Headline

Jim Kandt & Nathan Williams
2004

YOU'LL ADORE LUXE
Hollywood Classic

Luxe

Nathan Williams
2003

totally hip
& GROOVY

the quick brown
fox jumped over
the lazy dog.

THE QUICK BROWN
FOX JUMPED OVER
THE LAZY DOG.

AaBbCcDdEeFfGgHhIiJjKkLlMmNnOoPpQq
RrSsTtUuVvWw123456789o([<!?>])*%$#@

Maxime Regular

AaBbCcDdEeFfGgHhIiJjKkLlMmNnOoPpQqRrSsTtUu

Maxime Italic

AaBbCcDdEeFfGgHhIi

Maxime Bold

AaBbCcDdEeFfGgHhIi

Maxime Bold Italic

AaBbCcDdEeFfGgHh

Maxime Shadow

AaBbCcDdEeFfGgHhIiJjKkLlMmNnOoPpQq

Maxime Regular

systematic

Maxime Bold

systematic

Maxime Shadow

systematic

Maxime Regular

WOW!

Maxime Outline

WOW!

Maxime Shadow & Regular

WOW!

Momentum Italic

EXTRA CHUNKY

Momentum Regular

AaBb

Momentum Bold

AaBb

Momentum Bold Italic

AaBb

AaBbCcDdEeFfGgHhIiJjKkLlM
mNnOoPpQqRrSsTtUuVvWwXx
YyZz1234567890!@#$%^&*({[

**AaBbCcDdEeFfGgHhIiJjKkLlM
mNnOoPpQqRrSsTtUuVvWwXx
YyZz1234567890!@#$%^&*({[**

*AaBbCcDdEeFfGgHhIiJjKkLlM
mNnOoPpQqRrSsTtUuVvWwXx
YyZz1234567890!@#$%^&*({[*

Old Paris Nouveau

AaBbCcDdEeFfGgHhIiJjKkLlMmNnOoPpQqRrSsTt
UuVvWwXxYyZz1234567890!@$%^&*(([])?<

Nathan Williams
2003

Old Paris Nouveau Italic

AaBbCcDdEeFfGgHhIiJjKkLlMmNnOoPpQqRrSsTt
UuVvWwXxYyZz1234567890!@$%^&*(([])?<

Old Paris Nouveau Alternate

AaBbCcDdEeFfGgHhIiJjKkLlMmNnOoPpQqRrSsTt
UuVvWwXxYyZz1234567890!@$%^&*(([])?<

Old Paris Nouveau Titling

AaBbCcDdEeFfGgHhIiJjKkLlMmNnOoPpQqRrSsTt
UuVvWwXxYyZz1234567890!@$%^&*(([])?<

Old Paris Nouveau Titling Bold

AaBbCcDdEeFfGgHhIiJjKkLlMmNnOoPpQqRrSsTt
UuVvWwXxYyZz1234567890!@$%^&*(([])?<

Old Paris Nouveau Regular, Bold, Italic, & Alternate

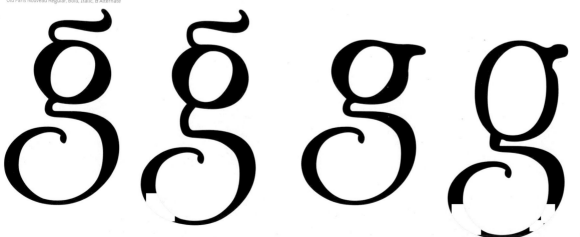

Old Times American Regular

AaBbCcDdEeFfGgHhIiJjKkLlMmNnOoPp

Old Times American Italic

AaBbCcDdEeFfGgHhIiJjKkLlMmNnOoPp

Old Times American Heavy

AaBbCcDdEeFfGgHhIiJjKkLlMmNnOoP

Old Times American Heavy Italic

AaBbCcDdEeFfGgHhIiJjKkLlMmNnOoP

Old Times American Titling

AABBCCDDEEFFGGHHIIJJKKLLMM

Old Times American Titling Heavy

AABBCCDDEEFFGGHHIIJJKKLLMM

Old Times American Regular

the quick brown fox jumped over the lazy dog.

Old Times American Italic

the quick brown fox jumped over the lazy dog.

HIP TO BE SQUARE.

AaBbCcDdEeFfGgHhIiJjKkLlMmNnOoPpQqRrSsTt
UuVvWwXxYyZz1234567890!@$%&*([])?<

boxy

Pippen

Nathan Williams
2004

Rodeo Rope

Nathan Williams
2004

Rodeo Rope Regular

Yeehaw!

Rodeo Rope Headline

ABCDE

Rodeo Rope Superchunk

Yeehaw!

Rodeo Rope Wranglers

Rodeo Rope Superchunk Dingbats

Rodeo Rope Regular

AaBbCcDdEeFfGgHhIiJjKkLlM

Rodeo Rope Headline

ABCDEFGHIJKLMNOPQ

Rodeo Rope Superchunk

AaBbCcDdEeFfGgHhIiJjKk

Slab American Regular

Bold ★ American

Slab American Regular

AaBbCcDdEeFfGgHh

Slab American Titling

AaBbCcDdEeFfG

Slab American Titling Heavy

AaBbCcDdEeFt

Tuscan Condensed

MIRACLE CURE

Tuscan Condensed

AaBbCcDdEeFfGgHhI

Tuscan Loose

SNAKE OIL3

Tuscan Loose

AaBbCcDdEeFfGg

Woodgrit

Nathan Williams
2002

Woodgrit Thin

BOLD HEADLINES ALLOWED

Woodgrit Medium

BOLD HEADLINES ALLOWED

Woodgrit Heavy

BOLD HEADLINES ALLOWED

Woodgrit Heavy

GENTLE JACKHAMMER

Woodgrit Heavy

He was almost perfect, save for his flaws.

Woodgrit Thin

roughly

Woodgrit Medium

roughly

Woodgrit Heavy

roughly

Woodgrit Thin

AaBbCcDdEeFfGgHhIiJjKkLlMm

Woodgrit Thin

AaBbCcDdEeFfGgHhIiJjKkLlMm
NnOoPpQqRrSsTtUuVvWwXxYy
Zz1234567890!@$%&*({[]})?

Woodgrit Medium

AaBbCcDdEeFfGgHhIiJjKkLlMm
NnOoPpQqRrSsTtUuVvWwXxYy
Zz1234567890!@$%&*({[]})?

Woodgrit Heavy

AaBbCcDdEeFfGgHhIiJjKkLlMm
NnOoPpQqRrSsTtUuVvWwXxYy
Zz1234567890!@$%&*({[]})?

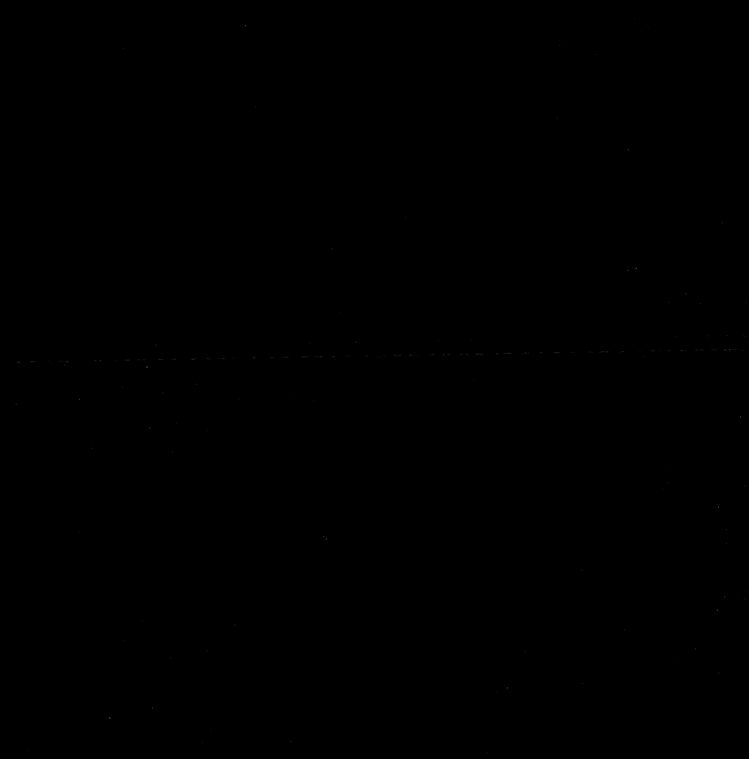

eyeliner
STOP*LiSTeN
MODULAR
LEATHEreTTE

eyeliner
STOP*LiSTeN
MODULAR
LEATHEreTTE

TALKING ORACLE SPIRITS *from* BEYOND

ABCDEFGHIJKLMNOPQRSTUV
WXYZABCDEFGHIJKLMNOPQRSTU
VWXYZ$1234567890 (?!@#&)

FORTUNE TELLER.

PALM READER

EST. 1892

COSTUME CARNIVAL

Taroca Extras

Jess Latham
2005

Taroca Extras is loaded with icons, word banners, and flourishes. When using the OpenType version, simply select the ornaments feature.

Macrame Super Tri

Jess Latham
2002

Here & now
1982
fashion expo

Gros Marqueur

Jess Latham
2004

Natural Ingredients

This is my own handwriting drawn
with a large chisel edged marker.

www.bvfonts.com

100% Organic

bluevinyl@bvfonts.com

YIN & YANG

Please slurp your soup?

KARATE!

Import Warehouse

Green Tea

SUMI BRUSH WORK

VERY ZEN

Azuki

Jess Latham
2005

The OpenType version of Azuki contains contextual alternates.

Blue Vinyl

Pink Martini

Jess Latham
2001

The Pink Martini family contains
5 typefaces: Regular, Italic, Bold,
Bold Italic, and Icons.

Bongo Lounge

Dig That Fun Retro Style

Je Ne Sais Quoi

martini

Going To Vegas

Let's Play Poker

Is it happy hour yet?

Jess Latham
2001

Blue Vinyl

Pink Martini Regular

ABCDEFGHIJKLMNOPQRSTUVWXYZ
abcdefghijklmnopqrstuvwxyz
123456789!@#$%^&*-."etc...

Pink Martini Regular Italic

ABCDEFGHIJKLMNOPQRSTUVWXYZ
abcdefghijklmnopqrstuvwxyz
123456789!@#$%^&*-."etc...

Pink Martini Bold

ABCDEFGHIJKLMNOPQRSTUVWXYZ
abcdefghijklmnopqrstuvwxyz
123456789!@#$%^&*-."etc...

Pink Martini Bold Italic

ABCDEFGHIJKLMNOPQRSTUVWXYZ
abcdefghijklmnopqrstuvwxyz
123456789!@#$%^&*-."etc...

Pink Martini Icons

bluevinyl@bvfonts.com

Delicious Aroma
chocolate cake & lemon pie
CREAM PUFF
What's On The Menu?
Hand Dipped Nuts

Meringue

Jess Latham
2002

Blue Vinyl

Caramel Creme
Secret Herbal Grimoire
Rose Beads
Sunflowers At The Tuscany Villa

Delorita

Jess Latham
2003

Rodeo Girl

Jess Latham
2003

Don't forget to make a grocery list!
Handwriting fonts are always popular
On Sale! 25% Off
Step away from the doughnuts.
Bananas, Soy Burgers, Whole Wheat Crackers
Did I forget the onions?

Majorette

Jess Latham
2000

Glitter
and shine

bluevinyl@bvfonts.com

Brownies
sprinkle fairy dust
Pink Lady

Hot Fudge

Jess Latham
2003

Blue Vinyl

Tis The Season

Jess Latham
2003

MIGRAINE HEADACHE

RAINY DAYS

mornings are the worst

It's depressing to get up that early

Playing In The Sun

BLUE SKIES

little puffy clouds

GOLDEN RAYS

bluevinyl@bvfonts.com

Wish You Were Here!

Shimmer looks just like real cursive handwriting, because that's exactly what it is! The letters were meticulously hand traced from actual samples of handlettering and great care was taken to keep the strokes natural and fluid.

Shimmer

Jess Latham
2004

Blue Vinyl

Hit Me With A Left Hook

But not too hard please cause it might hurt.

The Gloves Are On!

What's in those things, lead?

Left Hook

Jess Latham
2000

Fun and Casual

You Can Do Magic

Abra Cadabra!

SUPER FRIENDLY

Perfect for all age groups.

BABY ELEPHANT

If you make a mess please clean it up.

SOFTEN ALL THE EDGES

bluevinyl@bvfonts.com

SMASH & GRAB

MODEL

F.SHION MAGAZINE

STYLE

GLAMOROUS LIFE

Fashionista

Jess Latham
2001

Blue Vinyl

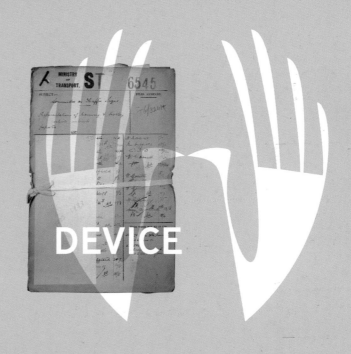

DEVICE

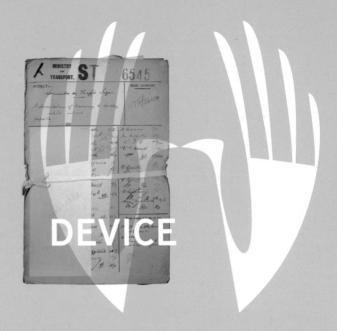

DEVICE

Fonts available for immediate download:
www.devicefonts.co.uk

The font arm of Rian Hughes's Device studio, Device Fonts, has been releasing innovative type designs since 1995. Device also produces graphic design, logo design, illustration, and custom font design for a broad range of clients in advertising, fashion, editorial, music, toys, corporate, and comic books. An online portfolio is available at the above web address.

A commemorative specimen book produced to celebrate Device Fonts' recent ten-year anniversary is available from the Device website. Released in both paperback and limited edition hardback, it features articles, extensive sample settings that cover all available weights, and even more fonts.

info@devicefonts.co.uk
rianhughes@aol.com

ABCDEFGHIJKLMNOPQRSTUVWXYZ
ABCDEFGHIJKLMNOPQRSTUVWXYZ
1234567890 (&£$¥€?!%ffi@®)

PRAGUE LIGHTS

DF Absinthe

Rian Hughes
2004

ABCDEFGHIJKLMNOPQRSTUVWXYZ
abcdefghijklmnopqrstuvwxyz
1234567890 [&£$¥€?!%®@□]

Power

DF Acton

Rian Hughes
1998

Entire family consists of One, One Italic, Two, and Two Italic.

ABCDEFGHIJKLMNOPQRSTUVWXYZ
abcdefghijklmnopqrstuvwxyz
1234567890 [&£$¥€?!%®@®]

South Bank Festival

DF Ainsdale

Rian Hughes
1992

Entire family consists of Medium, Medium Italic, Bold, and Bold Italic.

ABCDEFGHIJKLMNOPQRSTUV
ABCDEFGHIJKLMNOPQRSTUV
1234567890 (&£$¥€?!%ÆAT

TRACE

DF Amorpheus

Rian Hughes
1995

Entire family consists of Regular and Alternates.

DF Autofont

Rian Hughes
1997

ABCDEFGHIJKLMNOPQRSTUVWX
ABCDEFGHIJKLMNOPQRSTUVWX
1234567890 (&£$¥??!%Æ@®)

BRONX

DF Battery Park

Rian Hughes
2006

ABCDEFGHIJKLMNOPQRST
ABCDEFGHIJKLMNOPQRST
1234567890 (&£$¥€?!%

99 FLAVOURS! SPRINKLES

DF Bingo

Rian Hughes
1997

ABCDEFGHIJKLMNOPQRS
abcdefghijklmnopqrstuvwxyz
1234567890 (&£$¥€?!%

Candies

DF Blackcurrant

Rian Hughes
1997-1999

Entire family consists of Black, Squash, Black Alternates, and Squash Alternates.

Device

DF Bullroller

Rian Hughes
1999

ABCDEFGHIJKLMNOPQRSTUVWX
abcdefghijklmnopqrstuvwxy
1234567890 (&£$¢?!%Æ@®)

punchy

DF Cantaloupe

Rian Hughes
1998-2003

ABCDEFGHIJKLMNOPQRSTU
abcdefghijklmnopqrstuvwxy
1234567890 (&£$¥€?!%Æ@®)

Green

DF Catseye

Rian Hughes
2005

Entire family consists of Medium,
Medium Italic, Bold, Bold Italic,
Narrow, and Narrow Italic.

ABCDEFGHIJKLMNOPQRSTUVWXYZ
abcdefghijklmnopqrstuvwxyz
1234567890 (&£$¥€?!%Æ@®)

Gryff's Enigma

DF Chantal

Rian Hughes
1993

Entire family consists of Light,
Light Italic, Medium, Medium
Italic, Bold, and Bold Italic.

ABCDEFGHIJKLMNOPQRSTUVWX
ABCDEFGHIJKLMNOPQRSTUVW
1234567890 (&£$¥€?!%Æ@®)

SKETCH

DF Chase

Rian Hughes
2005

ABCDEFGHIJKLM
NOPQRSTUVWXYZ
1234567890 (&?!%)

ROT!

DF Cheapside

Rian Hughes
2006

ABCDEFGHIJKLMNOPQRSTUVWXYZ
abcdefghijklmnopqrstuvwxyz
1234567890 (&£$¥?!%Æ@®)

Ratcheted

DF Citrus

Rian Hughes
1999

ABCDEFGHIJKLMNO
abcdefghijklmnopqrs
1234567890 (&£$¥€

eggs

DF Coldharbour Gothic

Rian Hughes
2006

ABCDEFGHIJKLMNOPQRS
ABCDEFGHIJKLMNOPQRS
1234567890 (&£$¥?!%@

WOOD

info@devicefonts.co.uk

AGCDEFGHIJKLM NOPQRSTUVWXY 1234567890 &E

DF Contour

Rian Hughes
1992

Entire family consists of Regular, Outline, Shaded, and Italic.

abcdefghijklmnopqrstu abcdefghijklmnopqrstu 1234567890 (&≠£§y?!∞?)

sixties

DF Cottingley

Rian Hughes
1993

Entire family consists of Regular, Word Beginnings, and Word Endings.

ABCDEFGHIJKLMNOPQRSTUVWXYZ abcdefghijklmnopqrstuvwxyz 1234567890 (&£$¥€?!%Æ@®)

Rhubarb

DF Custard

Rian Hughes
2005

Entire family consists of Regular and Condensed.

abcdefghijklmnopqrstuvwxyz 1234567890 (&£¥€?!ojoœ@®)

international

DF Darkside

Rian Hughes
1995

Entire family consists of Regular, Italic, and Bright.

ABCDEFGHIJKLMNOPQR ABCDEFGHIJKLMNOPQRS 1234567890 (&£$¥€?!%

DF Data 90

Rian Hughes
2002

Entire family consists of Regular, Outline, and Shaded.

ABCDEFGHIJKLMNOPQRSTUVWXYZ ABCDEFGHIJKLMNOPQRSTUVWXYZ 1234567890 (&£$¥€?!%ÆA@®)

BOUDOIR

DF Dauphine

Rian Hughes
2004

Entire family consists of Regular, Alternates, and Foliage.

ABCDEFGHIJKLMNOPQRST ABCDEFGHIJKLMNOPQRST 1234567890 (&£$¥€?!%Æ

CIAO!

DF Dazzle

Rian Hughes
2006

Entire family consists of Regular, Solid, and Underprint.

ABCDEFGHIJKLMNOPQRSTUVWX ABCDEFGHIJKLMNOPQRSTUVWX 1234567890 (&£$¥€?!%Æ@®)

METAL

DF Diecast

Rian Hughes
2005

Device

DF Doom Platoon	ABCDEFGHIJKLMNOPQRST	**ZONED**
Rian Hughes 2002	ABCDEFGHIJKLMNOPQRST	
Entire family consists of Medium and Bold.	1234567890 (&£$¥€?!%Æ	

| **DF Drexler** | abcdefghijklmnopqrstuv | **nano** |
| Rian Hughes 1994 | 1234567890 (&?!/.) | |

DF Dynasty	ABCDEFGHIJKLMNOPQRSTUVW	**Tidal Shore**
Rian Hughes 1998-2004	abcdefghijklmnopqrstuvwxyz	Dungeness Point Overview
Entire family consists of 14 fonts–Thin, Extra Light, Light, Medium, Demi Bold, Bold, Heavy, and their accompanying Italics.	1234567890 (&£$¥€?!%Æ@®)	

DF Egret	ABCDEFGHIJKLMNOPQRSTUVWX	Modern
Rian Hughes 2003	abcdefghijklmnopqrstuvw	
Entire family consists of Light and Light Flourish.	1234567890 (&£$¥€?!%Æ@®)	

DF Electrasonic	ABCDEFGHIJKLMNOPQ	Lipgloss
Rian Hughes 2005	abcdefghijklmnopqrstuvwxyz	
Entire family consists of XX Fine, X Fine, and Fine.	1234567890 (&£¢¥€?!%	

DF Elektron	ABCDEFGHIJKLMNOPQRSTU	**Fermion**
Rian Hughes 1992	abcdefghijklmnopqrstuvwxyz	
Entire family consists of Light, Medium, Bold, and Shaded.	1234567890 [&£$¥€!0JoÆ	

DF English Grotesque	ABCDEFGHIJKLMNOPQRSTU	Brake Adjustment
Rian Hughes 1998	abcdefghijklmnopqrstuvwxyz	**ENGLISH CLASSICS**
Entire family consists of Thin, Light, Medium, Bold, Heavy, Extra Bold, and Black.	1234567890 (&£$¥€?!%Æ@®)	

DF Flak	ABCDEFGHIJKLMNOPQRSTUVWXYZ	**Crash**
Rian Hughes 2002	abcdefghijklmnopqrstuvwxyz	
Entire family consists of Regular, Nailed, Spraycard, and Heavy.	1234567890 [&£$¥€?!%Æ@®]	

info@devicefonts.co.uk

ABCDEFGHIJKLMNOPQRSTUVW
abcdefghijklmnopqrstuvwxy
1234567890 (&£$¥€?!%Æ)

Angels

DF Foonky

Rian Hughes
1995

Entire family consists of Heavy and Starred.

ABCDEFGHIJKLMNOPQRSTUVWXY
ABCDEFGHIJKLMNOPQRSTUVWX
1234567890 (&£$¥??!%Æ@?)

MANHOLE

DF Forge

Rian Hughes
2006

ABCDEFGHIJKLMNOPQRST
abcdefghijklmnopqrstuvwx
1234567890 (&£$¥€?!%Æ

Chicago

DF Galicia

Rian Hughes
2004

Entire family consists of Light, Light Italic, Medium, and Medium Italic.

ABCDEFGHIJKLMNOPQR
STUVWXYZ 123456789
(&£$¥€?!%Æ@R)

SCORE

DF Game Over

Rian Hughes
1999

ABCDEFGHIJKLMNOPQRSTUV
abcdefghijklmnopqrstuvwxyz
1234567890 (&£$¥?!%Æ@R)

Concept

DF Gentry

Rian Hughes
2005

Entire family consists of Medium and Bold.

ABCDEFGHIJKLMNOPQRSTUVWXYZ
abcdefghijklmnopqrstuvwxyz
1234567890 (&£$¥€?!%Æ@®)

Disco 81

DF Glitterati

Rian Hughes
2004

Entire family consists of Light and Alternates.

ABCDEFGHIJKLMNOPQR
abcdefghijklmnopqrstuvw
1234567890 (&£$¥€?!

Turbo

DF Gran Turismo

Rian Hughes
1998

Entire family consists of Regular, Italic, Outline, Shaded, Extended, and Extended Italic.

ABCDEFGHIJKLMNOPQRSTUVWXYZ
abcdefghijklmnopqrstuvwxyz
1234567890 (&£$¥€?!%Æ@®)

InterCityXP

DF Gravel

Rian Hughes
2003

Entire family consists of Light, Light Italic, Medium, Medium Italic, Bold, and Bold Italic.

Device

DF Gridlocker

Rian Hughes
2004

Entire family consists of One and Two.

ABCDEFGHIJKLMNOPQRST
ABCDEFGHIJKLMNOPQRST
1234567890 [&£$¥€?!%Æ

DF Griffin

Rian Hughes
1997

Entire family consists of Black, Italic, Shaded, and Dynamo Caps.

ABCDEFGHIJKLMNOPQRS
abcdefghijklmnopqrstu
1234567890 (&£$¥€?!%

Dynamic
RANGE VALUE

DF Gusto

Rian Hughes
2004

Entire family consists of Regular, Highlight, and Solid.

ABCDEFGHIJKLMNOPQR
STUVWXYZ 1234567890
(&£$¥€?!%ÆÆ▲®)

GLOSS

DF Hawksmoor

Rian Hughes
2006

ABCDEFGHIJKLM
NOPQRSTUVWXYZ
1234567890 (&£$¥)

GRIT

DF Hounslow

Rian Hughes
1998

Entire family consists of Solid, Solid Italic, Open, and Open Italic.

ABCDEFGHIJKLMNOPQR
STUVWXYZ 1234567890
[&£$¥€?!%Æ]

BOXED

DF Iconics

Rian Hughes
2000

Entire family consists of One, Two, Three, and Four.

DF Interceptor

Rian Hughes
1998

Entire family consists of Regular, Italic, Nitro, Nitro Italic, and Heavy.

ABCDEFGHIJKLMNO
PQRSTUVWXYZ
1234567890 (&£$¥)

ACTION
OVERHEAD CAMSHAFT

DF Ironbridge

Rian Hughes
2006

ABCDEFGHIJKLMNOPQRST
ABCDEFGHIJKLMNOPQRST
1234567890 (&£$¥?!%Æ@®)

PLATE

info@devicefonts.co.uk

ABCDEFGHIJKLMNOPQR
ABCDEFGHIJKLMNOPQR
1234567890 (&£$¥€?!

OFFWORLD SHUTTLE
TERMINUS

DF Klaxon

Rian Hughes
2003

Entire family consists of One and Two.

ABCDEFGHIJKLMNOPQRS
abcdefghijklmnopqrstuvwx
1234567890 (&£$¥€?!%

Minx

DF Klickclack

Rian Hughes
2006

Entire family consists of Regular and Swash.

ABCDEFGHIJKLMNOPQRSTUVW
ABCDEFGHIJKLMNOPQRSTUVW
1234567890 (&£$¥€?!%@)

SWOON!

DF Laydeez Nite

Rian Hughes
1997

ABCDEFGHIJKLMNOPQRSTUVWXYZ
abcdefghijklmnopqrstuvwxyz
1234567890 (&£$¥€?!?.ÆÆ@®)

Microgroove

DF Lusta

Rian Hughes
1995

Entire family consists of Forty Sans, Forty Serif, Eighty Sans, Eighty Serif, One Twenty Sans, One Sixty Sans, and Two Hundred Sans.

ABCDEFGHIJKLMNOPQRSTUVWXYZ
abcdefghijklmnopqrstuvwxyz
1234567890 (&£$¥€?!%off@®)

Interior Design

DF Mercano Empire

Rian Hughes
2003

Entire family consists of Regular, Regular Italic, Condensed, Condensed Italic, Lined, and Lined Italic.

ABCDEFGHIJKLMNOPQRSTU
ABCDEFGHIJKLMNOPQRST
1234567890 (&£$¥€?!%Æ@

RANDOM ACTS OF
VIOLETS

DF Metropol Noir

Rian Hughes
1995

DF MenSwear

Rian Hughes
1998

ABCDEFGHIJKLMNOPQRSTUVW
ABCDEFGHIJKLMNOPQRSTUVW
1234567890 (&£$¥€?!%@)

STACK

DF Mastertext

Rian Hughes
1994

Entire family consists of Light, Plain, Heavy, Boxed, Icons, Symbols One, and Symbols Two.

Device

ABCDEFGHIJKLMNOPQRSTUV
abcdefghijklmnopqrstuvwxyz
1234567890 (&£$¥€?!%Æ@®)

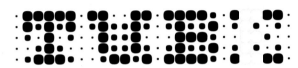

Torquay Pier
WORTHING & BRIGHTON

ABCDEFGHIJKLMNOPQRSTUVWXYZ
abcdefghijklmnopqrstuvwxyz
1234567890 (&£$¥€?!%Æ@®)

San Marco 1797

ABCDEFGHIJKLMNOP
ABCDEFGHIJKLMNOP
1234567890 (&£$¥

ABCDEFGHIJKLMNOPQRSTUVWXYZ
abcdefghijklmnopqrstuvwxyz
1234567890 (&£$¥€?!%Æ@®)

COVEN 13

ABCDEFGHIJKLMNOPQRST
ABCDEFGHIJKLMNOPQRST
1234567890 (&£$¥€?!%)

IRON

ABCDEFGHIJKLMNOP
ABCDEFGHIJKLMNOP
1234567890 (&£$¥?)

abcdefghijklmnopqr
stuvwxyz 1234567890
[&£$¥€?!%©@®]

ABCDEFGHIJKLMNOPQR
abcdefghijklmnopqrstuvw
1234567890 (&£$¥€?!%Æ

Floral

info@devicefonts.co.uk

ABCDEFGHIJKLMNOP
abcdefghijklmnop
1234567890 (&£\$¥

altair
SUPERNOVA

DF Outlander Nova

Rian Hughes
1993-2004

Entire family consists of Light,
Light Italic, Medium, Medium,
Italic, Bold, Bold Italic, Black,
and Black Italic.

ABCDEFGHIJKLMNOPQRSTUV
abcdefghijklmnopqrstuvwxyz
1234567890 (&£\$¥€?!%Æ@)

Clarity

Text Weights:
Thin & *Italic*
Extra Light & *Italic*
Light & *Italic*
Medium & *Italic*
Demi Bold & ***Italic***
Bold & ***Italic***
Heavy & ***Italic***

DF Paralucent

Rian Hughes
2000-2001

Entire family consists of 14
fonts–Thin, Extra Light, Light,
Medium, Demi Bold, Bold, Heavy,
and their accompanying Italics.

ABCDEFGHIJKLMNOPQRSTUVWXYZ
abcdefghijklmnopqrstuvwxyz
1234567890 (&£\$¥€?!%Æ@)

Elegant

Text Weights:
Thin & *Italic*
Extra Light & *Italic*
Light & *Italic*
Medium & *Italic*
Demi Bold & ***Italic***
Bold & ***Italic***
Heavy & ***Italic***

DF Paralucent Condensed

Rian Hughes
2000-2002

Entire family consists of 14
fonts–Thin, Extra Light, Light,
Medium, Demi Bold, Bold, Heavy,
and their accompanying Italics.

ABCDEFGHIJKLMNOPQRST
abcdefghijklmnopqrstuvwx
1234567890 (&£\$¥€?!%)

Giants

DF Paralucent Stencil

Rian Hughes
2003

Entire family consists of Extra
Light, Medium, and Heavy.

ABCDEFGHIJKLMNOPQ
ABCDEFGHIJKLMNOPQ
1234567890 (&£\$¥%

DROP THE
BOMB!

DF Payload

Rian Hughes
2004-2005

Entire family consists of Regular,
Wide, Narrow, Outline, and
Spraycan.

DF Pic Format

Rian Hughes
1995–1997

ABCDEFGHIJKLMNOPQRSTUVWXYZ
abcdefghijklmnopqrstuvwxyz
1234567890 [&£\$¥€?!%Æ@R]

MERLOT BIN 9

DF Pitshanger

Rian Hughes
2004

Entire family consists of Regular
and Initial Capitals.

ABCDEFGHIJKLMNOPQR
abcdefghijklmnopqrstuv
1234567890 [&£\$¥€?!]

Chain

DF Platinum

Rian Hughes
2002

Entire family consists of Regular
and Inline.

DF Popgod
Rian Hughes
2003

ABCDEFGHIJKLMNOPQRST
abcdefghijklmnopqrstuvw
1234567890 (&£$¥€?!%)

Quids

DF Profumo
Rian Hughes
2006

ABCDEFGHIJKLMNOPQRSTUVWXYZ
ABCDEFGHIJKLMNOPQRSTUVWXYZ
1234567890 (&£$¥€?!%Æ@®)

SECRET

DF Quagmire
Rian Hughes
1997

Entire family consists of 12 fonts—
Medium, Demi Bold, Bold, Black,
Medium Extended, Bold Extended
and their accompanying Italics.

ABCDEFGHIJKLMNOPQRSTU
abcdefghijklmnopqrstuvw
1234567890 (&£$¥€?!%Æ)

Corporate
Finance

DF Radiogram
Rian Hughes
1997

Entire family consists of Regular,
Tall, Solid, and Solid Tall.

ABCDEFGHIJKLMNOPQRSTUVWXYZ
abcdefghijklmnopqrstuvwxyz
1234567890 (&£$¥€?!%@®)

Valve Powered

DF Range
Rian Hughes
2000

Entire family consists of Light,
Medium, Bold, Extra Bold, and
Black.

ABCDEFGHIJKLMNOPQRSTUVWX
abcdefghijklmnopqrstuvwxyz
1234567890 (&£$¥€?!%Æ@®)

DJ Rap

DF Reasonist
Rian Hughes
1992

Entire family consists of Medium
and Medium Italic.

ABCDEFGHIJKLMNOPQRS
ABCDEFGHIJKLMNOPQRSTUVW
1234567890 (&£$¥€?!%)

CHERRY

DF Register Condensed
Rian Hughes
2000

Entire family consists of Bold and
Bold Italic.

ABCDEFGHIJKLMNOPQRSTUVWXY
abcdefghijklmnopqrstuvwxyz
1234567890 [&£$¥€?!%Æ@]

IN THE STUDIO
LAYING DOWN THE BEATS

DF Register
Rian Hughes
2000

Entire family consists of 10
fonts—Extra Light, Light, Medium,
Demi Bold, Bold, and their
accompanying Italics.

ABCDEFGHIJKLMNOPQRSTUVW
abcdefghijklmnopqrstuvwxyz
1234567890 [&£$¥€?!%Æ@]

Sport 6

info@devicefonts.co.uk

ABCDEFGHIJKLMNOPQR
abcdefghijklmnopqrstuv
1234567890 (&£$¥€?!)

Trunk

DF Register Wide

Rian Hughes
2000

Entire family consists of 10 fonts–Extra Light, Light, Medium, Demi Bold, Bold, and their accompanying Italics.

ABCDEFGHIJKLMNOPQRSTUV
abcdefghijklmnopqrstuvwxyz
1234567890 (&£$¥€?!%Æ@)

Utility

DF Regulator

Rian Hughes
1993-1997

Entire family consists of 11 fonts–Thin, Light, Medium, Bold, Heavy, and their accompanying Italics, plus a cameo version.

ABCDEFGHIJKLMNOPQ
abcdefghijklmnopqrstuv
1234567890 (&£$¥€?!)

Controls
airborne refuelling manœuvre

DF Ritafurey

Rian Hughes
1992-2004

Entire family consists of 10 fonts–Extra Light, Light, Medium, Demi Bold, Bold, and their accompanying Italics.

ABCDEFGHIJKLMNOPQRSTUVWXYZ
ABCDEFGHIJKLMNOPQRSTUVWXYZ
1234567890 (&£$¥€?!%Æ@)

OVERPASS ⬆

DF Roadkill

Rian Hughes
2005

Entire family consists of Regular, Alternates, and Symbols.

ABCDEFGHIJKLMNOPQRSTU
ABCDEFGHIJKLMNOPQRSTU
1234567890 (&£$¥€?!%)

EXIT 14

DF Roadkill Heavy

Rian Hughes
2006

ABCDEFGHIJKLMNOPQRSTUVW
abcdefghijklmnopqrstuvwxy
1234567890 (&£$¥€?!%)

Industry

DF Rogue Sans

Rian Hughes
2004

Entire family consists of Light, Light Italic, Medium, Medium Italic, Bold, and Bold Italic.

ABCDEFGHIJKLMNOPQRSTUVW
abcdefghijklmnopqrstuvwxy
1234567890 (&£$¥€?!%)

Mission

DF Rogue Sans Cond.

Rian Hughes
2004

Entire family consists of Light, Light Italic, Medium, Medium Italic, Bold, and Bold Italic.

ABCDEFGHIJKLMNOPQRSTUVW
abcdefghijklmnopqrstuvwxy
1234567890 (&£$¥€?!%)

Loaded

DF Rogue Sans Extended

Rian Hughes
2004

Entire family consists of Light, Light Italic, Medium, Medium Italic, Bold, and Bold Italic.

Device

DF Rogue Serif

Rian Hughes
2004

Entire family consists of Light, Light Italic, Medium, Medium Italic, Bold, and Bold Italic.

ABCDEFGHIJKLMNOPQRSTUVWXY
abcdefghijklmnopqrstuvwxyz
1234567890 (&£$¥€?!%)

Finance

DF Saintbride

Rian Hughes
2006

ABCDEFGHIJKLMNOPQRSTUVWXYZ
ABCDEFGHIJKLMNOPQRSTUVWXYZ
1234567890 (&£$¥€?!%)

CLOISTER

DF Scrotnig

Rian Hughes
1993-1997

Entire family consists of Medium, Medium Italic, Heavy, Heavy Italic, Condensed, Condensed Italic, Hexes 1, and Hexes 2.

ABCDEFGHIJKLMNOPQRS
TUVWXYZ 1234567890
(&£$¥€?!%⊞⊠⊛Ⓐⓡ)

ZARJAZ

DF September

Rian Hughes
2001-03

Entire family consists of Medium, Medium Italic, Bold, Bold Italic, Heavy, and Heavy Italic.

ABCDEFGHIJKLMNOPQRSTUV
abcdefghijklmnopqrstuvwxyz
1234567890 (&£$¥€?!)

Report

DF Shenzhen Industrial

Rian Hughes
2006

ABCDEFGHIJKLMNOPQRSTUVWXYZ
ABCDEFGHIJKLMNOPQRSTUVWXYZ
1234567890 (&£$¥€?!)

CLASSIFIED

DF Silesia

Rian Hughes
1998

ABCDEFGHIJKLMNOPQRST
abcdefghijklmnopqrstuvwxyz
1234567890 [&£$¥€?!]

**Electronica
Synthesizer romance**

DF Sinclair

Rian Hughes
1999

Entire family consists of Biform and Display.

ABCDEFGHIJKLMNOPQRSTUVWXYZ
abcdefghijklmnopqrstuvwxyz
1234567890 (&£$¥€?!)

Reactor Core

DF Skylab

Rian Hughes
2000

Entire family consists of Regular, Capsule, and Code.

ABCDEFGHIJKLMNOPQRS
ABCDEFGHIJKLMNOPQRS
1234567890 [&£$¥€?!]

ABCDEFGHIJKLMNOPQRSTUVWXYZ
abcdefghijklmnopqrstuvwxyz
1234567890 [&£$¥€?!%]

EuroTunnel Break

DF Slack Casual

Rian Hughes
1998

Entire family consists of Medium, Medium Italic, Bold, and Bold Italic.

ABCDEFGHIJKLMNOPQRSTUVWXYZ
1234567890
(&£$¥€?!%)

RAYGUN

DF Space Cadet

Rian Hughes
1993

ABCDEFGHIJKLMN
OPQRSTUVWXYZ
1234567890 (&£$¥€?!%)

OXFORD
GREAT YARMOUTH ATTRACTIONS

DF Sparrowhawk

Rian Hughes
2004

ABCDEFGHIJKLMNOPQRSTUVWXY
abcdefghijklmnopqrstuvwxyz
1234567890° (&$¥€?!%)(◼◼)

la Mode

DF Stadia

Rian Hughes
1996

Entire family consists of Regular and Outline.

ABCDEFGHIJKLMNOPQRSTUVWXYZ
abcdefghijklmnopqrstuvwxyz
1234567890 (&£$¥€?!%)

Beige

DF Straker

Rian Hughes
1997-2004

ABCDEFGHIJKLMNOPQRSTU
ABCDEFGHIJKLMNOPQRSTU
1234567890 (&£$¥€?!%€€)

RELAY

DF Substation

Rian Hughes
2002

ABCDEFGHIJKLMNOPQRSTUV
ABCDEFGHIJKLMNOPQRSTUV
1234567890 (&£$¥€?!%Æ)

SCANNER

DF Telecast

Rian Hughes
1996

Entire family consists of Regular and Spare Parts.

ABCDEFGHIJKLMNOPQRSTUVWXYZ
abcdefghijklmnopqrstuvwxyz
1234567890 (&£$¥€?!%)

Lunar Module

DF Telstar

Rian Hughes
2004

Device

DF Terrazzo

Rian Hughes
1997

DF Tinderbox

Rian Hughes
2006

ABCDEFGHIJKLMNOPQRS
abcdefghijklmnopqrstuvwxyz
1234567890 (&£$¥€?!%ÆŒ@)

Da Gama

DF Transmat

Rian Hughes
1995

Entire family consists of Regular
and Terminals.

ABCDEFGHIJKLMNOPQRSTUVW
ABCDEFGHIJKLMNOPQRSTUVW
1234567890 [&£$¥€?!%ÆŒ]

CATHODE

DF Untitled 1

Rian Hughes
1994

ABCDEFGHIJKLMNOPQR
ABCDEFGHIJKLMNOPQR
1234567890 [&£$¥€?!]

GRUNT

DF Valise Montréal

Rian Hughes
1989-2005

ABCDEFGHIJKLMNOPQRSTUVWXYZ
abcdefghijklmnopqrstuvwxyz
1234567890 [&£$¥€?!%ÆŒ@]

Girlfriend

DF Vanilla

Rian Hughes
2006

ABCDEFGHIJKLMNOPQR
STUVWXYZ 1234567890
(&£$¥€?!%ÆŒ@)

CREAM

DF Vertex

Rian Hughes
1999

Entire family consists of Light,
Medium, Demi Bold, Bold, and
Inline.

ABCDEFGHIJKLMNOPQRSTUV
abcdefghijklmnopqrstuvw
1234567890 (&£$¥€?!%)

extras

DF Westway

Rian Hughes
2002

Entire family consists of
Eastbound and Westbound.

ABCDEFGHIJKLMNOPQR
STUVWHYZ 1234567890
(&£$¥€?!%ÆŒ@)

FUTURE

info@devicefonts.co.uk

ABCDEFGHIJKLMNOPQRST
abcdefghijklmnopqrstuvwx
1234567890 (&£$¥€?!%)

DF Wexford Oakley

Rian Hughes
1997

Entire family consists of Regular and Alternates.

DF Why Two Kay

Rian Hughes
1999

ABCDEFGHIJKLM
ABCDEFGHIJKLMNOPQ
1234567890 (&?!%)

PRINTER &
DECORATOR

DF Wormwood Gothic

Rian Hughes
2006

ABCDEFGHIJKLMNOPQRSTUVWXYZ
abcdefghijklmnopqrstuvwxyz
1234567890 (&£$¥€?!%‰@®)

Cosmology 101

DF Xenotype

Rian Hughes
2004

Entire family consists of Regular and Shaded.

ABCDEFGHIJKLMNOPQRST
abcdefghijklmnopqrstuvw
1234567890 [&£$¥€?!%]

Stamp™

DF Yellow Perforated

Rian Hughes
2005

Entire family consists of Regular and Solid.

ABCDEFGHIJKLMNOPQRSTUVWXYZ
abcdefghijklmnopqrstuvwxyz
1234567890 (&£$¥€?!%Æ@®)

Queen

DF Yolanda

Rian Hughes
2004

Entire family consists of Countess, Duchess, and Princess.

ABCDEFGHIJK
abcdefghijkl
1234567890
?&£$¥€?!‰Æ

zap

DF Zinger

Rian Hughes
2000

Entire family consists of Regular and Italic.

ABCDEFGHIJKLMNOPQRSTUVWXYZ
ABCDEFGHIJKLMNOPQRSTUVWXYZ
1234567890 (&£$¥€?!%Æ@®)

PROTEST NOW!

DF Zond Diktat

Rian Hughes
2005

Entire family consists of Medium and Bold.

Device

Urgent Matter:
OPEN WITHOUT DELAY

RECEIVER'S NUMBER

DATE

TIME FILED

CHECK

SENDING STATION:

E-PHEMERA
Vintage Fonts for a Digital World

SYMBOLS: DL·DAY LETTER NL·NIGHT LETTER LC·DEFERRED CABLE
NLT·CABLE NIGHT LETTER SR·SHIP RADIOGRAM

A
MAIL

AN · ACTUAL LETTER ON ACTUAL PAPER · ELABORATELY OVERDONE · PLEASE WRITE BACK SOON!

FOR OFFICIAL USE ONLY

RESPONSE OPTIONS:
(PARTIAL LISTING)

MAIL....... | VIA USPS TO SENDER
TELEPHONE
(CELL)... | 323 646 4798
(LAND).. | 323 227 5527
E-MAIL.... | EPHEMERA@AHLEMAN.COM
RETRO-GRAM | WWW.RETRO-GRAM.COM

E-PHEMERA FONTS

WWW.AHLEMAN.COM   WWW.MYFONTS.COM

489 MAVIS DRIVE
LOS ANGELES, CA
90065

In the course of work as a prop designer for movies, television, and gaming, I often need fonts that accurately replicate the look of older, nondigital printing technologies. When I can't find them, I make them myself. Over the years, I have amassed a considerable and growing collection of these vintage fonts, and now make them available through www.myfonts.com.

E-phemera fonts are meant to revive type from years gone by in a way that captures the feeling of pre-digital printing technology. "Ephemera" is a term used to describe all manner of printed items that were not intended to last very long: pamphlets, circulars, dance cards, tickets, and the like. E-phemera fonts are inspired by this old printed and hand-lettered material and are usually designed a little rough and a little irregular, in deliberate defiance of the crisp perfection and merciless uniformity of modern digital fonts. Multiple letterforms and ligatures are provided when possible and practical. As a lover of letters and a user of fonts myself, I believe in keeping prices low and license terms generous. Although I love computers and wouldn't do without them, I also wish to remember and celebrate the days when every letter was an individual piece of metal or wood and not just a collection of BCP data.

Print, they say, is dead. Long live print!

Andrew W. Leman

Andrew Leman

Cablegram Regular

LEWISTON ME 725P PLANE TRIP CANCELLED. HOME ON TRAIN. SEE YOU TUESDAY. LOVE =MAC.

ABCDEFGHIJKLMNOPQRSTUVWXYZ
ÅBÇDÉFGHÎJKLMÑÒPQRSTÜVWXYZ1234567890!@©®™#$¢%&*"''()[]{}¶

Cablegram Urgent

= KEEP DESTINATION QUIET.
EXPECT GREAT REVELATIONS.
ABCDEFGH
IJKLMNOPQ
RSTUVWXYZ
ÅBÇDÉFGHÎJKLMÑÒPQRSTÜVWXYZ
1234567890!?.,:;
@©®™#$¢%&*"''()[]{}¶

Cablegram Ottoman

abcdefghijklm
nopqrstuvwxyz
åbçdéfghîjklm
ñòpqrstüvwxyz
1234567890
!?.,:;@©®™$¢*"''¶
shipper states cod $13.04
covers both ctns. on hand

Cablegram Madras

WR16 KUALALUMPUR 5 1027 - LC
- SANGANITHI MADRAS - RECEIVE
1000 MERCANTILE - SIDAMBARAM *
ABCDEFGHIJKLM
NOPQRSTUVWXYZ
ÅBÇDÉFGHÎJKLMÑÒPQRSTÜVWXYZ
1234567890
!?.,:;@©®™#$
¢%&*"''()[]{}¶

Cablegram Zagreb

Paris 24437 15 16 9 = Profondevens Peines Grand Valheur Prions Avoir Courage Vous Embrassons Attristes
ABCDEFGHIJKLMNOPQRSTUVWXYZabcdefghijklmnopqrstuvwxyz
ÅÇÉÑÒÜÆæŒŒœ†‡1234567890!@©®™№$¢ZŁ*"''()()[]{}

Cablegram

Andrew Leman
2000

The members of the Cablegram family are replicas of a variety of typewriters used on international telegrams from the 1920s and '30s and were designed originally for www.retro-gram.com. In keeping with their mechanical origins and to better capture the look of the source material, the fonts are monospaced and have no kerning pairs.

For Digestion's Sake...
Made from better, more expensive
tobaccos than any other popular brand!

Aa Bb Cc Dd Ee Ff Gg Hh Ii Jj Kk Ll Mm
Nn Oo Pp Qq Rr Ss Tt Uu Vv Ww Xx Yy Zz
1234567890!@©®™#$¢%¢*"''()[]{}¶
ε s εε ſſ tt dd pp bb æ ll ff gg s ª º Æ Ø

Satisfaction

Andrew Leman
2003

This casual script font was inspired by hand-lettered cigarette ads appearing in 1930s magazines. It features alternate letterforms and ligatures to help create a handwritten feel.

E-phemera

Shipley

Andrew Leman
2004

This font was based on the type used in a 1920s pamphlet from the now-defunct Science League of America. The piece was retrieved from the ephemera bin of a Chicago used bookstore many years ago. "I loved the type but couldn't identify it," designer Andrew Leman said. "So I made my own version in a crisp, clean roman and italic and four rougher weights that capture the feel of old metal type. It is named after Maynard Shipley, the president of the Science League who passionately defended science education and the teaching of evolutionary theory. Years later, I was finally able to identify the source font as Kennerley, originally designed by Frederic Goudy. Amazingly, the argument about teaching evolution rages on."

THE SCIENCE LEAGUE OF AMERICA

Maynard [1927] Shipley

Shipley Rough

123ABCDEFGHIJKLM456
78NOPQRSTUVWXYZ90
abcdefghijklmnopqrstuvwxyz
.,:;?!/[]()@#$%&*©™†§¶fifIffiffl
"ÅÄÇÉÈÎÑÕÕÜåäçéèîñöü"

Shipley Rough SC

123ABCDEFGHIJKLM456
78NOPQRSTUVWXYZ90
ABCDEFGHIJKLMNOPQRSTUVWXYZ
.,:;?!/[]()@#$%&*©™†§¶
"ÅÄÇÉÈÎÑÕÕÜåäçéèîñöü"

Shipley Rough Italic

123ABCDEFGHIJKLM456
78NOPQRSTUVWXYZ90
abcdefghijklmnopqrstuvwxyz
.,:;?!/[]()@#$%&*©™†§¶fifIffiffl
"ÅÄÇÉÈÎÑÕÕÜåäçéèîñöü"

An Alarming Situation

There could be no greater mistake than to assume that the sudden death of William Jennings Bryan means the passing of Bryanism. Bryan's son, indeed, has announced that he will continue his father's anti-evolution activities. Nor does freedom in teaching and in *learning* depend upon the outcome of the Scopes test case. "This is a matter for the nation: there's no compromise possible. It's a fight to the finish."

"I believe that with a vigorous effort such a law or proscription can be and will be established in fifteen or twenty states. The next step will be to banish such teaching from all schools; and we may witness the spectacle in this country of men and women facing prosecution who decline to accept the literal statement of the Old Testament upon geography, geology, and astronomy and the origin of human life, and to construct their theology on the foundation of a flat earth."

Shipley Regular

123ABCDEFGHIJKLM456
78NOPQRSTUVWXYZ90
abcdefghijklmnopqrstuvwxyz
.,:;?!/[]()@#$%&*©™†§¶fifIffiffl
"ÅÄÇÉÈÎÑÕÕÜåäçéèîñöü"

Shipley Italic

123ABCDEFGHIJKLM456
78NOPQRSTUVWXYZ90
abcdefghijklmnopqrstuvwxyz
.,:;?!/[]()@#$%&*©™†§¶fifIffiffl
"ÅÄÇÉÈÎÑÕÕÜåäçéèîñöü"

Shipley Rough Italic Alternate

123ABCDEFGHIJKLM456
78NOPQRSTUVWXYZ90
abcdefghijklmnopqrstuvwxyz
.,:;?!/[]()@#$%&*©™†§¶fifIffiffl
"ÅÄÇÉÈÎÑÕÕÜåäçéèîñöü"

Coldstyle

Andrew Leman
2004

This font was inspired by the classic Old Style No. 1 found in a Linotype catalog from the 1930s. It's gently aged to capture the feel of old metal type.

COLD MOUNTAIN

Four score and seven years ago our fathers brought forth upon this continent a new nation, conceived in liberty and dedicated to the proposition that all men are created equal. Now we are engaged in a great civil war, testing whether that nation — or any nation so conceived and so dedicated — can long endure. We are met on a great battlefield of that war. We have come to dedicate a portion of that field as a final resting place for those who here gave their lives that this nation might live. It is altogether fitting and proper that we should do this.

But, in a larger sense, we cannot dedicate, we cannot consecrate, we cannot hallow this ground. The brave men, living and dead, who struggled

Coldstyle Roman

123ABCDEFGHIJKLM456
78NOPQRSTUVWXYZ90
abcdefghijklmnopqrstuvwxyz
.,:;?!/[]()@№$%&*©™†§¶fifl
"ÅÄÇÉÈÎÑÕÕÜåäçéèîñöü"

Coldstyle Italic

123ABCDEFGHIJKLM456
78NOPQRSTUVWXYZ90
abcdefghijklmnopqrstuvwxyz
.,:;?!/[]()@#$%&*©™†§¶
"ÅÄÇÉÈÎÑÕÕÜåäçéèîñöü"

Coldstyle SC

ABCDEFGHIJKLM
NOPQRSTUVWXYZ
ABCDEFGHIJKLM
NOPQRSTUVWXYZ
.,:;?!/[]()@№$%&*©™†§¶

here have consecrated it far above our poor power to add or detract. The world will little note nor long remember what we say here, but it can never forget what they did here.

It is for us — the living — rather to be dedicated here to the unfinished work which they who fought here have thus far so nobly advanced. It is rather for us to be here dedicated to the great task remaining before us: that from these honored dead we take increased devotion to that cause for which they gave the last full measure of devotion. That we here highly resolve that these dead shall not have died in vain, that this nation, under God, shall have a new birth of freedom, and that this government of the people, by the people, and for the people shall not perish from the earth.

ephemera@ahleman.com

ABCDEFGHIJKLMNOPQRSTUVWXYZ
abcdefghijklmnopqrstuvwxyz
1234567890.,:;?!-/'''"\\"()«»—&~ß©~æ œff ffiflŒÆ

Andrew Leman
2005

This friendly font was inspired by the hand lettering of Fred G. Cooper, whose work decorated the pages of *Life* magazine in the 1920s. It was originally developed for use in the screen credits and intertitles of an independent motion picture shot in the style of a classic silent film.

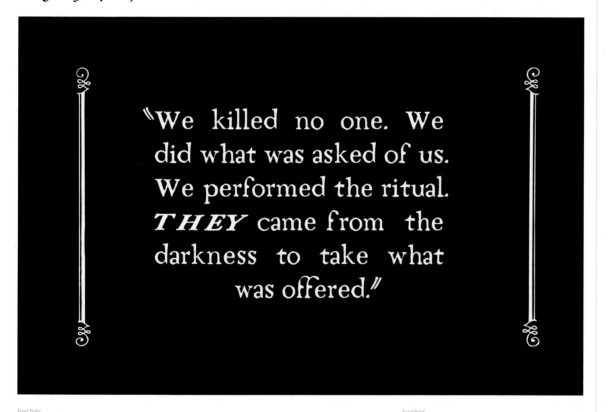

"We killed no one. We did what was asked of us. We performed the ritual. *THEY* came from the darkness to take what was offered."

Fred Italic

ABCDEFGHIJKLM
NOPQRSTUVWXYZ
abcdefghijklmnopqrstuvwxyz
1234567890.,:;?!-'''""()—&~ffffififl

Fred Bold

ABCDEFGHIJKLM
NOPQRSTUVWXYZ
abcdefghijklm
nopqrstuvwxyz
1234567890
.,:;?!-/'''""()—
&©~æœffffififl

E-phemera

Journalistic	
Andrew Leman	
2006	

The Morning Journal

ABCDEFGHIJKLMNOPQRSTUVWXYZabcdefghijklmnopqrstuvwxyz№1234567890.,;:&

Temporal
Andrew Leman
2006

The Daily Times

ABCDEFGHIJKLMNOPQRSTUVWXYZabcdefghijklmnopqrstuvwxyz1234567890.,;:&&

Transcriptural
Andrew Leman
2006

The Evening Transcript

ABCDEFGHIJKLMNOPQRSTUVWXYZabcdefghijklmnopqrstuvwxyz.,;:

Exilis
Andrew Leman
2004

EARHART FORCED DOWN AT SEA

ABCDEFGHIJKLMNOPQRSTUVWXYZabcdefghijklmnopqrstuvwxyz.,;:1234567890?!@#$%&*()[]{}©®™§¶ß€

Glendale Gothic
Andrew Leman
2006

APPEAL TO THE KING REVEALED

ABCDEFGHIJKLMNOPQRSTUVWXYZabcdefghijklmnopqrstuvwxyz.,;:1234567890?!@№$%&()ÄÇÉÍÑ

Toronto Gothic
Andrew Leman
2003

HOOVER SKEPTICAL OF SUCCESS

ABCDEFGHIJKLMNOPQRSTUVWXYZABCDEFGHIJKLMNOPQRSTUVWXYZ.,;:1234567890?!@#$%&()

Subhead One
Andrew Leman
2004

Demand For Statute in Capital

ABCDEFGHIJKLMNOPQRSTUVWXYZabcdefghijklmnopqrstuvwxyz.,;:1234567890?!$&()

Subhead Two
Andrew Leman
2004

Truce Expected at Once

ABCDEFGHIJKLMNOPQRSTUVWXYZabcdefghijklmnopqrstuvwxyz.,;:1234567890?!$&

EXTRA! EXTRA

LATEST NEWS

HOME EDITION

EVENING EDITION

FINAL EDITION

HOME EDITION

COMPLETE FINANCIAL

FINAL HOME EDITION

HOME

HOME EDITION

EARLY SPORTS

Extra Extra

Andrew Leman
2005

This dingbat font, along with the fonts on the opposite page, was designed for use in creating vintage prop newspapers. The designs were inspired by a variety of North American newspapers and tabloids from the 1920s and '30s.

E-phemera

Satinheime

Andrew Leman
2004

Satinheime is a digitization of hand-drawn poster lettering by Otto Heim from 1925. The regular style can be used on its own, or you can use the base style in conjunction with the left and/or right styles for a multicolored effect. Interesting effects can be achieved by using all four styles together with the regular style on top and slightly out of register.

DARK ADVENTURE

Satinheime Regular

ABCDEFGHIJKLM
NOPQRSTUVWXYZ
abcdefghijklmnopqrstuvwxyz
1234567890.,;:?!-//''''""—

Satinheime Base

ABCDEFG
HIJKLM
NOPQRST
UVWXYZ
abcdefghijklm
nopqrstuvwxyz

Satinheime Left

ABCDEFG
HIJKLM
NOPQRST
UVWXYZ
abcdefghijklm
nopqrstuvwxyz

Satinheime Right

ABCDEFG
HIJKLM
NOPQRST
UVWXYZ
abcdefghijklm
nopqrstuvwxyz

Hadank

Andrew Leman
2004

Hadank is a display typeface developed from hand-lettered words in a German printer's letterhead from the 1920s.

Hadank Regular

ABCDEFGHIJKLM
NOPQRSTUVWXYZ
abcdefghijklmnopqrstuvwxyz
1234567890.,;:?!-/'''""—-$¢€£¥©®@&★

★GESCHÄFTSBÜCHER

Hadank Engraved

ABCDEFGHIJKLM
NOPQRSTUVWXYZ
abcdefghijklmnopqrstuvwxyz
1234567890.,;:?!-/'''""—-$¢€£¥©®@&★

ABCDEFGHIJKLM
NOPQRSTUVWXYZ
ABCDEFGHIJKLMNOPQRSTUVWXYZ
1234567890.,:;?!-/'''""—&*$¢€£¥ÆŒ
UNITED STATES OF AMERICA
2576

ABCDEFGHIJKLM
NOPQRSTUVWXYZ
ABCDEFGHIJKLMNOPQRSTUVWXYZ
1234567890.,:;?!.-/'''""—&*$¢€£¥ÆŒ

Stentorian

Andrew Leman
2003

Stentorian was inspired by some captions for illustrations found in a book about sign lettering from the early 1900s. The uppercase letters have smoother outlines than the lowercase set, for use at various sizes. The engraved style can be used over the regular style to create a two-color effect.

ABCDEFGHIJKLM
NOPQRSTUVWXYZ
abcdefghijklmnopqrstuvwxyz
1234567890.,:;?!-'''""—_

Golden Ticket

Andrew Leman
2003

Golden Ticket is a digitization of hand-drawn poster lettering by Otto Heim from 1925. The regular style is meant to be used on its own, while the other three styles are meant to be used atop one another in three different colors to create a 3-D effect. For best results, set the base style on the bottom, the fill style directly above in a second color, and the highlight style layered on top in a third color.

ABCDEFG
HIJKLM
NOPQRST
UVWXYZ
abcdefghijklm
nopqrstuvwxyz

ABCDEFG
HIJKLM
NOPQRST
UVWXYZ
abcdefghijklm
nopqrstuvwxyz

ABCDEFG
HIJKLM
NOPQRST
UVWXYZ
abcdefghijklm
nopqrstuvwxyz

MYSTERY STORIES

E-phemera

Compliments

Andrew Leman
2003

Compliments was inspired by a few hand-lettered words found on a 1930s Western Union brochure entitled *The Yellow Blank Is Correct for Every Social Need.* This design contains some common double-letter pairs to help create the look of hand lettering.

Compliments Regular

ABCDEFGHIJKLMNOPQRSTUVWXYZ
abcdefghijklmnopqrstuvwxyz
1234567890 .,:;?!
- / ' ' " " — № $ % ¢ ( ) @© ss rr ff*

Compliments of the Management

Compliments Upright

ABCDEFGHIJKLMNOPQRSTUVWXYZ
abcdefghijklmnopqrstuvwxyz
1234567890 .,:;?!
- / ' ' " " — № $ % ¢ ( ) @© ss rr ff*

Landry Gothic

Andrew Leman
2003

Landry Gothic was inspired by a wood type alphabet by an unknown designer. It was digitized in order to make prop signage for movies and television. Its imperfect lines and rounded corners are meant to capture the feeling of real wood or metal type that's worn from use. Landry Gothic works very well for cutting vinyl signage.

ABCDEFGHIJKLM
NOPQRSTUVWXYZ
ABCDEFGHIJKLMNOPQRSTUVWXYZ
1234567890.,:;?!-/'"""–$©@&*

CAUTION
COMPUTER CONTROLLED
DO NOT INTERFERE

YOU MUST READ THIS WORD FOR WORD! INFORMATION THAT YOU MAY NOT RECEIVE AGAIN SO PLEASE TAKE IT SERIOUSLY!! WOULD YOU LIKE TO.... RECEIVE $500, $1,500, $3,500 CASH DAILY? IF YES, CLICK HERE NOW! PEOPLE ARE MAKING REAL FORTUNES NO HYPE – NO FALSE PREDICTIONS! HAVE UNLIMITED CASH FLOW POTENTIAL.

ABCDEFGHIJKLM NOPQRSTUVWXYZ

ABCDEFGHIJKLMNOPQRSTUVWXYZ
1234567890.,:;?!-/''""–&*$#@©®℗™

Policy Gothic

Andrew Leman
2003

Policy Gothic was inspired by boilerplate text found on an insurance policy from the 1920s.

Lanier Small Caps

ABCDEFGHIJKLM NOPQRSTUVWXYZ
abcdefghijklmnopqrstuvwxyz
1234567890.,:;?!-/''""(℗®©)
th wh ff ct ſp ſt and ch dd pp ll

The Harlequin of Dreams

Lanier Regular

Aa Bb Cc Dd Ee Ff Gg Hh Ii Jj Kk Ll Mm Nn Oo Pp Qq Rr Ss Tt Uu Vv Ww Xx Yy Zz

Swift, through
some trap mine
eyes have
never found,
Dim-panelled in
the painted scene of
sleep,
Thou, giant
Harlequin of
Dreams, dost leap
Upon my
spirit's stage.

Lanier

Andrew Leman
2004

Lanier is based on the handwriting of American poet and novelist Sidney Lanier, as seen in a letter he wrote in 1875. The font features numerous special ligatures and letter combinations to better mimic the feel of real, if rather hard-to-read, handwriting.

E-phemera

Mercantile

Andrew Leman
2005

Mercantile was adapted from a 1923 type specimen book and was designed for use on vintage prop stock certificates and government licenses.

ABCDEFGHIJKLMNOPQRSTUVWXYZ
ABCDEFGHIJKLMNOPQRSTUVWXYZ
1234567890.,:;?!-''""-$&

CHAIRMAN OF THE BOARD

Mercantile Card

ABCDEFGHIJKLMNOPQRSTUVWXYZ
ABCDEFGHIJKLMNOPQRSTUVWXYZ
1234567890.,:;?!-''""-$&

CHIEF FINANCIAL OFFICER

Mercantile Oblique

ABCDEFGHIJKLMNOPQRSTUVWXYZ
ABCDEFGHIJKLMNOPQRSTUVWXYZ
1234567890.,:;?!-''""-$&

PRESIDENT

Saccovanzetti

Andrew Leman
2003

This slanted display type was inspired by hand-lettered advertisements from the 1920s.

ABCDEFGHIJKLMNOPQRSTUVWXYZ
abcdefghijklmnopqrstuvwxyz
1234567890.,:;?!-/''""–#$&()

Vogue

Andrew Leman
2003

Vogue was extrapolated from text found in a 1930s brochure from Western Union called *The Vogue of the Social Telegram*.

ABCDEFGHIJKLMNOPQRSTUVWXYZ
ABCDEFGHIJKLMNOPQRSTUVWXYZ
1234567890.,:;?!-/''""–Nº$&()@

ephemera@ahleman.com

A B CDEFGHIJKLMN OPQRSTUVWXYZ

Nate Ward

Andrew Leman
2003

Nate Ward is based on nineteenth-century display type.

ABCDEFGHIJKLM
NOPQRSTUVWXYZ
abcdefghijklmnopqrstuvwxyz
1234567890.,.:;?!-'""" $&@ggttddffft
fresh Summer air all winter long

Reinert

Andrew Leman
2003

Reinert is inspired by the hand lettering of 1930s advertising layout artist Allen Reinert. It features letter pairs, ligatures, and alternate characters.

Impersonal Regular

I'm complicated, yet simple. I'm decent yet wild. But the main thing is I know when to be what. And when I'm anything (e.g. hot) I know how to be that. Too complex for you?? I hope you can handle. I would like to meet a girl that's decent and sexy. An easy going girl who is simple. One who will turn me hot and makes me go wild on the bed. I like both sides of life and try to explore. I am changing all the time according my surrounding, so if you don't match, don't worry, stay with me and I'll change. Rock on. Waiting for (your name goes here).

ABCDEFGHIJKLM
NOPQRSTUVWXYZ
abcdefghijklmnopqrstuvwxyz
[1234567890.,:;?!-''""""®*€$&@©™]

Impersonal

Andrew Leman
2004

Impersonal is a detailed replica of type appearing in *La Plume*, a 1950s personal ads magazine. The magazine billed itself as "The correspondence medium devoted to the connoisseur of the 'unusual'." Impersonal is a monospaced typewriter font with no kerning pairs.

ABCDEFGHIJKLM
NOPQRSTUVWXYZ
abcdefghijklmnopqrstuvwxyz
[1234567890.,:;?!-''""""®*€$&@©™]

Impersonal Light

I need someone in my life. Every committed relationship I've been in has ended on a sour note. And here I am, putting myself out there just in case my soul-mate is using this site too. I've searched for him, but in vain. Maybe now he'll find me.... Note to my soul-mate: If you're out there, please find me soon. My heart is aching without you & I'm not sure how much more loneliness I can withstand. I've loved you on paper for years... Isn't it time to love you in real life? NOTE: Does no one believe in MARRIAGE any more??????

Blackburn

Andrew Leman
2006

Blackburn is one of a series of types intended for use at small text sizes to capture the feel of vintage letterpress printing. Blackburn was inspired by a French type sample dating from the turn of the twentieth century.

ABCDEFGHIJKLMNOPQRSTUVWXYZ

Blackburn abcdefghijklmnopqrstuvwxyz

1234567890.,:;?!-''""—$ÆŒ æœ fifl @©

When we compare the individuals of the same variety or sub-variety of our older cultivated plants and animals, one of the first points which strikes us is, that they generally differ more from each other than do the individuals of any one species or variety in a state of nature. And if we reflect on the vast diversity of the plants and animals which have been cultivated, and which have varied during all ages under the most different climates and treatment, we are driven to conclude that this great variability is due to our domestic productions having been raised under conditions of life not so uniform as, and somewhat different from, those to which the parent species had been exposed under nature. There is, also, some probability in the view propounded by Andrew Knight, that

Epistre

Andrew Leman
2006

Epistre was inspired by a French type sample from the mid-1600s. It includes traditional ligatures and archaic letterforms, including the long s.

ABCDEFGHIJKLMNOPQRSTUVWXYZ

Epistre abcdefghijklmnopqrstuvwxyz

. , : ; ! - '' "" & ¶ ß ®©™ ff st ct ſſ ſt us is ſbſ

seems clear that organic beings must be exposed during several generations to new conditions to cause any great amount of variation; and that, when the organisation has once begun to vary, it generally continues varying for many generations. No case is on record of a variable organism ceasing to vary under cultivation. Our oldest cultivated plants, such as wheat, still yield new varieties: our oldest domesticated animals are still capable of rapid improvement or modification. As far as I am able to judge, after long attending to the subject, the conditions of life appear to act in two ways, directly on the whole organisation or on certain parts alone, and indirectly by affecting the reproductive system. With respect to the direct action, we must bear in mind that in every case, as Professor Weismann has lately insisted, and as I have incidentally shown in my

Offerman

Andrew Leman
2006

Offerman is based on a French type sample dating from 1470 and contains classic typographical ligatures.

ABCDEFGHIJKLMNOPQRSTUVWXYZ

Offerman abcdefghijklmnopqrstuvwxyz

(1234567890.,:;?!-@ ÆŒ æœ fi fl ff ffi ffl « »)

seems to be much the more important; for nearly similar variations sometimes arise under, as far as we can judge, dissimilar conditions; and, on the other hand, dissimilar variations arise under conditions which appear to be nearly uniform. The effects on the offspring are either definite or indefinite. They may be considered as definite when all or nearly all the offspring of individuals exposed to certain conditions during several generations are modified in the same manner. It is extremely difficult to come to any conclusion in regard to the extent of the changes which have been thus definitely induced. There can, however, be little doubt about many slight changes, such as size from the amount of food, colour from the nature of the food, thickness of the skin and hair from climate, etc. Each of the endless variations which we see in the plumage

Derham

Andrew Leman
2005

Derham was inspired by the italic type used extensively in the encyclopedic footnotes of *Physico-Theology: or, A Demonstration of the Being and Attributes of God, from His Works of Creation* (Third Edition, Corrected), by W. Derham, Rector of Upminster in Essex, published in St. Paul's Church Yard in 1716. It features archaic ligatures and alternate characters, including the long s.

ABCDEFGHIJKLMNOPQRSTUVWXYZ

Derham abcdefghijklmnopqrstuvwxyz

1234567890.,:;-' & *@©®ct st ſh ſ ſl ſſ ſt as is k ll ff

(65) The Contrivance of the Legs, Feet and Nails of the Opoſſum ſeems very advantageous to this Animal in climbing Trees (which it doth very nimbly) for preying upon Birds. But that which is moſt ſingular in this Animal, is the Structure of its Tail, to enable it to hang on Boughs. The Spines, or Hooks — in the middle of the under ſide of the Vertebræ of the Tail, are a wonderful piece of Nature's Mechaniſm. The firſt three Vertebræ had none of theſe Spines, but in all the reſt they were obſerved. They were placed juſt at the Articulation of each Joynt, and in the middle from the Sides. For the performing this Office [of hanging by the Tail] nothing, I think, could be more advantageouſly contrived. For when the Tail is twirled about a Stick, this Hook of the Spine eaſily ſuſtains the Weight, and there is but little labour of the Muſcles required. See Dr. Tyson's Anat. of the Opoſſ. in Phil. Tranſ. No. 239

ABCDEFGHIJKLMNOPQRSTUVWXYZ
abcdefghijklmnopqrstuvwxyz Garamold Roman
1234567890.,:;?!-''""& Æ Œ æ œ ff fi fl ffl ſt ſ ſl ſt

Garamold

Andrew Leman
2006

Garamold is a digitization of letters designed by Claude Garamond dating from 1540. It includes traditional ligatures and alternate letterforms, including the long s.

Therewith he spake to Hermes, his dear son: "Hermes, forasmuch as even in all else thou art our herald, tell unto the nymph of the braided tresses my unerring counsel, even the return of the patient Odysseus, how he is to come to his home, with no furtherance of gods or of mortal men. Nay, he shall sail on a well-bound raft, in sore distress, and on the twentieth day arrive at fertile Scheria, even at the land of the Phæacians, who are near of kin to the gods. And they shall give him all worship heartily as to a god, and send him on his way in a ship to his own dear country, with gifts of bronze and gold, and raiment in plenty, much store, such as never would Odysseus have won for himself out of Troy, yea, though he had returned unhurt with the share of the spoil that fell to him. On such wise is he fated to see his friends, and come to his high-roofed home and his own country."

So spake he, nor heedless was the messenger, the slayer of Argos. Straightway he bound beneath his feet his lovely golden sandals, that wax not old, that bare him alike over the wet sea and over the limitless land, swift as the breath of the wind. And he took the wand wherewith he lulls the eyes of whomso he will, while others again he even wakes from out of sleep. With this rod in his hand flew the strong slayer of Argos.

ABCDEFGHIJKLMNOPQRSTUVWXYZ
abcdefghijklmnopqrstuvwxyz Garamold Italic
1234567890.,:;!-''"" & Æ Œ æ œ ct

And lo, there about the hollow cave trailed a gadding garden vine, all rich with clusters. And fountains four set orderly were running with clear water, hard by one another, turned each to his own course. And all around soft meadows bloomed of violets and parsley, yea, even a deathless god who came thither might wonder at the sight and be glad at heart. There the messenger, the slayer of Argos, stood and wondered. Now when he had gazed at all with wonder, anon he went into the wide cave; nor did Calypso, that fair goddess, fail to know him, when she saw him face to face; for the gods use not to be strange one to another, the immortals, not though one have his habitation far away. But he found not Odysseus, the greathearted, within the cave, who sat weeping on the shore.

ABCDEFGHIJKLMNOPQRSTUVWXYZ
abcdefghijklmnopqrstuvwxyz Hale
1234567890.,:;?!-''""& ſ ſi ſſi ſb ſſ ct æ œ

Hale

Andrew Leman
2006

Hale was inspired by a French type sample dating from the turn of the twentieth century. It includes traditional typographic ligatures and archaic letterforms, including the long s.

But if the destruction of the Union by one, or by a part only, of the States be lawfully possible, the Union is less perfect than before the Constitution, having lost the vital element of perpetuity.

It follows from these views that no State, upon its own mere motion, can lawfully get out of the Union; that resolves and ordinances to that effect are legally void; and that acts of violence, within any State or States, against the authority of the United States, are insurrectionary or revolutionary, according to circumstances.

I therefore consider that, in view of the Constitution and the laws, the Union is unbroken; and to the extent of my ability I shall take care, as the Constitution itself expressly enjoins upon me, that the laws of the Union be faithfully executed in all of the States. Doing this I deem to be only a simple duty on my part; and I shall perform it, so far as practicable, unless my rightful masters, the American people, shall withhold the requisite means, or in some Authoritative manner direct the contrary. I trust this will not be regarded as a menace, but only as the declared purpose of the Union that it will constitutionally defend and maintain itself.

In doing this there needs to be no bloodshed or violence; and there shall be none, unless it be forced upon the national authority. The power confided to me will be used to hold, occupy, and possess the property and places belonging to the Government, and to collect the duties and imposts; but beyond what may be

E-phemera

Andrew Leman
2004

The members of the Vatican family were inspired by samples from the type specimen book of the Vatican Press dating from 1628. The types all feature archaic ligatures and alternate character forms, including the long s, which was commonly used at that time. Vatican was developed for use in a prop book of seventeenth-century magic and sorcery.

Vatican Clement

ABCDEFGHIJKLMNOPQRSTUVWXYZ

VATICAN abcdefghijklmnopqrstuvwxyz CLEMENT

1234567890.,:;?!-'''""— $ & ſſ ſt ff fi fl ct æ

Adonai, Elohim, El, Eheieh Aſher Eheieh, Prince of Princes, Exiſtence of Exiſtences, have mercy upon me, and caſt thine eyes upon thy ſervant (N.) who invoketh thee moſt devoutly, and ſupplicateth thee by thy holy and tremendous name, Tetragrammaton, to be propitious and to order thine angels and ſpiritſ to come and take up their abode in this place; O ye angels and ſpirits of the ſtars, O all ye angels and elementary ſpirits, O all ye ſpirits preſent before the face of God, I the miniſter and faithful ſervant of the moſt high conjure ye, let God himſelf, the Exiſtence of Exiſtences, conjure ye to come and be preſent at this operation; I the ſervant of God, moſt humbly entreat ye. Amen.

Vatican Gregory

ABCDEFGHIJKLMNOPQRSTUVWXYZ

VATICAN abcdefghijklmnopqrstuvwxyz GREGORY

1234567890.,:;?!-'''""— $ & ff ffl fi fl ct st es is as us æ œ † ſſ ſh ſp

It being underſtood that in this operation we have to do with a great and powerful enemy, whom through our own weakneſs and human ſtrength or ſcience we cannot reſſiſt without particular aid and aſſiſtance from the holy angels and from the Lord of the good ſpirits; it is neceſſary that each one ſhould always have God before his eyes, and in no way offend Him. On the other hand, he muſt always be upon his guard, and abſtain as from a mortal ſin from flattering, obeying, regarding, or having reſpect to the demon, and to his viperine race; neither muſt he ſubmit himſelf unto him in the ſlighteſt thing, for that would be his ruin and the fatal loſs of his soul.

As it happened unto all the ſeed deſcended from Noah, Lot, Iſhmael, and others who did poſſeſs the bleſſed land (before our forefathers)

Vatican Innocent

ABCDEFGHIIKLMNOPQRSTVVVVXYZ

VATICAN abcdefghijklmnopqrstuvvvxyz INNOCENT

1234567890.,:;?-'''""$ & ſ ſſ ſt ct fi Æ æ

I exhort you, ye vvho read, to have the fear of God, and to ſtudy juſtice, becauſe infallibly unto you ſhall be opened the gate of the true vviſdom vvhich God gave unto Noah and unto his deſcendants Iaphet, Abraham, and Iſhmael; and it vvas his vviſdom that delivered Lot from the burning of Sodom. Moſes learned the ſame vviſdom in the deſert, from the Burning Buſh, and he taught it unto Aaron his brother. Ioſeph, Samuel, David, Solomon, Elijah, and the Apoſtles, and Saint Iohn particularly (from vvhom vve hold a moſt excellent book of prophecy) poſſeſſed it. Let every one then knovv that this, this vvhich I teach, is that ſame vviſdom and magic, and vvhich is in this ſame book, and independent of any other ſcience, or vviſdom, or magic, ſoever. It is, hovvever, certainly true that theſe miraculous operations have much in common vvith the Qabalah; it if alſo true that there are other arts vvhich have ſome ſtamp of vviſdom; the vvhich alone vvould be nothing vvorth vvere they not mingled vvith the foundation of

Vatican Urban

ABCDEFGHIJKLMNOPQRSTVVVWXYZ

VATICAN abcdefghijklmnopqrstuvvvwxyz VRBAN

(1234567890.,:;?!-'''"" & Æ æ s ct ſt)

THE NETHERMOST CAVERNS ARE NOT FOR THE FATH-OMING OF EYES THAT SEE; FOR THEIR MARVELS ARE STRANGE AND TERRIFIC. Curſed the ground vvhere dead thoughts live nevv and oddly bodied, and evil the mind that is held by no head. Wiſely did Ibn Schacabao ſay, that happy is the tomb vvhere no vvizard hath lain, and happy the tovvn at night vvhoſe vvizards are all aſhes. For it is of old rumour that the ſoul of the devil-bought haſtes not from his charnel clay, but fats and inſtructs the very vvorm that gnavvs; till out of corruption horrid life ſprings, and the dull ſcavengers of earth vvax crafty to vex it and ſvvell monſtrous to plague it. Great holes are digged vvhere earth's pores ought to ſuffice, and things have learnt to vvalk that ought to cravvl.

Buchstaben

A B C D E F G H I J K L M
N O P Q R S T U V W X Y Z
a b c d e f g h i j k l m n o p q r s t u v w x y z
1 2 3 4 5 6 7 8 9 0 . , : ; ? ! ‹ ‚ ' ' ' ‚ ' — $ ₡
ſ z ſt ch ſi ll ſt tt ßk ßß ck tz ſt th
$ ¢ £ © @ ™ Æ œ Œ œ

Buchstabenzusammenzückungen

The Necronomicon

Nor is it to be thought, that man is either the oldest or the last of earth's masters, or that the common bulk of life and substance walks alone. The Old Ones were, the Old Ones are, and the Old Ones shall be. Not in the spaces we know, but between them, They walk serene and primal, undimensioned and to us unseen. Yog-Sothoth knows the gate. Yog-Sothoth is the gate. Yog-Sothoth is the key and guardian of the gate. Past, present, future, all are one in Yog-Sothoth. He knows where the Old Ones broke through of old, and where They shall break through again.

Buchstaben

Andrew Leman
2006

Buchstaben was inspired by an illuminated manuscript dating from 1488. It contains ligatures and letterforms traditional in German blackletter type.

It is well also to recall that which I have said in the first book, viz., that in the greater part of their conjurations there was not the slightest mention made of God almighty, but only of invocations of the Devil, together with very obscure Chaldean words. Surely it would be a rash thing of a man who should deal with God by the intermediary of His holy angels, to think that he ought to address Him in a jargon, neither knowing what he saith nor what he demandeth. Is it not an act of madness to wish to offend God and His holy angels? Let us then walk in the right way, let us speak before God with heart and mouth alike opened, in our own maternal language, since how can ye pretend to obtain any grace from the Lord, if ye yourselves know not what ye ask?

Schreibweise

A B C D E F G H I J K L M
N O P Q R S T U V W X Y Z
a b c d e f g h i j k l m n o p q r s t u v w x y z
1 2 3 4 5 6 7 8 9 0 . , : ; ? ! ‹ ‚ ' ' " " ~ $ ₡
ſ z ſt ch ſi ll tt ö tt ß k ßß ck tz fl ffi
$ ¢ £ © @ ™ Æ œ Œ œ

George Washington Carver

Schreibweise

Andrew Leman
2006

Schreibweise was inspired by an illuminated manuscript dating from 1492. It contains ligatures and letterforms traditional in German blackletter type.

E-phemera

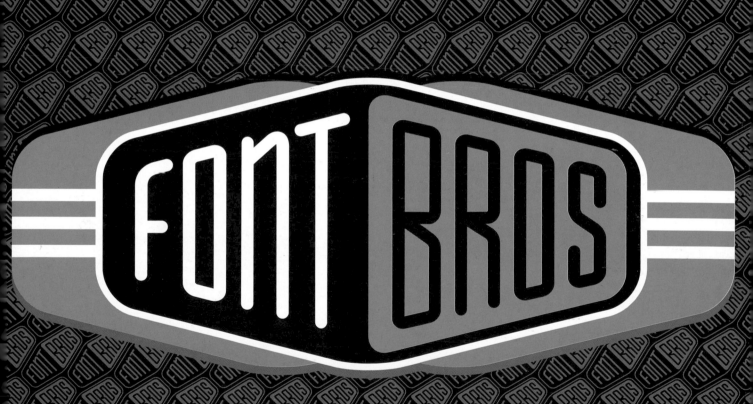

TYPOGRAPHY SUPPLY COMPANY

FONTS | MERCHANDISE | FREE FONTS

FONT BROS

FONT SETS | DESIGN KITS | SUPPORT

C B d O

SPECIMEN | CHARACTER SET

California
Seafood Raw
treasure chest of fun!
Beach Blanket Seaside Partytime

Manhattan Cocktail Dinner Theatre Seating

Bounce Script
by **CBdO**
Only $35.00

About: Bounce Script is a nice hand lettered upright font that has an appealing "bounce" character. Great for headings, logos or where a brush script is needed.

Platform:
Macintosh ▲▼

How Many Users:
Up to 5 ▲▼

ADD TO CART

SELECTRONIC

SANS SERIF
SERIF
SCRIPTS: CASUAL
SCRIPTS: FORMAL
ART DECO (1910-1935)
RETRO (1936-1965)
GROOVY (1966-1978)
NEW WAVE (1980s)
FUN/WACKY
DISTRESSED
DINGBAT
FUTURISTIC
HANDWRITTEN
GRAFFITI/URBAN
SPECIAL EFFECT
HISTORICAL

SERIAL NO. 07828

ADDITIONAL PRODUCTS   Sort by: Most Recent ▲▼

Sarah Script with Peppercorn Ra   MORE

MOTENACITY MADCAP HYJINX ENSUES SCRAM   MORE

Belair Light Streamline Co   MORE

AboutFace is sometimes better meaning

AaBbCcDdEeFfGgHhIiJjKkLlMmNnOoPpQqRrSsTtUuVvWwXxYyZz1234

AboutFace
Robbie de Villiers
2005

AboutFace Thin

AboutFace Thin is sometimes better than

AaBbCcDdEeFfGgHhIiJjKkLlMmNnOoPpQqRrSsTtUuVvWwXxYyZz1234

ACADEMY COLLEGE FOOTBALL HOMECOMING

ABCDEFGHIJKLMNOPQRSTUVWXYZ1234567890!@#$%^&★(),.<>?

Academy
Ben Balvanz
2002

Academy Outline

ACADEMY OUTLINE
FRATERNAL ORDER
SOPHOMORE LEVEL

Academy Stencil

ACADEMY STENCIL
HELICOPTER PILOT

Academy Stunted

ACADEMY STUNTED
UNDERGRADUATE
FOOTBALL SEASON

Americratika inspires a sense liberty and Freedom

AaBbCcDdEeFfGgHhIiJjKkLlMmNnOoPpQqRrSsTtUuVvWwXxYyZz1234567890!@#$%^&

Americratika
Ethan Dunham
1997

Annabelle is like Summertime Picnics

AaBbCcDdEeFfGgHhIiJjKkLlMmNnOoPpQqRrSsTtUuVvWwXxYyZz123456

Annabelle
Ethan Dunham
2004

ARCHITECTURAL LETTERING IS INSPIRING

AABBCCDDEEFFG·GHHIIJJKKLLMMNNOOPPQQRRSSTTUUVVWWXxYyZZ1234

Architectural Lettering
Rae Kaiser
1999

BadDog crouches in the lawn making trouble

AaBbCcDdEeFfGgHhIiJjKkLlMmNnOoPpQqRrSsTtUuVvWwXxYyZz1234567890!@#$%^&

Bad Dog
Ethan Dunham
1996

BAMBOOZLED FROM PIRATES RUM GROG

AaBbCcDDEeFFGgHHIIJKLLMMNnOoPQRRSSTTUUVWYYYZ0123456789

Bank Gothic MD

Michael Doret
2006

Bank Gothic MD Extends the Usefulness

AaBbCcDdEeFfGgHhIiJjKkLlMmNnOoPpQqRrSsTtUuVvWwXxY

Bank Gothic MD Condensed

Bank Gothic MD Condensed Extends the Usefulness

AaBbCcDdEeFfGgHhIiJjKkLlMmNnOoPpQqRrSsTtUuVvWwXxYyZz1234567890

Belair

Clive Piercy & Robbie de Villiers
2005

Belair Regular Streamline Travellers

AaBbCcDdEe FfGgHhIiJjKkLlMmNnOoPpQqRrSsTtUuVvWw

Belair Light

*Belair Light Has
Classic Inspired*

Belair Shadow

*Belair Shadow
Shiny Emblem*

Billo

Ben Balvanz
2002

billo shiny happy kitten pretty

abcdefghijklmnopqurstuuwнyzIz345678g0!☺#$%/?=+\"

Bello Shadow

**billo shadow playful
dimensional sparkly**

Bello Dream

**billo dream gives
daytime playtime**

Borneo

Ben Balvanz
2002

BORNEO BIG ISLAND ADVENTURES

AABBCCODEEFFGGHHIIJJKKLLMMNNODPPQ Q RRSSTTUUVWWXXYZ

Butterfinger with Chocolate Covering

AaBbCcDdEeFfGgHhIiJjKkLlMmNnOoPpQqRrSsTtUuVvWwXxYyZz12345678

Butterfinger Serif

Butterfinger serif contains Krispy

AaBbCcDdEeFfGgHhIiJjKkLlMmNnOoPpQqRrSsTtUuVvWwXxYyZz12

Kennedy Limes Barbara Underling Quotes
ABCDEFGHIJKLMNOPQRSTUVWXYZabcdefghijklmnopqrstuvwxyz

Californiard Eleven Property Uniform Songs

Calypsico

Calypsico slammin' popsicle

Calypsico Sans

Calypsico Sans disco dancing player

Calypsico Latino

Calypsico Latino bongo lounge

CARAMBA! FASHIONABLE LETTERING FOR THE GIRLS

AaBbCcDdEeFfGgHhIiJjKkLlMmNnOoPpQqRrSsTtUuVvWwXxYyZz1234567890!@#$%^&*(),.<>?

Cat Scratch
Ethan Dunham
2001

CAT SCRATCH FEVER CAUSES HAIRBALL GROWTH

AABBCCDDEEFFGGHHiiJjKkLLMmNnOOPPQQRRSStTuuVvWwXxYYZz1234567890!@#$%^&*

Caterpillar
Ethan Dunham
1999

Caterpillar makes Beautifully Small Cocoons

AaBbCcDdEeFfGgHhIiJjKkLlMmNnOoPpQqRrSsTtUuVvWwXxYyZz1234567890!@#$%^&*(),.<>?

Catnip
Ethan Dunham
2001

CATNiP Scented to DRiVE YOUR FELiNE BONKERS

AABBCCDDEEFFGGHHiiJJKkLLMmNnOOPPQQRRSStTuuVvWwXxYYZz1234567890!@#$%^&*(

Celsius
Robbie de Villiers
2005

Celsius enhances any degree of chill

AaBbCcDdEeFfGgHhIiJjKkLlMmNnOoPpQqRrSsTtUuVvWwXxYyZz1234567890!@#$%^

CherishFont
Andreas Ekberg
2005

CherishFont Swedish Modern Fashion

AaBbCcDdEeFfGgHhIiJjKkLlMmNnOoPpQqRrSsTtUuVvWwXxYyZz123456

Chickabiddies
Ben Balvanz
2002

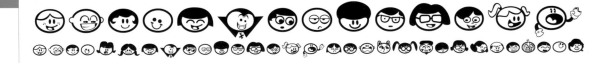

Cilantro
Robbie de Villiers
2005

Cilantro makes authentic Mexican dishes muy bueno

AaBbCcDdEeFfGgHhIiJjKkLlMmNnOoPpQqRrSsTtUuVvWwXxYyZz1234567890!@#$%^

Cinnamon
Robbie de Villiers
2005

Cinnamon makes my gingerbread houses warming

AaBbCcDdEeFfGgHhIiJjKkLlMmNnOoPpQqRrSsTtUuVvWwXxYyZz1234567890!@#$% &*(),.<>?

Cinnamon Sprinkles
Robbie de Villiers
2005

[decorative ornament samples]

Circus Dog
Ethan Dunham
2000

circusdog performs fantastic tricks
AaBbCcDdeeFfGgHhiiJjKkLlMmNnOoPpQqRrSsTtUuVvWwXxYyzz1234567890!@#$

CornDog
Ethan Dunham
2004

CornDog batterfried in Golden
AaBbCcDdEeFfGgHhIiJjKkLlMmNnOoPpQqRrSsTtUuVvW

Creaky
Derek Yaniger
2004

Creaky Frank
CREAKY FRANK WIGGLING GREASY GEARS
AABBCCDDEEFFGGHHIIJJKKLLMMNNOOPPQQRRSSTTUUVVWWXXYYZZ123456

Creaky Tiki
CREAKY TIKI WIGGLING ISLAND DRUMS
AABBCCDDEEFFGGHHIIJJKKLLMMNNOOPPQQRRSSTTUUVVWWXXYYZZ123456

Croissant
Ethan Dunham
2004

Croissant Smeared with Hot Camembert Cheese
AaBbCcDdEeFfGgHhIiJjKkLlMmNnOoPpQqRrSsTtUuVvWwXxYyZz1234567890!@#$% &*().~?

CynCyn
Andreas Ekberg
2004

CYNCYN DEVELOPS FUN COMPUTER SCREEN
AABBCCDDEEFFGGHHIIJJKKLLMMNNOOPPQQRRSSTTUUVVWWXXYYZZ1234567

Dance Party
Ethan Dunham
1998

DANCEPARTY FEATURES JAMMING DJ'S
AABBCCDDEEFFGGHHIiJJKKLLMMNNOOPPQQRRSSTTUUVVWWXXYYZZ1234567890!@

Dannette

Ethan Dunham
2004

Dannette gently kisses the bright

AaBbCcDdEeFfGgHhIiJjKkLlMmNnOoPpQqRrSsTtUuVvWwXxYy

Dannette Outline

Dannette Outline gently breezes

AaBbCcDdEeFfGgHhIiJjKkLlMmNnOoPpQqRrSsTtUuVvWwXxYy

Daydream

Ethan Dunham
2004

DayDream of Candy Licorice Morsels

AaBbCcDdEeFfGgHhIiJjKkLlMmNnOoPpQqRrSsTtUuVvWwXxYyZz1234567890!@#$%

Derekbats

Derek Yaniger
2005

Dimitri Swank

Ben Balvanz
2002

DiMiTRi SWANK RUSSIAN DiSCOPiMP

AABBCCDDEEFFGGHHIiJJKKLLMMNNOOPPQQRRSSTTUUVVWWXXYYZZ1234567890!?

Diva Doodles

Rae Kaiser
2005

Doyourthing

Andreas Ekberg
1998

DOYOURTHING WITHOUT ANOTHER

AABBCCDDEEFFGGHHIIJJKKLLMMNNOOPPQQRRSSTTUUVVWWXXYYZZ

Eerie

A.J. Garces & Emery Wang
1997

EERIE SHRIEKING SOUNDS BRING

ABCDEFGHIJKLMNOPQRSTUVWXYZ1234567890!@#$%^&*()[]|[]\,./<>?

Eyeliner produces clean streak-free

AaBbCcDdEeFfGgHhIiJjKkLlMmNnOoPpQqRrSsTtUuVvWwXxYyZz1234567

Eyeliner

Brian Bonislawsky
2006

FLASH IS THE SPEEDIEST

A B C D E F G H I J K L M N O P Q R S T U V W X Y

Flash

A.J. Garces & Emery Wang
1997

FLIMFLAM SAYS GEEZER JOE WHILE RECEIVING

AABBCCDDEEFFGGHHIIJJKKLLMMNNOOPPQQRRSSTTUUVVWWXXYYZZ1234567890!@#$%^&*(),<>

Flim Flam

Ethan Dunham
1995

Freestyle digweed tangobop

aabbccddeeffgghhiijjkkllmmnnooppqqrrssttuuvvwwxx

Freestyle

Ben Balvanz
2002

FREEZE CHILLY ARCTIC POPSICLES

ABCDEFGHIJKLMNOPQRSTUVWXYZ1234567890!@#$%^&*()[]\|,./<>?

Freeze

A.J. Garces & Emery Wang
1997

FRESHBOT SCIENTIFICALLY OPENS

aabbccddeeffgghhiijjkkllmmnnooppqqrrssttuuvvwwxxyyzz

Freshbot

Ben Balvanz
2002

Garanimals

Ben Balvanz
2002

Glee Club

Ben Balvanz
2002

Gelato
Robbie de Villiers
2005

Gelato Light with delicate frothy foam
AaBbCcDdEeFfGgHhIiJjKkLlMmNnOoPpQqRrSsTtUuVvWwXxYyZz 123456

Gelato Regular

Gelato Regular with creamery butter
AaBbCcDdEeFfGgHhIiJjKkLlMmNnOoPpQqRrSsTtUuVvWwXxYyZz 123456

Gelato Bold

Gelato Bold featuring whipped cream
AaBbCcDdEeFfGgHhIiJjKkLlMmNnOoPpQqRrSsTtUuVvWwXxYyZz 123456

Gemini
Ben Balvanz
2002

gemini transcends astrological distance
AaBbCcDdEeFfGgHhIiJjKkLlMmNnOoPpQqRrSsTtUuVvWwXxYyZz1234567890!@#$%^&@(),.‹›

Gemini Outline

gemini outline spirographics

Gemini Alternate

Gemini Alternate italic modernism

Gemini 1972

Gemini 1972 man superfunkyfresh

Grit
Ethan Dunham
1997

GRIT YOUR BICUSPIDS ON ANOTHER
AABBCCDDEEFFGGHHIIJJKKLLMMNNOOPPQQRRSSTTUUVVWWXXYYZZ1234

Henparty
Crystal Kluge
2006

henparty conversation leads to neighborhood gossip
abcdeghijklmnopqrstuvwxyz 1234567890 $¢@&# ‹›

Henparty Sans

henparty conversation leads to neighborhood gossip
abcdeghijklmnopqrstuvwxyz 1234567890 $¢@&# ‹›

orders@fontbros.com

Holy Cow! Save Big on Everything Today!

AaBbCcDdEeFfGgHhIiJjKkLlMmNnOoPpQqRrSsTtUuVvWwXxYyZz123456789

Holy Cow

Ethan Dunham
1995

Hot Coffee Steaming Cream

AaBbCcDdEeFfGgHhIiJjKkLlMmNnOoPpQqRrSsTtUuVvWw

Hot Coffee

Ethan Dunham
1995

Joybug Cabbage Seattle, Washington

Joybug

Crystal Kluge
2006

Kinescope New Animated Featurettes Nightly

AaBbCcDdEeFfGgHhIiJjKkLlMmNnOoPpQqRrSsTtUuVvWwXxYyZz1234567890!@#$%&*

Kinescope

Mark Simonson
2006

Laundromat Dry Cleaning Aids the Modern Homemaker

AaBbCcDdEeFfGgHhIiJjKkLlMmNnOoPpQqRrSsTtUuVvWwXxYyZz1234567890!@#$%

Laundromat

Mark Simonson
2006

LEFTSIDE THINKING INSPIRING ME

AaBbCcDdEeFfGgHhIiJjKkLlMmNnOoPpQqRrSsTtUuVvWw

Leftside

Andreas Ekberg
1998

Lindkvist1

Andreas Ekberg
1998

Lindkvist2

Andreas Ekberg
1998

Font Bros

Loosie Goosie

Robbie de Villiers
2004

Loosie Goosie saw freddie Pickle digging

AaBbCcDdEeFfGgHhIiJjKkLlMmNnOoPpQqRrSsTtUuVvWwXxYyZz12345

Loosie Goosie Thin

Loosie Goosie Thin saw freddie Pickle digging

AaBbCcDdEeFfGgHhIiJjKkLlMmNnOoPpQqRrSsTtUuVvWwXxYyZz1234567890!@

LordRat

Brian Bonislawsky
2003

LordRat scavenging sewage

AaBbCcDdEeFfGgHhIiJjKkLlMmNnOoPpQqRrSsTtU

Marshmallow

Ben Balvanz
2002

marshmallow campfire smores

aabbccddeeffgghhiijjkkllmmnnooppqqrrssttuuvvw

Marshmallow Italic

marshmallow italic creates smooth emphasis clearly

Marshmallow Outline

marshmallow outline styles

Marshmallow SuperPuff Italic

marshmallow superpuff italic brings the flava

Meatball The Font

Andreas Ekberg
1998

Meatball The Font Tastes Like Spaghetti

AaBbCcDdEeFfGgHhIiJjKkLlMmNnOoPpQqRrSsTtUuVvWwXxYY

Metroscript

Michael Doret
2006

Metroscript Cosmopolitan Manhattan Skyway Living

AaBbCcDdEeFfGgHhIiJjKkLlMmNnOoPpQqRrSsTtUuVvWwXxYyZz1234567890!@#$%^&

Mo Tenacity

Brian Bonislawsky
2006

MO TENACITY MADCAP HIJINKS ENSUES SCRAMBLING TOAST

AaBbCcDdEeFfGgHhIiJjKkLlMmNnOoPpQqRrSsTtUuVvWwXxYyZz1234567890!@#$%^&*(),.<>?

Moderna Contemporary Styling Salon
AaBbCcDdEeFfGgHhIiJjKkLlMmNnOoPpQqRrSsTtUuVvWwXxYyZz

Moderna
Ben Balvanz
2002

Mondo Loose is how to wear the latest
aabbcedefffghiijjkkllmmnnooppqqrrsttuuvvwwxxyyzz1234567890!@#$%^&*()_.<>?

Mondo Loose
Ethan Dunham
1995

ODYSSEUS SUPERCHARGED EQUALIZER
AABBCCDDEEFFGGHHIIJJKKLLMMNNOOPPQQRRSSTTUUUUVVWWXXYY

Odysseus
Ben Balvanz
2002

Old Glory helped American Founding
AaBbCcDdEeFfGgHhIiJjKkLlMmNnOoPpQqRrSsTtUuVvWwXxYyZz1234567890!@#$%^&*().

Old Glory
Ethan Dunham
2001

OOZE DRIPPING FROM SWAMPWATER
ABCDEFGHIJKMLNOPQRSTUVWXYZ1234567890!@#$%^&*()<>/?

Ooze
A.J. Garces & Emery Wang
1997

Orion Intergalactic Constellation Upper
AaBbCcDdEeFfGgHhIiJjKkLlMmNnOoPpQqRrSsTtUuVvWwXxYyZz1234567890!@

Orion MD
Michael Doret
2003

Paella is a delightful Spainish specially made
AaBbCcDdEeFfGgHhIiJjKkLlMmNnOoPpQqRrSsTtUuVvWwXxYyZz1234567890

Paella Regular
Robbie de Villiers
2005

PLASTIC BAG CRINKLING IN A LUNCHBOX
ABCDEFGHIJKLMNOPQRSTUVWXYZ1234567890!@#$%^&*()<>/?

PlasticBag
Andreas Ekberg
2005

Pinball
Ben Balvanz
2002

PINBALL ELECTROMECHANICAL WIZARDRY

AABBCCDDEEFFGGHHIIJJKKLLMMNNOOPPQQRRSSTTUUVWWXXY

Pinball Wizard

PINBALL WIZARD TURNS TILT INTO HIGH SCORE

Pinball Galaxy

PINBALL GALAXY FUN BRINGS DREAMY FUN

Plush
Ben Balvanz
2002

PLUSH tigerstriped jungle freshness

AOBBCCDDEEFFGGHHIIJJKKLLMMNNOOPPQQRRSSTTUUVVWWXXYY

PlzPrint
Rae Kaiser
2002

PlzPrint Creates Exciting Handlettered Fun

AaBbCcDdEeFfGgHhIiJjKkLlMmNnOoPpQqRrSsTtUuVvWwXxYyZz123

PlzScript
Rae Kaiser
2000

PlzScript is Expressive & Inspires Passion

AaBbCcDdEeFfGgHhIiJjKkLlMmNnOoPpQqRrSsTtUuVvWwXxYyZz1234

Popalicious
Crystal Kluge
2006

Popalicious Buenos Dias Ithaca Kitty Kat

AaBbCcDdEeFfGgHhIiJjKkLlMmNnOoPpQqRrSsTtUuVvWwXxYyZz

Powerstation Block
Michael Doret
2006

POWERSTATION BLOCK WAREHOUSE

AABBCCDDEEFFGGHHIIJJKKLLMMNNOOPPQQRRSSTTUUVVWWXXYYZZ1234

Powerstation Block Wide

POWERSTATION BLOCK WIDE

AABBCCDDEEFFGGHHIIJJKKLLMMNNOOPPQQRRSSTTUU

Randisious
Ethan Dunham
1996

RANDISIOUS SUMMERTIME CARNIVAL FUNHOUSE

AaBBCCDDEeFFGGHHIIJ JKKLLMMNNOoPPQaRRSSTTUUWWXXYYZZ/1234567890!@#$%&*().

RunTron 1983
Ben Balvanz
2002

RUNTRON 1983 ENTOURAGE PLAYAS

AABBCCDDEeFFGGNNIIJJKKLLMMNNOoPPOORRSSTTUUDDWWXXYY2212

Rustler
Ben Balvanz
2002

RUSTLER WILD WESTERN BUCKEROO SHOOTOUT

AABBCCDDEEFFGGHHIIJJKKLLMMNNOOPPQQRRSSTTUUVVWWXXYYZZ1234567890!@#$%&?

Rustler Fancy

RUSTLER FANCY HAS MANY GUNSLINGERS

Rustler Rawhide

RUSTLER RAWHIDE COWPOKE WRANGLER

Rustler Saloon

RUSTLER SALOON IN OLD WHISKY BOTTLES

Seasoned Hostess
Crystal Kluge
2006

SEASONED HOSTESS MAKES SNAPPY HORS D'OEUVRES

A B C D E F G H I J K L M N O P Q R S T U V W X Y Z O 1 2 3 4 5 6 7 8 9 O ! ? @ $ ¢ % + & #

Silverstein
Crystal Kluge
2006

SILVERSTEIN APPLES, CHEESES, & LOTS OF BREAD

A B C D E F G H I J K L M N O P Q R S T U V W X Y Z O 1 2 3 4 5 6 7 8 9 % + ¿ ¢ # $ £ €¢ @

Ski-Pop!
Ben Balvanz
2002

Snicker
Mark Simonson
2006

Snicker BBQ Chicken Market

AaBbCcDdEeFfGgHhIiJjKkLlMmNnOoPpQqRrSsTtUuVvWwXxYyZ

Terry Wüdenbachs
2005

SNiPLaSH QUaCKeR MONKeY BaNaNaS

aaBBCCDDEeFFGGHHiiJjKKLLMMNNOOPPQQRRSSTTUUVVWWXXYYZZ1234567

Sniplash Bold

SNiPLaSH BOLD QUaCKeR MONKeYFUN

aaBBCCDDEeFFGGHHiiJjKKLLMMNNOOPPQQRRSSTTUUVVWWXXYYZZ123456

Robbie de Villiers
2004

Sprout through a new big Adventure!

AaBbCcDdEeFfGgHhIiJjKkLlMmNnOoPpQqRrSsTtUuVvWwXxYyZz1234567

A.J. Garces & Emery Wang
1997

STUBBY VINTAGE MOVIE POSTER MAGIC

ABCDEFGHIJKLMNOPQRSTUVWXYZ 1234567890!@#

Crystal Kluge
2006

aabcdefdeefghlmmijkklmnoppqrsstuvwxyz

Brian Bonislawsky
2006

Swimsuit Boys diving in polluted Miller's Pond teeming with algae

AaBbCcDdEeFfGgHhIiJjKkLlMmNnOoPpQqRrSsTtUuVvWwXxYyZz1234567890!@#$%^&*(),.<>?

Swimsuit Boys Alternate Caps

SWIMSUIT BOYS ALTERNATE CAPS FOR RANDOM LOOKING BOUNCE

AABBCCDDEEFFGGHHIIJJKKLLMMNNOOPPQQRRSSTTUUVVWWXXYYZZ1234567890!@#$%^&*(),.<>?

Ben Balvanz
2002

TABLETRON FEATURING BLEEPS

AABBCCDDEEFFGGHHIIJJKKLLMMNNOOPPQQRRSSTTUUVVWWH

The Kids

Ben Balvanz
2002

THUG CREEPIN THROUGH DA NEIGHBORHOOD

AABBCCDDEEFFGGHHIIJJKKLLMMNNOOPPQQRRSSTTUUVVWWXXYYZZ123

Thuglife

Ben Balvanz
2002

TOON MAKING FRIENDLY FELLOWS BETTER

ABCDEFGHIJKMNOPQRSTUVWXYZ1234567890!@#$%^&*()<>/?

Toon

A.J. Garces & Emery Wang
1997

TWOBYFOUR FRAMING CRAFSTMAN

AABBCCDDEEFFGGHHIIJJKKLLMMNNOOPPQQRRSSTTUUVVWWXXYYZZ12345

TwoByFour

Ethan Dunham
1998

typing with Rudolf Proves to be interesting

aaBBccDDeeffGGHHiijjKKLLMMNNooppqqRRssttuuvVwwxxyyzz1234567890!@#$%^&*[]..<>?

Typing with Rudolf

Raymond Brekelmans
2006

VERYMERRY CHRISTMAS SUGARPLUM FAIRY

AABBCCDDEEFFGGHHIIJJKKLLMMNNOOPPQQRRSSTTUUVVWWXXYYZZ1234567890!@#$

VeryMerry

Ethan Dunham
1998

WELTRON URBAN HARDCORE GHETTOSTYLE

AABBCCDDEEFFGGHHIIJJKKLLMMNNOOPPQQRRSSTTUUVVWWXXYYZZ1234567890!@#$%^&-

Weltron Urban

Ben Balvanz
2002

WOODY TREEHOUSE CLUB ONLY

ABCDEFGHIJKMNOPQRSTUVWXYZ1234567890!@#$%^&*()<>/?

Woody

A.J. Garces & Emery Wang
1997

Founded in the spring of 2003, Handselecta is an evolving
project dedicated to the documentation and translation of the
many geographic styles of urban calligraphy. We are a type
foundry dedicated to creating innovative and
collaborative new products with some of the
world's most gifted graffiti practitioners.

Handselecta fonts are available for sale
in Mac and PC formats at:

HANDSELECTA.COM

info@handselecta.com

Simile Silva Id Est Interdum. Quod Facit
Ut Mirer Quomodo Prohibeo Ne Subeam.
Simile Silva Id Est Interdum. Quod Facit
Ut Mirer Quomodo Prohibeo Ne Subeam.

Hualus Ubique Fractus. Vulgus Meit
In Ocalas. Ocito Curarent Haud.
Percellit Me Et Foetor, Et Clamor
Nullam. Pecuniam Ad Exeuntem Habeo.

Conjecto Me Nullam Optionem
Habere. Mures In Grontica,
Blattae In Postica. Drodis Dediti
In Andiportu Cum Clava Golli.

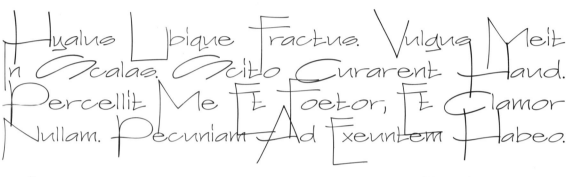

Joker Straight Letter

Joker & Christian Acker
2006

Light family:
 Regular
 Swash Caps A
 Swash Caps B

Entire family consists of 9
fonts–3 weights, each
containing 3 styles.

Handselecta

Joker & Christian Acker
2006

Medium family:
  Regular
  Swash Caps A
  Swash Caps B

Entire family consists of 9
fonts–3 weights, each
containing 3 styles.

Tetendi Fugere Sed Non
Nequivi Procul Ire Quoniam
Vir Cum Vehiculo Ad Remulco
Trahendum Receperat Currum Meum

Non Urgue Me Quod
Propinquus Ad Margine Eum
Tetendi Non Perdere Capitum
Eheu, Eheu Simile Silva Id

Est Interdum Quod Facit
It Mirer Quomodo Prohibeo
Ne Subeam Sto In
Principe Scamno Pendeo Ex Fenestra

info@handselecta.com

Specto Cuncta Autocineta
Meare Fremo Sicut Flamina
Adflant Delira Mulier,
Colit In Sacco Edit Ex Lacu

Quisquilliae Fuerat Cinaeda Dixit
Se Saltare Tangum
Peroulta Fandangum Levum
Principiasa Zircon Perdere

Genus Se Visus Erat
Deorsus Ad Spectaculum
Tuetur Monstra Ut Posset

Joker Straight Letter

Joker & Christian Acker
2006

Bold family:
Regular
Swash Caps A
Swash Caps B

Handselecta

Aa̋ Aa B B Bb C C Cc D D Dd FLEe F QF Ff G G Gg H H Hh I I Ii J J Jj K K Kk L L Ll M M Mm N N Nn O O Oo P P Pp Q Q Qq R R Rr s s ss T T Tt U U Uu V V Vv W W Ww X X Xx Y Y Yu Z Z Zz
0 1 2 3 4 5 6 7 8 9 ½ ¼ ¾ ' " $ £ ¥ € ¢ ‡ † ‰ ® © ® ( ) [ ] { } ✻ + − ×
, - . / < > = ÷ ″ ˝ ` ^ ′ ○ ∞ Á á À à Â â Ä ä Ã ã Å å Ç ç Ð ð È è É é Ê ê Ë ë Í í Ì ì Î î Ï ï
Ò ò Ó ó Ö ö Õ õ Ø ø Ú ú Ù ù Û û Ü ü Ÿ ÿ Ž ž Þ þ Æ æ Œ œ ƒ A ff . , : ; " " " " ✻ ° ✿

Mene One Mexicali

Mene One & Christian Acker
2006

Regular
Swash Caps

Entire family consists of 2 fonts—
1 weight with 2 styles.

Narrare Historias Suas Ad
Puellas Doma Ibat Urbem Et
Accepit Securitatem Socialem

Acquirendum Est Lenem Hot
Posset Prosperare Per Se
Non Urgue Me Quod Propinquus

Mesh One & Christian Acker
2006

Light family:
Regular
Swash Caps A
Swash Caps B

Entire family consists of 9 fonts—3 weights, each containing 3 styles.

Ad Margine Sum Tetendi Non Perdere Capitum Eheu, Eheu Simile Silva Id Est Interdum

Quod Facit Ut Mirer Quomodo Prohibeo Ne Subeam, Simile Silva Id Est Interdum Quod

facit Ut Mirer Quomodo Prohibeo Ne Subeam frater facit Cito In Televisione Matris Dicit Se Nimium Spectare, Non Est Sanus

Aa Aa Aa Bb Bb Bb Cc Cc Cc Dd Dd Dd Ee Ee Ee Ff Ff Ff Gg Gg Gg Hh Hh Hh Ii Ii Ii Jj Jj Jj Kk Kk Kk Ll Ll Ll Mm Mm Mm Nn Nn Nn Oo Oo Oo Pp Pp Pp Qq Qq Qq Rr Rr Rr Ss Ss Ss Tt Tt Tt Uu Uu Uu Vv Vv Vv Ww Ww Ww Xx Xx Xx Yy Yy Yy Zz Zz Zz 0 1 2 3 4 5 6 7 8 9 ½ ¼ ¾ ¹ ² ³ $ ¢ £ ¥ € ƒ # & @ ¡ ¿ § ™ % ‰ © ® ( ) [ ] { } ? * + ÷ × , - ⁄ < > ≤ ≥ = ≠ ¨ ` ^ ˜ ´ ◇ ← → Áá Àà Ââ Ää Ãã Åå Çç Đđ Òò Óó Ôô Öõ Íí Ìì Îî Ïï Ññ Òò Óó Ôô Õõ Šš Úú Ùù Ûû Üü Ýý Žž Þp Ææ Œœ ƒ fl fi . , ¡ ; " " „ " › ‚ ° · ⟨mesh⟩

Mesh One & Christian Acker
2006

Medium family:
  Regular
  Swash Caps A
  Swash Caps B

Entire family consists of 9
fonts–3 weights, each
containing 3 styles.

Omnis Liberorum Meorum Interdiu,
Dallas Nocte Non Possum Vel
Ludum Vel Pugnam Sacchari Magis

Videre Coactores Telephonum Meum
Timmirent Et Mulierem Terrent Quando
Non Num Domi Cultus Futilis

Habeo, Inflatio Gemino Tramen
Non Me Invehit Ad Negotium
Operistitem Est In Statio

Aa Aa Bb Cc Dd Ee Ff Gg Hh Ii Jj Kk
Ll Mm Nn Oo Pp Qq Rr Ss Tt Uu Vv
Ww Xx Yy Zz 0 1 2 3 4 5 6 7 8 9 ½ ¼ ¾ 1 2 0 $ ¢ ¥ € ƒ # &
@ !¡ ?¿ § ™ ‰ © ® ( ) [ ] { } * + ÷ × , - / < > ≤ ≥ = ≠ ¨ ` ^ ' ~ ‹ ‹‹ Áá
Àà Ââ Ää Ãã Åå Çç Ðð Èè Éé Êê Ëë Íí Ìì Îî Ïï Ññ Òò Óó Ôô Õõ Šš Ùù Úú Ûû Üü Ýý
Žž Þþ Ææ Œœ ƒ fl fi . , : ; " " ^ ^ " " > ° ˙

info@handselecta.com

King Kong Stet In Tergum
Nequeo Consistere, Sacrolacium Mutilum
Est Hemicrania Meditulla, Membrana

Canceratus Interdum Credo Me
Delirare Adjuro Me Planum
Capturum Esse. Simile Silva

Id Est Interdum Quod
Facit Et Mixer Quomodo
Prohibeo Ne Subeam Filius

Mesh One AOK

Mesh One & Christian Acker
2006

Bold family:
Regular
Swash Caps A
Swash Caps B

Handselecta

Aa Aa Aa Bb Bb Cc Cc Dd Dd Ee Ee Ff Ff Gg Gg Hh Hh Ii Ii Jj Jj Kk Kk
Ll Ll Mm Mm Nn Nn Oo Oo Pp Pp Qq Qq Rr Rr Ss Ss Tt Tt Uu Uu Vv Vv
Ww Ww Xx Xx Yy Yy Zz Zz 0 1 2 3 4 5 6 7 8 9 ½ ¼ ¾ ¹ ² ⁰ $ ¢ £ € ƒ # &
@ ¡¡ ? ¿ § ℳ % ‰ © ® ( ) [ ] { } * + ÷ × , - . / < > ≤ ≥ = ≠ ¨ ` ^ ˝ ´ ◇ ⬌ Áá
Àà Ââ Ää Ãã Åå Çç Ðð Éé Èè Êê Ëë Íí Ìì Îî Ïï Ññ Óó Òò Ôô Õõ Šš Úú Ùù Ûû Üü Ýý
Žž Þþ Ææ Œœ ƒ fl fi . , : ; " " " " → ° ° ᵐᵉˢʰ

Meskyle Laid Back

Mesk One & Christian Acker
2006

Light family:
 Regular
 Swash Caps A
 Swash Caps B

Entire family consists of 9
fonts—3 weights, each
containing 3 styles.

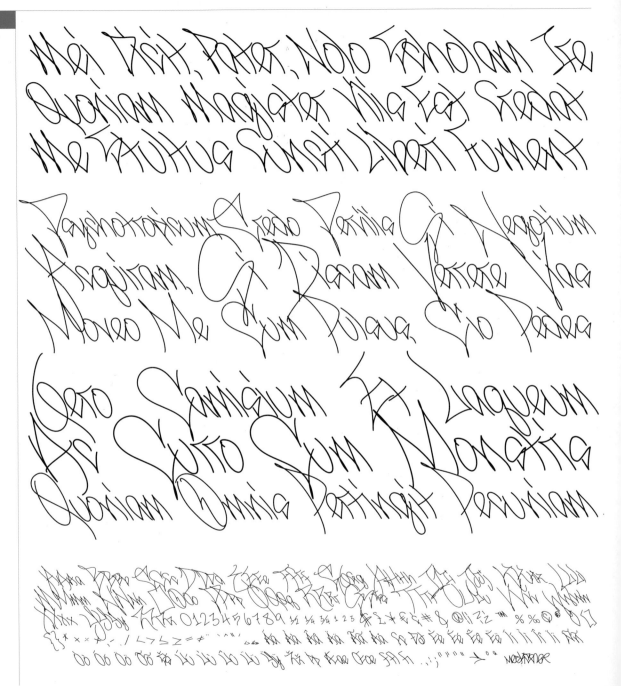

info@handselecta.com

Meskyle Laid Back

Mesk One & Christian Acker
2006

Medium family:
Regular
Swash Caps A
Swash Caps B

Handselecta

Meskyle Laid Back

Mesk One & Christian Acker
2006

Bold family:
 Regular
  Swash Caps A
  Swash Caps B

Entire family consists of 9
 fonts–3 weights, each
 containing 3 styles.

info@handselecta.com

Comprehensio Caecus Propositibus Mundi Deus Te
Subridet Sed Quoque Comminetur Quoque
Deus Solus Scit Quod Pateris Nasceris

In Cunabulis, Vivis Tempiter Et Oculi Tui
Cantabunt Carmen Odii Profundi Loci Ubi
Ludas Et Ubi Manes Videtur Simile

Immanis Angiportus Suspicies Cuncta
Annotatores Numeri Dentifrangibuli, Lenones,
Venditores, Divites Agentes Magna Carra,

Sabe & Christian Acker
2006

Regular
Swash Caps A
Swash Caps B

Entire family consists of 3 fonts–
1 weight with 3 styles.

Handselecta

Mene One & Christian Acker
2006

Outline
Fill
Outline & Fill used in layers

Entire family consists of 2 fonts–
1 weight with 2 styles.

ABSUMENTES UICENI ET DENI
ET UELAS FATUS EST SIMILE EAS
SUBINTRODUCTORES, UADURES, PURGATORES,

DEINDE DEFUNCTORIS LYCEO SIMILE
SILUA ID EST INTERDUM
QUOD FACIT UT MIRER

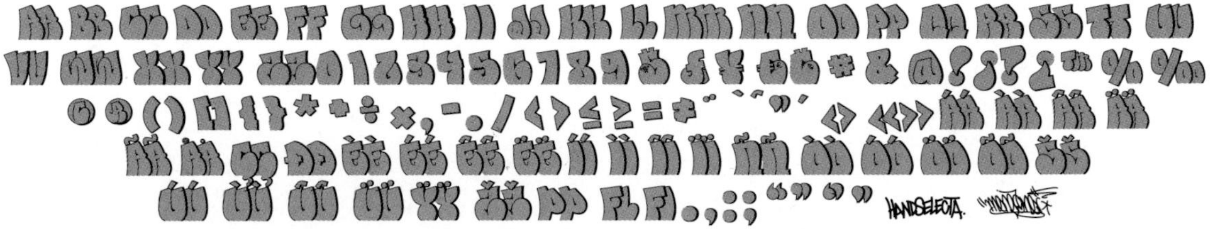

info@handselecta.com

Simile silva id est interdum Quod facit ut mirer quomodo prohibeo ne subeam Simile silva id est interdum Quod facit ut mirer quomodo prohibeo ne subeam Hyalus ubique fractus Vulgus meit in scalas Ocito curarent haud Percellit me et foetor, et clamor Nullam pecuniam ad exeuntem habeo Conjecto me nullam optionem habere Mures in frontica, blattae in postica Orodis dediti in andiportu cum clava folli Tetendi fugere sed non nequivi procul ire Quoniam vir cum vehiculo ad remulco trahendum Receperat currum meum Non urgue me quod propinquus ad margine sum Tetendi non perdere capitum Eheu, eheu Simile silva id est interdum Quod

Joker Straight Letter

Joker & Christian Acker
2006

Light Regular
Medium Swash Caps A
Bold Swash Caps B

Entire family consists of 9 fonts–3 weights, each containing 3 styles.

Handselecta

facit ut mirer quomodo prohibeo ne subeam sto in principe scamno pendo ex fenestra specto cuncta autocineta meare freno sicut faxina adfima delito mulier, colit in sacco coit ex locu autsoutillus furut cinctus dixit se soltore tangum persulto fandangum lauum Principissa Virgon perdere venus se vivus erat Deorsus ad spectaculum tuetur Monstra Ut posset narrare historias suas ad puellae doma Ibat urbem et accepit securitatem socialem Acquirendum est lenem Non posset prosperare per se Non urgue me quod propinquus ad margine sum Tetendi non perdere capitum Eheu, eheu Simile silva id est interdum Quod facit ut mirer quomodo prohibeo ne subeam Simile silva id est interdum Quod facit ut mirer quomodo

Mene One Mexicali

Mene One & Christian Acker
2006

Regular
Swash Caps

Entire family consists of 2 fonts–1 weight with 2 styles.

Mesh One AOK

Mesh One & Christian Acker
2006

Light Regular
Medium Swash Caps A
Bold Swash Caps B

Entire family consists of 9
fonts–3 weights, each
containing 3 styles.

prohibeo ne subeam Frater fecit cito in televisione matris Dicit se nimium spectare, non est sanus Omnis Liberorum Meorum interdiu, Dallas nocte Non possum vel ludum Vel pugnam Sacchari Rayis videre Coactores telephonum meum, timuirent Et mulierem + habeo, inflatio gemino Tramen non me invehit ad negotium Aperistitem est in statio King Kong stet in tergum Nequeo consistere, sacrolacium mutilum est Hemicrania meditulla, membrana canceratus Interdum credo me delirare Adjuro me planum capturum esse.

Meskyle Laid Back

Mesk One & Christian Acker
2006

Light Regular
Medium Swash Caps A
Bold Swash Caps B

Entire family consists of 9
fonts–3 weights, each
containing 3 styles.

info@handselecta.com

conspit iterum bracchium lexnt illum in pectore Dabant
transplantem ante novum initium Nequeo ingredi per agri
quoniam nocte delicius est Manus remanet ad pistolium
Quoniam faciunt ut curram Videor simile proscriptus
Strepebam maxillam terminalem Audio illos dicere te velle plus
Habito in fulcro. Simile silva id est interdum
Quod facit ut mixer quomodo prohibeo ne subeam Libellus
notus est sine conprehensio Caecus propositibus mundi
Deus te subridet sed quoque comminetur Quoque
Deus solus scit quod pateris Nasceris in canabulis, vivis tempiter
Et oculi tui cantabunt carmen odii profundi Loci ubi ludas et ubi

Sabe Ghetto Gothic

Sabe & Christian Acker
2006

Regular
Swash Caps A
Swash Caps B

Entire family consists of 3 fonts–
1 weight with 3 styles.

Handselecta

MANES VIDETUR SIMILE IMMANIS ANGIPORTUS
SUSPINES CUNTA ANNOTATORS NUMERI
DENTIFRANGIBUL, LENONES, VENDITORES, DIVITES
AGENTES MAGNA CARRA, ABSUMENTES VICEM
ET DEIN ET VELLAS FACTUS ESSE SIMILE
EOS SUBINTRODUCTORES, VADIRES, BURSATORES
ALUMNES FURES, INSTITORES, QUIDEM ROGATORES
DICAS ME CLARIS, DICAS ME NON STULTUS
DEINDE DEFUNGERE LEGEM SIMILE SILVA ID
EST INTERDUM QUOD FACIT UT MIXER QUOMODO
PROHIBEO NE SUBEAM NUNCIOSUS ES, OMNIS

Mene One NY Throwie

Mene One & Christian Acker
2006

Regular
Regular & Fill

Entire family consists of 2 fonts–
1 weight with 2 styles.

Jeremy Tankard Typography designs, manufactures, and retails high-quality typefaces for digital use. All our fonts are in the OpenType font format, and many have extensive character sets that take advantage of this technology. OpenType fonts are fully cross-platform compatible and function on Mac OS 8.6 and higher and Windows 95 and higher.

In addition to the general retail collection, some companies are benefiting from specially commissioned typefaces. An example of how Jeremy Tankard Typography works with existing and prospective clients to produce a typeface to suit specialist use is a commission for Arjowiggins. In 2006, the international paper manufacturer, Arjowiggins, introduced a new range of uncoated papers called Inuit. Jeremy Tankard Typography was commissioned by Blast, a design company working for Arjowiggins, to create a unique typeface based on the Inuktitut syllabic alphabet used by the Inuit people of northern Canada.

The Arjowiggins Inuit font is included on the CD that accompanies this book.

arjowiggins inuit

● ● ●

The following pages illustrate the typefaces currently being marketed by Jeremy Tankard Typography. For purchasing and further font information, please visit **www.typography.net.**

123 4⁵/₆ £78.90

ALLEGRO

effloresce

TELEPHONE

The long and the short

Talar þú ensku?

Aspect

Jeremy Tankard
2002-2006

Light
Regular
Bold
ExtraBold
Heavy

Aspect is an OpenType font.

OpenType features include:
Ligatures
Discretionary Ligatures
Swash
Stylistic Alternates
Stylistic Sets
Proportional Lining Figures
Tabular Lining Figures
Proportional Old Style Figures
Tabular Old Style Figures
Superior Figures
Inferior Figures
Numerators
Denominators
Fractions
Alternative Fractions
Ordinals

The concept behind Aspect was to produce an upright script typeface. Understanding of the term "script" varies. It can refer to an individual writing style of any kind, writing informed by a cursive or flowing construction (and especially as practiced by the writing master), or the informal brush script of the commercial lettering artist. To take even the most specific idea of a script–as a series of letter- or type forms following a flowing construction–is then further riddled with difficulty. When does a calligraphic form become a typographic form?

To preserve the sense of the calligraphic within this typeface, Aspect introduces many alter-nate character forms reflecting the formal diversity of writing. In fact, the freedom of approach adopted during the early design stages of Aspect has resulted in some intriguing character variations and combinations, with more than 200 single and ligatured forms on offer. (continued)

Jeremy Tankard

Jeremy Tankard
2002-2006

(continued)
These many unusual and unique forms all add to the distinctive appearance of Aspect. Yet Aspect can still be used in a more traditional manner by setting text with only the standard character forms and the basic ligatures such as fi and fl. Or customization of a text might be limited to the considered use of a single special character. From simple finial forms and swashes to incredibly elaborate ligatured swashes, Aspect certainly offers huge flexibility. If you should choose to pursue a more exotic design path, the many creative possibilities readily available are clear.

123 4 $\frac{5}{6}$ £78.90

ALEGRO

effloresce

TELEPHONE

The long and the short

Talar þú ensku?

orders@typography.net

supermercado

THE GREEN ROOM

Jekk joghogbok

COMISARÍA

documentation

Bliss Pro (Latin)

Jeremy Tankard
1996–2006

ExtraLight
ExtraLight Italic
Light
Light Italic
Regular
Italic
Medium
Medium Italic
Bold
Bold Italic
ExtraBold
ExtraBold Italic
Heavy
Heavy Italic

Bliss Pro is an OpenType font.

OpenType features include:
Small Capitals
Stylistic Alternates
Stylistic Sets
Superiors
Proportional Lining Figures
Tabular Lining Figures
Proportional Old Style Figures
Tabular Old Style Figures
Superior Figures
Inferior Figures
Numerators
Denominators
Fractions
Alternative Fractions
Historical Forms
Ordinals

In 1906, Edward Johnston's seminal book, *Writing & Illuminating & Lettering,* was first published. The ideas Johnston put forward, both in this book and in his lectures, were to inspire a revival of interest in calligraphy and to inform the wider fields of lettering and type in England. One of Johnston's ideas was a belief that a block sans serif form could be made more harmonious and acceptable if it were derived from the proportions of the Roman square capital letter. Bliss began with a nod of recognition to this idea.

However, during the development of Bliss, five typefaces in all were studied, each with a unique and interesting history: Johnston's Underground, Gill Sans, the Transport typeface, Syntax, and Frutiger. (continued)

Text below shows various weights and styles, set 8.5 on 11 pt.

DONEC POSUERE. NAM ALIQUET vehicula velit. Duis vel velit. Praesent tincidunt, diam et bibendum pretium, elit felis euismod metus, *vitae nonummy lorem dolor in tellus.* Donec bibendum suscipit tellus. Quisque a felis. Pellentesque erat justo, gravida nec, **malesuada** in, posuere sed, urna. Morbi ac ligula. Mauris *condimentum ultricies* nisi. Vestibulum placerat eros non dolor. Cras id quam in urna tempus suscipit. *Curabitur ut pede. Nunc porta quam in turpis.* Nullam nonummy lacus nec magna. Donec viverra. *SUSPENDISSE* potenti. Donec scelerisque iaculis risus. Duis a libero at sapien aliquam **pellentesque**. Curabitur at purus. Sed metus. In semper, metus non pretium blandit, ante quam **tristique** lacus, ut faucibus massa metus at purus. ALIQUAM LECTUS felis, pulvinar at, eleifend ac, pellentesque non, orci. Curabitur lacus. Curabitur feugiat faucibus magna. FUSCE FACILISIS feugiat sem. Aliquam elit nibh, adipiscing hendrerit, tempus et, ullamcorper sit amet, lacus. **Duis sollicitudin varius diam.** *Aenean orci lacus,* **laoreet et, vehicula quis, laoreet a, lorem.** Cras iaculis mauris sit amet lectus. Fusce nunc pede, tincidunt nec, egestas dignissim, convallis venenatis,

(continued)
With the Underground type, Johnston put into practice his ideas of a linear block sans serif. Eric Gill, a friend and collaborator of Johnston, draws heavily on Johnston's example for his own Gill Sans of c. 1928. Transport, designed for the Department for Transport, utilizes features and ideas from Johnston and Gill as well as concepts found in some of the continental type forms of the 1950s (such as the single bowl form of the **g**). The designer, Jock Kinneir, also worked hard to avoid ambiguity between characters sharing similar basic forms.

Hans Eduard Meier developed the idea of a dynamic structure within the normally rigid forms of a sans serif type. His Syntax typeface is drawn over the structure of an Old Face letter. As with Gill Sans, it has humanistic subtleties of proportion together with weighted shading and open forms, but differs in that it has oblique terminals to the stokes. The underlying influence of the pen-written forms has resulted in an energetic type form.

Adrian Frutiger developed his Frutiger type from the design of a legible signage typeface for Roissy Airport in France. Looking at the optics of letters seen at a distance, it became obvious that the forms had to be open, making them individually more readable and resulting in clearer word shapes.

In developing Bliss, forms were chosen for their simplicity, legibility, and "Englishness" (where forms are typically softer, more flowing, and generous in their curves). The lowercase forms demonstrate some of these ideas. For example, the **l** is clearly different in form to a capital **I** and a number **1**; the roman two-bowled **g** is traditionally found in English sans serif designs. A great deal of the character of Bliss is found in the lowercase letters. Influenced by Meier's reasoning of "dynamic structure," the resulting letters have a more natural feel and flow to them.
(continued)

Λεξικό

Χάρτης της Ελλάδας

ΠΛΗΡΟΦΟΡΙΕΣ

Ταχυδρομείο

Τα τελευταία Ελληνικά τραγούδια

Text below shows various weights and styles, set 8.5 on 11 pt.

ΕΠΕΙΔΗ Η ΑΝΑΓΝΩΡΙΣΗ της αξιοπρέπειας, που είναι σύμφυτη σε όλα τα μέλη της ανθρώπινης οικογένειας, καθώς και των ίσων και αναπαλλοτρίωτων *δικαιωμάτων τους* αποτελεί το θεμέλιο της ελευθερίας, της δικαιοσύνης και της ειρήνης στον κόσμο. **Επειδή η παραγνώριση και η *περιφρόνηση των δικαιωμάτων του ανθρώπου*** οδήγησαν σε πράξεις βαρβαρότητας, που εξεγείρουν την *ανθρώπινη συνείδηση*, και η προοπτική ενός κόσμου όπου οι άνθρωποι θα *ΕΙΝΑΙ ΕΛΕΥΘΕΡΟΙ* να μιλούν και να πιστεύουν, **λυτρωμένοι** από τον τρόμο και την αθλιότητα,

έχει διακηρυχθεί ως η πιο υψηλή επιδίωξη του ανθρώπου. Επειδή έχει **ΟΥΣΙΑΣΤΙΚΗ ΣΗΜΑΣΙΑ** να προστατεύονται τα ανθρώπινα δικαιώματα από ένα καθεστώς δικαίου, ώστε ο άνθρωπος να μην αναγκάζεται να προσφεύγει, ως *έσχατο καταφύγιο, στην εξέγερση κατά της* τυραννίας και της καταπίεσης. Επειδή έχει ουσιαστική σημασία να ΕΝΘΑΡΡΥΝΕΤΑΙ η ανάπτυξη φιλικών σχέσεων ανάμεσα στα έθνη. Επειδή, με τον καταστατικό Χάρτη, **οι λαοί των Ηνωμένων** Εθνών διακήρυξαν και πάλι την πίστη τους στα θεμελιακά δικαιώματα του ανθρώπου, στην αξιοπρέπεια και την αξία

Большое спасибо за информацию

спасибо

Я благодарен Вам за помощь

Пожалуйста

СТОЯНКА ЗАПРЕЩЕНА!

Bliss Pro (Cyrillic)

Jeremy Tankard
1996-2006

(continued)
In contrast to the nineteenth-century tradition of grotesque sans serifs, in which the proportions of the capitals tend to be even, the proportions of Bliss have been influenced by the Roman square capital, resulting in a varied width to their forms. The horizontal top strokes of E, F, T, and Z have oblique cuts that are balanced by the same detail in the rounded lower strokes of C, J, Q, and S. These terminal details are expanded in the lowercase.

The complement italic of Bliss follows a more flowing structure, reminiscent of its written ancestor. Beyond this structural difference, the four key lowercase characters have been drawn in sympathy with the rest of Bliss. The sloped forms of a and e are retained so not to make the type too soft, whereas cursive forms of f and g are included to maintain the rhythm and flow.

Bliss Pro sees the addition of Greek and Cyrillic scripts across the whole family of weights.

All three scripts share, in part, a common heritage in form, which can easily be seen through common characters. The lowercase, though, differs quite extensively. In the Greek lowercase, all the characters except the omicron differ from Latin. In the Cyrillic lowercase, several characters are the same as Latin, while others appear to be strongly influenced by Latin.

While this visual continuity can help to harmonize the three scripts across the design of a font family, it can also make it difficult to maintain the individual integrity of each script. One must remember that each script has its own rhythm and structure; forcing the principles of Latin into either Greek or Cyrillic will result in an unsuccessful character set.

The simplicity and legibility of form that underpin the design of the original Bliss font were applied to the design of the Greek and Cyrillic. Having begun with the essential underlying structure of each character, these forms were then harmonized and brought together as coherent scripts and then a complete family.

Jeremy Tankard

Text below shows various weights and styles, set 8.5 on 11 pt.

Принимая во внимание, что признание достоинства, присущего всем *членам человеческой семьи, и равных* и неотъемлемых прав их ***является*** основой свободы, справедливости и **всеобщего** мира; и принимая во внимание, что пренебрежение и ПРЕЗРЕНИЕ к правам человека привели к варварским актам, которые **возмущают совесть человечества, и что** создание такого мира, в котором люди будут иметь свободу слова и убеждений и будут свободны от страха и нужды, **провозглашено как** *высокое стремление людей; и принимая во внимание, что*

необходимо, чтобы права человека охранялись властью закона в целях обеспечения того, чтобы человек не был вынужден прибегать, в **качестве последнего средства,** *к восстанию* **против** *тирании* и угнетения; и принимая во внимание, что необходимо содействовать развитию дружественных ОТНОШЕНИЙ между народами; и **ПРИ-НИМАЯ** во внимание, что народы Объединенных Наций подтвердили в Уставе *свою веру в основные права человека, в достоинство и ценность человеческой* **лич**ности и в равноправие мужчин и женщин и решили

Jeremy Tankard
1999–2004

Regular
Italic
Bold
Bold Italic

Enigma is an OpenType font.

OpenType features include:
Ligatures
Small Capitals
Proportional Lining Figures
Tabular Lining Figures
Proportional Old Style Figures
Tabular Old Style Figures
Superior Figures
Inferior Figures
Numerators
Denominators
Fractions
Ordinals

Does the enigma of the typeface hide in the character forms of each letter? It is incredible that a simple mark (such as the letter **a**) can take on a seemingly endless number of visual guises. And it is certainly a puzzle to try and see through those guises and reveal any sense of form beneath. As Eric Gill pointed out, "letters are things, not pictures of things." They must be allowed to bend and move and fill their own spaces, to relax against one another and create unique rhythms that excite the mind.

If there is a place to excite the mind of the type designer, it is surely the Plantin-Moretus Museum Antwerp. This unique space provides a glimpse into a way of life long past, and a business much changed since. We find not only the home of printer Christophe Plantin (c. 1520–1589) but also the type foundry, printshop, and bookshop of a major printing dynasty that lasted some 300 years. On display is a small percentage of a vast collection showing types and books of many languages and styles. In the midst of all this diversity, while staring at the letterforms of the punchcutter Hendrik van den Keere, thoughts towards the Enigma typeface began. (continued)

ART & DESIGN MUSEUMS

biðstöð

Travelling from A *to* B

İMDAT!

Enigma Regular 9 on 11.5 pt.

INTEGER MAGNA FELIS, SAGITTIS ID, ornare nec, ultricies vel, leo. Quisque non tellus non est euismod facilisis. Maecenas nisi. Aliquam erat volutpat. Cras mauris libero, consequat eget, convallis ac, pharetra sed, massa. Aenean pretium nisl quis eros. Morbi adipiscing fringilla metus. In et erat. Mauris sagittis. Cras rhoncus felis. Morbi euismod nibh non nibh luctus aliquam. Etiam eu erat. Nunc nec est quis magna malesuada dictum. Phasellus dolor sapien, posuere vel, nonummy quis, nonummy sit amet, urna. Fusce sit amet dui. Donec non elit ut lectus congue scelerisque. Vivamus

Enigma Italic 9 on 11.5 pt.

AENEAN AC TURPIS. MORBI FACILISIS libero vitae massa. Curabitur sed justo. Fusce pulvinar accumsan lorem. Morbi ac felis congue odio commodo bibendum. Proin risus felis, porta et, congue sed, volutpat quis, sem. Suspendisse sed nulla id ligula pharetra pellentesque. Etiam interdum lobortis est. Pellentesque habitant morbi tristique senectus et netus et malesuada fames ac turpis egestas. Integer eget dui. Nulla nunc justo, mattis non, lacinia nec, gravida eget, ligula. Maecenas lobortis semper mi. Suspendisse potenti. Aenean vel lacus. Vivamus nisl erat, tincidunt ornare, condimentum vel, consequat quis, dolor. Sed vestibulum, nibh cursus

orders@typography.net

l'agence de presse

Dziękuję

Science Fiction

Magazines & Newspapers

Enigma

Jeremy Tankard
1999-2004

(continued)
As Enigma developed, other influences took hold. The rotunda letter (a broken script form) influenced the initial look of the lowercase. The intention was to incorporate formal rotunda elements in those Enigma characters that shared similarities of underlying structure. The Electra typeface, designed c. 1935 by W.A. Dwiggins for Linotype, shows internal curves that are given a definite cut. Intended to convey the speed and streamlined style of the age, these help to build the horizontal movement of the type. With this and the rotunda letter in mind, Enigma developed, resulting in a typeface that is clear and legible, bringing color and a unique image to both text and display setting.

Jeremy Tankard

Enigma Bold 9 on 11.5 pt.

IN PHARETRA RISUS AC ARCU. Vivamus nunc. Ut eu nulla. Donec lobortis dui ac velit. Fusce justo tortor, accumsan ut, vulputate non, vestibulum vel, ante. Cras at neque eget quam aliquet auctor. Pellentesque a nisl quis erat sodales iaculis. Aliquam accumsan viverra ante. Cras sed purus. Etiam posuere ipsum egestas turpis. Integer volutpat. Sed in elit. In congue magna eget mi. Vestibulum lectus. Nullam varius pellentesque est. Nullam aliquam nunc. Proin hendrerit, libero eget iaculis egestas, leo felis elementum

Enigma Bold Italic 9 on 11.5 pt.

PRAESENT FAUCIBUS MAGNA ID FELIS. Nulla luctus, enim non fringilla luctus, pede quam euismod nunc, malesuada pharetra risus mi ac massa. Nulla facilisi. Quisque placerat lectus eu risus. Vestibulum porttitor felis a lectus. Curabitur condimentum semper mauris. Mauris vitae mauris scelerisque lectus porttitor vestibulum. Pellentesque sem dui, ullamcorper sit amet, porta quis, ultrices nec, ligula. Suspendisse non lectus eget dolor mollis gravida. Donec molestie fringilla elit. Donec sollicitudin nunc id ligula. Aliquam scelerisque. Fusce vulputate ante quis lectus. In viverra. Proin commodo,

Jeremy Tankard
2005

Display
Display Italic
Regular
Italic
Bold
Bold Italic
Heavy
Heavy Italic

Kingfisher is an OpenType font.

OpenType features include:
Ligatures
Small Capitals
Swash
Stylistic Alternates
Stylistic Sets
Proportional Lining Figures
Tabular Lining Figures
Proportional Old Style Figures
Tabular Old Style Figures
Superior Figures
Inferior Figures
Numerators
Denominators
Fractions
Alternative Fractions
Ordinals

The concept of making text type interesting to the eye, and in so doing make the reading experience a better one, has been discussed many times. An interesting view is that the punchcutter was well aware of the need for subtle irregularities in the letterforms he cut. It can be suggested that these irregularities break the systematic monotony of the reading experience.

The theory is that character irregularities will, when the type is set, give the text a lively pattern—nothing startling—but with just enough interest to entice the eye. Perhaps today the irregularities of punchcutting, once lost to industrialization, could be reintroduced in an attempt to reinvigorate the reading experience. This idea was developed through the design of Kingfisher. (continued)

Enlighten

ARCHITECTURE STUDIO

Gjörðu svo vel

Kingfisher

Quiero un billete para Bilbao

Memorable date

orders@typography.net

Jeremy Tankard
2005

(continued)
A slight irregularity has been added to the letters to make the overall flow of the type seem less rigid. Several of the lowercase letters, for example, incorporate some degree of movement, and the illusion of a slight slope has been added to the verticals. All this imparts a very subtle restlessness to the text. As the font design progressed, it was tested for text-setting suitability. A model double-page book spread was set up and printed using each new trial version of Kingfisher. Seeing the letters perform together as text made it easier to weed out problems. It also made it possible to evaluate the desirable color of the developing font. Modifications could be made, and slowly the letters came together.

Act Two, Scene One

MARIA: No.

BOYET: What then, do you see?

ROSALINE: Ay, our way to be gone.

BOYET: You are too hard for me.

Exeunt.

III.1

Enter Braggart and Boy.
Song.

BRAGGART: Warble child, make passionate my sense of hearing.

BOY: Concolinel.

BRAGGART: Sweet air, go tenderness of years: take this key,
give enlargement to the swain, bring him festinately hither:
I must employ him in a letter to my love.

BOY: Will you win your love with a French brawl?

BRAGGART: How meanst thou, brawling in French?

BOY: No my complete master, but to jig off a tune at the tongue's
end, canary to it with the feet, humour it with turning up
your eye: sigh a note and sing a note, sometime through the
throat: as if you swallow'd love with singing love, sometime
through the nose as if you snuff'd up love by smelling love
with your hat penthouse-like o'er the shop of your eyes, with
your arms cross'd on your thinbelly boublet, like a rabbit
on a spit, or your hands in your pocket, like a man after the
old painting, and keep not too long in one tune, but a snip
and away: these are complements, these are humours, these
betray nice wenches that would be betrayed without these,
and make them men of note: do you note men that most are
affected to these?

BRAGGART: How hast thou purchased this experience?

Example in Kingfisher
(after Jan Tschichold)

Jeremy Tankard
2000-2004

Light Condensed
Light Condensed Italic
Condensed
Condensed Italic
Bold Condensed
Bold Condensed Italic
ExtraBold Condensed
ExtraBold Condensed Italic
Heavy Condensed
Heavy Condensed Italic
Light
Light Italic
Regular
Italic
Bold
Bold Italic
ExtraBold
ExtraBold Italic
Heavy
Heavy Italic
Light Wide
Light Wide Italic
Wide
Wide Italic
Bold Wide
Bold Wide Italic
ExtraBold Wide
ExtraBold Wide Italic
Heavy Wide
Heavy Wide Italic

Shaker is an OpenType font.

OpenType features include:
Ligatures
Small Capitals
Proportional Lining Figures
Tabular Lining Figures
Proportional Old Style Figures
Tabular Old Style Figures
Superior Figures
Inferior Figures
Numerators
Denominators
Fractions
Ordinals

Beyond the infamous oval box, the Shakers' intelligent approach to the creation of useful objects was one of simplicity and practicality. Their culture resulted not only in a now famous furniture style but many other things that we take for granted. The metal pen nib, the flat broom, the circular saw, and a method for waterproofing cloth are a few of their innovations. The Shaker typeface pays homage to the fullness of their vision. (continued)

Whitewater

TJALDSVÆÐI

Material Manufacturer

fizetővendég

Text below shows various weights and styles of Shaker Condensed, set 8.5 on 11 pt.

AENEAN AC TURPIS. MORBI FACILISIS LIBERO vitae massa. Curabitur sed justo. Fusce pulvinar **accumsan** lorem. Morbi ac felis congue odio commodo bibendum. Proin risus felis, porta et, congue sed, volutpat quis, sem. *Suspendisse sed nulla id ligula* pharetra pellentesque. Etiam interdum lobortis est. Pellentesque habitant morbi tristique senectus et netus et malesuada fames ac turpis egestas. Integer e get dui. Nulla nunc justo, mattis non, lacinia nec, gravida eget, ligula. Maecenas lobortis semper mi. **Suspendisse potenti.** Aenean vel lacus. Vivamus nisl erat, tincidunt ornare, CONDIMENTUM vel, consequat quis, dolor. Sed vestibulum, nibh cursus lobortis gravida, nisi turpis posuere eros, ut vehicula quam felis eget augue. **Donec nec erat. Maecenas aliquam, est ac egestas mollis,** *velit risus dapibus magna,* **in gravida nunc ligula quis dui. Etiam at neque vitae metus lobortis scelerisque.** Aliquam ante. Etiam condimentum aliquet elit. Nullam laoreet tristique elit. Donec ante. Pellentesque tincidunt accumsan nunc. Maecenas tempus, diam faucibus rutrum commodo, turpis diam sodales diam, vitae ultrices ante libero eu eros. Proin ut odio. Cras semper accumsan sapien. **Praesent accumsan.** *Nullam* **elementum.** Ut scelerisque ante gravida velit. Duis dolor lectus, aliquet sit amet, aliquet et, pellentesque non, velit. Praesent eu odio. Ut et est. Sed faucibus dictum augue.

orders@typography.net

Strassenbahnhaltestelle

New Hampshire

Háið í lögregluna!

Prašau

Shaker (Regular)

Jeremy Tankard
2000–2004

(continued)
The difficulty presented by a sans-serif design is how to evenly distribute the detailing that will give the font its overall character or personality. No one letter should carry all the style; conversely, too much style added throughout will result in a poor text type. Shaker began as a complement to the Enigma typeface. As such, it needed to carry enough visual reference to Enigma to convey a family likeness. Early stages of the design involved pursuing ideas tentatively explored in Enigma, such as the inclusion of definite cuts to the inside of several curved letterforms. However, some features of Enigma proved to be too overpowering for Shaker, such as the lead-in stroke of the n. Other letters also needed to be simplified, including the g and u.

The simplicity of the basic uppercase forms of a sans serif means that there is still less room for detailing. In Shaker, cuts made along some of the horizontal strokes complement the same detail found in the lowercase and help bind the whole typeface together.

In their simplicity, sans serif types are thought able to withstand a huge degree of modulation. They can be compressed, stretched, made thin or heavy, and still retain their basic styling. Throughout the development of Shaker, variations of width and weight were explored. From the start of the project, it was always intended that Shaker should also have condensed and wide versions. This has resulted in a typeface that is more than simply a sans serif version of Enigma— rather, it is one that offers a great deal of functionality across a wide range of possible uses.

Jeremy Tankard

Text below shows various weights and styles of Shaker Regular, set 8.5 on 11 pt.

PRAESENT FAUCIBUS MAGNA ID FELIS. Nulla luctus, enim non fringilla luctus, pede quam euismod nunc, malesuada pharetra risus mi ac massa. *Nulla facilisi.* Quisque placerat lectus eu risus. Vestibulum porttitor felis a lectus. Curabitur **condimentum** semper mauris. Mauris vitae mauris scelerisque lectus porttitor vestibulum. Pellentesque sem dui, ullamcorper sit amet, porta quis, ultrices nec, ligula. Suspendisse non lectus eget dolor mollis gravida. **Donec molestie fringilla elit. Donec sollicitudin nunc id ligula.** *Aliquam scelerisque.* **Fusce vulputate ante quis lectus.** In viverra. Proin commodo, turpis quis ultrices congue,

massa nulla posuere erat, sit amet placerat dolor ligula nec nisl. ***Nullam bibendum, tellus eu vestibulum*** fermentum, sapien lorem elementum massa, id ALIQUAM neque arcu at tellus. Sed in mi. In hac habitasse platea dictumst. Donec non lectus. Maecenas mollis. *Class aptent taciti sociosqu ad litora torquent per conubia nostra, per inceptos hymenaeos.* Sed id dui. Nulla venenatis. Morbi faucibus sagittis est. Curabitur adipiscing lectus nec ipsum. Nam dui sapien, sollicitudin quis, congue in, aliquam laoreet, felis. **Duis tincidunt libero vitae magna. Cras ante.** *Maecenas* **at orci lobortis nisl tincidunt tempor.**

COMMUNITIES

Orario di Apertura

Gæti ég fengið tveggjamannaherbergi

öğleden sonra

Union Village

Text below shows various weights and styles of Shaker Wide, set 8.5 on 11 pt.

Vivamus sagittis justo a mauris. Praesent quis arcu et nunc vehicula pharetra. *Maecenas nulla.* Proin consectetuer gravida mi. Proin metus. Donec elementum, pede eget malesuada CONSECTETUER, velit lectus posuere urna, vitae **tempor** orci est vitae augue. Integer aliquam. In nisl. Pellentesque eget nibh. Suspendisse rutrum. **Sed luctus est pharetra est. Nunc enim odio, fringilla nec, varius id,** *mollis sit amet,* **magna. In a erat id massa hendrerit eleifend.** Curabitur ac felis. Nunc non eros. Pellentesque habitant morbi tristique

senectus et netus et malesuada fames ac turpis egestas. Nulla convallis quam quis justo. **Donec ligula neque, tincidunt vel, porta vitae, ultrices id, turpis. Proin accumsan, ligula ac** *imperdiet porta,* **tellus felis faucibus nisi,** in malesuada eros odio quis mauris. Donec cursus, erat vel scelerisque vestibulum, orci tellus adipiscing lectus, *in ornare eros diam a tellus. Integer massa.* **Curabitur** *augue pede, suscipit sit amet,* suscipit vitae, vulputate eu, sem. Nunc non odio in justo sodales lobortis. Aenean tincidunt. Cras a orci. Quisque purus

orders@typography.net

SØNDAG

POMERIGGIO

UNDERGROUND CAVERNS

BANNAÐ

HIGHLANDS OF SCOTLAND

PARLA INGLESE?

TABLE

La catena di montagne

The Shire Types

Jeremy Tankard
1998-2004

Cheshire
Derbyshire
Shropshire
Staffordshire
Warwickshire
Worcestershire

The Shire Types are in the
OpenType font format.

OpenType features include:
Ligatures
Fractions (pre-built only)
Ordinals

The Shire Types are a collection of six typefaces inspired by a time when England's midland counties were changing–A time when parts of rural England changed the plow for the steam hammer and the shire horse for the steam engine. The resulting Shire Types bring together a heavy, solid notion of the Industrial Revolution mixed with ideas about specific localities. The individual typefaces take their names from six of the Shires that are grouped together around the Black Country and neighboring rural areas.

The concept behind the Shire Types was to create a dense black letterform that would make a dark, tight textural mass when set. Inspiration for the basic shapes came from the Grotesque and Egyptian lettering styles of the nineteenth century, from examples of lettering cast in iron, painted on locomotives, shop fascias, and street nameplates. The vigor and robustness of these forms belie their beauty. Once commonplace, many examples have now gone, these letterforms having fallen out of favor. The intent here was not to pastiche but to revitalize.

There are no ascenders or descenders in The Shire Types. Accented characters shrink to fit the character height and capital letters mix happily with their less stately comrades; it is a classless and caseless system. The resulting word shapes from this linguistic interaction can be both eccentric and interesting or plainly bold, all hybrids of a familiar typescape.

Jeremy Tankard

Jeremy Tankard
2006

Light
Light Italic
Regular
Italic
Medium
Medium Italic
SemiBold
SemiBold Italic
Bold
Bold Italic
Heavy
Heavy Italic

Wayfarer is an OpenType font.

OpenType features include:
Ligatures
Small Capitals
Superiors
Stylistic Alternates
Stylistic Sets
Proportional Lining Figures
Tabular Lining Figures
Proportional Old Style Figures
Tabular Old Style Figures
Superior Figures
Inferior Figures
Numerators
Denominators
Fractions
Alternative Fractions
Ordinals

The typeface was originally commissioned for use with a new wayfinding system for the city of Sheffield in the UK. As Sheffield was home to the Stephenson, Blake & Co. type foundry, it had been thought that their Granby Condensed would be suitable. The Granby family of types was developed during the 1930s as Stephenson, Blake's contribution to the general cashing in of other foundries on the popularity of Monotype's Gill Sans and the geometric sans serifs being introduced by the continental type foundries.

Application of the original Granby Condensed type was, however, difficult practically. It was not available in digital form and was felt to be too condensed, with the proportion of ascender to x-height too uncomfortable for use on the signing project. So there arose an opportunity to design a new typeface and, at the same time, tailor it to the specific needs of the Sheffield project.
(continued)

Iškvieskite policiją

Eastern

Vă tog arătați-mi pe hartă

Junction 5

Wayfarer Light 8 on 11 pt.

IN PHARETRA RISUS AC ARCU. Vivamus nunc. Ut eu nulla. Donec lobortis dui ac velit. Fusce justo tortor, accumsan ut, vulputate non, vestibulum vel, ante. Cras at neque eget quam aliquet auctor. Pellentesque a nisl quis erat sodales iaculis. Aliquam accumsan *viverra ante. Cras sed purus. Etiam posuere ipsum egestas turpis. Integer volutpat. Sed in elit. In congue magna eget mi. Vestibulum lectus. Nullam varius pellentesque est. Nullam aliquam nunc. Proin hendrerit, libero*

Wayfarer Regular 8 on 11 pt.

CURABITUR AT PURUS. SED METUS. In semper, metus non pretium blandit, ante quam tristique lacus, ut faucibus massa metus at purus. Aliquam lectus felis, pulvinar at, eleifend ac, pellentesque non, orci. Curabitur lacus. Curabitur feugiat *faucibus magna. Fusce facilisis feugiat sem. Aliquam elit nibh, adipiscing hendrerit, tempus et, ullamcorper sit amet, lacus. Duis sollicitudin varius diam. Aenean orci lacus, laoreet et, vehicula quis, laoreet a,*

Wayfarer Medium 8 on 11 pt.

CRAS IACULIS MAURIS SIT AMET LECTUS. Fusce nunc pede, tincidunt nec, egestas dignissim, convallis venenatis, metus. Morbi mattis turpis vel lectus. Duis molestie, massa sed volutpat interdum, risus massa fringilla nunc, in iaculis sem arcu eget nisl. *Aenean molestie mattis sapien. Maecenas vel purus non magna ornare aliquam. Donec urna. Donec ante. Proin metus urna, porttitor vulputate, lobortis ut, feugiat vel, odio. Mauris auctor, urna ornare egestas*

Sheffield

upplýsingaþjónustu fyrir ferðafólk

Peak District National Park

London R^D

Wayfarer

Jeremy Tankard
2006

(continued)
It was also an opportunity to widen the typographic references for the new font. I was keen to look at other early sans serif types, especially those from Stephenson, Blake and, most notably, their Grotesque series. These most idiosyncratic of designs are full of warmth and have an informal rhythm and a vitality to their shapes, all of which help create interesting word patterns. The rhythm of Wayfarer is similar to that of Granby but is combined with an approach to character detailing which echoes the informal variety found in the Grotesques. There is an extensive character set and, as a feature of Wayfarer, superior small capitals have been included. Examples of their use can typically be found in contractions on older street name lettering and in some business names.

Wayfarer SemiBold 8 on 11 pt.

VIVAMUS SCELERISQUE. Sed justo dolor, rhoncus at, fringilla eu, elementum sed, elit. Duis et metus. Aliquam congue rhoncus neque. Praesent nulla. Sed diam diam, lobortis at, semper vitae, molestie a, tellus. Aliquam vitae velit. Duis ante. *Aliquam fringilla sodales lectus. Morbi elementum metus quis urna. In diam. Donec sit amet tortor. Curabitur id elit. Praesent pretium nibh sit amet nisl. Vestibulum ipsum. Integer neque nisl, tristique vel,*

Wayfarer Bold 8 on 11 pt.

PROIN TINCIDUNT. PRAESENT NON nibh non nisl eleifend condimentum. Suspendisse metus mauris, venenatis sed, accumsan eget, laoreet eu, enim. Etiam sodales. Aliquam erat volutpat. Sed vulputate tellus nec nisl. Vestibulum molestie varius *libero. Nullam orci mi, rhoncus id, tincidunt at, congue ac, ipsum. Aliquam lacinia faucibus tortor. In turpis lacus, elementum at, adipiscing non, dictum vitae, eros. Praesent eget sapien. Donec elit. Morbi*

Wayfarer Heavy 8 on 11 pt.

INTEGER INTERDUM LECTUS nec nisi. Ut ut justo id ipsum ultrices ultricies. Donec est. In varius. Aliquam aliquet arcu vitae odio. Pellentesque id mauris bibendum risus scelerisque pulvinar. Sed ut purus tempus turpis tincidunt laoreet. Praesent commodo. *Integer sed dolor sit amet enim volutpat facilisis. Suspendisse potenti. Fusce vel turpis. Vestibulum ante ipsum primis in faucibus orci luctus et ultrices posuere cubilia*

kenn
munk
. com

Kenn Munk is a design army of one. ———His work ranges from graphic design and type design to product and toy design. The force is strong in this one, Topped only by his ability to appeal to something that's definitely not the mainstream. This goes both for his fonts and certainly also for his self-published series of hunting trophy paper kits called "Antlor - The Deer Departed————————." His designs usually have a commenting nature - his fonts change how people write, **Urbanregent**, for instance, doesn't really work with long words and works best ——When Every Word Starts With A Capital. His hunting trophies are a comment on the weird combination that is hunting and interior decoration - for some reason, it's not considered gross to chop the head off an animal, stick it to a wooden plate, and hang it on the wall. ———People find it more strange when they see one of Kenn's environmentally-friendly ——paper ——heads... He's also tried to change the way silence looks by designing a —font for the space between words, to attach some quality Other than nothingness to silence. This font is free, as people generally don't like being charged for **nothingness**————————————————Contact:

Kenn Munk - Ingerslevs Boulevard 4, 2.tv - DK-8000 Aarhus C - Denmark

www.kennmunk.com - info@kennmunk.com

phone +45 2674 0242 - skype kennmunk

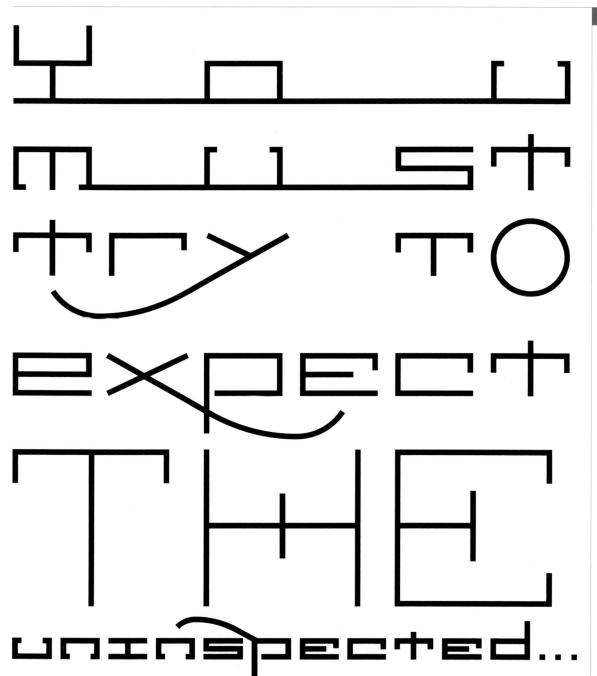

YOU MUST TRY TO EXPECT THE uninspected...

Replywood

Kenn Munk
2004

Monospaced

Alternate underscore works
as a connector.

Kenn Munk

Replywood

Kenn Munk
2004

Monospaced

Alternate underscore works
as a connector.

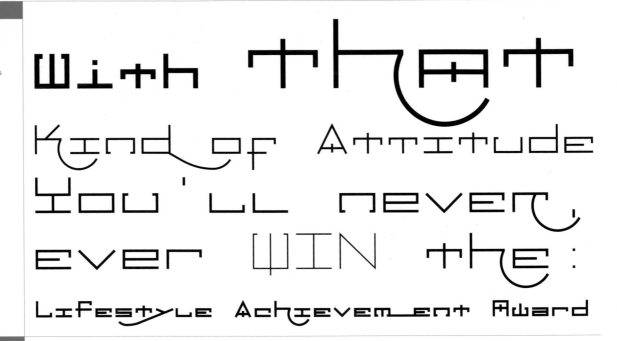

With that
Kind of Attitude
You'll never,
ever WIN the:
Lifestyle Achievement Award

From: afnqmin544@shixicker.net
Subject: specs for techs this
weekend endses [BREAKING NEWS]
confessional: homicide
Date: May 14, 2006 5:11:22 AM

Meta symbol: XAPRMZ 41
Obvious Price: $0.21
Short Term Projected: $0.85
Watch this one, huge PR campaign
strong quasiantipotential!

In nex Announces Joint Venture
and Option Agreement Extension
LAS VEGAN, May 5/- In nex AdVentures Inc. and its Board of
Directors are not pleased...

The Region has a tradition
of mining dating back to 1876.
Several high-grade gold skarns
were mined in the area. The
table is MINTT ogzF/516

March 6, 2006 - Animal Manufacturing Associates, Inc. [Punk
Genome Projects:
AYPM - OLDS], announced today
that management is very lost.

Feb. 24, 2006 - Pink Armour
Manufacturing Associates, Inc.
Metal Sheets (Lot of 56):
APFM, announced tonight that yet
another step towards damnation

Replywood Thin

Kenn Munk
2004

The thin weight is half the width
of the regular weight.

Replywood Thin Alternate

Kenn Munk
2004

Replywood Bold

Kenn Munk
2004

The regular weight is half the
width of the bold weight.

Replywood Bold Alternate

Kenn Munk
2004

Kenn Munk

Kenn Munk
1999

And then Davin Fraser said: "You should try a lifesize woman."

That must be one of the best insults

All verified dr@gs collected at one Licensed online store! Great choice of Wonderful meds to give you Long-awaited relief... Operative support. fast Shipping. 24-7 secure p@yment free process (92-56) and Complete lack of confidentiality!

info@kennmunk.com

Kenn Munk
2003

Aether is a companion dingbat to Acetone.

Aether is to be used for writing silence, breaks, sighs, and pauses.

Kenn Munk

sharks are not poisonous

[Neither are fonts that are a mix of bitmap and blackletter...]

This week peaks! New News just out. Should Spark No Growth. Big Quilts just Out! PRICE: 0.535 Day expected 2.26 The store is very verified and will close Tuesday May 9, 2:09 pm ET

info@kennmunk.com

a white caffé
latte con leche, please
and could i have milk with that?

big news just way out of print!
price: 0.54, 3 day job. unexpected
32.26 linebreaking the news.
cantexana energy corps of 1974

Circlejerk Bold

Kenn Munk
2003

any cold coffee
based drink would do
wonderful wonders for me, luv

san retonio ~ september 19th 1969s
cantexana energy corps has been
receiving several phonecalls from
23 shareholders who are all dead.

Circlejerk Light

Kenn Munk
2003

Kenn Munk

Lineman actually is a script _ s point _ font for a simpler more digital a g e.

The Clams are located on Tex Island, B.C. This REGION has a long, and dull history of mining data. BACK in 1876 Several high grade Mb were found. There are no spiritual or material changes in The Company. Honestly.

Infinox AdVentures Inc. (NoFX) Price: 0.80 Already started to stink. This did very well, VERY! No really. It did... Get it here, there, everywhere: Canadian online Spark. Nice growth sir! NM2-store

WE would like to offer licensed meds from our Canadian store! - worldwide delivery, including off-world shipping and customs - 24/7 customer support service

Linemap Bold

Kenn Munk
2002

Identifying THESE 596 mishaps in THE EARLiEST STAGES allows us TO accelerate business development and fully REALIZE our complete lack of potential...

Linemap Bold Alternate

Kenn Munk
2002

Soma 780 Phentermine 767 Am+ien 760 - Valium 430 Xanax 320 Viagra 7 Cialis 90 Operative Support. fast shipping, secure prayment. Free process + complete confidentiality!

Linemap Extended

Kenn Munk
2002

THE STORE is APPROVED BY visa! www.spam.biz/905392 Winter sale on Wiiagra::::..? [ATHER Drugs Great choice of wonderful meds to give you long-awaited sideeffects!

Linemap Extended Alt.

Kenn Munk
2002

Kenn Munk

info@kennmunk.com

Kenn Munk

Kenn Munk
2003

Building block dingbat system.

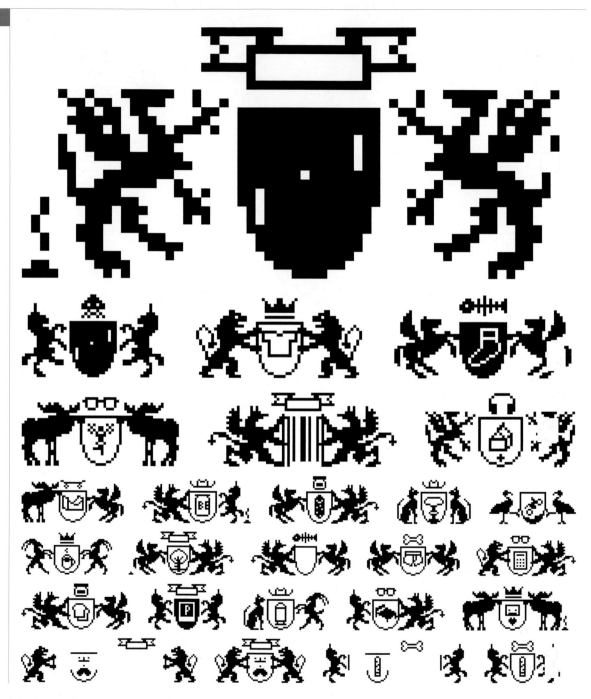

info@kennmunk.com

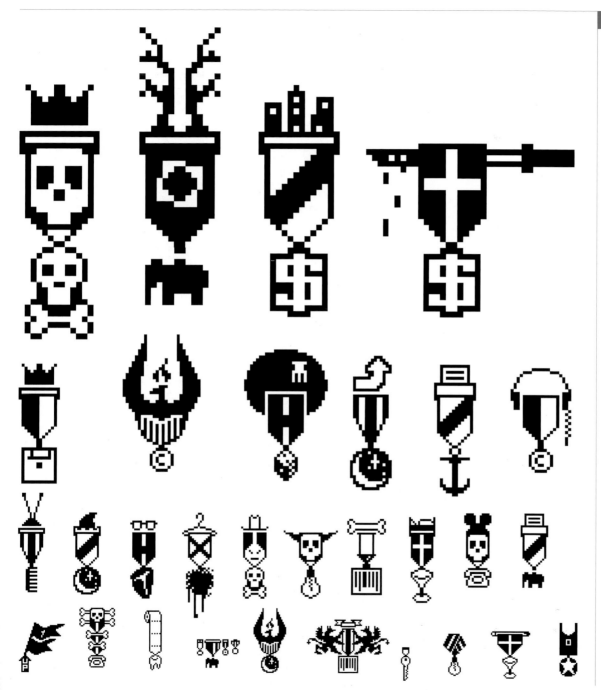

Kenn Munk

Kenn Munk
2001

Building block dingbat system.

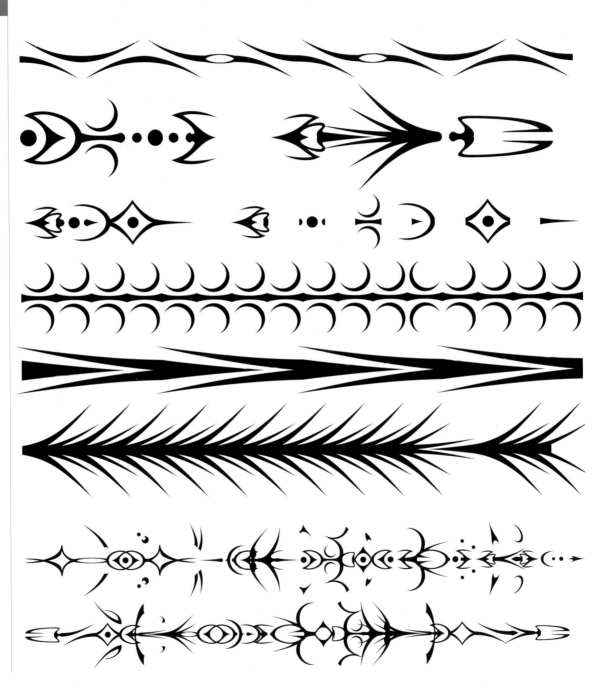

info@kennmunk.com

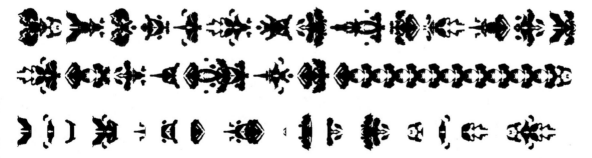

When faced with an ever-growing list of fonts, choosing the right one can be an overwhelming task for the designer today. But when you understand that each font is really a tool in its own right, you are on your way to choosing the correct fonts quickly and with confidence.

Fonts are like people in some ways. They come in all shapes and sizes. And they even have personalities. Some give off a stern and serious vibe, while others are playful. But if you don't take the time to get to know your fonts by using them and experimenting with them, than you won't know which to use when the right time comes.

Some designers make the mistake of using the wrong font for the task at hand. This can mean using an inappropriate font, such as an ultra-serious Blackletter style for a light-hearted purpose (maybe a children's party). But more often it means compressing or extending a font in an attempt to make it fit an area it doesn't naturally fit. Sometimes this is the result of trying to appease an overbearing customer who demands that you "Make it bigger."

A good example is Helvetica. This overused font is commonly compressed by inexperienced designers so that the horizontal cross strokes of the letter E are thicker than the vertical strokes. But that's not the way the original creator of Helvetica (Max Miedinger) designed it. The horizontal cross strokes of Helvetica have been purposely created slightly thinner to enable the letters to be read more easily and to carry the eye through the message. This subtlety is destroyed by compressing the letters just 50 percent.

With that said, nothing is wrong with compressing (or stretching) a font within its capacity. The problem arises when a font has been compressed beyond its ability to retain a pleasing and readable effect. Rather than risk murdering a font by compressing and stretching, it would be better to try to find a font that fits the space of the design.

FREE TODAY!

Helvetica murdered, er... compressed in an attempt to fill the space. Horizontal crosstrokes on the *E* are now thicker than the vertical strokes.

FREE TODAY!

A better choice would be a vertical font such as Compacta, which was designed for a space such as this.

A good way to choose fonts is to categorize them ahead of time as either Condensed, Extended, or Neutral. Examples of Condensed fonts might be Impact, Compacta, and, of course, Helvetica Condensed. In your Extended category, you might list styles like Microgramma, Serpentine, or Copperplate. Fonts such as Helvetica, Futura, and perhaps Optima might fall into the Neutral category. Once you've made a mental note of which fonts belong to which categories, the next step is to determine the space you have to fill. Is the space horizontal or vertical in shape? Then choose a Horizontal or Vertical font. Is the shape square? Maybe one of the Neutral fonts would work best.

Designing in this manner will free you up to begin thinking about creative treatments of the letters. But always remember, 3-D bevels and special effects can't save a poor design. You must assess your area and begin with the proper font.

For more tips like this, visit www.letterheadfonts.com

Little Smoking Putz

Mini Cigarillos

for The Effeminate Man

Letterhead

Fightin' Fogies

2006 Senior Ultimate Fighting Champions

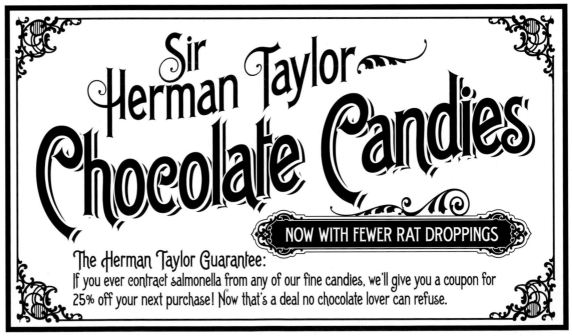

LHF Bulldog

John Studden
2002

Bulldog was originally created for a project requiring a 1930s-1940s feel.

LHF Casablanca

John Studden
2003

This elegant display face was inspired by Casablanca ceiling fan company logos and signage.

LHF Classic Caps

John Studden
2002

Originally created by Studden for his own shop logo, Classic Caps has an old-fashioned western appeal.

LHF English Rose

Dave Smith
2006

English Rose captures the feel of England during the Victorian era.

LHF Ephemera

Tom Kennedy
2002

This old-fashioned script was inspired by letterheads from the late 1800s and early 1900s. Included are more than 58 different swashes designed to attach to the ends of the Ephemera letters.

Letterhead

LHF Esoteric 3

Chuck Davis
2004

This outspoken design is the latest in the Esoteric Trilogy, which began in 1999 with Davis's first font, Esoteric. This set features three fonts.

LHF Fairground

John Studden
2002

As a young boy in Mudflats, England, Studden was raised within the topsy-turvy world of the circus. This font is the result of his trauma.

LHF Firehouse

Tom Kennedy
2004

With its highly unique swirls and serifs, Firehouse represents the late 1800s quite well.

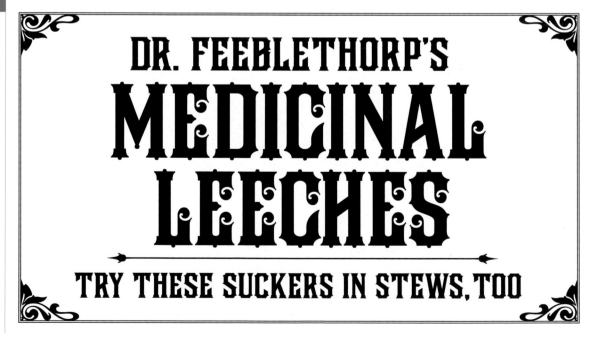

YOU MAY HAVE MORE HAIR IN YOUR EARS THAN ON YOUR HEAD BUT WE STILL ASK FOR ID

LHF Garner

Duncan Wilkie
2006

Born out of necessity, Garner captures the feel of an old sign painter's gothic. Slight quirks and imperfections give the appearance of hand lettering.

Letterhead

LHF Hamilton Ornate

John Studden
2006

This narrow design was inspired by glass signage dating back to the 1870s.

Hole in One Dentistry and Jack Hammering Service

"One stop shop for all your dentistry and jack hammering needs"

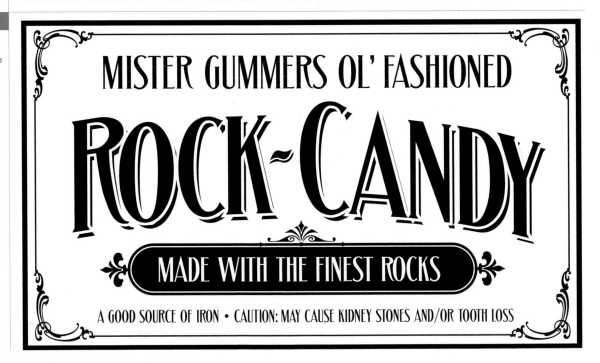

BEAT STREET

PARACHUTE PANTS · KANGOLS · BAD ACTING

LHF Menace

Chuck Davis
2004

This two-part font flows with old-school graffiti style.

Letterhead

Get bossed around by college dropouts who take this stuff way too seriously.

Relive the life of a real pirate!*

Pirate's Cove

Fun for the whole family!

* Not responsible for bouts of cholera or the black plague

Swab the deck! · Eat rat meat! · Get scurvy!

LHF Orange Grove

Mike Frickson
2003

This whimsical typeface uses calligraphy-style nicks and cuts to achieve a hand lettered appearance.

LHF Prentice

Dave Correll
2006

This set includes 6 fonts consisting of variations of plain, swashes, and spurs.

ILL ADVISORS
HEALTH CONSULTATION
S E R V I C E S
"WHERE ALL ADVICE IS ILL-ADVISED"

LHF Quadrex

Chuck Davis
2005

Print it. Scale it. With its groundbreaking prismatic style comprises 4 separate sides, Quadrex allows for more realistic vector-based 3-D effects than ever before. By itself, the Quadrex BASE font is handsome enough, but add the other layers, and you've got a surefire head-turner. Quadrex includes 5 separate fonts to create the look shown here.

SURFER DUDE
MAGAZINE
NOW WITH FEWER BIG WORDS

LHF Sarah Script

Charles Borges de Oliveira
2004

One of our most popular fonts, Sarah Script is perfect for all forms of advertising where a brush script is needed.

LHF Sofia Script

Chuck Davis
2005

Sofia is a hand-lettered script with alternate characters. This typeface looks especially nice when used in conjunction with bolder letter styles for good contrast.

Chuck Davis
2003

Stanford is an unusual, fun-to-use script featuring many alternate ending characters for creating custom hand-painted looks. This typeface is especially suited to vehicle signage and looks great when used with bolder lettering.

John Studden
2004

This sophisticated design can be used in place of more traditional and overused light-face fonts such as University Roman.

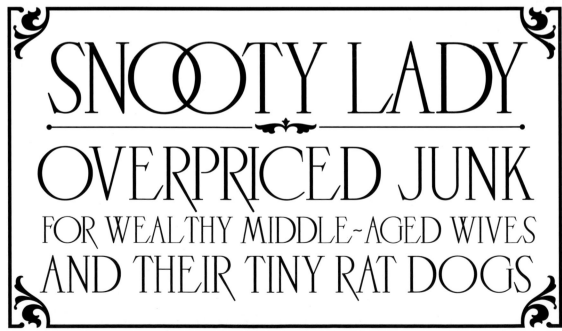

LHF Stevens Percepta

Arthur Vanson
2003

Inspired by legendary showcard writer and designer Mike Stevens, this typeface has loads of personality. The six-font set makes a smart alternative to Optima.

Letterhead

WE'VE CHANGED OUR NAME! DHUM MASS WILL NOW BE KNOWN AS...

Dhum Schmuck

ATTORNEYS AT LAW

BETWEEN THE GOODWILL & TACO HEAVEN ON JEFFERSON

LHF Tideway Script

Arthur Vanson
2004

Arthur Vanson delivers two much-needed scripts that are neither too dainty nor too formal, yet retain an air of sophistication. Wide strokes allow for many creative possibilities. This set includes 2 styles: Tideway Regular and Tideway Classic (which features curly caps).

Thank You!

With dear Friends like you I never need any Enemies

LHF Timberlodge

Chuck Davis
2002

This extended typeface has half-circles cut out of the tops and bottoms. Timberlodge includes ornamental caps and is a perfect alternative to the overused Thunderbird font.

LHF Tonic

Tom Kennedy
2002

This classic style was used on old advertising tins in the late 1800s. This set includes 2 fonts for what ails you: Tonic Liver and Tonic Nerve.

DR. EMMA QUACK, MD

MEMORY LOSS INSTITUTE

"We'll help you forget your memory loss"

UNCLE DAD'S

GRITS & POSSUM INNARDS

We treat you like family

('Cause you just might be.)

LHF Tyler

Gary Godby
2004

Tyler is based on an old-fashioned engrossing style from the late 1800s and includes 3 variations.

Letterhead

LHF Wade Grotesque

Arthur Vanson
2003

This 6-font Roman-based grotesque was inspired by the work of Cecil Wade. This type of lettering was used for headlines on showcards and posters from the 1920s onward. Though not typically art deco, this sort of curvaceous style was often used to counterpoint and animate the more angular designs of the period.

pizzadude.dk is located in
Copenhagen, Denmark.
Type designer Jakob Fischer
does all the fonting,
graphics, and web design.
The style of pizzadude.dk is
loose, laid-back and
sometimes quite goofy,
but you quickly
get the picture!

Find out more at
www.pizzadude.dk,
or contact me at
jakob@pizzadude.dk

ABCDEFGHIJK
LMNOPQRST
UVWXYZ!"'#?
0123456789

FRESH!

LET'S PLAY THE FUNKY DRUMMER!

Sure Shot

Jakob Fischer
2004

ABCDEFGHIJK
LMNOPQRST
UVWXYZ!"#?
0123456789

BREAK!

I JUST CAN'T GET ENOUGH OF THIS!

Kickshaw

Jakob Fischer
2003

ABCDEFGHIJK
LMNOPQRST
UVWXYZ!"#?
0123456789

SPRAY!

i GET ON THE MIX LATE IN THE NIGHT!

TagBoyHardcore

Jakob Fischer
?003

ABCDEFGHIJKL
MNOPQRSTUV
WXYZ012345
6789!"'#&$^?

STYLE!

HEY! PUT THE OTHER RECORD ON!

Shake Your Head

Jakob Fischer
2003

Pizzadude

I Think
tonight
I fancy
myself

ABCDEFGHIJKLMNOPQRSTUVWXYZ
abcdefghijklmnopqrstuvwxyz
0123456789!?*@&...

jakob@pizzadude.dk

I think I'll die unless I kiss you, please don't murder me

Fligerish

Jakob Fischer
2005

ABCDEFGHIJKLMNOPQRSTUVWXYZ!?*&...
abcdefghijklmnopqrstuvwxyz0123456789

Please

Just a reminder

ABCDEFGHIJKLMNOPQRSTUVWXYZ
abcdefghijklmnopqrstuvwxyz!"#&*...

Stop

Is this what you want?

ABCDEFGHIJKLMNOPQRSTUVWXYZ
abcdefghijklmnopqrstuvwxyz!"#&*...

You are beautiful

at least that is what my friends keep telling me!

ABCDEFGHIJKLMNOPQRSTUVWXYZ?!#€%
abcdefghijklmnopqrstuvwxyz0123456789...

Hopeless Heart

Jakob Fischer
2004

I will fly away, disappear into air

but please keep an eye on me anyway!

ABCDEFGHIJKLMNOPQRSTUVWXYZ?!#€%
abcdefghijklmnopqrstuvwxyz0123456789...

Jerky Tash

Jakob Fischer
2004

jakob@pizzadude.dk

Nothing sounds
as good as
"I Remember That"
- Did you
feel it too ?

ABCDEFGHIJKLMNOPQRSTUVWXYZ?!#€%
abcdefghijklmnopqrstuvwxyz0123456789...

Oh my God,
you make
me work
so hard!

ABCDEFGH
IJKLMNOP
QRSTUVW
XYZ?!#€%
abcdefghi
jklmnopq
rstuvwxyz
0123456789...

jakob@pizzadude.dk

LET ME SHOW YOU SOMETHING VERY INTERESTING MY MAN!

BUT BE CAREFUL, YOU MAY NEVER HAVE SEEN SOMETHING LIKE THIS!

ABCDEFGHIJKLMNOPQRSTUVWXYZabcdefghijklmnopqrstuvwxyz

TalkSeek

Jakob Fischer
2004

Just kidding!

I am just very bad at joking, you know!

ABCDEFGHIJKLMNOPQRSTUVWXYZ
abcdefghijklmnopqrstuvwxyz0123456789!?

Krooked Teeth

Jakob Fischer
2002

UNDERSTAND

THAT THESE CHANGES MAY TAKE SOME TIME!

ABCDEFGHIJKLMNOPQRSTUVWXY20123456789!?

Junkfool

Jakob Fischer
2004

THIS DOESN'T MAKE ANY SENSE AT ALL...DOES IT?

ABCDEFGHIJKLMNOPQRSTUVWXYZ0123456789!?

Hefty Galloon

Jakob Fischer
2004

Pizzadude

I was going to apologize for my rude behaviour, but then I heard you...

ABCDEFGHIJKLMNOPQRSTUVWXYZ!€%
abcdefghijklmnopqrstuvwxyz0123456789

You hypnotized me!
- Could you please turn me into a smoker again?!
ABCDEFGHIJKLMNOPQRSTUVWXYZ
abcdefghijklmnopqrstuvwxyz!#€%&?

SOMEONE ELSE?
ARE YOU REALLY DOING THE THINGS YOU DO?
ABCDEFGHIJKLMNOPQRSTUVWXYZ
0123456789!"#€%&/$<=>?+*(-)£@

jakob@pizzadude.dk

Keep me in mind!

but please forget everything I said about you!

ABCDEFGHIJKLMNOPQRSTUVWXYZ0123456789
abcdefghijklmnopqrstuvwxyz!"&*<=>?$@£+...

Who are we ?

And where excactly are going?

ABCDEFGHIJKLMNOPQRSTUVWXYZ
abcdefghijklmnopqrstuvwxyz!"&*<=>?$

Don't say no!

But I disagree if you are thinking of saying yes!

ABCDEFGHIJKLMNOPQRSTUVWXYZ
abcdefghijklmnopqrstuvwxyz!"#%&?

I was just kidding!

But I'm not sure if you knew it was a joke!

ABCDEFGHIJKLMNOPQRSTUVWXYZ
abcdefghijklmnopqrstuvwxyz!#€?

Mutaints
Jakob Fischer
2004

Omibez
Jakob Fischer
2005

Tomoli
Jakob Fischer
2005

Tomoli 2
Jakob Fischer
2005

jakob@pizzadude.dk

I wanted to make a list of all the things that crossed my mind today. But I quickly found out that it was not that easy...So, I just took the day off instead, and did nothing at all!

ABCDEFGHIJKLMNOP
QRSTUVWXYZ?!#€%
abcdefghijklmnopqrs
tuvwxyz0123456789

ABCDEFGHIJKLMNOP
QRSTUVWXYZ?!#€%
abcdefghijklmnopqrs
tuvwxyz0123456789

ABCDEFGHIJKLMNOP
QRSTUVWXYZ?!#€%
abcdefghijklmnopqrs
tuvwxyz0123456789

Talk to me!

In a language I can understand!

ABCDEFGHIJKLMNOPQRSTUVWXYZ!#€%
abcdefghijklmnopqrstuvwxyz0123456789

I WOULD LOVE TO ROCK THE BEAT!

AND, I WILL LOVE TO WALK THE STREET!

ABCDEFGHIJKLMNOPQRSTUVWX'.'Z

waiting for a phone call

And I really, really, really want that phone call to be from you!

ABCDEFGHIJKLMNOPQRSTUVWXYZ!"'#?
abcdefghijklmnopqrstuvwxyz0123456789

FunKadelika!

Why don't you come over to visit me sometime?

ABCDEFGHIJKLMNOPQRSTUVWXYZ
abcdefghijklmnopqrstuvwxyz!#&

Cruise the night!

Stop by my house, drinks are on me tonight!

ABCDEFGHIJKLMNOPQRSTUVWXYZ
abcdefghijklmnopqrstuvwxyz0123456789!"#&*...

jakob@pizzadude.dk

I'm not looking to disturb you, just a little to unnerve you

I hope that'll get your attention!

ABCDEFGHIJKLMNOPQRSTUVWXYZ!#€%&...
abcdefghijklmnopqrstuvwxyz0123456789

Jilly Bean

Jakob Fischer
2005

A thousand words

Is not enough for me to say I care

ABCDEFGHIJKLMNOPQRSTUVWXYZ!?
abcdefghijklmnopqrstuvwxyz0123456789

Fig Bun

Jakob Fischer
2005

Hands up!

And get those legs down!

ABCDEFGHIJKLMNOPQRSTUVWXYZ
abcdefghijklmnopqrstuvwxyz!?

Elevator Boy

Jakob Fischer
2003

 **positype** THE TYPE DESIGNS OF NEIL SUMMEROUR

Positype is an independent digital type design and lettering studio developing original and custom type for advertising, corporate, publishing, online, and broadcast clients. It was founded in 2002 by Athens, Georgia-based designer Neil Summerour {b. 1972}. Summerour began developing typefaces in 1996 with that year's Olympic Park's Brick Paver Project in Alanta. He is the managing partner and senior designer of the interactive, design, and marketing firm **Sliced Bread**. He is also an instructor of electronic design in the Lamar Dodd School of Art's Graphic Design Program at the University of Georgia.

In 2001, Summerour published his first 2 type designs with T-26 Digital Type Foundry in Chicago, Illinois. Since then, he has released more than 50 typeface families {more than 420 fonts} including Japanese Hiragana and Katakana fonts. Positype fonts are available online, and are sold arround the world by TheTypeTrust, Veer, T-26, and MyFonts. com.

www.positype.com
706.546.9353 phone
706.543.7322 fax

type sales

TheTypeTrust
312.226.2563
www.typetrust.com

Veer
877.297.7900
www.veer.com

T26
888.826.3668
www.t26.com

MyFonts
www.myfonts.com

Photograph previous page: Ritsurin-koen, Takamatsu, Kagawa Prefecture, Japan. © Neil Summerour.   Featured text: *Haiku* by Bashō.

Kari Pro

is now OpenType

Kari Pro

Neil Summerour
2006

Entire family consists of Normal,
Italic, Wide, and Wide Italic.

OpenType features include:
Expanded ligatures set
Discretionary ligatures
Stylistic alternates
Swashes
Old style numerals

aæbcçdðefghijklłmnnoøœpq
rsßtuvwxyzAÆBCÇDÐEFGHIJK
LŁMNOØŒPQRSTUVWXYZ0123
456789$¢€£¥f {[(@&;:!?¿¡%<>)]}
fiflfffbfhfjfrftfygigylypytvtwty
ffbffhffiffjfflffirfftffygogyttyaabb
ccddeeffgghhiijjjkkllmmnnoo
ppqqrrsttuuvvwwxxyyzzabcde
fghijklmnopqrstuvwxyzelryll

Anthology

Aaux Pro

Neil Summerour
2004

Entire family consists of 38 styles
including true italics.

OpenType features include:
Proportional figures
Old style figures
Small caps

Aaux Pro Thin

Neil Summerour
2004

aæbcçdðefghijklłmnoøœpqrsßtuvwxyz
AÆBCÇDÐEFGHIJKLŁMNOØŒPQRSTUVWXYZ
A ÆBCÇDÐEFGHIJKLŁMNOØ ŒPQRSTUVWXYZ
0123456789 0123456789 0123456789
$¢€£¥ƒ {[(@&;:!?¿i%<>)]} fifl

Aaux Pro Thin Italic

Neil Summerour
2004

aæbcçdðefghijklłmnoøœpqrsßtuvwxyz
AÆBCÇDÐEFGHIJKLŁMNOØŒPQRSTUVWXYZ
AÆBCÇDÐ EFGHIJKLŁMNOØ ŒPQRSTUVWXYZ
0123456789 0123456789 0123456789
$¢€£¥ƒ {[(@&;:!?¿i%<>)]} fifl

aæbcçdðefghijklłmnoøœpqrsßtuvwxyz
AÆBCÇDÐEFGHIJKLŁMNOØŒPQRSTUVWXYZ
AÆBCÇDÐEFGHIJKLŁMNOØŒPQRSTUVWXYZ
0123456789 0123456789 0123456789
$¢€£¥ƒ {[(@&;:!?¿¡%<>)]} fifl

aæbcçdðefghijklłmnoøœpqrsßtuvwxyz
AÆBCÇDÐEFGHIJKLŁMNOØŒPQRSTUVWXYZ
AÆBCÇDÐEFGHIJKLŁMNOØŒPQRSTUVWXYZ
0123456789 0123456789 0123456789
$¢€£¥ƒ {[(@&;:!?¿¡%<>)]} fifl

aæbcçdðefghijklłmnoøœpqrsßtuvwxyz
AÆBCÇDÐEFGHIJKLŁMNOØŒPQRSTUVWXYZ
A ÆBCÇDÐEFGHIJKLŁMNOØ ŒPQRSTUVWXYZ
0123456789 0123456789 0123456789
$¢€£¥ƒ {[(@&;:!?¿¡%<>)]} fifl

aæbcçdðefghijklłmnoøœpqrsßtuvwxyz
AÆBCÇDÐEFGHIJKLŁMNOØŒPQRSTUVWXYZ
AÆBCÇDÐEFGHIJKLŁMNOØŒPQRSTUVWXYZ
0123456789 0123456789 0123456789
$¢€£¥ƒ {[(@&;:!?¿¡%<>)]} fifl

aæbcçdðefghijklłmnoøœpqrsßtuvwxyz
AÆBCÇDÐEFGHIJKLŁMNOØŒPQRSTUVWXYZ
AÆBCÇDÐEFGHIJKLŁMNOØŒPQRSTUVWXYZ
0123456789 0123456789 0123456789
$¢€£¥f {[(@&;:!?¿¡%<>)]} fifl

aæbcçdðefghijklłmnoøœpqrsßtuvwxyz
AÆBCÇDÐEFGHIJKLŁMNOØŒPQRSTUVWXYZ
AÆBCÇDÐEFGHIJKLŁMNOØŒPQRSTUVWXYZ
0123456789 0123456789 0123456789
$¢€£¥f {[(@&;:!?¿¡%<>)]} fifl

aæbcçdðefghijklłmnoøœpqrsßtuvwxyz
AÆBCÇDÐEFGHIJKLŁMNOØŒPQRSTUVWXYZ
AÆBCÇDÐEFGHIJKLŁMNOØŒPQRSTUVWXYZ
0123456789 0123456789 0123456789
$¢€£¥f {[(@&;:!?¿¡%<>)]} fifl

aæbcçdðefghijklłmnoøœpqrsßtuvwxyz
AÆBCÇDÐEFGHIJKLŁMNOØŒPQRSTUVWXYZ
AÆBCÇDÐEFGHIJKLŁMNOØŒPQRSTUVWXYZ
0123456789 0123456789 0123456789
$¢€£¥f {[(@&;:!?¿¡%<>)]} fifl

info@positype.com

aæbcçdðefghijklłmnoøœpqrsßtuvwxyz
AÆBCÇDÐEFGHIJKLŁMNOØŒPQRSTUVWXYZ
AÆBCÇDÐEFGHIJKLŁMNOØŒPQRSTUVWXYZ
0123456789 0123456789 0123456789
$¢€£¥ƒ {[(@&;:!?¿¡%‹›)]} fifl

aæbcçdðefghijklłmnoøœpqrsßtuvwxyz
AÆBCÇDÐEFGHIJKLŁMNOØŒPQRSTUVWXYZ
AÆBCÇDÐEFGHIJKLŁMNOØŒPQRSTUVWXYZ
0123456789 0123456789 0123456789
$¢€£¥ƒ {[(@&;:!?¿¡%‹›)]} fifl

ABCDEFGHIJKLMNOPQRSTUVWXYZabcdefghijklmnopqrstuvwxyz

Ultra Weight

VARIABLE
SUSPENSE

Positype

Neil Summerour
2003, 2005

Entire family consists of 24 styles
including:
Narrow
Narrow Oblique
Narrow SC
Narrow SC Oblique
Narrow Biform
Narrow Biform Oblique
Medium
Medium Oblique
Medium SC
Medium SC Oblique
Medium Biform
Medium Biform Oblique
Wide
Wide Oblique
Wide SC
Wide SC Oblique
Wide Biform
Wide Biform Oblique
UltraWide
UltraWide Oblique
UltraWide SC
UltraWide SC Oblique
UltraWide Biform
UltraWide Biform Oblique

Eight

PROVINCES DUELING WITH STRATEGISTS

Time for the 10th day

MUROMACHI PERIOD

of Kanei (1645)

TRADITIONAL GUIDANCE IS HERE

Iwato of Higo in Kyushu

Nito ichi

RYU

AƎAa AƎAa AƎAa AƎAa

AƎAa AƎAa AƎAa AƎAa

info@positype.com

Mure-cho Takamatsu

aæbcçdɜefghijklltmno øœpqrrsʒßtuvwx
yzÆBCçDDEFGHIJKKLLMMN
NOøœPQQRRSSTUVWXYZ0123456789$¢
£¥ƒ@&¡;:!?%

Baka

Neil Summerour
2005

This rough but elegant handwriting script is available in OpenType format.

Nihonjin ni naritai!

aæbcçdɜefghijklltmnoøœpqrrsʒßtu
vwxxyyzAÆBBᵦCçDDDEFGH
IJKKLLMMNNOøœPQQRRSSTU
VWXYZ0123456789$¢ £¥ƒ@&¡;:!?%
fiflffiffflfrffrftfftttrtrtroost

Baka Too

Neil Summerour
2006

This rough but elegant handwriting script is available in OpenType format.

Positype

Neil Summerour
2005

Entire family consists of 12 styles
including:
Regular
Italic
Regular OSF
Italic OSF
Small Caps
Small Caps Italic
Bold
Bold Italic
Bold OSF
Bold Italic OSF
Bold Small Caps
Bold Small Caps Italic

Language support includes:
Central European

Donatora

ABCDEFGHIJKLMNOPQRSTUVWXYZ·abcdefg
hijklmnopqrstuvwxyz·ABCDEFGHIJKLMNOPQRST
UVWXYZ·0123456789·0123456789·*ABCDEFGHIJ*
KLMNOPQRSTUVWXYZ·abcdefghijklmnopqrstuv
wxyz·ABCDEFGHIJKLMNOPQRSTUVWXYZ·*0123456789*·
0123456789·**ABCDEFGHIJKLMNOPQRSTUV**
WXYZ·**abcdefghijklmnopqrstuvwxyz**·ABC
DEFGHIJKLMNOPQRSTUVWXYZ·**0123456789**·**o**
123456789·***ABCDEFGHIJKLMNOPQRSTUVWX***
YZ·***abcdefghijklmnopqrstuvwxyz***·ABCDEFGHI
JKLMNOPQRSTUVWXYZ·*0123456789*·*0123456789*

Donatora

info@positype.com

Regular

ABCDEFGHIJKLMNOPQRSTUVWXYZ abcdefghijklmnopqrstuvwxyz
ABCDEFGHIJKLMNOPQRSTUVWXYZ 0123456789 0123456789 $¢€£¥ƒ
{[(@&;:!?¿¡%<>)]} fifl

Italic

ABCDEFGHIJKLMNOPQRSTUVWXYZ abcdefghijklmnopqrstuvwxyz
ABCDEFGHIJKLMNOPQRSTUVWXYZ 0123456789 0123456789 $¢€£¥ƒ
{[(@&;:!?¿¡%<>)]} fifl

Medium

ABCDEFGHIJKLMNOPQRSTUVWXYZ abcdefghijklmnopqrstuv
wxyz ABCDEFGHIJKLMNOPQRSTUVWXYZ 0123456789 0123456789
$¢€£¥ƒ {[(@&;:!?¿¡%<>)]} fifl

Medium Italic

ABCDEFGHIJKLMNOPQRSTUVWXYZ abcdefghijklmnopqrstuvwxyz
ABCDEFGHIJKLMNOPQRSTUVWXYZ 0123456789 0123456789 $¢€£¥ƒ
{[(@&;:!?¿¡%<>)]} fifl

Bold

ABCDEFGHIJKLMNOPQRSTUVWXYZ abcdefghijklmnopq
rstuvwxyz ABCDEFGHIJKLMNOPQRSTUVWXYZ 0123456789
0123456789 $¢€£¥ƒ {[(@&;:!?¿¡%<>)]} fifl

Bold Italic

ABCDEFGHIJKLMNOPQRSTUVWXYZ abcdefghijklmnopqrstuv
wxyz ABCDEFGHIJKLMNOPQRSTUVWXYZ 0123456789 0123456789
$¢€£¥ƒ {[(@&;:!?¿¡%<>)]} fifl

Neil Summerour
2005

Entire family consists of 18 styles, including:
Regular
Italic
Regular OSF
Italic OSF
Small Caps
Small Caps Italic
Medium
Medium Italic
Medium OSF
Medium Italic OSF
Medium Small Caps
Medium Small Caps Italic
Bold
Bold Italic
Bold OSF
Bold Italic OSF
Bold Small Caps
Bold Small Caps Italic

Language support includes:
Central European

Positype

Headcold

Neil Summerour
2004

This playful futuristic design is available in regular and shadowed styles.

AaBbCcDdEeFfGgHhIiJjKkLlMmNnOo
PpQqRrSsTtUuVvWwXyYyZzⓐⓡⓒⓟtm
0123456789&$¢€¥ƒ.:;ⓢⓢⓤⓤⓤⓢⓢFiFl

AaBbCcDdEeFfGgHhIiJjKkLlMmNnOo
PpQqRrSsTtUuVvWwXyYyZzⓐⓡⓒⓟtm
0123456789&$¢€¥ƒ.:;ⓢⓢⓤⓤⓤⓢⓢFiFl

Juicy

Neil Summerour
2004

Entire family consists of 6 styles, including:
Regular
Regular Italic
Bold
Bold Italic
Black
Black Italic

Black

AaBbCcDdEeFfGgHhIiJjKk
LlMmNnOoPpQqRrSsTtUu
VvWwXxYyZʒ0123456789
&$¢€¥ƒ {[(@&;:!?¿¡%<>)]}

Black Italic

AaBbCcDdEeFfGgHhIiJjKk
LlMmNnOoPpQqRrSsTtUu
VvWwXxYyZʒ0123456789
&$¢€¥ƒ {[(@&;:!?¿¡%<>)]}

Bold

AaBbCcDdEeFfGgHhIiJjKk
LlMmNnOoPpQqRrSsTtUu
VvWwXxYyZʒ0123456789
&$¢€¥ƒ {[(@&;:!?¿¡%<>)]}

Bold Italic

AaBbCcDdEeFfGgHhIiJjKk
LlMmNnOoPpQqRrSsTtUu
VvWwXxYyZʒ0123456789
&$¢€¥ƒ {[(@&;:!?¿¡%<>)]}

Regular

AaBbCcDdEeFfGgHhIiJjKk
LlMmNnOoPpQqRrSsTtUu
VvWwXxYyZʒ0123456789
&$¢€¥ƒ {[(@&;:!?¿¡%<>)]}

Regular Italic

AaBbCcDdEeFfGgHhIiJjKk
LlMmNnOoPpQqRrSsTtUu
VvWwXxYyZʒ0123456789
&$¢€¥ƒ {[(@&;:!?¿¡%<>)]}

Sneakers Script

Neil Summerour
2004

Wake, butterfly- it's late, we've miles to go together. egggggss Pretending to drink sake from my fan, sprinkled with cherry petals.

228   info@positype.com

Light and Light Italic

AaBbCcDdEeFfGgHhIiJjKkLlMmNnOoPpQqRrSsTtUuVvWwXxYyZz
0123456789&$¢€¥ƒ {[(@&;:!?¿¡%<>)]}

AaBbCcDdEeFfGgHhIiJjKkLlMmNnOoPpQqRrSsTtUuVvWwXxYyZz0123456789

Regular and Italic

AaBbCcDdEeFfGgHhIiJjKkLlMmNnOoPpQqRrSsTtUuVvWwXxYyZz
0123456789&$¢€¥ƒ {[(@&;:!?¿¡%<>)]}

AaBbCcDdEeFfGgHhIiJjKkLlMmNnOoPpQqRrSsTtUuVvWwXxYyZz0123456789

Medium and Medium Italic

AaBbCcDdEeFfGgHhIiJjKkLlMmNnOoPpQqRrSsTtUuVvWwXx
YyZz 0123456789&$¢€¥ƒ {[(@&;:!?¿¡%<>)]}

AaBbCcDdEeFfGgHhIiJjKkLlMmNnOoPpQqRrSsTtUuVvWwXxYyZz0123456789

Bold and Bold Italic

**AaBbCcDdEeFfGgHhIiJjKkLlMmNnOoPpQqRrSsTtUuVvWw
XxYyZz 0123456789&$¢€¥ƒ {[(@&;:!?¿¡%<>)]}**

AaBbCcDdEeFfGgHhIiJjKkLlMmNnOoPpQqRrSsTtUuVvWwXxYyZz0123456789

Altar

Neil Summerour
2003

Entire family consists of 8
styles, including:
Regular
Small Caps
Petite Caps
Fractions
Bold
Bold Small Caps
Bold Petite Caps
Bold Fractions

Regular, Small Caps, Petite Caps, and Fractions

AaBbCcDdEeFfGgHhIiJjKkLlMmNnOoPpQqRrSsTtUuVvWwXxYyZz 0123456789
ABCDEFGHIJKLMNOPQRSTUVWXYZ ABCDEFGHIJKLMNOPQRSTUVWXYZ ⅛¼½⅔ ✺ * ✺

Bold, Small Caps, Petite Caps, and Fractions

AaBbCcDdEeFfGgHhIiJjKkLlMmNnOoPpQqRrSsTtUuVvWwXxYyZz 012345
ABCDEFGHIJKLMNOPQRSTUVWXYZ ABCDEFGHIJKLMNOPQRSTUVWXYZ ⅛¼½⅔✺ ✺

Mirroring each other: white narcissi, paper screen.

Plastek

Neil Summerour
2005

Entire family consists of 4
styles, including:
Regular
Outline
Left Shadow
Right Shadow

Left Shadow

Regular

AaBbCcDdEeFfGgHhIiJjKkLlMmNn
OoPpQqRrSsTtUuVvWwXxYyZz
0123456789&$¢€¥ƒ ﬂ&;:!?%

plastek outline
plastek left shadow
plastek right shadow

Cen Pro Light

Neil Summerour
2006

OpenType features include:
Proportional, lining, and old style figures, and small caps

Language support includes:
Central European

aæbcçdðefghijklłmnooœpqrsßtuvwxyz AÆBCÇDÐEFGHIJKLŁMNOØ ŒPQRSTUVWXYZ AÆBCÇDEFGHIJKLMNOØŒPQRSTUVWXYZ 0123456789 0123456789 0123456789 $¢€£¥ƒ {[(@&;:!?¿¡%<>)]} fifl

Cen Pro Light Italic

Neil Summerour
2006

OpenType features include:
Proportional, lining, and old style figures, and small caps

Language support includes:
Central European

aæbcçdðefghijklłmnooœpqrsßtuvwxyz AÆBCÇDÐEFGHIJKLŁMNOØ ŒPQRSTUVWXYZ AÆBCÇDEFGHIJKLMNOØŒPQRSTUVWXYZ 0123456789 0123456789 0123456789 $¢€£¥ƒ {[(@&;:!?¿¡%<>)]} fifl

Cen Pro Normal

Neil Summerour
2006

OpenType features include:
Proportional, lining, and old style figures, and small caps

Language support includes:
Central European

aæbcçdðefghijklłmnooœpqrsßtuvwxyz AÆBCÇDÐEFGHIJKLŁMNOØ ŒPQRSTUVWXYZ AÆBCÇDEFGHIJKLMNOØŒPQRSTUVWXYZ 0123456789 0123456789 0123456789 $¢€£¥ƒ {[(@&;:!?¿¡%<>)]} fifl

Cen Pro Normal Italic

Neil Summerour
2006

OpenType features include:
Proportional, lining, and old style figures, and small caps

Language support includes:
Central European

aæbcçdðefghijklłmnooœpqrsßtuvwxyz AÆBCÇDÐEFGHIJKLŁMNOØ ŒPQRSTUVWXYZ AÆBCÇDEFGHIJKLMNOØŒPQRSTUVWXYZ 0123456789 0123456789 0123456789 $¢€£¥ƒ {[(@&;:!?¿¡%<>)]} fifl

Cen Pro Bold

Neil Summerour
2006

OpenType features include:
Proportional, lining, and old style figures, and small caps

Language support includes:
Central European

aæbcçdðefghijklłmnooœpqrsßtuvwxyz AÆBCÇDÐEFGHIJKL ŁMNOØŒPQRSTUVWXYZ AÆBCÇDEFGHIJKLMNOØŒPQRSTUVWXYZ 0123456789 0123456789 0123456789 $¢€£¥ƒ {[(@&;:!?¿¡%<>)]}

Cen Pro Bold Italic

Neil Summerour
2006

OpenType features include:
Proportional, lining, and old style figures, and small caps

Language support includes:
Central European

aæbcçdðefghijklłmnooœpqrsßtuvwxyz AÆBCÇDÐEFGHIJKL ŁMNOØŒPQRSTUVWXYZ AÆBCÇDEFGHIJKLMNOØŒPQRSTUVWXYZ 0123456789 0123456789 0123456789 $¢€£¥ƒ {[(@&;:!?¿¡%<>)]}

Mure-cho, Takamatsu

Cynapse

Cynapse Pro

Neil Summerour
2005

Entire family consists of 12
styles, including:
Regular
Italic
Bold
Bold Italic
SC Regular
SC Italic
SC Bold
SC Bold Italic
OSF Regular
OSF Italic
OSF Bold
OSF Bold Italic

Language support includes:
Central European

aæbcçdðefghijklłmnooœpqrsßtuvwxyz AÆBCÇDÐEF
GHIJKLŁMNOØŒPQRSTUVWXYZAÆBCÇDÐ EFGHIJKLŁ
MNOØŒPQRSTUVWXYZ 0123456789 0123456789
0123456789 $¢€£¥ƒ {[[@&;:!?¿¡%<>]]} fifl

aæbcçdðefghijklłmnooœpqrsßtuvwxyz AÆBCÇD
ÐEFGHIJKLŁMNOØŒPQRSTUVWXYZAÆBCÇDÐ E
FGHIJKLŁMNOØŒPQRSTUVWXYZ 0123456789
0123456789 0123456789 $¢€£¥ƒ {[[@&;:

A

Cynapse Regular 5 on 6 pt.

Buddha's death–day—old hands clicking rosaries. While moon sets atop the trees, leaves cling
to the rain. How pleasant—just once not to see Fuji through mist. Bright moon: I stroll around
the pond—hey, dawn has come. Buddha's death–day—old hands clicking rosaries. While moon
sets atop the trees, leaves cling to the rain. How pleasant—just once not to see Fuji through
mist. Bright moon: I stroll around the pond—hey, dawn has come. Buddha's death–day—old
hands clicking rosaries. While moon sets atop the trees, leaves cling to the rain. How
pleasant—just once not to see Fuji through mist. Bright moon: I stroll around the pond—hey,
dawn has come. Buddha's death–day—old hands clicking rosaries. While moon sets atop the
trees, leaves cling to the rain. How pleasant—just once not to see Fuji through mist. Bright

Cynapse Regular 6 on 7.2 pt.

Buddha's death–day—old hands clicking rosaries. While moon sets atop the
trees, leaves cling to the rain. How pleasant—just once not to see Fuji through
mist. Bright moon: I stroll around the pond—hey, dawn has come. Buddha's
death–day—old hands clicking rosaries. While moon sets atop the trees,
leaves cling to the rain. How pleasant—just once not to see Fuji through mist.
Bright moon: I stroll around the pond—hey, dawn has come. Buddha's death–
day—old hands clicking rosaries. While moon sets atop the trees, leaves cling
to the rain. How pleasant—just once not to see Fuji through mist. Bright moon: I
stroll around the pond—hey, dawn has come. Buddha's death–day—old hands
clicking rosaries. While moon sets atop the trees, leaves cling to the rain. How

Cynapse Regular 8 on 9.6 pt.

Buddha's death–day—old hands clicking rosaries. While
moon sets atop the trees, leaves cling to the rain. How
pleasant—just once not to see Fuji through mist. Bright
moon: I stroll around the pond—hey, dawn has come.
Buddha's death–day—old hands clicking rosaries. Whil
moon sets atop the trees, leaves cling to the rain. Ho
pleasant—just once not to see Fuji through mist. Brig
moon: I stroll around the pond—hey, dawn has com
Buddha's death–day—old hands clicking rosaries.
moon sets atop the trees, leaves cling to the rain.
pleasant—just once not to see Fuji through mist.
moon: I stroll around the pond—hey, dawn has
Buddha's death–day—old hands clicking rosari
moon sets atop the trees, leaves cling to the r

Positype

Ayumi

Neil Summerour
2004

Entire family consists of 8
styles, including:
Light
Light Italic
Regular
Regular Italic
Medium
Medium Italic
Bold
Bold Italic

How I long to see ¶ among dawn flowers, ¶ the face of God.

AaBbCcDdEeFfGgHhIiJjKkLlMmNnOoPpQqRrSsTtUuVv
WwXxYyZz 0123456789&$¢€¥f {[(@&;:!?¿¡%<>)]}

AaBbCcDdEeFfGgHhIiJjKkLlMmNnOoPpQqRrSsTtUuVv
WwXxYyZz 0123456789&$¢€¥f {[(@&;:!?¿¡%<>)]}

Pretending to drink
sake from my fan,
sprinkled with cherry petals.

How pleasant—just once *not* to see Fuji through mist.

Buddha's death-day—old hands clicking rosaries. While moon sets atop the trees, leaves cling to the rain. How pleasant—just once *not* to see Fuji through mist. Bright moon: I stroll around the pond—hey, dawn has come. *Buddha's death-day—old hands clicking rosaries. While moon sets atop the trees, leaves cling to the rain. How pleasant—just once not to see Fuji through mist. Bright moon: I stroll around the pond—hey, dawn has come.* **Buddha's death-day—old hands clicking rosaries.** While moon sets atop the trees, leaves cling to the rain. How pleasant—just once *not* to see Fuji through mist. Bright moon: I stroll around the pond—hey, dawn has come. *Buddha's death-day—old hands clicking rosaries. While moon sets atop the trees, leaves cling to the rain. How pleasant—just once not to see Fuji through mist. Bright moon: I stroll around the pond—hey, dawn has come.*

Ayumi

info@positype.com

One

AaBbCcDdEeFfGgH
hIiJjKkLlMmNnOoP
pQqRrSsTtUuVvW
wXxYyZz 01234567

Two

AaBbCcDdEeFfGgH
hIiJjKkLlMmNnOoP
pQqRrSsTtUuVvW
wXxYyZz 01234567

Three

AaBbCcDdEeFfGgH
hIiJjKkLlMmNnOoP
pQqRrSsTtUuVvW
wXxYyZz 01234567

One Bold

AaBbCcDdEeFfGgH
hIiJjKkLlMmNnOoP
pQqRrSsTtUuVvW
wXxYyZz 01234567

Two Bold

AaBbCcDdEeFfGgH
hIiJjKkLlMmNnOoP
pQqRrSsTtUuVvW
wXxYyZz 01234567

Three Bold

AaBbCcDdEeFfGgH
hIiJjKkLlMmNnOoP
pQqRrSsTtUuVvW
wXxYyZz 01234567

Luce

Neil Summerour
2004

Entire family consists of 6 styles, including:
One
One Bold
Two
Two Bold
Three
Three Bold

UltraLight

AaBbCcDdEeFf
GgHhIiJjKkLlMmN
nOoPpQqRrSsTt
UuVvWwXxYyZz
Bright moon: I stroll
around the pond-

Light

AaBbCcDdEeFf
GgHhIiJjKkLlMmN
nOoPpQqRrSsTt
UuVvWwXxYyZz
Bright moon: I stroll
around the pond-

Bold

AaBbCcDdEeFf
GgHhIiJjKkLlMmN
nOoPpQqRrSsTt
UuVvWwXxYyZz
Bright moon: I stroll
around the pond-

UltraLight Oblique

AaBbCcDdEeFf
GgHhIiJjKkLlMmN
nOoPpQqRrSsTt
UuVvWwXxYyZz
Bright moon: I stroll
around the pond-

Light Oblique

AaBbCcDdEeFf
GgHhIiJjKkLlMmN
nOoPpQqRrSsTt
UuVvWwXxYyZz
Bright moon: I stroll
around the pond-

Bold Oblique

AaBbCcDdEeFf
GgHhIiJjKkLlMmN
nOoPpQqRrSsTt
UuVvWwXxYyZz
Bright moon: I stroll
around the pond-

Truss

Neil Summerour
2004

Entire family consists of 6 styles, including:
UltraLight
UltraLight Oblique
Light
Light Oblique
Bold
Bold Oblique

Positype

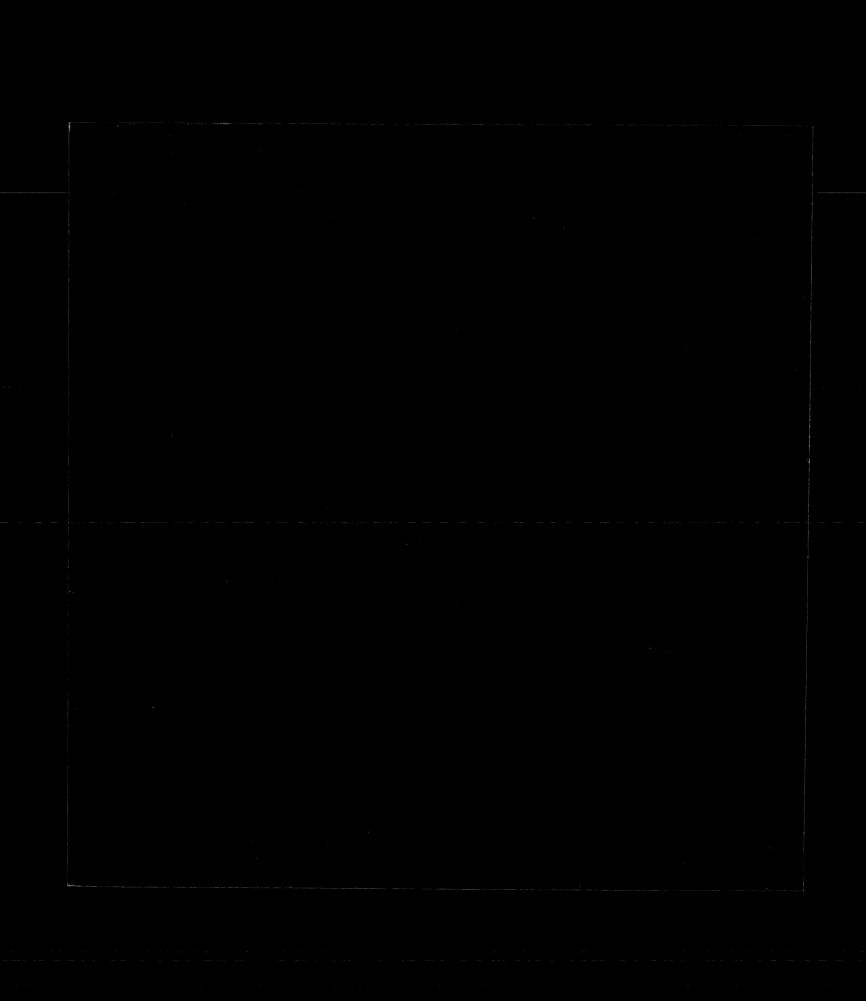

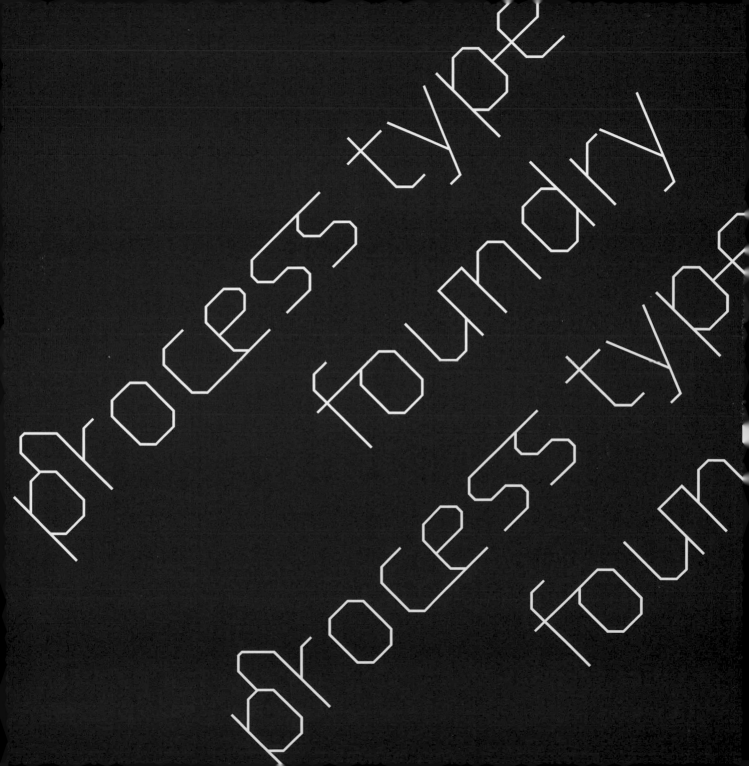

Buy online:
www.processtypefoundry.com

Contact:
info@processtypefoundry.com

Process Type Foundry

now transliterate

Writers suggest it's usually best to kick things off with a capital letter

Crafted Round Mechanics

Changes in lettering standards have left some room for digital fonts

VISUAL ADDITION

Several stations are set to offer hand lettering

15 Reductions

Lettering will appear under different conditions

Home Election Board

Sometimes the pleasures of working can be free

BRANCH 328

Regional notes and corrections seem provincial

2 pouty
manatees
↓ ↓ ↓
pouty
manatees

Bryant 2

Eric Olson
2002–2005

Bryant 2 is a completely re-drawn and updated version of the typeface Bryant, originally modeled around the popular Wrico lettering kits used by draftsmen and amateur sign makers in the 1960s and 1970s, Bryant 2 features four weights, each with a companion alternate including different versions of oft-used characters. It is suitable for anything from worldwide branding projects to simple one-off posters.

Entire family consists of Light, Light Alternate, Regular, Regular Alternate, Medium, Medium Alternate, Bold, and Bold Alternate.

Bryant Light 8 on 11 pt.

Place the guide holder in position where the lettering is to be done. The rubber and cork composition runners on the under side of the guide holder and the right hand free to operate the scriber. Before using the guide holder, the surface should be wiped with a cloth to remove any dust which might interfere with the smooth movement of the guide. If grit collects in the track in which the tail pin of the scriber slides, the track should be wiped with a cloth. The chart shown in figure 4 illustrates the

Bryant Regular 8 on 11 pt.

Place the guide holder in position where the lettering is to be done. The rubber and cork composition runners on the under side of the guide holder and the right hand free to operate the scriber. Before using the guide holder, the surface should be wiped with a cloth to remove any dust which might interfere with the smooth movement of the guide. If grit collects in the track in which the tail pin of the scriber slides, the track should be wiped with a cloth. The chart shown in figure 4 illustrates the characters made with

Process

Eric Olson
2002–2005

Bryant 2 Pro adds to the capabilities of Bryant 2 with the addition of small caps, italics, and multiple numeral styles.

Entire family consists of Light, Light Alternate, Light Italic, Regular, Regular Alternate, Regular Italic, Medium, Medium Alternate, Medium Italic, Bold, Bold Alternate, and Bold Italic.

Bryant 2 Pro Light 8 on 11 pt.

Select the WRICO LETTERING GUIDE for the size of character required. The number in the upper right-hand corners of the guides indicates *the size of character and whether the guide is for capitals, lower case letters, numerals, or capitals and numbers.* For example, "Guide No. G 100 CN" indicates "Capital and Numerals .100" in height" and "Guide No. G 240 C" indicates "Capitals .240" in height. Place the lettering guide in position where the *lettering is to be done.* The rubber and cork composition runners

Bryant 2 Pro Regular 8 on 11 pt.

Select the WRICO LETTERING GUIDE for the size of character required. The number in the upper right-hand corners of the guides indicates the size of character and whether the guide is for capitals, lower case letters, numerals, or capitals and numbers. For example, "Guide No. G 100 CN" indicates "Capital and Numerals .100" in height" and "Guide No. G 240 C" indicates "Capitals .240" in height. Place the lettering guide in position where the *lettering is to be done.* The rubber and cork composition runners

SHACHIHOKO

Open during 9 AM, 11 AM, and 6 PM only

Minneapolis

Z technických důvodů zavřeno

NEVER ENDER

DO NOT GIVE OR RECEIVE INFORMATION

District →41

Ok then, I declare a microphone brawl

DEERWOOD

26 Lower Chambers

Bryant 2 Pro Light complete character set

abcdefghijklmnopqrstuvwxyzABFCDEFGHIJKLMNOPQRSTUVWXYZABCDEFGHIJK
LMNOPQRSTUVWXYZáăâäæǽàāąãååćčçĉćďđéěĕêëèēęğĝģġħĥíîïìīįijĵķĺľļŀłńňñ
ñóöőôöœòőōøǿõřŕŗśšşŝßţ̌țúùûüùûűůũŵŵŵẃýŷ̈ÿ́źž̇żðŋþfifláăâäæǽàāąãååćčç
ĉćďđéěĕêëèēęğĝģġħĥíîïìīįijĵķĺľļŀłńňñ̃óöőôöœòőōøǿõřŕŗśšşŝșţ̌țúùû
üùûűůũŵŵŵẃýŷ̈ÿ́źž̇żðŋþfifláăâäæǽàāąãååćčçĉćďđéěĕêëèēęğĝģ
ġħĥíîïìīįijĵķĺľļŀłńňñ̃óöőôöœòőōøǿõřŕŗśšşŝșţ̌țúùûüùûűůũŵ
ŵŵẃýŷ̈ÿ́źž̇żðŋþ0123456789<-×÷+±=≠≈>#$¢£¥€ƒ0123456789<-×÷+±=≠≈>
#$¢£¥€ƒ0123456789<-×÷+±=≠≈>$¢£¥€ƒ0123456789<-×÷+±=≠≈>$¢£¥
€ƒαυýáăâäàāąåååúýûỳýù||◊∞∫∂√ΔΩΠΣμπ¬≤≥~^%‰/¼½¾¹²³ªº№℮ℓ¤(){}[]()[]{}/\
¶@&!?¡¿¿¡†‡°©®™•.*:„"""‹›«»‗–‒— ' ‛   " "
←↙↗↖↘↓↑←↔→↗↖↙↓↑↓■▲▼▶◀▲▽

   info@processtypefoundry.com

POSITION 1

Our neighbor is holding us hostage

5 Felt Pens

Moving in silence is for the neighbors

Pen No. 6

If we could erase his stereo speakers

Ink Cleaner

Express lettering stations for holiday

86 PYRALIN

Sunday is almost always before Monday

PEN GUIDE

Holding before a mirror reveals system

Bryant Condensed Light 8 on 11 pt.

Place the guide holder in position where the lettering is to be done. The rubber and cork composition runners on the under side of the guide holder and the right hand free to operate the scriber. Before using the guide holder, the surface should be wiped with a cloth to remove any dust which might interfere with the smooth movement of the guide. If grit collects in the track in which the tail pin of the scriber slides, the

Bryant Condensed Regular 8 on 11 pt.

Place the guide holder in position where the lettering is to be done. The rubber and cork composition runners on the under side of the guide holder and the right hand free to operate the scriber. Before using the guide holder, the surface should be wiped with a cloth to remove any dust which might interfere with the smooth movement of the guide. If grit collects in the track in which the tail pin of the

Bryant Compressed Light 8 on 11 pt.

Place the guide holder in position where the lettering is to be done. The rubber and cork composition runners on the under side of the guide holder and the right hand free to operate the scriber. Before using the guide holder, the surface should be wiped with a cloth to remove any dust which might interfere with the smooth movement of the guide. If grit collects in the track in which the tail pin of the scriber slides, the track should be wiped with a cloth. The lettering platter will now be ready for you

Bryant Compressed Regular 8 on 11 pt.

Place the guide holder in position where the lettering is to be done. The rubber and cork composition runners on the under side of the guide holder and the right hand free to operate the scriber. Before using the guide holder, the surface should be wiped with a cloth to remove any dust which might interfere with the smooth movement of the guide. If grit collects in the track in which the tail pin of the scriber slides, the track should be wiped with a cloth. The lettering platter will now be ready for you prepare a lettered sign or

Bryant Condensed

Eric Olson
2002–2005

Bryant Condensed is the mid-width family of the Bryant series. Though condensed in name, this family shares a page color and body width similar to many standard grotesques. In other words, it's equally suited for text or display work.

Entire family consists of Light, Regular, Medium, and Bold.

Bryant Compressed

Eric Olson
2002–2005

Designed for situations in which large point sizes and maximum letter counts need to coexist, Bryant Compressed is the narrowest of the Bryant families. Sharp stem joins and increased contrast—stylistic departures from the other weights and widths—allow this face to keep the Bryant style while maintaining a narrow width.

Entire family consists of Light, Regular, Medium, and Bold.

Process

Eric Olson
2001-2002

FIG—named after the FIGlet application created by Frank Sheeran, Ian Chai, and Glenn Chappell—is a set of three typefaces in the spirit of early email and ASCII art explorations. Written in 1991 using the programming language C, the FIGlet application allows users to create fonts with basic ASCII characters. The FIG types capture the simplicity and beauty of the FIGlets with a family that includes a sans, a serif, and a script.

Entire family consists of Sans, Serif, and Script.

5 2 0 9 2 . 7 8 1 3

3 3 . 5 2 5 1 0 1 0

Newish Singles

vacuous adventures in fictional writing

FINISH AUDIO

I could be mistaken, but that looks Canadian

Delightful Deception

* * *

Accomplished

Negotiation and compromise needed

* * *

Coffee Power

Vegan vitamins for the nervous system

Roselin Pourpré

Known to feed in my newly installed bird feeder

WATCHING

All stone material was culled from local sources

Richard
&
C-Bear

info@processtypefoundry.com

International

Sound was a deliberate distortion

2415.8769.019351.01

infrastructure

Flying in rented information tubes

Certified

nbf

Your prayers have been answered

SIMULTANEOUSLY

901

SYNCHRONIZE CLOCKS AND EVENTS AROUND THE WORLD

Effectively

Transmit the exchange of data packets

Researchers

Started in 1974 with two glow sticks

Prospects: Coffee As Healing Force

The inside of the tank had some previous damage from the first round of action. I know, I know, really an obsession with minor particulars but this kind of thing is usually very important. But exactly, first glance would reveal virtually no damage but the thing was pretty screwed up. I didn't test any esoteric areas but focused almost exclusively on the frontal lobe. As you know, those areas are impressively flexible and able to recover quickly from rather traumatic accidents. Uplifting, I know. It restores an amount of faith in the healing powers of organic coffee.

```
---------------------------------
Fourth Quarter By Year ---------
---------------------------------
1994 Q4......................387
1995 Q4......................425
1996 Q4......................442
1997 Q4......................463
1998 Q4......................452
1999 Q4......................445
2000 Q4......................507
2001 Q4......................507
---------------------------------
```

Operations	2005	2006
NET PRODUCTION		
United States	4533	4525
International	1228	1195
Worldwide	1681	1647
OTHER VOLUMES INTERNATIONAL		
United States	1750	2719
International	1894	1692
Worldwide	2644	2411
SALES OF REFINED FIBS		
United States	1534	1462
International	2332	2331
Worldwide	3866	3793
United Credulity	2365	5678

Kettler

Eric Olson
2002

Courier, originally designed in 1955 by Howard G. Kettler for the IBM bar typewriter, has become a ubiquitous presence on the computer. The twelve pitch mono type family Kettler pays tribute to the simplicity of Kettler's monospaced classic by revisiting the smooth letter fit and efficiency of form.

Entire family consists of Regular and Bold.

Process

Eric Olson
2003

Lingua dwells on the attraction designers have for ligatures and the new possibilities OpenType has created. When used without its ligatures, Lingua is a geometric typeface with strong angles and few sympathies. With the discretionary ligatures turned on, it transforms into a modern, nearly upright script.

Entire family consists of Light and Regular.

Lingua Regular 8 on 11 pt.

The inside of the tank had some previous damage from the first round of action. I know, I know, really an obsession with minor particulars but this kind of thing is usually very important. But exactly, first glance would reveal virtually no damage but the thing was pretty screwed up. I didn't test any esoteric areas but focused almost exclusively on the frontal lobe. As you know, those areas are impressively flexible and able to recover quickly from rather traumatic accidents. Uplifting, I know. It restores an amount of faith in the recovery process but you have to remain critical of the whole thing. What if it never heals? You could

026

at

⇒) lingua (⇐

Then where do first like our new and have

Stanchions

Could he/his/she/her some most like they

The of and to

Before been had not their which one these

candidates

More no new way even no if out well would

also said who

Only must way can other over by that is was

62 listeners

By its nature, the stacks seem to store time

Downtowner

More no new way even no if out well would

delicate move

info@processtypefoundry.com

Show Available Discs Only

Replace With

InvalidObject %macro.end

Save Version

Document Preset / File Info

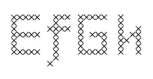

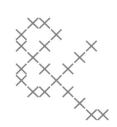

Move Paste From Clipboard

Encoding:

SQL syntax error 0215.76g

Uninstall

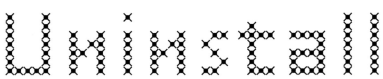

FindReplace

Eric Olson
2003-2004

FindReplace is an exploration of the generative possibilities of current type software and simple grid structures.

Entire family consists of Thin, Light, Regular, Medium, Bold, and Black.

Process

Eric Olson
2003–2004

Klavika is a flexible family of sans serifs for editorial and identity design. Features such as small caps, true italics, multiple language support, and several numeral styles make it an ideal workhorse typeface.

Entire family consists of Light, Light Italic, Regular, Regular Italic, Medium, Medium Italic, Bold, and Bold Italic.

Klavika Light & Italic 8 on 11 pt.

The inside of the tank had some previous damage from the first round of action. I know, I know, really an obsession with minor particulars but this kind of thing is usually very important. But exactly, first glance would reveal virtually no damage but the thing was pretty screwed up. I didn't test any esoteric areas but focused almost exclusively on the frontal lobe. As you know, those areas are impressively flexible and able to recover quickly from *rather traumatic accidents*. Uplifting, I know. It restores an amount of faith in the recovery process but you have to remain critical of the whole thing. WHAT IF IT NEVER HEALS? You could purchase a new pair of lungs but then you would have to cross your fingers for continued low interest rates. No, *seriously* I'm just kidding. But new lungs *may* improve your stamina. Please understand, this kind

Klavika Regular & Italic 8 on 11 pt.

The inside of the tank had some previous damage from the first round of action. I know, I know, really an obsession with minor particulars but this kind of thing is usually very important. But exactly, first glance would reveal virtually no dam-age but the thing was pretty screwed up. I didn't test any esoteric areas but focused almost exclusively on the frontal lobe. As you know, those areas are impressively flexible and able to recover quickly from *rather traumatic ac-cidents*. Uplifting, I know. It restores an amount of faith in the recovery process but you have to remain critical of the whole thing. WHAT IF IT NEVER HEALS? You could purchase a new pair of lungs but then you would have to cross your fingers for continued low interest rates. No, *seriously* I'm just kidding. But new lungs *may* improve your stamina. Please understand, this kind of thing needs to

Joining me to talk more about these developments

NEW DETAILS EMERGE

Recently launched a sustained distortion to convince

FIRST THIS OLD NEWS

She joins us from the phone in her compound

Reliable Office

OUTSIDE THE COUNTY COURTHOUSE AWAITING FURTHER WORD

In Studio ʔa

FANTASTIC, WE SHOULD OVEREMPHASIZE THIS STORY

Demands for transparency

For the second time in as many days authorities point to

editorial & opinion

Weekend storms have left many residents without power

LINKED TO EVIDENCE

Speaking of which, can you describe how that works?

Continue Now

BEFORE OUR BREAK YOU WERE SAYING HOW MEDIA COVERAGE

ROVING WIRETAPS

Auto Responder, Legacy Of Outsider

State school leaders meet to push for further legislation this Thursday

Labor Department points to rise in

ELECTED OFFICIALS POINT TO PINKO ITALIAN GREYHOUND OWNERS

It wasn't articulated well enough

RIGOROUS DEBATE ESSENTIALLY RULES YOUR OPINION LOST ON ME

5 Recent Surveys Of World Music

Given your record, it looks like you've just set a new world record

LOCATION CODES →	
Service Time	00.0231.02360201.25
Adjustment	00.6234.85420232.00
30 Days	00.5633.88112022.66
Tab Balanced	11.6234.85420232.00
12 months	00.5623.69852522.00
Issued Tab	88.1121.21560111.86
Payable Line	12.6234.85420232.00

IMPACT CODES →	
Line Code	51.5511.02363252.62
Wiretap	45.8401.30215890.81
Balanced	89.0136.01012248.00
Credit Line	48.0136.45742632.11

Klavika

Eric Olson
2003-2004

Entire family consists of Light, Light Italic, Regular, Regular Italic, Medium, Medium Italic, Bold, and Bold Italic.

Btűníɢ Q₅1őy Gɋ/71ɕSdięħŭ

Klavika Light complete character set

abcdefghijklmnopqrstuvwxyzABCDEFGHIJKLMNOPQRSTUVWXYZABCDEFGHIJKLMNOPQRS TUVWXYZáăâäæǽàāąååáćçĉċďđéěêëëèêęǧĝģġħĥíĩîïìiĩįijĵķĺľļŀłńňņñóõôöœòőōøǿõŕřŗśŝ şšşßŧťțúũûüùūűųůûŵẁẅẃýŷỳýźžżðŋþÁĂÂÄÆǼÀĀĄÅÅÁĆÇĈĊĎĐÉĚÊËËÈÊĘĜĜĢĠĦĤÍĨÎÏÌĨ ĲĴĶĹĽĻŁŃŇŅÑÓÕÔÖŒÒŐŌØǾÕŔŘŖŚŜŞŠŞŦŤÚŨÛÜÙŪŰŲŮŴŴẂẃÝŶỲÝŹŽŻÐŊÞÁĂÂÄÆ ÀĀĄÅÅÁĆÇĈĊĎĐÉĚÊËËÈÊĘĜĜĢĠĦĤÍĨÎÏÌIĨĲĴĶĹĽĻŁŃŇŅÑÓÕÔÖŒÒŐŌØǾÕŔŘŖŚŞŞ ŦŤÚŨÛÜÙŪŰŲŮŴŴẂẃÝŶỲÝŹŽŻÐŊÞfiflfffiffifjffjffl FI FL 0123456789#$¢£¥€ƒ∫¤%‰01 23456789 #$¢£¥€ƒ∫-×<=>-÷0123456789 #$¢£¥€ƒ∫%‰0123456789 #$¢£¥€ƒ∫-×<=>- ÷0123456789 #$¢£¥€ƒ∫%‰0123456789#$¢£¥€ƒ∫-×<=>-÷|¦◊∞∫∂√∆ΩΠΣμπ№℮ℓªº ¹²³/¼½¾%‰-×÷+±=≠¬≈~<>≤≥^ (){}[]¶¶@@&&Ǥ!?¡¿!?¡¿†‡©®™•*/\:;,,....''""‹›«»_- --

Eric Olson
2002–2003

Originally proposed as a custom typeface for the Design Institute at the University of Minnesota, Locator is now a complete family of 12 fonts with a true italic.

Entire family consists of Ultra Light, Ultra Light Italic, Light, Light Italic, Regular, Regular Italic, Medium, Medium Italic, Bold, Bold Italic, Black, and Black Italic.

Locator Light & Italic 8 on 11 pt.

The inside of the tank had some previous damage from the first round of action. I know, I know, really an obsession with minor particulars but this kind of thing is usually very important. But exactly, first glance would reveal virtually no damage but the thing was pretty screwed up. I *didn't test any esoteric areas* but focused almost exclusively on the frontal lobe. As you know, those areas are *impressively flexible* and able to recover quickly from rather traumatic accidents. Uplifting, I know. It restores an amount of faith in the recovery process but you have to remain critical of the whole thing. What if it never heals? You could purchase a new pair of lungs but then you *would have to cross your fingers* for continued low interest rates. No, seriously I'm just kidding. But new lungs may improve

Locator Regular & Italic 8 on 11 pt.

The inside of the tank had some previous damage from the first round of action. I know, I know, really an obsession with minor particulars but this kind of thing is usually very important. But exactly, first glance would reveal virtually no damage but the thing was pretty screwed up. I *didn't test any esoteric areas* but focused almost exclusively on the frontal lobe. As you know, those areas are *impressively flexible* and able to recover quickly from rather traumatic accidents. Uplifting, I know. It restores an amount of faith in the recovery process but you have to remain critical of the whole thing. What if it never heals? You could purchase a new pair of lungs but then you *would have to cross your fingers* for continued low interest rates. No, seriously I'm just kidding. But new lungs may improve

OPEN MARKET GATHERING

I think you've become unfairly fixated on your neighbor

The Beaumont Home

Is that his music? Not sure. It sounds like salsa or something

DUPONT

Really? I thought he was cleaning his chainsaw

Washburn Ave.

IN HIS APARTMENT? REMEMBER, THE GUY IS SURELY NUTS

HENNEPIN AVENUE NORTH

Oh, right. We should have him trim the brush out front tonight

LYNDALE

Excellent idea. I wonder if our association will be cool with it

Moved To Emerson

They already gave us clearance. He's set to trim the whole complex

CITY HALL ANNEX

HE'S USUALLY DRUNK THOUGH. WHAT IF HE CUTS OFF A LIMB?

HARDING

I suppose we could request he wear a suit of armor while working

WINNING MINNEAPOLIS MOCK DOCK

info@processtypefoundry.com

ƐBFR1

Locator Display

Eric Olson
2002 - 2003

Originally drawn as the companion to Locator, Locator Display is a family of six capital fonts flexible enough for a range of design work. Designed to fit with Locator, all six weights share the same line weight, cap height, and spacing approach.

Entire family consists of Ultra Light, Light, Regular, Medium, Bold, and Black.

HUMBOLDT

MUST BE YOUR WONDERFUL NEIGHBOR AGAIN. ALL OF OUR LOVE OK!

BLUEBERRY HILL

MAYBE HE CAN'T TAKE HIS SHOES OFF. I HAVE THOUGHT OF THAT

MINNƐHAHA

LIKE PERMANENT SHOES, YES! BUT WITH CEMENT SOLES BUT EVEN LOUDER

GLENWOOD AVENUE

YOU MEAN CONCRETE RIGHT? WHATEVER. IMAGINE THOSE FLOORS

HOMƐ FREMONT

GOOD POINT. YOU THINK HE WOULD WEAR THROUGH THEM QUICKLY

WINNƐTKA

MAYBE NOT. WHAT IF THEY'RE MAPLE? THEY WOULD LAST A LONG TIME

ZEALAND AVENUE

EXCELLENT POINT. I WOULD CARE FOR SOMETHING MUCH DARKER MYSELF

Maple is a flamboyant family of types inspired by the irregular grotesques of the nineteenth and early twentieth centuries. The family features four weights, companion italics, and multiple language support.

Entire family consists of Regular, Regular Italic, Medium, Medium Italic, Bold, Bold Italic, Black, and Black Italic.

Maple Regular & Italic 8 on 11 pt.

The inside of the tank had some previous damage from the first round of action. I know, I know, really an obsession with minor particulars but this kind of thing is usually very important. But exactly, first glance would reveal *virtually no damage* but the thing was pretty screwed up. I didn't test any esoteric areas but focused almost exclusively on the frontal lobe. As you know, those areas are *impressively flexible* and able to recover quickly from rather traumatic accidents. Uplifting, I know. It restores an amount of faith in the recovery process but you have to remain critical of the whole thing. *What if it never heals?* You could purchase a new pair

Maple Medium & Italic 8 on 11 pt.

The inside of the tank had some previous damage from the first round of action. I know, I know, really an obsession with minor particulars but this kind of thing is usually very important. But exactly, first glance would reveal *virtually* no damage but the thing was pretty screwed up. I didn't test any esoteric areas but focused almost exclusively on the frontal lobe. As you know, those areas are *impressively flexible* and able to recover quickly from rather traumatic accidents. Uplifting, I know. It restores an amount of faith in the recovery process but you have to remain critical of the whole thing. *What if it never heals?* You could

MORE SACRED HARP AND SHAPE NOTE SINGING

BIOGRAPHY

We will be sending new messages

Redirecting

Please run along and alert the others

Climb

IT APPEARS TO HAVE HAS JUST ONE STRING

Homesteade

The echo sound is really like nothing else

DISTINCTION

New messages from recent days remain unread

burn and shoulder

Final

The central dogmas find no support in science

info@processtypefoundry.com

F LUM
Northern

Maple

Eric Olson
2002–2005

Entire family consists of Regular, Regular Italic, Medium, Medium Italic, Bold, Bold Italic, Black, and Black Italic.

No sweat, you're covered. I'm sweaty though, no AC today

ONE ARMED SCISSOR OK

Notice of Sales Tax Delinquency. For the snow monkey bender?

Pattern Against 32510 Users

The hightops and sweats were bangin' though! Ok, not really

➜ ➜ ➜

Hollow Are The Bones Of Lonely

The faux erudite historical observations are a distraction

Reading One Thousand Faces

Show your source. That's what I thought. You don't have one

That takes the weight of 95

Easy killer, the edge hasn't gone dull. Great, that means nothing

OAK
Boxelder
F INE

ASH
Mountain

Conversations: Prospects for recovery?

The inside of the tank had some previous damage from the first round of action. I know, I know, really an obsession with minor particulars but this kind of thing is usually very important. But exactly, first glance would reveal *virtually no damage* but the thing was pretty screwed up. I didn't test any esoteric areas but focused almost exclusively on the frontal lobe. As you know, those areas are *impressively flexible* and able to recover quickly from rather traumatic accidents. Uplifting, I know. It restores an amount of faith in the recovery process but you have to remain critical of the whole thing. *What if it never heals?* You could buy a new pair of lungs but then you would have to cross your fingers.

Maple Regular complete character set

abcdefghijklmnopqrstuvwxyzABCDEFGHIJKLMNOPQRSTUVWXYZáăâäæǽàāąã
åǻćčçĉċďđéěêëèēeęǧĝģġğħíĭîïìīįijĵķĺľļłŀńňņŋñóŏôöœòőōøǿõŕřŗśšşŝşßŧťţúŭûüùűū
ųůũẁŵẃẅýŷÿýźžżðŋþÁĂÂÄÆǼÀĀĄÃÅǺĆČÇĈĊĎĐÉĚÊËÈĒĘĞĜĢĠĦÍĬÎÏÌĪĮIJ
ĴĶĹĽĻŁĿŃŇŅŊÑÓŎÔÖŒÒŐŌØǾÕŔŘŖŚŠŞŜŞŦŤŢÚŬÛÜÙŰŪŲŮŨẀŴẂẄÝŶŸÝŹŽ
ŻÐŊÞ fi fl ff ffi ffl 0123456789#$¢£¥€ƒ§¤%‰/−×÷+±=≠¬≈~<>≤≥^‖◊∞∫∂√ΔΩΠ
Σμπ(){}[]¶@&!?¡¿†‡©®™ªº•*/\:;,„….''""‹›«»_–—←→←→

Eric Olson
2003-2004

Stratum is a family of typefaces built from a synthesis of contemporary and historical sources. The austere geometry of early twentieth-century display faces paired with a desire for a contemporary lowercase have merged to produce this family of six weights.

Shown on this page, Stratum 1 has angled or clipped terminals.

Entire Stratum 1 family consists of Thin, Light, Regular, Medium, Bold, and Black.

Sb6C

Stratum1 Thin 8 on 11 pt.

The inside of the tank had some previous damage from the first round of action. I know, I know, really an obsession with minor particulars but this kind of thing is usually very important. But exactly, first glance would reveal virtually no damage but the thing was pretty screwed up. I didn't test any esoteric areas but focused almost exclusively on the frontal lobe. As you know, those areas are impressively flexible and able to recover quickly from rather traumatic accidents. Uplifting, I know. It restores an amount of faith in the

Stratum1 Light 8 on 11 pt.

The inside of the tank had some previous damage from the first round of action. I know, I know, really an obsession with minor particulars but this kind of thing is usually very important. But exactly, first glance would reveal virtually no damage but the thing was pretty screwed up. I didn't test any esoteric areas but focused almost exclusively on the frontal lobe. As you know, those areas are impressively flexible and able to recover quickly from rather traumatic accidents. Uplifting, I know. It restores an amount of faith in the recovery process but you have to remain

WE FOUND A NEW HOME TO FOLD INTO PACKETS

heritage to be shared

Sound In Time: Constellations, a proper set of bookends

Picture 91 Shows

A Data Learn The Language: {tequesta +}

32 SECTIONS

She landed a small part in the chorus singing

Hi Chuck

People came out to say goodbye to their trees

Take or leave it dude

WELL IT SEEMS THE OTHER BOYS SPENT THE NIGHT

info@processtypefoundry.com

G2aR

Stratum 1 and 2

Eric Olson
2003-2004

Shown on this page, Stratum 2 has flat terminals.

Entire Stratum 2 family consists of Thin, Light, Regular, Medium, Bold, and Black.

GEORGE WILL WAS REPEATEDLY DROPPED AS A CHILD

Remote Channel 25

Our square houses are still permitted on the 689 block?

Index Please

NOTIFICATION QUIETLY UPDATED AND SENT

All These Blues

Hymning Slews, Loops and Verses, A Final Shaking

often denied

YOU'RE RIGHT, SCIENCE IS OFTEN TOO FACT BASED

Michael Bloomfield

Come to think of it, that would be my suggestion

Stratum2 Regular 8 on 11 pt.

The inside of the tank had some previous damage from the first round of action. I know, I know, really an obsession with minor particulars but this kind of thing is usually very important. But exactly, first glance would reveal virtually no damage but the thing was pretty screwed up. I didn't test any esoteric areas but focused almost exclusively on the frontal lobe. As you know, those areas are impressively flexible and able to recover quickly from rather traumatic accidents. Uplifting, I know. It restores an amount of faith in the

Stratum2 Medium 8 on 11 pt.

The inside of the tank had some previous damage from the first round of action. I know, I know, really an obsession with minor particulars but this kind of thing is usually very important. But exactly, first glance would reveal virtually no damage but the thing was pretty screwed up. I didn't test any esoteric areas but focused almost exclusively on the frontal lobe. As you know, those areas are impressively flexible and able to recover quickly from rather traumatic accidents. Uplifting, I know. It restores an amount of faith in the recovery process

Process

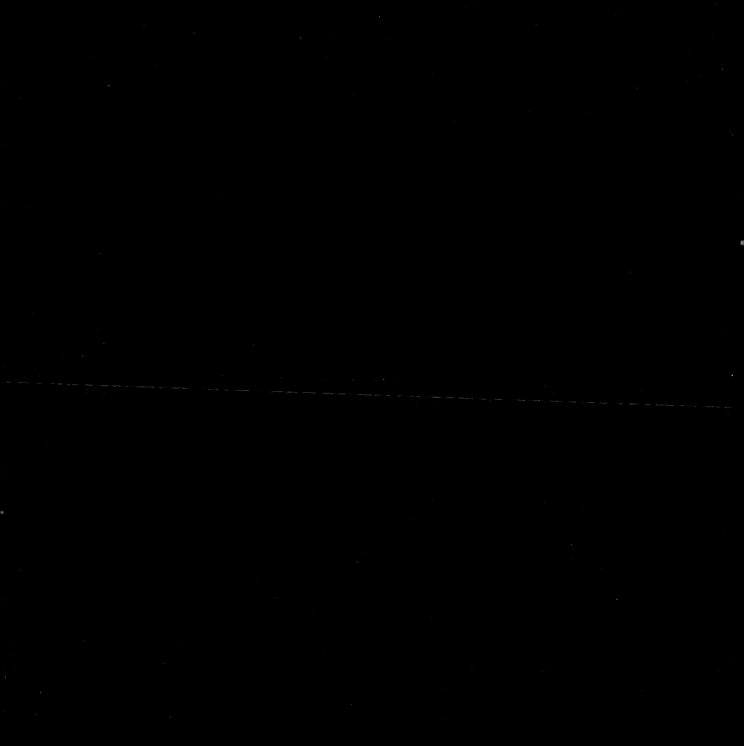

Rimmer Type Foundry

It is a rare typographic craftsman who is fully at ease cutting metal typefaces by hand and working those same designs with Bezier curves on a Macintosh computer. Jim Rimmer is this craftsman and more. He has designed typefaces for his own books, which he designs, illustrates, prints, and occasionally writes himself. P22 is proud to be the exclusive outlet for Rimmer's digital fonts. He has created more than 200 digital faces, including the imposing 60-font Dokument family. Digital offerings such as Albertan Oldstyle, Alexander Quill, Fellowship, and Lancelot all have metal counterparts among the proprietary fonts found at Rimmer's Pie Tree Press in Vancouver, British Columbia. Other faces, such as Zigarre Script, Poster Paint, Cotillion, and Amethyst, are designs developed exclusively for digital use. Rimmer also made the digital versions of the Cloister, Deepdene, and Garamont fonts for the Lanston Type Company. He served as Lanston's type director while the company was based in Vancouver.

Available online at www.p22.com/rtf

Albertan

Aa *Aa*

Aa *Aa*

Aa *Aa*

AaAa

Turning sharply to the north, we travel two hundred miles, and draw into where Edmonton, the capital of **Alberta**, sits smiling on the banks of her silver Saskatchewan. As he sees us digging out our tents and dunnage, the porter asks, "*Then yer not comin' back?*" "No." "*You are goin' to the North Pole, then, the place you wuz hollerin' fer!*"

¶ With the exception of Victoria, Edmonton has the most charming location of all cities of Western Canada. High Hope stalks her streets. There is a spirit of initiative and assuredness in this virile town, a culture & thoughtfulness in her people, expectancy in the very air. It is the city of contrasts; the ox-cart dodges the automobile; in the track of French heel treads the moccasin; the silk hat salutes the Stetson.

¶ Edmonton is the end of steel. Three lines converge here: the *Canadian Northern, the Canadian Pacific*, & *the Grand Trunk Pacific*. The Canadian Northern arrived first, coming in four years ago. Now that Edmonton has arrived, it seems the most natural thing in the world that there should have sprung up on the Saskatchewan this rich metropolis, anticipating for itself a future expansion second to no city in commercial Canada. But some one had to have faith and prescience before Edmonton got her start, and the god-from-the-machine was the Canadian Northern, in other words, *William Mackenzie* and *D.D. Mann*. Individuals and nations as they reap a harvest are apt to forget the hands that sowed the seed in faith, nothing doubting. When this railroad went into Edmonton, as little was known of the valley of the Saskatchewan as is known now of the valley of the Peace. Without exception, Canadian men of letters go to other

RTF Albertan Family

Jim Rimmer
1982–2005

18 Styles~8 OpenType

OpenType Pro versions combine regular and small caps with old style figures and other features.

Albertan Light Pro
Incorporates the fonts:
Albertan Light
Albertan Light SC

Albertan Light Italic Pro
Incorporates the fonts:
Albertan Light Italic
Albertan Light Italic SC

Albertan Regular Pro
Incorporates the fonts:
Albertan
Albertan Titling
Albertan SC

Albertan Regular Italic Pro
Incorporates the fonts:
Albertan Italic
Albertan Titling
Albertan Italic SC

Albertan Bold Pro
Incorporates the fonts:
Albertan Bold
Albertan Bold SC

Albertan Bold Italic Pro
Incorporates the fonts:
Albertan Bold Italic
Albertan Bold Italic SC

Albertan Black Pro
Incorporates the font:
Albertan Black

Albertan Bold Italic Pro
Incorporates the font:
Albertan Black Italic

Albertan Titling Inline

Albertan Titling Inline Italic

Rimmer

Jim Rimmer
1982-2005

Albertan Roman was designed and cut in metal at the 16 pt. size by Jim Rimmer in 1982 as a proprietary type for use in his private press and foundry, Pie Tree Press & Type Foundry. Only the roman was cut for casting at the foundry. It was intended for use in the hand-setting and printing of limited edition books. At about that time, the Mac was taking hold very strongly, and it seemed like a sound idea to render the type in digital format.

Albertan Italic was drawn in 1985 to accompany the Roman. It was designed to a narrow set width and has a very slight incline. The capitals were taken from the Roman face and have been condensed about 10 percent to blend with the lowercase forms. The face has a full set of ligatures and a font of italic small capitals.

Albertan Light is a complete family of types, comprising a Roman, Italic, Small Caps, Italic Small Caps, and both lining and hanging (old style) figures. The regular weight of Albertan is of a substantial color, and Rimmer felt that a more slender version would make a good addition to the family. This weight will print well down to five point, and will hold up in reverse to about nine or ten point. In the occasional place where letterpress or foil stamping is called for, the light face works beautifully. This type is well suited to book, magazine, corporate print, and advertising typography.

Albertan Light Italic and its companion Italic Small Caps have been produced for situations in which the text requires delicate handling. This design exactly follows that of the regular weight italic, but is slightly more open in its general appearance, adding a bit more air throughout a line of type.

Albertan Bold was redrawn in 2005. The original Albertan Bold has been rechristened Albertan Black.

RTF Albertan Light Pro - Roman & Italic with Small Caps 13pt.

We prefer jazz music while having our taxes done quickly by Ed.

JOEY QUESTIONED A WAX MUSEUM ABOUT HAVING HIS LIKENESS CRAFTED IN MARZIPAN.

Jamy was frazzled but showed Alex his "No Mercy Policy" when it came to Viking Quips.

WOOL VACUUM PUMPS KNOCK THE SOCKS OFF ZACH'S DO-HICKY-MA-JIGGY!

0123456789 0123456789 0123456789 0123456789 0123456789 0123456789 0123456789 0123456789

À Á Â Ã Ä Å à á â ã ä å À Á Â Ã Ä Å à á â ã ä å

RTF Albertan Pro - Roman & Italic with Small Caps & Titling 13pt.

From Algiers to the brick pavement of the Quarter, reedy jazz sax wails.

JOEY QUESTIONED A WAX MUSEUM ABOUT HAVING HIS LIKENESS CRAFTED IN MARZIPAN.

Your equiped with a heavy duty ziploc bag to put fresh melted butter on extra Cracker Jacks.

RUBBING ZINC OXIDE PASTE FOR FUN MAKES A QUITE WHITE AND VILE PASTE.

QUITE LAZY EXECUTIVE IN RIGHT JUSTIFIED WORK PROBLEM

LAZY FOX QUORUM KERNS VAGUE CAP WIDTH JOB

RTF Albertan Bold Pro - Roman & Italic with Small Caps 13pt.

Abacuses defog highly equivocal math puzzles for nitwitted jocks with sox.

QUICK WIZARDS BECOME FOXY WHEN JUMPING OVER TELEVISIONS.

Seven ewes quietly jumped and frolicked about in the azaleas and phlox each morning.

JACK FORGOT I PLAYED AN EXTRA IN A MOVIE ABOUT A QUIZ SHOW.

0123456789 0123456789 0123456789 0123456789 0123456789 0123456789 0123456789 0123456789

À Á Â Ã Ä Å à á â ã ä å À Á Â Ã Ä Å à á â ã ä å

RTF Albertan Black Pro - Roman & Italic with Small Caps 13pt.

Crazy weasel, hopped up on Tang, mixed vaquero-style jerked beef.

Zesty cole slaw, hamburgers, and waxy fries pique Jack's voracity.

Pangrams by: (Top to Bottom) [1] RTF Albertan Light *Kim Tyburski*, [2] RTF Albertan Light Small Caps *Kim Tyburski*, [3] RTF Albertan Light Italic *Jamy Sweet*, [4] RTF Albertan Light Italic Small Caps *Ken Gross*, [5] RTF Albertan Regular *Edward F. Gumnick*, [6] RTF Albertan Regular Small Caps *Kim Tyburski*, [7] RTF Albertan Italic *Kay Cloutier*, [8] RTF Albertan Italic Small Caps *Clayton T. Claymore*, [9] RTF Albertan Titling *Richard L. George*, [10] RTF Albertan Titling Italic *Richard L. George*, [11] RTF Albertan Bold *Lorraine Beaumont*, [12] RTF Albertan Bold Small Caps *Kelly McGuire*, [13] RTF Albertan Bold Italic *Camontcu*, [14] RTF Albertan Bold Italic Small Caps *Kim Tyburski*, [15] RTF Albertan Black *Mark Bennett*, [16] RTF Albertan Black Italic *Lorraine Beaumont*.

A2Z

RTF Albertan Titling Inline

ALBERTAN INLINE
ABCDEFGHIJKLMNOPQRSTUVWXYZ

A2Z

RTF Albertan Titling Inline

ALBERTAN INLINE ITAL
ABCDEFGHIJKLMNOPQRSTUVWXYZ

Albertan Inline

Jim Rimmer
2005

This an all caps inline titling companion font to the Albertan family. The Q has no descender.

AaBbCcDdEeFf
GgHhIiJjKkLlMmNnOoPpQqRrSsTtUuVvWwXxYyZz
1 2 3 4 5 6 7 8 9 0 & @ ? ! # $ { [( ) }] å é î ø ű
The Quill Is Mightier Than The Brown Fox & Lazy Dog

Alexander Quill

Jim Rimmer
2005

Alexander Quill was designed in the early 1980s. The intention was to cut the type in 14 point for casting into foundry type for the setting and printing of limited edition books at Rimmer's private sanctum, Pie Tree Press & Type Foundry.

CADMUS PERICLES
SPARTICUS
ABCDEFGHIJKLMNOPQRSTUVWXYZ
1 2 3 4 5 6 7 8 9 0 & ? ! # $ @ { [( ) }]
Æ Å Á Ç Đ Ë É Î Ì K Ł Ñ Ø Õ Œ Þ Š Ü Û Ý Ÿ Ž € ¥ £

Cadmus

Jim Rimmer / Robert Foster
2005

Cadmus is Rimmer's reworking of Pericles, a design by Robert Foster. The design is based closely on early inscriptional Greek but is less formal than the sans types of Foster's time. Cadmus retains the proportions of Pericles but is less quirky overall than the Foster face.

Canadian Syllabics

Jim Rimmer & Paul Hunt
2006

This font was conceived as a more calligraphic version of the syllabary developed by Reverend James Evans in the early 1800s for the languages of the native tribes of the Canadian provinces. Originally, Jim Rimmer designed characters for East and West Cree to be cut as a metal font. The digital version grew to include all characters of the Canadian Syllabics Unicode block along with roman capitals for further usability.

Jim Rimmer
2002

28 Styles–8 OpenType

OpenType Pro versions combine regular and small caps with old style figures and full Central European character sets.

Amethyst Light Pro
Incorporates the fonts:
Amethyst Light
Amethyst Light SC

Amethyst Light Italic Pro
Incorporates the fonts:
Amethyst Light Italic
Amethyst Light Italic SC
Amethyst Light Italic Sorts
Amethyst Light Italic Swash
Amethyst Light Italic Swash SC

Amethyst Book Pro
Incorporates the fonts:
Amethyst Book
Amethyst Book SC

Amethyst Book Italic Pro
Incorporates the fonts:
Amethyst Book Italic
Amethyst Book Italic SC
Amethyst Book Italic Sorts
Amethyst Book Italic Swash
Amethyst Book Italic Swash SC

Amethyst Regular Pro
Incorporates the fonts:
Amethyst
Amethyst SC

Amethyst Regular Italic Pro
Incorporates the fonts:
Amethyst Italic
Amethyst Italic SC
Amethyst Italic Sorts
Amethyst Italic Swash
Amethyst Italic Swash SC

Amethyst Bold Pro
Incorporates the fonts:
Amethyst Bold
Amethyst Bold SC

Amethyst Bold Italic Pro
Incorporates the fonts:
Amethyst Bold Italic
Amethyst Bold Italic SC
Amethyst Bold Italic Sorts
Amethyst Bold Italic Swash
Amethyst Bold Italic Swash SC

RTF Amethyst Light - Regular, Italic, Small Caps, & Italic Small Caps 24 pt.

Amethyst
AMETHYST
Amethyst
AMETHYST

RTF Amethyst Book - Regular, Italic, Small Caps, & Italic Small Caps 24 pt.

Amethyst
AMETHYST
Amethyst
AMETHYST

RTF Amethyst - Regular, Italic, Small Caps, & Italic Small Caps 24 pt.

Amethyst
AMETHYST
Amethyst
AMETHYST

RTF Amethyst Bold - Regular, Italic, Small Caps, & Italic Small Caps 24 pt.

Amethyst
AMETHYST
Amethyst
AMETHYST

RTF Amethyst Light - Regular, Italic, Small Caps, Italic Small Caps & Swash 9 pt.

A very great industry indeed, comprising the crafts of HOUSE-BUILDING, PAINTING, JOINERY & CARPENTRY, SMITHS' WORK, POTTERY & GLASS-MAKING, WEAVING, and many others: a body of art most important to the public in general, but still more so to us handicraftsmen; since there is scarce anything that they use, and that we fashion, but it has always been thought to be unfinished till it has had some touch or other of decoration about it. True it is that in many or most cases we have got so used to this rnament, that we look upon it as if it had grown of itself, and note it no more than the mosses on the dry sticks with we light our fires. So much the worse! for there IS the decoration, or some pretence of it, and it has, or ought to have, a use and a meaning. For, and this is at the root of the whole matter, everything made by man's

RTF Amethyst Book - Regular, Italic, Small Caps, Italic Small Caps & Swash 9 pt.

hands has a form, which must be either beautiful or ugly; beautiful if it is in accord with *Nature*, and helps her; ugly if it is discordant with Nature, and thwarts her; it cannot be indifferent: we, for our parts, are busy or sluggish, eager or unhappy, and our eyes are apt to get dulled to this eventfulness of form in those things which we are always looking at. *Now it is one of the chief uses of decoration*, the chief part of its alliance with nature, that it has to SHARPEN OUR DULLED SENSES in this matter: for this end are those wonders of intricate patterns interwoven, those strange forms invented, which men have so long delighted in: forms and intricacies that do not necessarily imitate nature, but in which the hand of the craftsman is guided to work in the way that she does, till the WEB, the CUP, or the KNIFE, look as natural, nay as lovely, as the

RTF Amethyst - Regular, Italic, Small Caps, Italic Small Caps & Swash 9 pt.

green field, To give people pleasure in the things they must perforce USE, that is one great office of decoration; to give people pleasure in the things they must perforce MAKE, that is the other use of it. Does not our subject look important enough now? I say that without these arts, our rest would be vacant and uninteresting, our labour mere endurance, mere wearing away of body and mind. As for that last use of these arts, the giving us *pleasure in our work*, I scarcely know how to speak strongly enough of it; and yet if I did not know the value of repeating a truth again and again, I should have to excuse myself to you for saying any more about this, when I remember how a great man now living has spoken of it: I mean my friend *Professor John Ruskin*: if you read the chapter in the 2nd vol. of his

RTF Amethyst Bold - Regular, Italic, Small Caps, Italic Small Caps & Swash 9 pt.

Stones of Venice **entitled, 'ON THE NATURE OF GOTHIC, AND THE OFFICE OF THE WORKMAN THEREIN,' you will read at once the truest and the most eloquent words that can possibly be said on the subject. What I have to say upon it can scarcely be more than an echo of his words, yet I repeat there is some use in reiterating a truth, lest it be forgotten; so I will say this much further: we all know what people have said about the curse of labour, and what heavy and grievous nonsense are the more part of their words thereupon; whereas indeed the REAL CURSES OF CRAFTSMEN have been the curse of stupidity, and the curse of injustice from within and from without: no, I cannot suppose there is anybody here who would think it either a good life,**

Fact or *Affliction* Cromulent *filling station* aAAaaAAcA

¶ABCDEFGHIJKLMNOPQRSTUVWXYZabcdefghijklmnopqrstuvwxyz1234567890
0123456789 ⁰¹²³⁴⁵⁶⁷⁸⁹ ₀₁₂₃₄₅₆₇₈₉ ®©℗!"#$%&'()*+,-./:;<=>?@[\]^_`{|}
ÀÁÂÃÄÅÆÇÈÉÊËÌÍÎÏÐÑÒÓÔÕÖ×ØÙÚÛÜÝÞßàáâãäåçèéêëìíîïðñ
òóôõöøùúûüýþÿĀāĂăĄąĆćĈĉĊċČčĎďĐđĒēĔĕĖėĘęĚěĜĝĞğĠġĢģĤĥĦħĨĩĪīĬĭĮįİıĲĳĴĵĶķĸĹĺĻ
ļĽľĿŀŁłŃńŅņŇňŊŋŌōŎŏŐőŒœŔŕŖŗŘřŚśŜŝŞşŠšŢţŤťŦŧŨũŪūŬŭŮůŰűŲųŴŵŶŷŸŹźŻż
ŽžƒÁáÆæÓóŞşfiflfffiffl stæ~¡¢£€¥|÷µ,»ºį&™¼½¾⅓⅔⅛⅜⅝⅞
ABCDEFGHIJKLMNOPQRSTUVWXYZÀÁÂÃÄÅÆÇĆĈČĊĎĐÉÈÊĚËĒĔĘĢĜǦĠ
ĤĦÌÍÎĨÏĪĬİĮĲĴĶĹĽĿŁĻŃÑŇŅŊÒÓÔÕÖŌŎŐŐØŒŔŘŖŚŜŞşSSŤŢŦÙÚÛÜŨŪŬŮŰŴÝŶŸ
ABCDEFGHIJKLMNOPQRSTUVWYZÀÁÂÃÄÅÆÈÉÊËÑÒÓÔÕÖŒÐŁ
ÝŸŽABCDEFGHIJKLMNOPQRSTUVWYZÀÁÂÃÄÅÆÈÉÊËÑÒÓÔÕÖŒÐŁŠÝŸŽ
^˘˙¨º«¬¯˚±´——''‚""„†‡·…‰'"‹›/∂Π−·√∞≈≠≤≥◊Δ 卍

RTF Amethyst Book Pro- Roman & Italic 5 pt.

When in the Course of human events, it becomes necessary for one people to dissolve the political bands which have connected them with another, and to assume, among the Powers of the earth, the separate and equal station to which the Laws of Nature and of Nature's God entitle them, a decent respect to the opinions of mankind requires that they should declare the causes which impel them to the separation. We hold these truths to be self-evident, that all men are created equal, that they are endowed by their Creator with certain unalienable Rights, that among these are Life, Liberty, and the pursuit of Happiness.—That to secure these rights, Governments are instituted among Men, deriving their just powers from the consent of the governed,—That whenever any Form of Government becomes destructive of these ends, it is the Right of the People to alter or to abolish it, and to institute new Government, laying its foundation on such principles and organizing its powers in such form, as to them shall seem most likely to effect their Safety and Happiness. Prudence, indeed, will dictate that Governments long established should not be changed for light and transient causes; and accordingly all experience hath shown, that mankind are more disposed to suffer, while evils are sufferable, than to right themselves by abolishing the forms to which they are accustomed. But when a long train of ABUSES and USURPATIONS, pursuing invariably the same Object evinces a design to reduce them under absolute Despotism, it is their right, it is their duty, to throw off such Government, and to provide new Guards for their future

RTF Amethyst Light Pro - Roman & Italic 8 pt.

AMETHYST PRO Roman combines regular & SMALL CAPS plus a full set of Western & Central European accented characters.
ABCDEFGHIJKLMNOPQRSTUVWXYZ
abcdefghijklmnopqrstuvwxyz
ABCDEFGHIJKLMNOPQRSTUVWXYZ
1234567890 1234567890
Amethyst Pro Italic combines the regular & SMALL CAPS as well as Swash Caps and "sorts" which are swash small caps.
ABCDEFGHIJKLMNOPQRSTUVWXYZ
abcdefghijklmnopqrstuvwxyz
ABCDEFGHIJKLMNOPQRSTUVWXYZ
ABCDEFGHIJKLMNOPQRSTUVWXYZ
ABCDEFGHIJKLMNOPQRSTUVWXYZ
1234567890 1234567890

Jim Rimmer
2002

The Amethyst family of types is a complete series, well suited to the setting of bookwork or advertising text and display. The family contains four weights: light, Regular, Book, and Bold. Each weight includes Roman, Italic, Small Caps, Italic Small Caps, Swash Italic, Swash Italic Small Caps, plus Swashed Small Capitals (for restrained application by the font user).

Amethyst Book has been made just slightly heavier than Amethyst Light. Like the lighter weight, it carries all of the same characters, including two styles of figures and a complete suite of ligatures. This version reverses well and has been printed letterpress with fine results. The italic has been made at the same slight angle as the light face–it blends well with the roman but is strong enough to create emphasis in text.

For the purpose of advertising, a good type group needs a boldface. The Amethyst family is complete with a full complement of bold variants. This includes, as well as a roman font: Italic, Roman Small Caps, Italic Small Caps, and Italic Swash Small Caps. In addition, there is a sorts font of fully swashed italic small caps for judicious use by the adventurous typographer.

Jim Rimmer
2004

24 Styles–12 OpenType

OpenType versions combine regular and small caps with old style figures and full Central European character sets.

RTF Credo Extra Light [German] 8 pt.

Mäßig hochgewachsen, mager, bartlos und auffallend stumpfnäsig, gehörte der Mann zum rothaarigen Typ und besaß dessen milchige und sommersprossige Haut. Offenbar war er durchaus nicht bajuwarisch

RTF Credo Extra Light Italic [Catalan] 8 pt.

I el fill? ¿un fill no és més que una pesseta?-
Va exclamar la Tecla corferida pel silenci
de l'Andreu, que en sentir la Tecla va
redreçar-se tot d'una, s'alçà de l'escó,
donà un cop de puny a la taula i digué: Que

RTF Credo Extra Light Small Caps [French] 8 pt.

Ces prêtres qui montent éternellement élevant l'hostie. L'avion se pose enfin sans refermer les ailes. Le ciel s'emplit alors de millions d'hirondelles. À tire-d'aile viennent les corbeaux les faucons les

RTF Credo Extra Light Italic Small Caps [Spanish] 8 pt.

»¿Quién pudiera decir ahora los sobresaltos
que me dio el corazón mientras allí estuve,
los pensamientos que me ocurrieron, las
consideraciones que hice?, que fueron
tantas y tales, que ni se pueden decir ni aun

RTF Credo Light [Czech] 8 pt.

Nic vlastně. Někdy se jaksi pominou. Cosi, jako padoucnice, víte? Říká se tomu křeč Robotů. Najednou některý praští vším, co má v ruce, stojí, skřípá zuby - a musí přijít do stoupy. Patrně porucha organismu.

RTF Credo Light Italic [Italian] 8 pt.

Rimasi più d'un quarto d'ora in una specie
d'estasi rabbiosa, il tempo cioè che il
tenente impiegò; quindi la compagnia entrò
in sala, forse a prendere un caffè. No, la
guerra non è più bella dell'amore!

RTF Credo Light Small Caps [Finnish] 8 pt.

Mitä nyt vekseliin tulee, jota pyydät minun lunastamaan, niin kieltäydyn minä aivan jyrkästi. Mies, joka yhdessä vuodessa velkaantuu kaksituhatta markkaa, ei ansaitse mitään apua. Minua ilahduttaa

RTF Credo Light Small Caps Italic [Welsh] 8 pt.

Nodwedd bennaf plentyn iach, effro yw,
nas gall fod eiliad yn llonydd. Mae pob
gewyn ynddo ar fynd o hyd. Ac y mae mynd
yn yr hen hwiangerddi. Gorchest arwrol
gyntaf plentyn yw cael ei ddawnsio'n wyllt

RTF Credo Regular [Icelandic] 8 pt.

Hið þögla mál augnanna er öllum elskendum dýrmætara en nokkur orð og í einu augnatilliti getur falist meira en orð fá lýst, hvort sem það er ást, hatur eða fyrirlitning.harma hans.

RTF Credo Italic [Portugese] 8 pt.

Como se vê, Foville não faz senão seguir
a orientação psychologica de Lasègue,
que explicava pela intervenção de um
raciocinio a passagem, no delirio de
perseguições, do periodo prodromico ao

RTF Credo Small Caps [Polish] 8 pt.

Była to biedna jakaś babina, a snać nieco podpita, bo zataczając się z lekka, krzykliwie podśpiewywała coś sobie. Mała, krępa, okręcona czerwoną wełnianą chustką i w takiejże spódnicy, kołysała się

RTF Credo Small Caps Italic [Swedish] 8 pt.

Dagen därpå stod Viking vid sjön, och si!
som en havsörn, när han förföljer sitt
rov, flög in i viken ett drakskepp. Ingen
syntes därpå, ej en gång man märkte en
styrman, rodret dock lette sin buktiga

RTF Credo Bold 8 [English] pt.

"I see!" said the Queen, who had meanwhile been examining the roses. "Off with their heads!" and the procession moved on, three of the soldiers remaining behind to execute the unfortunate

RTF Credo Bold Italic [Dutch] 8 pt.

Voorzichtig snijdt hij er een gedeelte
van af en bergt de rest zorgvuldig
weer in 't papier en in de kast, waaruit
hij achtereenvolgens een stuk brood,
wat boter, een flesch met brandewijn

RTF Credo Bold Small Caps [Esperanto] 8 pt.

Miaj junaj amiko kaj amikino, kaj ankaŭ ilia patrino, iris hieraŭ al la parko. La infanoj diris al la patrino ke la parko estas agrabla, kaj ke ili volas promeni en ĝi. La knabino parolis al sia frato pri

RTF Credo Light Small Caps Italic [Middle English] 8 pt.

Take Chykenns and scald hem. take
parsel and sawge withoute eny opere
erbes. take garlec an grapes and stoppe
the Chikenns ful and seeþ hem in gode
broth. so þat þey may esely be boyled

Waffle
INK
Malarkey
CREDO
Blacker
Any
Pen
Kinks
Viktory

Contractual
OpenType
Tenacity
Eiffel Straße
Encyclopædiac

RTF Credo Black 8 pt.

Nevertheless there IS dull work to be done, and a weary business it is setting men about such work, and seeing them through it, and I would rather do the work twice over with my own

RTF Credo Black Italic 8 pt.

hands than have such a job: but now only let the arts which we are talking of beautify our labour, and be widely spread, intelligent, well understood both by the maker and the user, let

RTF Credo Black Small Caps 8 pt.

THEM GROW IN ONE WORD POPULAR, AND THERE WILL BE PRETTY MUCH AN END OF DULL WORK AND ITS WEARING SLAVERY; AND NO MAN WILL ANY LONGER HAVE AN EXCUSE FOR TALKING ABOUT THE CURSE OF

RTF Credo Black Italic Small Caps 8 pt.

LABOUR, NO MAN WILL ANY LONGER HAVE AN EXCUSE FOR EVADING THE BLESSING OF LABOUR. I BELIEVE THERE IS NOTHING THAT WILL AID THE WORLD'S PROGRESS SO MUCH AS THE ATTAINMENT OF THIS; I PROTEST

RTF Credo Extra Black 8 pt.

there is nothing in the world that I desire so much as this, wrapped up, as I am sure it is, with changes political & social, that in one way or another we all desire.

RTF Credo Extra Black Italic 8 pt.

Now if the objection be made, that these arts have been the handmaids of luxury, of tyranny, and of superstition, I must needs say that it is true in a sense; they have been

RTF Credo Extra Black Small Caps 8 pt.

SO USED, AS MANY OTHER EXCELLENT THINGS HAVE BEEN. BUT IT IS ALSO TRUE THAT, AMONG SOME NATIONS, THEIR MOST VIGOROUS AND FREEST TIMES HAVE BEEN THE VERY BLOSSOMING TIMES OF ART:

RTF Credo Extra Black Italic Small Caps 8 pt.

WHILE AT THE SAME TIME, I MUST ALLOW THAT THESE DECORATIVE ARTS HAVE FLOURISHED AMONG OPPRESSED PEOPLES, WHO HAVE SEEMED TO HAVE NO HOPE OF FREEDOM: YET I DO NOT THINK THAT

Credo Family

Jim Rimmer
2004

Credo is an original design by Jim Rimmer. It has been designed in six weights: Extra Light, Light, Regular, Bold, Black, and Extra Black. This design, like all types in the RTF Library, began as a pencil sketch and was then tightened up in pencil linear to be hand-digitized in Ikarus. The italic has style and vigor and is well suited to advertising and corporate print text and display. Credo has been thoroughly hand-kerned without overriding all the work that went into properly fitting the face in the first place. Without taking the time to tally, there are about 500 kerning pairs, give or take a few dozen.

Rimmer

60 styles

OpenType versions combine regular and small caps with old style figures.

Dokument is an expansive sans serif family that lends itself to many uses. Jim Rimmer explains: "Dokument was my attempt to make a Sans Grotesque in the general weight of News Gothic (for the Dokument regular) but took nothing from News Gothic. I used some of the basic forms of my Credo series but made many on-screen changes and broke away entirely from Credo on the range of weights. My plan was to make a typeface that would fill the requirements of financial document setting; things like annual reports and other such pieces of design. It is my hope that the large family of weights and variants will suit Dokument to this kind of work."

RTF Dokument Font Family

Dokument	Dokument Cond	Dokument Extra Cond
Dokument	*Dokument Cond*	*Dokument Extra Cond*
Dokument	Dokument Cond	Dokument Extra Cond
Dokument	*Dokument Cond*	*Dokument Extra Cond*
Dokument	Dokument Cond	Dokument Extra Cond
Dokument	*Dokument Cond*	*Dokument Extra Cond*
Dokument	Dokument Cond	Dokument Extra Cond
Dokument	*Dokument Cond*	*Dokument Extra Cond*
Dokument	Dokument Cond	Dokument Extra Cond
Dokument	*Dokument Cond*	*Dokument Extra Cond*
Dokument	Dokument Cond	Dokument Extra Cond
Dokument	*Dokument Cond*	*Dokument Extra Cond*
Dokument	Dokument Cond	Dokument Extra Cond
Dokument	*Dokument Cond*	*Dokument Extra Cond*
Dokument	Dokument Cond	Dokument Extra Cond
Dokument	*Dokument Cond*	*Dokument Extra Cond*
Dokument	Dokument Cond	Dokument Extra Cond
Dokument	*Dokument Cond*	*Dokument Extra Cond*
Dokument	Dokument Cond	Dokument Extra Cond
Dokument	*Dokument Cond*	*Dokument Extra Cond*

RTF Dokument Extra Condensed Light Pro - Regular & Italic 9pt

¶ One morning, when Gregor Samsa woke from troubled dreams, he found himself transformed in his bed into a horrible vermin. He lay on his armour-like back, and if he lifted his head a little he could see his brown belly, slightly domed & divided by arches into stiff sections. The bedding was hardly able to cover it and seemed ready to slide off any moment. His many legs, pitifully thin compared with the size of the rest of him, waved about helplessly as he looked.
¶ *"What's happened to me?"* he thought. It wasn't a dream. His room, a proper human room although a little too small, lay peacefully between its four familiar walls. A collection of textile samples lay spread out on the table - Samsa was a travelling salesman - and above it there hung a picture that he had recently cut out of an illustrated magazine & housed in a nice, gilded frame. It showed a lady fitted out with a fur hat & fur boa who sat upright, raising a heavy fur muff that covered the whole of her lower arm towards the viewer.
¶ Gregor then turned to look out the window at the dull weather. Drops of rain could be heard hitting the pane, which made him feel quite sad. *"How about if I sleep a little bit longer and forget all this nonsense"*, he thought, but that was something he was unable to do because he was used to sleeping on his right, & in his present state couldn't get into that position. However hard he threw himself onto his right, he always rolled back to where he was. He must have tried it a hundred times, shut his eyes so that he wouldn't have to look at the floundering legs, & only stopped when he began to feel a mild, dull pain there that he had never felt before.
¶ *"Oh, God"*, he thought, *"what a strenuous career it is that I've chosen! Travelling day in and day out. Doing business*

RTF Dokument Condensed Medium Pro - Regular & Italic 9pt

like this takes much more effort than doing your own business at home, and on top of that there's the curse of travelling, worries about making train connections, bad and irregular food, contact with different people all the time so that you can never get to know anyone or become friendly with them. It can all go to Hell!" He felt a slight itch up on his belly; pushed himself slowly up on his back towards the headboard so that he could lift his head better; found where the itch was, and saw that it was covered with lots of little white spots which he didn't know what to make of; and when he tried to feel the place with one of his legs he drew it quickly back because as soon as he touched it he was overcome by a cold shudder.
¶ He slid back into his former position. *"Getting up early all the time"*, he thought, *"it makes you stupid. You've got to get enough sleep. Other travelling salesmen live a life of luxury. For instance, whenever I go back to the guest house during the morning to copy out the contract, these gentlemen are always still sitting there eating their breakfasts. I ought to just try that with my boss; I'd get kicked out on the spot.*

RTF Dokument Bold Pro - Regular & Italic 9pt

But who knows, maybe that would be the best thing for me. If I didn't have my parents to think about I'd have given in my notice a long time ago, I'd have gone up to the boss and told him just what I think, tell him everything I would, let him know just what I feel. He'd fall right off his desk! And it's a funny sort of business to be sitting up there at your desk, talking down at your subordinates from up there, especially when you have to go right up close because the boss is hard of hearing. Well, there's still some hope; once I've got the money together to pay off my parents' debt to him - another five or six years I suppose - that's definitely what I'll do. That's when I'll make the big change. First of all though, I've got to get up, my train leaves at five."
¶ **And he looked over at the alarm clock, ticking on the chest of drawers. *"God in Heaven!"* he thought. It was half past six and the hands were quietly moving forwards, it was even later than half past, more like quarter to seven. Had the alarm clock not rung? He could see from the bed**

Dokum

Jim Rimmer
2005

60 styles

OpenType versions combine regular and small caps with old style figures.

Dokument is an expansive sans serif family that lends itself to many uses. Jim Rimmer explains: "Dokument was my attempt to make a Sans Grotesque in the general weight of News Gothic (for the Dokument regular) but took nothing from News Gothic. I used some of the basic forms of my Credo series but made many on-screen changes and broke away entirely from Credo on the range of weights. My plan was to make a typeface that would fill the requirements of financial document setting; things like annual reports and other such pieces of design. It is my hope that the large family of weights and variants will suit Dokument to this kind of work."

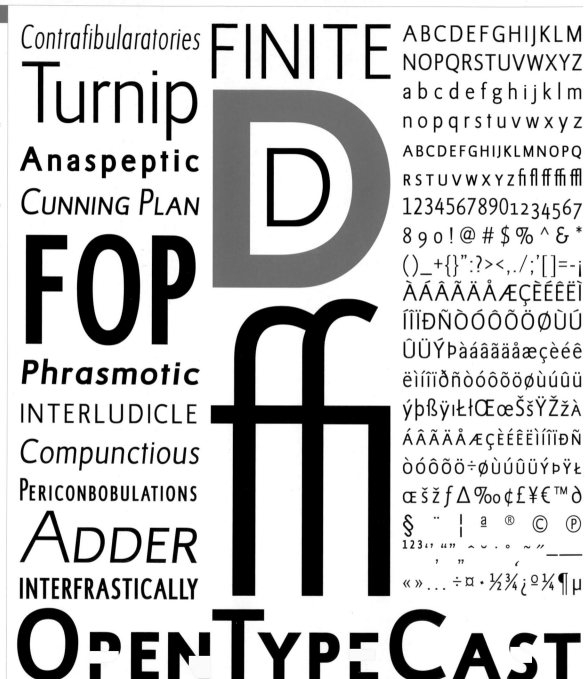

Contrafibularatories

FINITE

Turnip

Anaspeptic

CUNNING PLAN

FOP

D

Phrasmotic

INTERLUDICLE

Compunctious

PERICONBOBULATIONS

ADDER

INTERFRASTICALLY

ff

OPENTYPECAST

ABCDEFGHIJKLM
NOPQRSTUVWXYZ
abcdefghijklm
nopqrstuvwxyz
ABCDEFGHIJKLMNOPQ
RSTUVWXYZ fi fl ff ffi ffl
12345678901234567
890!@#$%^&*
()_+{}":?><,./;'[]=-¡
ÀÁÂÃÄÅÆÇÈÉÊËÌ
ÍÎÏÐÑÒÓÔÕÖØÙÚ
ÛÜÝÞàáâãäåæçèéê
ëìíîïðñòóôõöøùúûü
ýþßÿıŁŒœŠšŸŽžÀ
ÁÂÃÄÅÆÇÈÉÊËÌÍÎÏÐÑ
ÒÓÔÕÖ÷ØÙÚÛÜÝÞŸŁ
œšžƒΔ‰¢£¥€™∂
§¨|ªª®©℗
123'‚""‛^˜"__
' " ´ __
«»…÷¤·½¾¿º¼¶µ

RTF Cotillion

Cotillion

AaBbCc &¶

RTF Cotillion Italic

Cotillion

AaBbCc &¶

A B C D E F G H I J K L M
N O P Q R S T U V W X Y Z
ABCDEFGHIJKLMNOPQRSTUVWXYZ
abcdefghijklmnopqrstuvwxyz

broken flask filigree

broken flask filigree

A B C D E F G H I J K L M
N O P Q R S T U V W X Y Z
ABCDEFGHIJKLMNOPQRSTUVWXYZ
abcdefghijklmnopqrstuvwxyz

Cotillion Family

Jim Rimmer
1999

Cotillion
Cotillion Italic
Cotillion Small Caps
Cotillion Italic Small Caps

This face is suitable for many types of social print or for use in advertising anything from jewelry to fine automobiles. The typeface's very short x-height and tall ascenders are reminiscent of a number of designs that emerged in the late 1920s. The designer used the unusual dimensions of Bernhard Modern as a starting point but did not refer to it in the process of creating this face.

A B C D E F G H I J K L M
N O P Q R S T U V W X Y Z
abcdefghijklmnopqrstuvwxyz
1 2 3 4 5 6 7 8 9 0 fi fl ffi ffl ff ct st
á à â ã ä å ç é í ñ ô ü Ø
† § · ¶ ß & $ % ! ‡ « »
ð Ł Š þ ž ý Æ œ ¢ £ ¥ €

AaBbCc
American Typecasting Fellowship

Fellowship

Jim Rimmer
1981

Fellowship is a product of Rimmer's left-handed calligraphy. Designed as a tribute to members of the American Typecasting Fellowship (ATF), the face was cut by the designer in 24 point in the early 1980s and has been cast as fonts on the Thompson Typecasting Machine at Pie Tree Press.

RTF Isabelle

Isabelle

AäBbç

A B C D E F G H I J K L M
N O P Q R S T U V W X Y Z
abcdefghijklmnopqrstuvwxyz
1234567890123456789O

RTF Isabelle Italic

Isabelle

AaBbc

*A B C D E F G H I J K L M
N O P Q R S T U V W X Y Z
abcdefghijklmnopqrstuvwxyz
1234567890123456789O*

Isabelle Family

Jim Rimmer
2003

Isabelle
Isabelle Old Style Figures
Isabelle Italic
Isabelle Italic Old Style Figures

Isabelle Roman and its companion italic were designed as a pair by a woman type designer, cut and cast for decades by an historic German type foundry. The beautiful pair are noted for their graceful weights and delicate lines. Both the roman and italic are markedly condensed. Isabelle has been a favorite of fine printers and private presses since its emergence. Great care has been taken in the translation of this face to digital form.

The Honour of Your Presence is Hereby Requested on *The 31st of February 2024*
R.S.V.P. via the usual channels *by the usual time to the usual place* as per decorum

Lapis Family

Jim Rimmer
2001

12 Styles–6 OpenType

OpenType Pro versions combine regular and small caps with old style figures and other features.

Lapis Pro
Incorporates the fonts:
Lapis
Lapis Small Caps

Lapis Italic Pro
Incorporates the fonts:
Lapis Italic
Lapis Italic Small Caps

Lapis Medium Pro
Incorporates the fonts:
Lapis Medium
Lapis Medium Small Caps

Lapis Medium Italic Pro
Incorporates the fonts:
Lapis Medium Italic
Lapis Medium Italic SC

Lapis Bold Pro
Incorporates the fonts:
Lapis Bold
Lapis Bold Small Caps

Lapis Bold Italic Pro
Incorporates the fonts:
Lapis Bold Italic
Lapis Bold Italic Small Caps

Lapis ¶

Contextualizations

Contextualizations

Contextualizations

Contextualizations

Contextualizations

Contextualizations

It was the best of times, it was the worst of times, it was the age of wisdom, it was the age of foolishness, it was the *epoch of belief*, it was the *epoch of incredulity*, it was the season of Light, it was the season of **Darkness**, it was the *spring of hope*, it was the *winter of despair*, we had everything before us, we had nothing before us, we were all going direct to *Heaven*, we were all going direct the **other way**—in short, the period was so far like the present

Regular
SMALL CAPS

Regular
SMALL CAPS

Regular
SMALL CAPS

Regular
SMALL CAPS

Regular
SMALL CAPS

Regular
SMALL CAPS

ABCDEFGHIJKLMNOPQRSTUVWXYZ
abcdefghijklmnopqrstuvwxyz fi fl ff ffi ffl ß
ABCDEFGHIJKLMNOPQRSTUVWXYZ1234567890123
4567890!@#$%^&*()_+{}'":?><,./;'[]=-¡¢£¥ÀÁÂ
ÃÄÅÆÇÈÉÊËÌÍÎÏÐÑÒÓÔÕÖØÙÚÛÜÝÞ
àáâãäåæçèéêëìíîïðñòóôõöøùúûüýþÿıŁŒœŠ
šŸŽžÀÁÂÃÄÅÆÇÈÉÊËÌÍÎÏÐÑÒÓÔÕÖ÷ØÙÚÛÜÝÞŶŁŒ
š ž ƒ Δ Ω π ‰ € ™ ∂ Π § ¨ | ª ® © ℗ ² ³ ¹ Σ
ˆ ˇ ˙ ˚ ˜ ˝ ‘ ’ ‚ “ ” „ – — « » … ÷ ¤ • ½ ¾ ¿ º ¼ ¶ µ

Lapis

Lapis Family

Jim Rimmer
2001

The Lapis series of text types is a family best suited to the handling of advertising text and display than that of bookwork. Its angular, "edgy" curves give it a kind of tenseness. The design is based on (although not strictly) an Egyptian-style letter. The serifs are somewhat slabbed but are tapered just slightly in a kind of Latin-type serif. The design is made in three weights, with a full complement of refinements and small cap fonts.

Rimmer

Jim Rimmer
2002

Lancelot Titling and Lancelot Titling Light have been designed by Jim Rimmer as a pair of all-caps titling fonts. The fonts have a complete range of accented characters, punctuation, and figures along with the necessary euro symbol. The designer has altered the light face and engraved matrices in several sizes for casting into metal type at the Pie Tree foundry under the name Duensing Titling (named for American typographer Paul Hayden Duensing).

RTF Lancelot Titling Light

LANCELOT LIGHT

RTF Lancelot Titling

LANCELOT TITLE

ABCDEFGHIJKLMNOPQRSTUVWXYZ
0123456789!@#$%^&*()_+"{}:><,./;'[]=-
ÆÄĂÅÀÃÂÁÇÊÈËÉÍÎÏÌÑŒÓÔÒÕÕØÜÛÚÙ
ÐÞŠŸÝŽŁ¿¡«§£€¢¥¶™℗©®«»…—–""''÷/‹›',,,ˆ˜˜¨˝˘•–×!"~`\

PIE TREE PRESS

Jim Rimmer
2002

Posh Initials is a font of 27 characters designed for initial use. The name is pre-Spice Girls and actually hearkens from British ocean liner days. It has to do with the purported origin of the word: the part of the ship from which the privileged classes embarked and disembarked. In a word, the connotation was sort of "snooty." There have been a good many instances when the need for such a letter, to now, has not been completely addressed. It is hoped that this font and its lighter sister may fill the gap.

Posh works best as a lead initial letter and is not meant for typing out words.

RTF Posh Initials Light

RTF Posh Initials Light

POSTER PAINT STOUT ØL PILSNER

ABCDEFGHIJKLMNOPQRSTUVWXYZ
0123456789O!@#$%^&*() +"{}:><,./;'[]=-
ÄÅÀÃÂÁÇÊ?ËÉÍÎÏÌÑÓÔÒÖÕØÜÛÚÙ
ÐÞŠŸÝŽĿ¿¡«§ÆŒ£°™¥¶℗©®ΣΠΩ
«».. — """" ÷/‹›„‚‰ •½¼1¾³² ×?!"~`\^

Poster Paint

Jim Rimmer
2002

Poster Paint is an all-caps font with a full international character set. Jim Rimmer says of this face: "Poster Paint came about from my admiration of Goudy Stout. I liked this design in spite of the fact that Goudy detested it. In drawing Poster Paint, I resisted the temptation to look at Goudy's design but took my own approach to a similar design, relying on my impression of the original from memory."

Rimmer

Das Cabinet des Doktor Caligari

ABCDEFGHIJKLMNOPQRSTUVWXYZ
({[abcdefghijklmnopqrstuvwxyz1234567890]})
!@#$%^&*_ _+:"?›‹,./;'=-~ÄÅÀÃÂÁÇÈÉÈÉÑÖÜáàâ
äãåçèéêëìíîïñóòôöõúùûü°£ß´`ÆØ¥®ø¿¡f«»ÐŒœ—
""ÿŸÍÌÎÏÓÒÔÖÚÙÛÜfffiflfiÞ€®©®§Q%†‡¶П≤~ð£

Zigarre

Zigarre Script

Jim Rimmer
2002

Jim Rimmer designed this brush letter with a marker. Zigarre was inspired by a poster design found in one of those great books of German graphic design from the 1920s-1930s era. This font has a complete character set, including all accents and symbols.

A YOUNG MAN needs a big car, especially if he's just moved to Toronto from London.

So I bought a '66 Chevy Biscayne for $125, and since it was 1978, before long I was headed down to CBGB in New York.

Along the way I spied a vision on a hilltop: the sci-fi citadel of Empire State Plaza (then newly completed), in Albany. Astounded, I asked what the architects were smoking, but the locals weren't quite sure.

Literature—there must be some literature on this I reasoned, and went to the library of the Cultural Education Center at the Plaza. No, nothing on the present, but much about old New York State—and on one rack, a clearance of books.

I browsed. In pristine condition, two copies of *New York State Cabinet of Natural History, 23rd Annual Report, for the Year 1869,* full of hand-tinted plates of fungi and moths. Enchanted, I bought one for $45.

It's a book I've often returned to, not just for the delicacy of its illustrations but also to admire the beautiful typography, set in a Scotch Modern likely by George Bruce.

Over the years I've pieced together an understanding of type history, but one era has proved opaque—scholars have had little to say on the bulk of the nineteenth century, skipping from Bodoni to Morris as over a vast aberration.

How strange, since it was during these years that universal literacy,

mass media, and consumer culture emerged. In the United States, the type genre at the centre of this massive transformation was the Scotch Modern, fulfilling the evolutionary line that began with Jenson.

Looking at the *23rd Annual Report,* one can see why the Scotch would later fall from grace. Bruce's text type is a marvel of punch-cut virtuosity, printed with exquisite letterpress finesse, but this subtle quality of hand craft would be absent from subsequent technological renderings, chilling its effect.

In general, type redesigners have balked at the exaggerated features of the Scotch Modern—huge serifs and a tiny aperture—and sacrificed the charm of its letterpress idiosyncracies at the altar of mechanical consistency.

And so in 2004 I began a micro-detailed revival of the Bruce face (named Austin after the originator of the genre), with a matching sans, Figgins. But that's another story.
—NICK SHINN

While working as a creative director and graphic designer during the 1980s and 1990s, Nick Shinn designed several typefaces. Fontesque, published by FontShop International, was the most popular. In 1999, he founded Shinntype and went into the font business full time. Most of the typefaces shown here are published by Shinntype. Please check online for up-to-date information on available font formats.

Austin
Alphaville
Artefact
Beaufort
Bodoni Egyptian
Brown Gothic
Eunoia
Figgins
Fontesque
Fontesque Sans
Goodchild
Handsome
Merlin
Morphica
Nicholas
Oneleigh
PANOPTICA
Paradigm
Preface
SoftMachine
Walburn
Worldwide

Shinn Type Foundry Inc.
364 Sunnyside Avenue
Toronto, Ontario
Canada M6R 2R8
(416) 769-1078
nick@shinntype.com
www.shinntype.com

Austin Pro

Nick Shinn
2007

Austin is a revival of a type attributed to George Bruce, c. 1860. This design is named after the originator of the Scotch Roman genre, Richard Austin. The Cyrillic and Greek glyphs are new. Figgins is a matching sans serif.

Language support includes:
Latin 1
Central and Eastern European
Cyrillic
Greek Monotonic & Polytonic

OpenType features include:
Small Caps (excl. Cyrillic, Greek)
Standard Ligatures
Discretionary Ligatures
Fractions: Slash
Fractions: Nut
Case, including Cap-Height Figs.
Superior Figures
Inferior Figures
Ordinals
Kerning

Shinntype

The *formal* qualities of

ABCDEFGHIJKLMNOPQRSTUVWXYZ
abcdefghijklmnopqrstuvwxyz $€0123456789%

ABCDEFGHIJKLMNOPQRSTUVWXYZ
abcdefghijklmnopqrstuvwxyz $€0123456789%

АБВГДЕЖЗИКЛМНОПРСТУФХЦЧШЩЪЭЮЯ
абвгдежзиклмнопрстуфхцчшщъыьэюя

АБВГДЕЖЗИКЛМНОПРСТУФХЦЧШЩЪЭЮЯ
абвгдежзиклмнопрстуфхцчшщъыьэюя

ΑΒΓΔΕΖΗΘΙΚΛΜΝΞΟΠΡΣΤΥΦΧΨΩ
αβγδεζηθικλμνξοπρστυφχψως

ΑΒΓΔΕΖΗΘΙΚΛΜΝΞΟΠΡΣΤΥΦΧΨΩ
αβγδεζηθικλμνξοπρστυφχψως

Regular

THE FORMAL qualities of a typeface energize, facilitate and inform the typographic layout. Skilled typographers will leverage the attributes of judiciously chosen fonts to maxi-

Italic

THE FORMAL qualities of a typeface energize, facilitate and inform the typographic layout. Skilled typographers will leverage the attributes of judiciously chosen fonts to maxi-

Bold and Bold Italic

The formal qualities of a typeface energize, facilitate and inform the typographic layout. *Skilled typographers will leverage the attributes of judiciously chosen fonts to max-*

Cyrillic

Номинальные качества гарнитуры шрифта усиливают и облегчают печатный набор. Опытные тайпографы используют качества тщательно

Cyrillic Italic

Номинальные качества гарнитуры шрифта усиливают и облегчают печатный набор. Опытные тайпографы используют качества тщательно

Central European

Oficjalny krój czcionki ożywia, ułatwia czytanie, i ilustruje typografię. Profesjonalny typograf wykorzysta cechy starannie dobranych czcionek tak aby zmaksymalizować wyrazi-

Greek

Οἱ τυπικές ἰδιότητες ἑνός τυπογραφικοῦ στοιχείου δίνουν ροή, διευκολύνουν καί τροφοδοτοῦν τήν τυπογραφική διάταξη. Ἐπιδέξιοι τυπογράφοι θά δώσουν ἔμφαση στά

Greek Italic

Οἱ τυπικές ἰδιότητες ἑνός τυπογραφικοῦ στοιχείου δίνουν ροή, διευκολύνουν καί τροφοδοτοῦν τήν τυπογραφική διάταξη. Ἐπιδέξιοι τυπογράφοι θά δώσουν ἔμφαση στά

Central European Italic

Oficjalny krój czcionki ożywia, ułatwia czytanie, i ilustruje typografię. Profesjonalny typograf wykorzysta cechy starannie dobranych czcionek tak aby zmaksymalizować wyrazi-

Light

The formal qualities of a type

ABCDEFGHIJKLMNOPQRSTUVWXYZabcdefghijklmnopqrstuvwxyz$€0123456789%

Light

The formal qualities of a typeface energize, facilitate and inform the typographic layout. Skilled typographers will leverage the attributes of judiciously chosen fonts to maximize the personality of the page,

Regular

The formal qualities of a typeface energize, facilitate and inform the typographic layout. Skilled typographers will leverage the attributes of judiciously chosen fonts to maximize the personality of the page,

Bold

The formal qualities of a typeface energize, facilitate and inform the typographic layout. Skilled typographers will leverage the attributes of judiciously chosen fonts to maximize

Ultra

The formal qualities of a

Thin

ABCDEFGHIJKLMNOPQRSTUVWXYZ
abcdefghijklmnopqrstuvwxyz $€0123456789%
abcdefghijklmnopqrstuvwxyz $€0123456789%

Thin

The formal qualities of a typeface energize, facilitate and inform the typographic layout. Skilled typographers will leverage the attributes of judiciously chosen fonts to maxi-

Thin Oblique

The formal qualities of a typeface energize, facilitate and inform the typographic layout. Skilled typographers will leverage the attributes of judiciously chosen fonts to maxi-

Medium

The formal qualities of a typeface energize, facilitate and inform the typographic layout. Skilled typographers will leverage the attributes of judiciously chosen

Medium Oblique

The formal qualities of a typeface energize, facilitate and inform the typographic layout. Skilled typographers will leverage the attributes of judiciously chosen

Light

The formal qualities of a typeface energize, facilitate and inform the typographic layout. Skilled typographers will leverage the attributes of judiciously chosen fonts to maxi-

Light Oblique

The formal qualities of a typeface energize, facilitate and inform the typographic layout. Skilled typographers will leverage the attributes of judiciously chosen fonts to maxi-

Bold

The formal qualities of a typeface energize, facilitate and inform the typographic layout. Skilled typographers will leverage the attributes of

Bold Oblique

The formal qualities of a typeface energize, facilitate and inform the typographic layout. Skilled typographers will leverage the attributes of

Regular

The formal qualities of a typeface energize, facilitate and inform the typographic layout. Skilled typographers will leverage the attributes of judiciously chosen fonts to maxi-

Oblique

The formal qualities of a typeface energize, facilitate and inform the typographic layout. Skilled typographers will leverage the attributes of judiciously chosen fonts to maxi-

Ultra

The formal qualities of a typeface energize, facilitate and inform the typographic layout. Skilled typographers will leverage the attributes of judiciously chosen fonts to maxi-

Outline

The formal qualities of a typeface energize, facilitate and inform the typographic layout. Skilled typographers will leverage the attributes of judiciously chosen fonts to maxi-

nick@shinntype.com

Nick Shinn
1997

Condensed Heavy

The *formal* qualities of a typeface

ABCDEFGHIJKLMNOPQRSTUVWXYZabcdefghijklmnopqrstuvwxyz$€0123456789%

Regular

The *formal* qualities of a type

ABCDEFGHIJKLMNOPQRSTUVWXYZabcdefghijklmnopqrstuvwxyz$€0123456789%

Extended Light

The *formal* qualities of

ABCDEFGHJKLMNOPQRSTUWXYZabcdefghjklmnopqrstuwxyz

Condensed Light

The formal qualities of a typeface energize, facilitate and inform the typographic layout. Skilled typographers *will leverage the attributes of judiciously chosen fonts to maximize the page's personality, thereby standing out from the crowd.*

Condensed Regular

The formal qualities of a typeface energize, facilitate and inform the typographic layout. Skilled typographers *will leverage the attributes of judiciously chosen fonts to maximize the page's personality, thereby standing out from*

Condensed Medium

The formal qualities of a typeface energize, facilitate and inform the typographic layout. Skilled typographers *will leverage the attributes of judiciously chosen fonts to maximize the page's personality, thereby standing out from*

Condensed Bold

The formal qualities of a typeface energize, facilitate and inform the typographic layout. Skilled typographers *will leverage attributes of judiciously chosen fonts to maximize the page's personality, thereby standing out from*

Condensed Heavy

The formal qualities of a typeface energize, facilitate and inform the typographic layout. Skilled typographers *will leverage attributes of judiciously chosen fonts to maximize the page's personality, thereby standing out from*

Light

The formal qualities of a typeface energize, facilitate and inform the typographic layout. *Skilled typographers will leverage the attributes of judiciously chosen fonts to maximize the personality*

Regular

The formal qualities of a typeface energize, facilitate and inform the typographic layout. *Skilled typographers will leverage the attributes of judiciously chosen fonts to maximize*

Medium

The formal qualities of a typeface energize, facilitate and inform the typographic layout. *Skilled typographers will leverage the attributes of judiciously chosen fonts to maximize*

Bold

The formal qualities of a typeface energize, facilitate and inform the typographic layout. *Skilled typographers will leverage the attributes of judiciously chosen fonts to maximize*

Heavy

The formal qualities of a typeface energize, facilitate and inform the typographic layout. *Skilled typographers will leverage the attributes of judiciously chosen fonts to maximize*

Extended Light

The formal qualities of a typeface energize, facilitate and inform the typographic layout. *Skilled typographers will leverage the attributes of*

Extended

The formal qualities of a typeface energize, facilitate and inform the typographic layout. *Skilled typographers will leverage the attributes of*

Extended Medium

The formal qualities of a typeface energize, facilitate and inform the typographic layout. *Skilled typographers will leverage the attributes of*

Extended Bold

The formal qualities of a typeface energize, facilitate and inform the typographic layout. *Skilled typographers will leverage the attributes*

Extended Heavy

The formal qualities of a typeface energize, facilitate and inform the typographic layout. *Skilled typographers will leverage the attributes*

Thin
The formal qualities of a type

Light
The formal qualities of a type

Regular and Italic
The *formal* qualities of a

Capitals
THE FORMAL QUALITIES OF

Bold and Bold Italic
The *formal* qualities of a

Shadow with Bold Fill
The formal qualities of a

ABCDEFGHIJKLMNOPQRSTUVWXYZabcdefghijklmnopqrstuvwxyz$€0123456789%
ABCDEFGHIJKLMNOPQRSTUVWXYZabcdefghijklmnopqrstuvwxyz$€0123456789%
ABCDEFGHIJKLMNOPQRSTUVWXYZABCDEFGHIJKLMNOPQRSTUVWXYZ$€0123456789%
ABCDEFGHIJKLMNOPQRSTUVWXYZabcdefghijklmnopqrstuvwxyz$€0123456789%
ABCDEFGHIJKLMNOPQRSTUVWXYZabcdefghijklmnopqrstuvwxyz$€0123456789%

Thin
The formal qualities of a typeface energize, facilitate and inform the typographic layout. Skilled typographers will leverage the attributes of judiciously chosen fonts to maximize

Light
The formal qualities of a typeface energize, facilitate and inform the typographic layout. Skilled typographers will leverage the attributes of judiciously chosen fonts to maximize

Shadow
The formal qualities of a typeface energize, facilitate and inform the typographic layout. Skilled typographers will leverage the attributes of judiciously chosen fonts to maximize

Regular
The formal qualities of a typeface energize, facilitate and inform the typographic layout. Skilled typographers will leverage the attributes of judiciously chosen fonts to maximize

Italic
The formal qualities of a typeface energize, facilitate and inform the typographic layout. Skilled typographers will leverage the attributes of judiciously chosen fonts to maximize

Capitals
THE FORMAL QUALITIES OF A TYPEFACE ENERGIZE, FACILITATE AND INFORM THE TYPOGRAPHIC LAYOUT. SKILLED TYPOGRAPHERS WILL LEVERAGE THE ATTRIBUTES OF JUDICIOUSLY CHOSEN FONTS

Bold
The formal qualities of a typeface energize, facilitate and inform the typographic layout. Skilled typographers will leverage the attributes of judiciously chosen fonts to maximize

Bold Italic
The formal qualities of a typeface energize, facilitate and inform the typographic layout. Skilled typographers will leverage the attributes of judiciously chosen fonts to maximize

nick@shinntype.com

The formal quality

The formal qualities

The formal qualities of a type

Nick Shinn
2000–2005

Designed for use with Walburn and Worldwide, which have similar semi-condensed proportions and x-height and a similar finish.

Light

ABCDEFGHIJKLMNOPQRSTUVWXYZabcdefghijklmnopqrstuvwxyz$€0123456789%
ABCDEFGHIJKLMNOPQRSTUVWXYZabcdefghijklmnopqrstuvwxyz$€0123456789%

Light

The formal qualities of a typeface energize, facilitate and inform the typographic layout. Skilled typographers will leverage the attributes of judiciously chosen fonts to maximize

Regular

The formal qualities of a typeface energize, facilitate and inform the typographic layout. Skilled typographers will leverage the attributes of judiciously chosen fonts to maximize

Medium

The formal qualities of a typeface energize, facilitate and inform the typographic layout. Skilled typographers will leverage the attributes of judiciously chosen fonts to maximize

Bold

The formal qualities of a typeface energize, facilitate and inform the typographic layout. Skilled typographers will leverage the attributes of judiciously chosen fonts to maxi-

Medium Condensed

The formal qualities of a typeface energize, facilitate and inform the typographic layout. Skilled typographers leverage the attributes of carefully selected fonts to enhance the personality of the page, thereby standing out

Light Italic

The formal qualities of a typeface energize, facilitate and inform the typographic layout. Skilled typographers will leverage the attributes of judiciously chosen fonts to maximize

Italic

The formal qualities of a typeface energize, facilitate and inform the typographic layout. Skilled typographers will leverage the attributes of judiciously chosen fonts to maximize

Medium Italic

The formal qualities of a typeface energize, facilitate and inform the typographic layout. Skilled typographers will leverage the attributes of judiciously chosen fonts to maximize

Bold Italic

The formal qualities of a typeface energize, facilitate and inform the typographic layout. Skilled typographers will leverage the attributes of judiciously chosen fonts to maxi-

Bold Condensed

The formal qualities of a typeface energize, facilitate and inform the typographic layout. Skilled typographers will leverage the attributes of judiciously chosen fonts to maximize the personality of the page, thereby standing

Heavy

The formal qualities of a typeface energize, facilitate and inform the typographic layout. Skilled typographers will leverage the attributes of judiciously chosen fonts to maxi-

Extra Bold

The formal qualities of a typeface energize, facilitate and inform the typographic layout. Skilled typographers will leverage the attributes of judiciously chosen fonts to maximize the personality

Black

The formal qualities of a typeface energize, facilitate and inform the typographic layout. Skilled typographers will leverage the attributes of judiciously chosen fonts to maximize the personality of the page,

Black Condensed

The formal qualities of a typeface energize, facilitate and inform the typographic layout. Skilled typographers will leverage the attributes of judiciously chosen fonts to maximize the personality of the page, thereby standing out

Extra Bold Condensed

The formal qualities of a typeface energize, facilitate and inform the typographic layout. Skilled typographers will leverage the attributes of judiciously chosen fonts to maximize the personality of the page, thereby standing out from the crowd. The formal qualities of

Shinntype

Regular and Condensed

The formal qualities of a typeface

Round and Round Condensed

The formal qualities of a typeface

Unicase and Unicase Condensed

THE FORMAL QUALITIES OF A TYPEFACE

ABCDEFGHIJKLMNOPQRSTUVWXYZabcdefghijklmnopqrstuvwxyz$€0123456789%

ABCDEFGHIJKLMNOPQRSTUVWXYZabcdefghijklmnopqrstuvwxyz$€0123456789%

ABCDEFGHIJKLMNOPQRSTUVWXYZabcdefghijklmnopqrstuvwxyz$€0123456789%

ABCDEFGHIJKLMNOPQRSTUVWXYZabcdefghijklmnopqrstuvwxyz$€0123456789%

ABCDEFGHIJKLMNOPQRSTUVWXYZabcdefghijklmnopqrstuvwxyz$€0123456789%

ABCDEFGHIJKLMNOPQRSTUVWXYZabcdefghijklmnopqrstuvwxyz$€0123456789%

The Bold Caps are a revival of a font by the London type founder, Vincent Figgins, c. 1835. The rest of the typeface is executed in as authentic a manner as possible, given the hypothetical nature of the exercise.

Figgins is proportioned to match Austin. The bold has the same cap and x-height, and the italic has the same slant as Austin Italic, 20°.

Regular

The *formal* qualities of a TYPE

Bold

The formal qualities of a

ABCDEFGHIJKLMNOPQRSTUVWXYZabcdefghijklmnopqrstuvwxyz$€0123456789%

ABCDEFGHIJKLMNOPQRSTUVWXYZABCDEFGHIJKLMNOPQRSTUVWXYZ$€0123456789%

ABCDEFGHIJKLMNOPQRSTUVWXYZabcdefghijklmnopqrstuvwxyz$€0123456789%

Regular

The formal qualities of a typeface energize, facilitate and inform the typographic layout. Skilled typographers will leverage the attributes of judiciously chosen fonts to maximize

Italic

The formal qualities of a typeface energize, facilitate and inform the typographic layout. Skilled typographers will leverage the attributes of judiciously chosen fonts to maximize

Semibold

The formal qualities of a typeface energize, facilitate and inform the typographic layout. Skilled typographers will leverage the attributes of judiciously chosen fonts to maximize

Small Caps

THE FORMAL QUALITIES OF A TYPEFACE ENERGIZE, FACILITATE AND INFORM THE TYPOGRAPHIC LAYOUT. SKILLED TYPOGRAPHERS WILL LEVERAGE THE ATTRIBUTES OF JUDICIOUSLY CHOSEN FONTS TO MAXIMIZE

Bold

The formal qualities of a typeface energize, facilitate and inform the typographic layout. Skilled typographers will leverage the attributes of judiciously chosen fonts to maxi-

Middle Caps

THE FORMAL QUALITIES OF A TYPEFACE ENERGIZE, FACILITATE AND INFORM THE TYPOGRAPHIC LAYOUT. SKILLED TYPOGRAPHERS WILL LEVERAGE THE ATTRIBUTES OF JUDICIOUSLY CHOSEN

The formal quality

The formal quality

The formal quality

The formal quality

The formal qualities of a type

The formal qualities of a

ABCDEFGHIJKLMNOPQRSTUVWXYZabcdefghijklmnopqrstuvwxyz$€0123456789%
ABCDEFGHIJKLMNOPQRSTUVWXYZabcdefghijklmnopqrstuvwxyz$€0123456789%
ABCDEFGHIJKLMNOPQRSTUVWXYZabcdefghijklmnopqrstuvwxyz$€0123456789%

Regular

The formal qualities of a typeface energize, facilitate and inform the typographic layout. Skilled typographers will leverage the attributes of judiciously chosen fonts to max-

Italic

The formal qualities of a typeface energize, facilitate and inform the typographic layout. Skilled typographers will leverage the attributes of judiciously chosen fonts to maximize

Bold

The formal qualities of a typeface energize, facilitate and inform the typographic layout. Skilled typographers will leverage the attributes of judiciously chosen fonts to max-

Bold Italic

The formal qualities of a typeface energize, facilitate and inform the typographic layout. Skilled typographers will leverage the attributes of judiciously chosen fonts to max-

Display

The formal qualities of a typeface energize, facilitate and inform the typographic layout. Skilled typographers will leverage the attributes of judiciously chosen fonts to max-

Nicholas

Nick Shinn
2005

Nicholas is the headline version of Goodchild.

Shinntype

Goodchild

Nick Shinn
2002

Goodchild is a revival of Nicholas Jenson's 1467 typeface.

FF Fontesque

Nick Shinn
1994

FF Fontesque is published by FontShop International.

Ornaments:
There is a Fontesque ornament for each key of the keyboard. The shift key flips the characters. There are four ornament fonts:
Fine
Regular (shown here)
Black
Sans

The Fine Ornaments are extremely fine and intended for use as frames at very large sizes. The Black Ornaments are solid. Each ornament font has a series of eight characters that create a border (not shown).

Regular
The formal qualities of a typeface

Italic
The formal qualities of a typeface

Bold
The formal qualities of a typeface

Bold Italic
The formal qualities of a typeface

Extra Bold
The formal qualities of a typeface

ABCDEFGHIJKLMNOPQRSTUVWXYZ
abcdefghijklmnopqrstuvwxyz $€0123456789%
ABCDEFGHIJKLMNOPQRSTUVWXYZ
abcdefghijklmnopqrstuvwxyz $€0123456789%

Regular
The formal qualities of a typeface

ABCDEFGHIJKLMNOPQRSTUVWXYZabcdefghijklmnopqrstuvwxyz $0123456789%

Regular
The formal qualities of a typeface energize, facilitate and inform the typographic layout. Skilled typographers will leverage the attributes of judiciously chosen fonts to maximize the personality of the page,

Italic
The formal qualities of a typeface energize, facilitate and inform the typographic layout. Skilled typographers will leverage the attributes of judiciously chosen fonts to maximize the personality of the page, thereby standing out

Bold and Bold Italic
The formal qualities of a typeface energize, facilitate and inform the typographic layout. Skilled typographers will leverage the attributes of judiciously chosen fonts to maximize the personality of the page,

Nick Shinn
2001

FF Fontesque Sans is published by FontShop International.

Shinntype

Ultra Light

The formal qualities of a typeface

Light

The *formal* qualities of a typeface

Regular

The *formal* qualities of a typeface

Bold

The *formal* qualities of a typeface

Extra Bold

The formal qualities of a type

ABCDEFGHIJKLMNOPQRSTUVWXYZ
abcdefghijklmnopqrstuvwxyz $€0123456789%
ABCDEFGHIJKLMNOPQRSTUVWXYZ
abcdefghijklmnopqrstuvwxyz $€0123456789%

Light

The formal qualities of a typeface energize, facilitate and inform the typographic layout. Skilled typographers will leverage the attributes of judiciously chosen fonts to maximize the personality of the page, thereby standing out

Regular

The formal qualities of a typeface energize, facilitate and inform the typographic layout. Skilled typographers will leverage the attributes of judiciously chosen fonts to maximize the personality of the page, thereby standing

Bold

The formal qualities of a typeface energize, facilitate and inform the typographic layout. Skilled typographers will leverage the attributes of judiciously chosen fonts to maximize the personality of the page,

Light Italic

The formal qualities of a typeface energize, facilitate and inform the typographic layout. Skilled typographers will leverage the attributes of judiciously chosen fonts to maximize the personality of the page, thereby standing out

Italic

The formal qualities of a typeface energize, facilitate and inform the typographic layout. Skilled typographers will leverage the attributes of judiciously chosen fonts to maximize the personality of the page, thereby standing

Bold Italic

The formal qualities of a typeface energize, facilitate and inform the typographic layout. Skilled typographers will leverage the attributes of judiciously chosen fonts to maximize the personality of the page,

Ultra Light

The formal qualities of a typeface energize, facilitate and inform the typographic layout. Skilled typographers will leverage the attributes of judiciously chosen fonts to maximize the personality of the page, thereby standing out

Extra Bold

The formal qualities of a typeface energize, facilitate and inform the typographic layout. Skilled typographers will leverage the attributes of judiciously chosen fonts to maximize

Handsome Pro

Nick Shinn
2005

The contextual alternates feature of OpenType is used to simulate the joining behavior of fully cursive handwriting.

Thin

The formal qualities of a typeface energize, facilitate and inform the typographic layout. Skilled typographers will leverage the attributes of judiciously chosen fonts to maximize the personality of the page, thereby standing

Regular

The formal qualities of a typeface energize, facilitate and inform the typographic layout. Skilled typographers will leverage the attributes of judiciously chosen fonts to maximize the personality of the page, thereby standing

Bold

The formal qualities of a typeface energize, facilitate and inform the typographic layout. Skilled typographers will leverage the attributes of judiciously chosen fonts to maximize the personality of the page, thereby standing

Extra Bold

The formal qualities of a typeface energize, facilitate and inform the typographic layout. Skilled typographers will leverage the attributes of judiciously chosen fonts to maximize the personality of the page, thereby standing

Rough

The formal qualities of a typeface energize, facilitate and inform the typographic layout. Skilled typographers will leverage the attributes of judiciously chosen fonts to maximize the personality of the page, thereby standing

Classic

The formal qualities of a typeface energize, facilitate and inform the typographic layout. Skilled typographers will leverage the attributes of judiciously chosen fonts to maximize the personality of the page, thereby standing

FF Merlin

Nick Shinn
1997

FF Merlin is published by FontShop International.

Regular

The formal qualities of a type

Italic

The formal qualities of a typeface

Bold

The formal qualities of a type

ABCDEFGHIJKLMNOPQRSTUVWXYZabcdefghijklmnopqrstuvwxyz $€0123456789%
ABCDEFGHIJKLMNOPQRSTUVWXYZabcdefghijklmnopqrstuvwxyz $€0123456789%
ABCDEFGHIJKLMNOPQRSTUVWXYZABCDEFGHIJKLMNOPQRSTUVWXYZ

Regular with Small Caps and Italic

THE FORMAL QUALITIES of a typeface energize, facilitate and inform the typographic layout. Skilled typographers *will leverage the attributes of judiciously chosen fonts to maximize the personality of*

Bold

THE FORMAL qualities of a typeface energize, facilitate and inform the typographic layout. Skilled typographers will leverage the attributes of judiciously chosen fonts to maximize the personality

Decorative Capitals

THE FORMAL QUALITIES OF A TYPEFACE ENERGIZE, FACILITATE AND INFORM THE TYPOGRAPHIC LAYOUT. SKILLED TYPOGRAPHERS WILL LEVERAGE

The formal qualities of a type

The formal qualities of a type

ABCDEFGHIJKLMNOPQRSTUVWXYZabcdefghijklmnopqrstuvwxyz $€0123456789%
ABCDEFGHIJKLMNOPQRSTUVWXYZabcdefghijklmnopqrstuvwxyz $€0123456789%

The formal qualities of a type

The formal qualities of a typeface

THE FORMAL QUALITIES OF A TYPE

The formal qualities of a type

The formal qualities of a type

The formal qualities of a

The formal qualities of a type

ABCDEFGHIJKLMNOPQRSTUVWXYZabcdefghijklmnopqrstuvwxyz $€0123456789%
ABCDEFGHIJKLMNOPQRSTUVWXYZabcdefghijklmnopqrstuvwxyz $€0123456789%
$€0123456789% ABCDEFGHIJKLMNOPQRSTUVWXYZ

FF Oneleigh

Nick Shinn
1998

FF Oneleigh is published by
FontShop International.

Shinntype

Regular with Small Caps and Italic
THE FORMAL QUALITIES of a typeface energize, facilitate and inform the typographic layout. *Skilled typographers will leverage the attributes of judiciously chosen fonts to maximize the personality*

Bold and Bold Italic
The formal qualities of a typeface energize, facilitate and inform the typographic layout. *Skilled typographers will leverage the attributes of judiciously chosen fonts to maximize*

Black and Black Italic
The formal qualities of a typeface energize, facilitate and inform the typographic layout. *Skilled typographers will leverage the attributes of judiciously chosen fonts to maximize*

Regular, Italic, and Octagonal

THE *FORMAL* QUALITIES

Egyptian, Script, and Pixel

THE FORMAL QUALITIES

Sans Regular, Sans Bold, and Doesburg

THE **FORMAL** QUALITIES

Sans Medium

abcDEFGHIJKLMNOPQRSTUVWXYZ $€0123456789%

Regular and Italic

THE FORMAL QUALITIES OF A TYPE FACE ENERGIZE, FACILITATE, AND INFORM THE TYPOGRAPHIC LAYOUT. *SKILLED TYPOGRAPHERS WILL LEVERAGE THE ATTRIBUTES OF JUDICIOUSLY CHOSEN FONTS TO MAXIMIZE*

Egyptian

THE FORMAL QUALITIES OF A TYPE FACE ENERGIZE, FACILITATE, AND INFORM THE TYPOGRAPHIC LAYOUT. SKILLED TYPOGRAPHERS WILL LEVERAGE THE ATTRIBUTES OF JUDICIOUSLY CHOSEN FONTS TO MAXIMIZE

Script

THE FORMAL QUALITIES OF A TYPE FACE ENERGIZE, FACILITATE, AND INFORM THE TYPOGRAPHIC LAYOUT. SKILLED TYPOGRAPHERS WILL LEVERAGE THE ATTRIBUTES OF JUDICIOUSLY CHOSEN FONTS TO MAXIMIZE

Octagonal

THE FORMAL QUALITIES OF A TYPE FACE ENERGIZE, FACILITATE, AND INFORM THE TYPOGRAPHIC LAYOUT. SKILLED TYPOGRAPHERS WILL LEVERAGE THE ATTRIBUTES OF JUDICIOUSLY CHOSEN FONTS TO MAXIMIZE

Pixel

THE FORMAL QUALITIES OF A TYPE FACE ENERGIZE, FACILITATE, AND INFORM THE TYPOGRAPHIC LAYOUT. SKILLED TYPOGRAPHERS WILL LEVERAGE THE ATTRIBUTES OF JUDICIOUSLY CHOSEN FONTS TO MAXIMIZE

Doesburg

THE FORMAL QUALITIES OF A TYPE FACE ENERGIZE, FACILITATE, AND INFORM THE TYPOGRAPHIC LAYOUT. SKILLED TYPOGRAPHERS WILL LEVERAGE THE ATTRIBUTES OF JUDICIOUSLY CHOSEN FONTS TO MAXIMIZE

Sans

THE FORMAL QUALITIES OF A TYPE FACE ENERGIZE, FACILITATE, AND INFORM THE TYPOGRAPHIC LAYOUT. SKILLED TYPOGRAPHERS WILL LEVERAGE THE ATTRIBUTES OF JUDICIOUSLY CHOSEN FONTS TO MAXIMIZE

Sans Medium

THE FORMAL QUALITIES OF A TYPE FACE ENERGIZE, FACILITATE, AND INFORM THE TYPOGRAPHIC LAYOUT. SKILLED TYPOGRAPHERS WILL LEVERAGE THE ATTRIBUTES OF JUDICIOUSLY CHOSEN FONTS TO MAXIMIZE

Sans Bold

THE FORMAL QUALITIES OF A TYPE FACE ENERGIZE, FACILITATE, AND INFORM THE TYPOGRAPHIC LAYOUT. SKILLED TYPOGRAPHERS WILL LEVERAGE THE ATTRIBUTES OF JUDICIOUSLY CHOSEN FONTS TO MAXIMIZE

Regular

The formal qualities of a type

Italic

The formal qualities of a typeface

ABCDEFGHIJKLMNOPQRSTUVWXYZabcdefghijklmnopqrstuvwxyz $0123456789%
ABCDEFGHIJKLMNOPQRSTUVWXYZabcdefghijklmnopqrstuvwxyz $0123456789%

Regular with Small Caps

THE FORMAL QUALITIES of a typeface energize, facilitate and inform the typographic layout. Skilled typographers will leverage the attributes of judiciously chosen fonts to maximize

Italic with Small Caps

THE FORMAL QUALITIES of a typeface energize, facilitate and inform the typographic layout. Skilled typographers will leverage the attributes of judiciously chosen fonts to maximize

Bold with Small Caps

THE FORMAL QUALITIES of a typeface energize, facilitate and inform the typographic layout. Skilled typographers will leverage the attributes of judiciously chosen fonts to maximize

nick@shinntype.com

Thin
The *formal* qualities of a

Book
The *formal* qualities of a

Bold
The *formal* qualities of a

Black
The *formal* qualities of a

Nick Shinn
2003

Shinntype

ABCDEFGHIJKLMNOPQRSTUVWXYZabcdefghijklmnopqrstuvwxyz $0123456789%

ABCDEFGHIJKLMNOPQRSTUVWXYZabcdefghijklmnopqrstuvwxyz $0123456789%

Thin
The formal qualities of a typeface energize, facilitate and inform the typographic layout. *Skilled typographers will leverage the attributes of judiciously chosen fonts to maxi-*

Light
The formal qualities of a typeface energize, facilitate and inform the typographic layout. *Skilled typographers will leverage the attributes of judiciously chosen fonts to maxi-*

Book
The formal qualities of a typeface energize, facilitate and inform the typographic layout. *Skilled typographers will leverage the attributes of judiciously chosen fonts to maxi-*

Regular
The formal qualities of a typeface energize, facilitate and inform the typographic layout. *Skilled typographers will leverage the attributes of judiciously*

Bold
The formal qualities of a typeface energize, facilitate and inform the typographic layout. *Skilled typographers will leverage the attributes of judiciously*

Black
The formal qualities of a typeface energize, facilitate and inform the typographic layout. *Skilled typographers will leverage the attributes of judiciously*

Softmachine Pro

Nick Shinn
2006

Softmachine is a single font designed for outlines and special effects.

Language support includes:
Latin 1
Central and Eastern European

OpenType features include:
Contextual Alternates
Stylistic Alternates (not shown)

Regular
The formal qualities

Regular
The formal qualities

Regular
The formal qualities

Regular
The formal qualities

ABCDEFGHIJKLMNOPQRSTUVWXYZabcdefghijklmnopqrstuvwxyz $0123456789%

Walburn

Nick Shinn
1996–2005

Walburn is a revival in the Walbaum genre.

Brown Gothic is a matching sans serif, with similar semi-condensed proportions, cap and x-height, and finish.

Tooled

FORMAL QUALITY

Light

The formal qualities

Bold

The formal *qualities*

Ultra

The formal qualities

Regular

The formal qualities of a typeface energize

The formal qualities of a typeface energize

Text Light

ABCDEFGHIJKLMNOPQRSTUVWXYZabcdefghijklmnopqrstuvwxyz$€0123456789%

ABCDEFGHIJKLMNOPQRSTUVWXYZabcdefghijklmnopqrstuvwxyz$€0123456789%

Black

The formal qualities of a typeface energize and *inform the typographic*

Text Light

The formal qualities of a typeface energize, facilitate and inform

Text Light

The formal qualities of a typeface energize, facilitate and inform the typographic layout. Skilled typographers

Text

The formal qualities of a typeface energize, facilitate and inform the typographic layout. Skilled typographers will leverage the attributes of judiciously chosen fonts to maximize

Text Light Italic

The formal qualities of a typeface energize, facilitate and inform

Text Light Italic

The formal qualities of a typeface energize, facilitate and inform the typographic layout. Skilled typographers

Text Italic

The formal qualities of a typeface energize, facilitate and inform the typographic layout. Skilled typographers will leverage the attributes of judiciously chosen fonts to maximize

Nick Shinn
1999-2005

Worldwide is a revival in the Century genre.

Brown Gothic is a matching sans serif, with similar semi-condensed proportions and finish.

Shinntype

Ultra

The formal qualities of

Headline Regular

The formal qualities

Headline Italic

The formal qualities

Headline Bold

The formal qualities

Headline Black

The formal quality

Bold Condensed

The formal qualities of a

Regular

ABCDEFGHIJKLMNOPQRSTUVWXYZabcdefghijklmnopqrstuvwxyz$€0123456789%

ABCDEFGHIJKLMNOPQRSTUVWXYZ$€0123456789%

ABCDEFGHIJKLMNOPQRSTUVWXYZabcdefghijklmnopqrstuvwxyz$€0123456789%

Regular

The formal qualities of a typeface energize, facilitate and inform the typographic layout. Skilled typographers will leverage the attributes of judiciously chosen fonts to maxi-

Italic

The formal qualities of a typeface energize, facilitate and inform the typographic layout. Skilled typographers will leverage the attributes of judiciously chosen fonts to maxi-

Small Caps

The formal qualities of a typeface energize, facilitate and inform the typographic layout. Skilled typographers will leverage the attributes of judiciously

Bold

The formal qualities of a typeface energize, facilitate and inform the typographic layout. Skilled typographers will leverage the attributes of judiciously chosen

Bold Italic

The formal qualities of a typeface energize, facilitate and inform the typographic layout. Skilled typographers will leverage the attributes of judiciously chosen

Black

The formal qualities of a typeface energize, facilitate and inform the typographic layout. Skilled typographers will leverage the attributes of judiciously

sparky type

SparkyType is an independent foundry based in Wellington, New Zealand.

As well as creating commercial typefaces, SparkyType offers services from font repair or alteration to full customized design and development.

For details, check www.sparkytype.com or

Contact	David Buck
E-mail	david@sparkytype.com
Phone	+64 4 977 0495
Mail	PO Box 9590
	Marion Square
	Wellington
	New Zealand

MASTERFUL

TRANS-OCEANIC ADVENTURE

CRUISIN' LIKE TOM

ꝛ ONLY $1485, IT'S SUPAVALUE

ABCDEFGHIJKLMNOPQRSTUVWXYZ 123456789
ABCDEFGHIJKLMNOPQRSTUVWXYZ (!ꝛ#$%&*;)

Amoeba

David Buck
2006

DANGEROUS

my posse's got velocity

Razor-sharp &

Frighteningly effective

AaBbCcDdEeFfGgHhIiJjKkLlMmNnOoPp
QqRrSsTtUuVvWwXxYyZz123456789?!

Antelope

David Buck
2006

SparkyType

Foxton fries

& milk from Bulls

Taupo will bring Rainbow Trout

Rotorua's cooking us eggs

BRING YOUR LAUGHING GEAR

After, we'll have Pav!

Light
AaBbCcDdEeFfGgHhIiJjKkLlMmNnOoPpQqRrSsTtUuVvWw
XxYyZz 123456789 {¿¡«<@#$£&*»!?}

Regular
AaBbCcDdEeFfGgHhIiJjKkLlMmNnOoPpQqRrSsTtUuVvWw
XxYyZz 123456789 {¿¡«<@#$£&*»!?}

Bold
AaBbCcDdEeFfGgHhIiJjKkLlMmNnOoPpQqRrSsTt
UuVvWwXxYyZz 123456789 {¿¡«<@#$£&*»!?}

info@sparkytype.com

QUARTERBACK
75% FRONT
time for a serious hustle
don't pass the ball yet
THEY DON'T STAND A CHANCE
try and kick for goal!

Billy Serif

David Buck
2006

SparkyType

Light

AaBbCcDdEeFfGgHhIiJjKkLlMmNnOoPpQqRrSsTtUuVv
WwXxYyZz 123456789 {¿¡«@#$£&*»!?}

Regular

AaBbCcDdEeFfGgHhIiJjKkLlMmNnOoPpQqRrSsTtUu
VvWwXxYyZz 123456789 {¿¡«@#$£&*»!?}

Bold

AaBbCcDdEeFfGgHhIiJjKkLlMmNnOoPpQqRr
SsTtUuVvWwXxYyZz 123456789 {¿¡@#$£&*!?}

David Buck
2000

$6 KOMBO
bucket of thigh
& a smidgen of pigeon

AaBbCcDdEeFfGgHhIiJjKkLlMmNnOoPpQqRr
SsTtUuVvWwXxYyZz 123456789 (!@#$%&*)

David Buck
2003

Your beauty is beyond compare
"my happiness depends on you."
I COULD NEVER LOVE AGAIN

AaBbCcDdEeFfGgHhIiJjKkLlMmNnOoPpQqRrSsTt
UuVvWwXxYyZz 123456789 {¿¡«@#$£&*»!?}

info@sparkytype.com

HEY, WHO'S WATCHING THE ALPACAS? they're freakin' everywhere! ROUND'M UP, KIDS or it's bedtime & no wages.

Farmer

David Buck
2004

Farmer comes with an extra set of capital letters as OpenType Titling Alternates.

SparkyType

AaBbCcDdEeFfGgHhIiJjKkLlMmNnOoPpQqRrSsTtUuVv
WwXxYyZz 123456789 ABCDEFGHIJKLMNOPQRSTUVWXYZ

Captain's Log: rolling with my HOMIEZ we badly require the MIDNIGHT emergency PIE-RUN

AaBbCcDdEeFfGgHhIiJjKkLlMmNnOo
PpQqRrSsTtUuVvWwXxYyZz 123456

info@sparkytype.com

LATE-BREAKING NEWS
Work is Boring
There aren't enough hours in the day.

ABCDEFGHIJKLMNOPQRSTUVWXYZ 123456789
abcdefghijklmnopqrstuvwxyz (!@#$%&*;)

JAR OF BRAIN
Taught a lesson by ninja teens
UNDERGROUND

Regular

AaBbCcDdEeFfGgHhIiJjKkLlMmNnOoPpQqRrSsTt
UuVvWwXxYyZz 123456789{¿¡«@#$£&*»!?}

Shadow

AaBbCcDdEeFfGgHhIiJjKkLlMmNnOoPpQqRr

David Buck
2001

Lowery Auto's fill style was intended to facilitate layouts on non-white backgrounds, but is a useful font in its own right.

A unique effect can be created by offsetting the fill style a small amount behind the regular style. This gives the impression of a mis-registered stencil or screen print.

LET ME FIX YOUR
HOLDEN
CHEERS, CUZ
REPAIRS
KILL THE RUST

Regular

A A B B C C D D E E F F G G H H I I J J K K L L M M N N O O
P P Q Q R R S S T T U U V V W W X X Y Y Z Z 1 2 3 4 5 6 7 8 9

Fill

A A B B C C D D E E F F G G H H I I J J K K L L M M N N O O P

info@sparkytype.com

KINDA CLUMPY

curl your lashes & clean the wand regularly

LIPSTICK ON YOUR MOLAR

AaBbCcDdEeFfGgHhIiJjKkLlMmNnOoPpQqRrSsTtUuVvWwXxYyZz 123456789

PEANUCKLE
Declare thumb war
Victory

AaBbCcDdEeFfGgHhIiJjKkLlMmNnOoPp
QqRrSsTtUuVvWwXxYyZz 123456789

Nisswa was inspired by the overabundance of cowboy-style signage in Northern Minnesota. These two styles are interchangeable for an authentic hand-picked effect.

RIP VAN WINKLE WAS MAD SLEEPY & WASTED 20 YEARS NAPPIN' SEIZE THE DAY GRAB SOMETHING MOUSTACHE

Plain

ABCDEFGHIJKLMNOPQRSTUVWXYZ 123456789?!@$%*

Fancy

ABCDEFGHIJKLMNOPQRSTUVWXYZ 123456789?!@$%*

Lovers in the air

fairy bread or cupcakes?

Best Halloween Ever!

- piles of candy, all wrapped

AABBCCDDEEFFGGHHIIJJKKLLMM
NNOOPPQQRRSSTTUUVVWWXXYZ

abcdefghijklmnopqrstuvwxyz ab-cdefghijk lmnopqrs tuvwxyz

Panhandler

David Buck
2003

Panhandler comes loaded with OpenType features, including contextual swash characters, an alternate swash uppercase set, and ligatures for common letter pairs to help replicate a hand-drawn effect.

SparkyType

David Buck
2005

While the geometry of Propane's upright styles is industrial strength, the italics' mixture of upright and slanted lines adds an unlikely beauty to the family.

Propane is confident enough to work at small sizes and interesting enough to be used as large as you like.

BURNING-HOT

there's no better way to grill

Can I ask you a question?

PRIVATELY.

"Who ate all the pies?"

Someone has to replace them

Regular

ABCDEFGHIJKLMNOPQRSTUVWXYZ 1234567890
abcdefghijklmnopqrstuvwxyz {¿i@$£&*!?}

Italic

AaBbCcDdEeFfGgHhIiJjKkLlMmNnOoPpQqRrSsTtUuVvWw

Bold

AaBbCcDdEeFfGgHhIiJjKkLlMmNnOoPpQqRrSsTtUuVv

Bold Italic

AaBbCcDdEeFfGgHhIiJjKkLlMmNnOoPpQqRrSsTtUuVv

I'M BAD

YOU KNOW IT

"GRUESOME DETAILS"

FASTPLANT

©MCMXVII (1987)

MAG RIMS

Ruby

David Buck
2005

Ruby comes with two additional highlighting styles for adding that precious sparkle.

Regular
ABCDEFGHIJKLMNOPQRSTUVWXYZ 123456789

Highlight
ABCDEFGHIJKLMNOPQRSTUVWXYZ 123456789

Shines
ABCDEFGHIJKLMNOPQRSTUVWXYZ 123456789

SparkyType

JEALOUSY
What, are you nuts?
He's my personal trainer.

ABCDEFGHIJKLMNOPQRSTUVWXYZ 1234567890
abcdefghijklmnopqrstuvwxyz {¿¡@$£&*!?}

Wait in line
STEADY

Regular

ABCDEFGHIJKLMNOPQRSTUVWXYZ1234567
abcdefghijklmnopqrstuvwxyz{¿¡@$£*?}

Light

ABCDEFGHIJKLMNOP
QRSTUVWXYZ1234567

Bold

ABCDEFGHIJKLMNOP
QRSTUVWXYZ123456

info@sparkytype.com

A tish is noi a pet
I WANT DOGS
of my own
Pinscher
gnawed CDs
wrecking machine

ABCDEFGHIJKLMNOPQRSTUVWXYZ 1234567
abcdefghijklmnopqrstuvwxyz {¿¡@$£&*!?}

Suitcase Type Foundry

Suitcase Type Foundry

WWW.SUITCASETYPE.COM

Suitcase is an independent Czech type foundry
established in Prague in 2003. The foundry designs
and produces high-quality fonts for the widest
typographic use. There are more than 200 weights
of original designs available. All of the high-quality
Suitcase fonts have accented characters with
corresponding kerning pairs for setting most
of the Latin-character languages. Suitcase
also offers custom type design services.

Suitcase Type Foundry
Soběslavská 27
130 00 Prague 3
Czech Republic

mail@suitcasetype.com
www.suitcasetype.com

ABCDEFGHIJKLMNOPQRSTUV
WXYZ&1234567890AABBCCD
EEFFGGHHIIJJKKLLMMNNOO
PQQRRSSTTUUVVWWXXYYYZ
Z&1234567890AABBCCDDEE
FFGGHHIIJJKKLLMMNNOOPPQ
QRRSSTTUUVVWWXXYYZZ&1
234567890AABBCCDDEEFFGG
HHIIJJKKLLMMNNOOPPQQRRS
STTUVVWWXXYYZZ&12345
67890ABCDEFGHIJKLMNOPQ
RSTUVWXYZ&1234567890AB
CDEFGHIJKLMNOPQRSTUVWX

Orgovan

Tomáš Brousil
2004

Orgovan's typical capitals were designed for versatile use on storefront and shop advertisements.

Slightly cut-off strokes at the beginning and end are characteristic, giving the font a certain softness and spontaneity. This model can be handled and used in many ways. It can be adapted for different uses, from small text to the biggest on the house fronts.

The base typeface of the Orgovan family is Brush, a font meant to demonstrate free writing with a flat brush. This style has been published since the early 1960s in Czechoslovak sign painter's handbooks.

Thanks to the many alterations of the character construction and a wider inner design, the font is easily readable, even at small sizes. Orgovan is excellent for even the most demanding typographic settings.

Entire family consists of Brush, Fat Cap, Flower Power, Hairy, Punk, and Rounded.

Suitcase

Pavel Teimer/Tomáš Brousil
1967/2006

AaBbCcDdEeFfG

Font is one of the most important elements of brand visualization. Suitable font makes it easy to distinguish your corporate identity

Font is one of the most important elements of brand visualization. Suitable font makes it easy to distinguish your corporate identity from

Font is one of the most important elements of brand visualization. Suitable font makes it easy to distinguish your corporate

Font is one of the most important elements of brand visualization. Suitable font makes it easy to distinguish your corporate identity from

Tomáš Brousil
2006

AaBbCcDdEeFfG

Font is one of the most important elements of brand visualization. Suitable font makes it easy to distinguish your corporate

Font is one of the most important elements of brand visualization. Suitable font makes it easy to distinguish your corporate identity

Font is one of the most important elements of brand visualization. Suitable font makes it easy to distinguish your

Font is one of the most important elements of brand visualization. Suitable font makes it easy to distinguish your corporate identity

Tomáš Brousil
2006

AaBbCcDdEeFfG

Font is one of the most important elements of brand visualization. Suitable font makes it easy to distinguish your corporate

Font is one of the most important elements of brand visualization. Suitable font makes it easy to distinguish your corporate

Font is one of the most important elements of brand visualization. Suitable font makes it easy to distinguish your

Font is one of the most important elements of brand visualization. Suitable font makes it easy to distinguish your corporate identity

Tomáš Brousil
2006

AaBbCcDdEeFfG

Font is one of the most important elements of brand visualization. Suitable font makes it easy to distinguish your corporate

Font is one of the most important elements of brand visualization. Suitable font makes it easy to distinguish your corporate

Font is one of the most important elements of brand visualization. Suitable font makes it easy to distinguish your

Font is one of the most important elements of brand visualization. Suitable font makes it easy to distinguish your corporate

mail@suitcasetype.com

A B C D E F G H I J K L M N O P Q R S T U V W X Y Z Æ Ŋ Ð IJ Œ Ø Þ Á Ă Â Ä À Ā Ą
Å Ã Ć Č Ĉ Ç Ð Ď É Ě Ě Ê Ë È Ē Ę Ğ Ĝ Ġ Ĥ Ħ Í Ï Î Ï Ì Ī Į Ĩ Ĵ Ķ Ĺ Ľ Ł Ł Ń Ň
Ñ Ņ Ñ Ó Ŏ Ô Ö Ò Ő Ō Õ Ŕ Ř Ŗ Ś Š Ŝ Ş Ş Ŧ Ť Ţ Ú Ŭ Û Ü Ù Ű Ū Ų Ů Ũ Ŵ Ý Ŷ Ÿ Ź Ž Ż Æ Ø

a b c d e f g h i j k l m n o p q r s t u v w x y z æ ŋ ð ß ij œ ø þ á ă â ä à ā ą å ã ç
ć č ĉ ď ď é ě ě ê ë è ē ę ğ ĝ ġ ĥ ħ í ï î ï ì ī į ĩ ĵ ķ ĺ ľ ļ ł ń ň ņ ñ ó ŏ ô ö
ő ō õ ŕ ř ŗ ś š ŝ ş ş ŧ ť ţ ú ŭ û ü ù ű ū ų ů ũ ŵ ý ŷ ÿ ź ž ż æ ø *ff fb fh fi fj fk fl ft ffb ffh ffi ffj ffk ffl* ſ a b c d e è
f g h i j k l m n o p q r s t u v w x y z *a b c d e f g h i j k l m n o p q r s t u v w x y z* $ ¢ £ ¥ ƒ € # ¤

0 1 2 3 4 5 6 7 8 9 0 0 1 2 3 4 5 6 7 8 9 $ ¢ £ ¥ ƒ € # 0 1 2 3 4 5 6 7 8 9 0 1 2 3 4 5
6 7 8 9 0 1 2 3 4 5 6 7 8 9 $ ¢ £ ¥ ƒ € # % ‰ / ^ ~ · + ± < = > | ¦ × ÷ − ∂ μ π Δ Π Σ Ω √ ∞
∫ ≈ ≠ ≤ ≥ ◊ ¬ ℮ ℓ ° ª º _ – — - ' " " « ‹ › » , „ " ' ` , . : ; … ? ¿ ! ¡ ( ) [ ] { } / \ * · § † ‡ ¶ ©
℗ ® ™ @ 0 1 2 3 4 5 6 7 8 9 ( ) + - = . , 0 1 2 3 4 5 6 7 8 9 ( ) + - = . , 0 1 2 3 4 5 6 7
8 9 ¼ ½ ¾ ⅛ ⅜ ⅝ ⅞ ⅓ ⅔ ¿ ¡ « » ‹ › — – - @ ? ! ¿ ¡ ° ' " § & ´ ˘ ˇ ` ˆ ˙ ¨ ˝ ˛ ˚ ˜ ¯

← ↑ → ↓ ↖ ↗ ↘ ↙ ↔ ↕ ▲ △ ▴ ▵ ▶ ▷ ▸ ▹ ▼ ▽ ▾ ▿ ◀ ◁ ◂ ◃ ● ○ ◑ ◒
■ □ ▪ ▫ ◎ ◉ ● ◇ ◆ ◈ ⊠ ✂ ❶ ❷ ❸ ❹ ❺ ❻ ❼ ❽ ❾ ❿ ① ② ③ ④ ⑤ ⑥ ⑦ ⑧ ⑨ ⑩ ℰ & ▤ ❋ ✦ ✚ ✢ ⊞

Res

Pavel Teimer/Tomáš Brousil
1967/2006

Typographer and graphic design-er Pavel Teimer (1935–1970) drew this modern roman and italics in 1967. When drawing this typeface, he took inspiration from the types of Walbaum and Didot rather than from Bodoni. He reevaluated these elemen-tary models of modern type in a rather individual way. He adjusted both height and width proportions and modified details of strokes, thus breaking away from these historical models. Teimer's antiqua has less body contrast: the whole construction of letters is softer and more lively. The rather wide propor-tions of the italics–which stand out with their calm, measured rhythm–were set by the purpose of the typeface, which was meant to be used in two-character ma-trices. Long serifs are a typical feature present throughout the typeface.

In 1967, Teimer's antiqua was submitted to the Czechoslovak Grafotechna type foundry with a full set of elementary glyphs, numerals, and diacritics. Unfortunately, the face was never manufactured.

At the beginning of 2005, Suitcase decided to rehabilitate this gem of Czech typography. As a template for digitization, the designers used a booklet entitled, "Teimer's antiqua– a design of modern type roman and italics," by Jan Solpera and Klára Kvízová from 1992. The model contains an elementary set of roman and italics types, including numerals and the ampersand.

Thanks to its fine, light construc-tion, the original digitized design remains the family's lightest member. Several heavier weights were added later. The family now consists of Light, Light Italic, Medium, Medium Italic, Semibold, Semibold Italic, Bold, and Bold Italic.

Dederon Light

Tomáš Brousil
2005

Entire family consists of 8 fonts. Shown here are Light and Light Italic.

AaBbCcDdEeFfGg

Font is one of the most important elements of brand visualization. Suitable font makes it easy to distinguish your corporate identity from

Font is one of the most important elements of brand visualization. Suitable font makes it easy to distinguish your corporate identity from

FONT IS ONE OF THE MOST IMPORTANT ELEMENTS OF BRAND VISUALIZATION. SUITABLE FONT MAKES IT EASY TO DISTINGUISH

FONT IS ONE OF THE MOST IMPORTANT ELEMENTS OF BRAND VISUALIZATION. SUITABLE FONT MAKES IT EASY TO DISTINGUISH YOUR CORPORATE

Dederon Regular

Tomáš Brousil
2005

Entire family consists of 8 fonts. Shown here are Regular and Italic.

AaBbCcDdEeFfGg

Font is one of the most important elements of brand visualization. Suitable font makes it easy to distinguish your corporate identity from

Font is one of the most important elements of brand visualization. Suitable font makes it easy to distinguish your corporate identity from

FONT IS ONE OF THE MOST IMPORTANT ELEMENTS OF BRAND VISUALIZATION. SUITABLE FONT MAKES IT EASY TO DISTINGUISH

FONT IS ONE OF THE MOST IMPORTANT ELEMENTS OF BRAND VISUALIZATION. SUITABLE FONT MAKES IT EASY TO DISTINGUISH YOUR

Dederon Semibold

Tomáš Brousil
2005

Entire family consists of 8 fonts. Shown here are Semibold and Semibold Italic.

AaBbCcDdEeFfGg

Font is one of the most important elements of brand visualization. Suitable font makes it easy to distinguish your corporate identity from

Font is one of the most important elements of brand visualization. Suitable font makes it easy to distinguish your corporate identity from

FONT IS ONE OF THE MOST IMPORTANT ELEMENTS OF BRAND VISUALIZATION. SUITABLE FONT MAKES IT EASY TO DISTIN

FONT IS ONE OF THE MOST IMPORTANT ELEMENTS OF BRAND VISUALIZATION. SUITABLE FONT MAKES IT EASY TO DISTINGUISH

Dederon Bold

Tomáš Brousil
2005

Entire family consists of 8 fonts. Shown here are Bold and Bold Italic.

AaBbCcDdEeFfG

Font is one of the most important elements of brand visualization. Suitable font makes it easy to distinguish your corporate identity

Font is one of the most important elements of brand visualization. Suitable font makes it easy to distinguish your corporate identity from

FONT IS ONE OF THE MOST IMPORTANT ELEMENTS OF BRAND VISUALIZATION. SUITABLE FONT MAKES IT EASY TO DISTIN

FONT IS ONE OF THE MOST IMPORTANT ELEMENTS OF BRAND VISUALIZATION. SUITABLE FONT MAKES IT EASY TO DISTINGUISH

AaBbCcDdEeFfGgH

Dederon Sans Light

Tomáš Brousil
2005

Entire family consists of 8 fonts. Shown here are Light and Light Italic.

Font is one of the most important elements of brand visualization. Suitable font makes it easy to distinguish your corporate identity from

Font is one of the most important elements of brand visualization. Suitable font makes it easy to distinguish your corporate identity from

FONT IS ONE OF THE MOST IMPORTANT ELEMENTS OF BRAND VISUALIZATION. SUITABLE FONT MAKES IT EASY TO DISTINGUISH YOUR CORPORATE IDENTITY FROM

FONT IS ONE OF THE MOST IMPORTANT ELEMENTS OF BRAND VISUALIZATION. SUITABLE FONT MAKES IT EASY TO DISTINGUISH YOUR CORPORATE IDENTITY FROM

AaBbCcDdEeFfGgH

Dederon Sans Regular

Tomáš Brousil
2005

Entire family consists of 8 fonts. Shown here are Regular and Italic.

Font is one of the most important elements of brand visualization. Suitable font makes it easy to distinguish your corporate identity from

Font is one of the most important elements of brand visualization. Suitable font makes it easy to distinguish your corporate identity from

FONT IS ONE OF THE MOST IMPORTANT ELEMENTS OF BRAND VISUALIZATION. SUITABLE FONT MAKES IT EASY TO DISTINGUISH YOUR CORPORATE IDENTITY FROM

FONT IS ONE OF THE MOST IMPORTANT ELEMENTS OF BRAND VISUALIZATION. SUITABLE FONT MAKES IT EASY TO DISTINGUISH YOUR CORPORATE IDENTITY FROM

AaBbCcDdEeFfGg

Dederon Sans Semibold

Tomáš Brousil
2005

Entire family consists of 8 fonts. Shown here are Semibold and Semibold Italic.

Font is one of the most important elements of brand visualization. Suitable font makes it easy to distinguish your corporate identity from

Font is one of the most important elements of brand visualization. Suitable font makes it easy to distinguish your corporate identity from

FONT IS ONE OF THE MOST IMPORTANT ELEMENTS OF BRAND VISUALIZATION. SUITABLE FONT MAKES IT EASY TO DISTINGUISH YOUR CORPORATE IDENTITY FROM

FONT IS ONE OF THE MOST IMPORTANT ELEMENTS OF BRAND VISUALIZATION. SUITABLE FONT MAKES IT EASY TO DISTINGUISH YOUR CORPORATE IDENTITY FROM

AaBbCcDdEeFfGg

Dederon Sans Bold

Tomáš Brousil
2005

Entire family consists of 8 fonts. Shown here are Bold and Bold Italic

Font is one of the most important elements of brand visualization. Suitable font makes it easy to distinguish your corporate identity from

Font is one of the most important elements of brand visualization. Suitable font makes it easy to distinguish your corporate identity from

FONT IS ONE OF THE MOST IMPORTANT ELEMENTS OF BRAND VISUALIZATION. SUITABLE FONT MAKES IT EASY TO DISTINGUISH YOUR CORPORATE IDENTITY FROM

FONT IS ONE OF THE MOST IMPORTANT ELEMENTS OF BRAND VISUALIZATION. SUITABLE FONT MAKES IT EASY TO DISTINGUISH YOUR CORPORATE IDENTITY FROM

Suitcase

AaBbCcDdEeFfGgHh

Font is one of the most important elements of brand visualization. Suitable font makes it easy to distinguish your corporate identity from rival companies. Custom designed fonts represent a fitted solution completely respecting client needs. Usage of custom fonts supports an advanced visual culture of the corporate design. We offer two possibilities to achieve original custom fonts. Either by redesigning typefaces from the offer of our type foundry or by designing new typeface according to client

ABCDEFGHIJKLMNOPQRSTUVWXYZ&abcdefghijklm
nopqrstuvwxyz0123456789fiflffßÞþĐđ()[]{}@.,:;/
\#/½¼'¾³²†‡°$¢£¥€§•·¶®©™'"*µ∂∑∏∩∫°°+=<>±÷≤
≥|∞!?¿¡¬√ƒ~≈«»…·-—""''„÷<>^_%‰ÁÂÄÀÅĄĀÃÆ
ÁáăâäàāąåãæǽĆČÇĊĆćĉċçĈĎÐďđÉĚÊËĔĖÈĘáěêë
ëèèęĜĞĠĢĝğġģĤĦĥħ(ĬĨÍÏÌİĪĮ)ıíìïìıĭĩīįĴĵJĶĸĹĽĿĻ
ŁĺľŀļŃŇÑŅ·ŋ·ňñņʼnŊÓÔÖÒŐŌÕØǾŒóôöòőōõøǿŔŘ
ŕřŚŠŞŜŞšŝşŞšŤŢŦťţtŧÚÛÜÙŰŪŮŲŴúûüùűūůųŴ
ŵÝŶŸýŷÿŹŽŻźžżż←↖↑↗→↘↓↙↺↻↵↩↪⇐⇑⇒⇓⇔...

AaBbCcDdEeFfGgHh

AaBbCcDdEeFfGgHh

AaBbCcDdEeFfGgHh

AaBbCcDdEeFfGgHh

AaBbCcDdEeFfGgHh

AaBbCcDdEeFfGgH

Vafle™

Suitcase Type Cooperation. Marek Pistora

Vafle

Marek Pistora/Tomáš Brousil
1997/2006

In the sixth issue of *Zivel* magazine, published in 1997, Vafle, a face by Marek Pistora, first appeared. The inspiration for its title was rather straightforward: the face came to life through a digitization of the insignia on Luftwaffe airplanes, where it originally would have conformed to some Deutsche Industrie-Norm. Vafle is soulless, purely utilitarian, and plain. Two versions were soon born–Vafle round and angular.

At the turn of 2005 and 2006, Suitcase decided to give Vafle a redesign. It was necessary to carry out some minor corrections of proportions and weight in the uppercase, lowercase, and numerals. The designers added missing glyphs to the character set, as well as accented characters of common Latin script languages. The resulting face is to be known as Vafle Classic. A stencil version adopts a new and complex morphology.

The family also includes new members: Vafle Blindy exposes its blind inner parts of letters, and Vafle Scratch features a scratched finish. Vafle Shadow casts a tiny elegant shadow and may be used alone or as a base for Vafle Classic. The monospace version with fixed character width of all glyphs is called Vafle Mono. Vafle Tape has diagonals instead of oblong shapes, thus giving the impression of characters composed of folded tape. Vafle Small Caps contributes to the family with a set of small caps which have the same x-height as lowercase. Vafle Condensed and Vafle Extended are, of course, the classic condensed and extended variants. Vafle Egyptienne has slab serifs, thus adding a serif variant to this sans family. Arrows, frames, and other glyphs come in the Vafle Picto cut.

Vafle is a perfect companion for the design of magazines, books, posters, or complete corporate systems.

Suitcase

Tomáš Brousil
2004

Entire family consists of 16 fonts. Shown here are Book, Book Italic, Book Small Caps, and Book Condensed.

AaBbCcDdEeFfGg

Font is one of the most important elements of brand visualization. Suitable font makes it easy to distinguish your corporate identity from

Font is one of the most important elements of brand visualization. Suitable font makes it easy to distinguish your corporate identity from

Font is one of the most important elements of brand visualization. Suitable font makes it easy to distinguish your corporate identity from

Font is one of the most important elements of brand visualization. Suitable font makes it easy to distinguish your corporate identity from rival companies. Custom

Stanislav Maršo/Tomáš Brousil
1956/2004

Entire family consists of 16 fonts. Shown here are Text, Text Italic, Text Small Caps, and Text Condensed.

AaBbCcDdEeFfGg

Font is one of the most important elements of brand visualization. Suitable font makes it easy to distinguish your corporate identity from

Font is one of the most important elements of brand visualization. Suitable font makes it easy to distinguish your corporate identity from

Font is one of the most important elements of brand visualization. Suitable font makes it easy to distinguish your corporate

Font is one of the most important elements of brand visualization. Suitable font makes it easy to distinguish your corporate identity from rival companies. Custom

Tomáš Brousil
2004

Entire family consists of 16 fonts. Shown here are Book Bold, Book Bold Italic, Book Small Caps Bold, and Book Bold Condensed.

AaBbCcDdEeFfG

Font is one of the most important elements of brand visualization. Suitable font makes it easy to distinguish your corporate identity from

Font is one of the most important elements of brand visualization. Suitable font makes it easy to distinguish your corporate identity from

Font is one of the most important elements of brand visualization. Suitable font makes it easy to distinguish

Font is one of the most important elements of brand visualization. Suitable font makes it easy to distinguish your corporate identity from

Tomáš Brousil
2004

Entire family consists of 16 fonts. Shown here are Text Bold, Text Bold Italic, Text Small Caps Bold, and Text Bold Condensed.

AaBbCcDdEeFfG

Font is one of the most important elements of brand visualization. Suitable font makes it easy to distinguish your corporate identity

Font is one of the most important elements of brand visualization. Suitable font makes it easy to distinguish your corporate identity

Font is one of the most important elements of brand visualization. Suitable font makes it easy to distinguish

Font is one of the most important elements of brand visualization. Suitable font makes it easy to distinguish your corporate identity from

RePublic

Tomáš Brousil
2004

The RePublic font family is a reinterpreted digitized version of the Public font by Stanislav Marso, published by Grafotechna in 1956.

It is a wonderful and proven font for newspaper and magazine setting. A high mid-height and clearly distinguishable characters with open forms guarantee perfect readability in small sizes, even if printed by the worst printers using the worst quality papers.

Delicately processed characters please the eye, even in poster sizes.

A B C D E F G H I J K L M N O P Q R S T U V W X Y Z Æ Ŋ Đ IJ Œ Ø Þ Á Ă Â Ä À Ā Ą Å Ã

Ć Č Ĉ Ç Đ Ď É Ě Ĕ Ê Ë Ė È Ē Ę Ğ Ĝ Ġ Ġ Ħ Í Ĭ Î Ï Ì Į Ī Ĵ Ķ Ĺ Ľ Ļ Ł Ń Ň Ņ Ñ Ó Ŏ Ô

Ö Ò Ő Ō Õ Ŕ Ř Ŗ Ś Š Ŝ Ş Ţ Ť Ţ Ú Ŭ Û Ü Ù Ű Ū Ų Ů Ũ Ŵ Ý Ŷ Ÿ Ź Ž Ż a b c d e f g h i j

k l m n o p q r s t u v w x y z æ ŋ ð ß ij œ ø þ á ă â ä à ā ą å ã ç ć č ĉ ď é ě ĕ ê ë è

ē ę ğ ĝ ġ ġ ħ í ĭ î ï ì į ī ij ĵ ķ ĺ ľ ļ ł ń ň ņ ñ ó ŏ ô ö ò ő ō õ ŕ ř ŗ ś š ŝ ş ţ ť ţ ú ŭ û

ü ù ű ū ų ů ũ ŵ ý ŷ ÿ ź ž ż A B C D E F G H I J K L M N O P Q R S T U V W X Y Z Æ Ŋ Đ SS IJ

Œ Ø Þ Á Ă Â Ä À Ā Ą Å Ã Ç Ć Č Ĉ Ċ Đ Ď É Ě Ĕ Ê Ë Ė È Ē Ę Ğ Ĝ Ġ Ġ Ħ Í Ĭ Î Ï Ì Į Ī Ĵ Ķ Ĺ Ľ

Ļ Ł Ń Ň Ņ Ñ Ó Ŏ Ô Ö Ò Ő Ō Õ Ŕ Ř Ŗ Ś Š Ŝ Ş Ţ Ť Ţ Ú Ŭ Û Ü Ù Ű Ū Ų Ů Ũ Ŵ Ý Ŷ Ÿ Ź Ž Ż fi

fl ffi ffl a b c d e f g h i j k l m n o p q r s t u v w x y z $ ¢ £ ¥ ƒ € # ¤ 0 1 2 3

4 5 6 7 8 9 0 1 2 3 4 5 6 7 8 9 0 1 2 3 4 5 6 7 8 9 % ‰ / ^ ~ · + ± < = > | ¦ × ÷ − ∂ µ

π Π Σ √ ∞ ∫ ≈ ≠ ≤ ≥ ¬ ° ª º _ – — - ‚ " " « ‹ › » „ " ' ' , . : ; … ? ¿ ! ¡ ( ) [ ] { } / \ * • § † ‡

¶ © Ⓟ ® ™ @ 0 1 2 3 4 5 6 7 8 9 (. , -) / 0 1 2 3 4 5 6 7 8 9 (. , -) ¼ ½ ¾ &

´ ˘ ˇ ¸ ˆ ¨ ˙ ` ˝ ¯ ˛ ˚ ˜ ↑ ↗ → ↘ ↙ ← ↖ ↕ ↔ ↨ ○ □ ⊗ ⊠ ◉ ◼ ● ■ ○ □ ● ▫

• ▪ ■ ▷ △ ◁ ▽ ▷ △ ◁ ▽ ▶ ▲ ◀ ▼ ▶ ▲ ◀ ▶ ▲ ◀ ▼ ★ ① ② ③ ④ ⑤ ⑥

⑦ ⑧ ⑨ ⑩ ❶ ❷ ❸ ❹ ❺ ❻ ❼ ❽ ❾ ❿ ✻ ✺ ❋ ❀ ✄ ☼ ⛅ ☁ ☁ ☂ ☈ ❄ ☽ ☁

Suitcase

Tomáš Brousil
2003

Entire family consists of 50 fonts. Shown here are Extra Condensed Thin, Extra Condensed Light, Extra Condensed Regular, Extra Condensed Semibold, Extra Condensed Bold, Condensed Thin, Condensed Light, Condensed Regular, Condensed Semibold, Condensed Bold, Medium Thin, Medium Light, Medium Regular, Medium Semibold, Medium Bold, Extended Thin, Extended Light, Extended Regular, Extended Semibold, Extended Bold, Extra Extended Thin, Extra Extended Light, Extra Extended Regular, Extra Extended Semibold, and Extra Extended Bold.

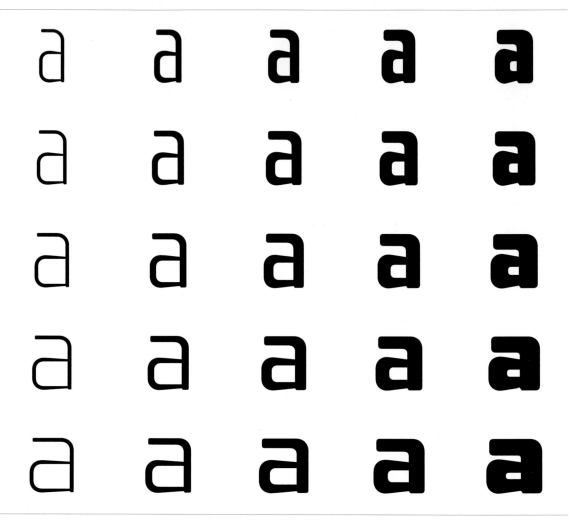

Fishmonger MR

Tomáš Brousil
2003

Entire family consists of 50 fonts. Shown here are Plain and Italic.

Font is one of the most important elements of brand visualization. Suitable font makes it easy to distinguish your corporate identity from rival companies. Custom designed fonts represent a fitted solution completely respecting client needs. Usage of custom fonts supports an advanced visual culture of the corporate design. We offer two possibilities to achieve original custom fonts. Either by redesigning typefaces from the offer of our type foundry or by designing new typeface according to client requirements. Every order needs a tailor-made approach, therefore primarily we make an

Font is one of the most important elements of brand visualization. Suitable font makes it easy to distinguish your corporate identity from rival companies. Custom designed fonts represent a fitted solution completely respecting client needs. Usage of custom fonts supports an advanced visual culture of the corporate design. We offer two possibilities to achieve original custom fonts. Either by redesigning typefaces from the offer of our type foundry or by designing new typeface according to client requirements. Every order needs a tailor-made approach, therefore primarily we make an

mail@suitcasetype.com

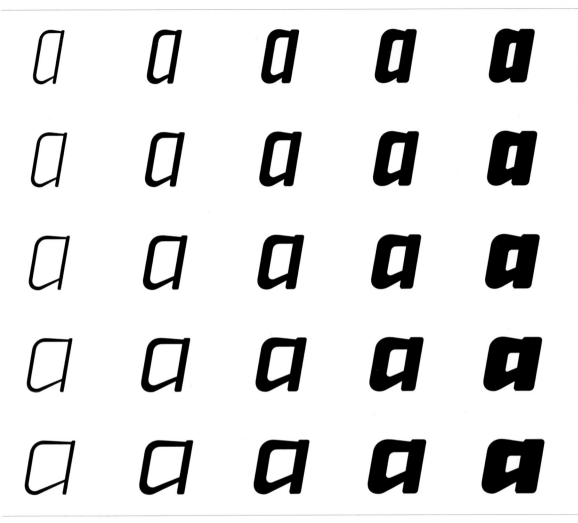

Fishmonger

Tomáš Brousil
2003

Entire family consists of 50 fonts. Shown here are Extra Condensed Thin Italic, Extra Condensed Light Italic, Extra Condensed Regular Italic, Extra Condensed Semibold Italic, Extra Condensed Bold Italic, Condensed Thin Italic, Condensed Light Italic, Condensed Regular Italic, Condensed Semibold Italic, Condensed Bold Italic, Medium Thin Italic, Medium Light Italic, Medium Regular Italic, Medium Semibold Italic, Medium Bold Italic, Extended Thin Italic, Extended Light Italic, Extended Regular Italic, Extended Semibold Italic, Extended Bold Italic, Extra Extended Thin Italic, Extra Extended Light Italic, Extra Extended Regular Italic, Extra Extended Semibold Italic, and Extra Extended Bold Italic.

ABCDEFGHIJKLMNOPQRSTUVWXYZ& abcd
efghijklmnopqrstuvwxyz0123456789
fi fl ff ffi ffl fj ffj ft ß þ Þ Ð đ ( ) [ ] { } @ . , : ; / \ # ½ ¼ ¹ ¾ ³
² † ‡ ° $ ¢ £ ¥ € § • · ¶ ® © ™ ' ' " * µ ∂ Σ Π ∫ ª º + − × = < >
± ≠ ≤ ≥ ¦ ¦ ∞ ! ? ¿ ¡ ¬ √ ƒ ~ ≈ « » … - - – — " " " ' ' ' , , ÷ ¤ < > ^ _
% ‰ Á Ä Â Ä À Ā Ą Å Å Æ á ä â à ā ą å ã æ Ć Č Ĉ Ċ ć č ç
ĉ ċ Ď Ī ď ō Ĕ Ē Ê Ė Ë È Ę é ĕ ě ê ê è ē ę ğ ĝ ġ ġ Ğ Ĝ Ġ
ħ ĥ Ħ ij jj ĵ Í Ï Î İ Ì Ū Į Ī í ï î ì ì ī ī Ĵ ĵ Ķ ķ Ł Ĺ Ľ Ļ Ŀ ł ĺ ľ ļ ŀ Ń Ñ
Ň Ñ ń ň ņ ñ Ó Ō Ô Ö Ò Õ Ő Ọ Œ ó ō ô ò ò ó ō õ ō œ Ŕ Ř Ŗ
ŕ ř ŗ Ś Š Ŝ Ş ś š ŝ ş Ť Ţ Ŧ ţ ŧ ŧ Ú Ū Û Ù Ǔ Ū Ų Ů Ū ú û
ü ù ű ū ų ů ū Ŵ ŵ Ý Ŷ Ÿ ý ŷ ÿ Ź Ż Ž ź ż ž

Fishmonger MR

Tomáš Brousil
2004

ABCDEFGHIJKLMNOPQRSTUVWXYZ& abcd
efghijklmnopqrstuvwxyz0123456789
fi fl ff ffi ffl fj ffj ft ß þ Þ Ð đ ( ) [ ] { } @ . , : ; / \ # ½ ¼ ¹ ¾ ³
² † ‡ ° $ ¢ £ ¥ € § • · ¶ ® © ™ ' ' " * µ ∂ Σ Π ∫ ª º + − × = < >
± ≠ ≤ ≥ ¦ ¦ ∞ ! ? ¿ ¡ ¬ √ ƒ ~ ≈ « » … - - – — " " " ' ' ' , , ÷ ¤ < > ^ _
% ‰ Á Ä Â Ä À Ā Ą Å Å Æ á ä â à ā ą å ã æ Ć Č Ĉ Ċ ć č ç
ĉ ċ Ď Ī ď ě Ĕ Ē Ê Ė Ë È Ę é ĕ ě ê ê è ē ę ğ ĝ ġ ġ Ğ Ĝ Ġ
ħ ĥ Ħ ij jj ĵ Í Ï Î İ Ì Ū Į Ī í ï î ì ì ī ī Ĵ ĵ Ķ ķ Ł Ĺ Ľ Ļ Ŀ ł ĺ ľ ļ ŀ Ń Ñ
Ň Ñ ń ň ņ ñ Ó Ō Ô Ö Ò Õ Ő Ọ Œ ó ō ô ò ò ó ō õ ō œ Ŕ Ř Ŗ
ŕ ř ŗ Ś Š Ŝ Ş ś š ŝ ş Ť Ţ Ŧ ţ ŧ ŧ Ú Ū Û Ù Ǔ Ū Ų Ů Ū ú û
ü ù ű ū ų ů ū Ŵ ŵ Ý Ŷ Ÿ ý ŷ ÿ Ź Ż Ž ź ż ž

Suitcase

THE SAN

ABCDEFGHIJKLMNOPQR

ABCDEFGHIJKLMNOPQRSTUVWXYZÆŊĐIJŒ ƏÞÁĂÂÄÀĀĄÅÃĆČĈÇĐ
ĎÉĚÊËÈĒĘĞĜĢĦÍĬÎÏÌĪĮĨĴĶĹĽĻŁŃŇŅÑÓŎÔÖÒŐŌÕŘŖŚŠŞ
ŞŦŤŢÚŬÛÜÙŰŪŲŮŨŴÝŶŸŹŽŻÆ ƏABCDEFGHIJKLMNOPQRSTUVWX
YZÆŊĐIJŒ ƏÞÁĂÂÄÀĀĄÅÃÇĆČĈĈĐĎÉĚÊËÈĒĘĞĜĢĦÍĬÎÏÌĪĮĨĴ
ĶĹĽĻŁŃŇŅÑÓŎÔÖÒŐŌÕŘŖŖŚŠŞŞŦŤŢÚŬÛÜÙŰŪŲŮŨŴÝŶŸŹŽŻÆ ə

$ ¢ £ ¥ ƒ € # ¤ º 0 1 2 3 4 5 6 7 8 9 # ‰ ‰ / ^ ~ · + ± < = > | ¦ × ÷ − ∂ µ π Δ Π Σ
Ω √ ∞ ∫ ≈ ≠ ≤ ≥ ° ‖ ° ‗ — – - ' " " « ‹ › » , „ "' ' , . · … ? ¿ ! ¡ [ ] [ ] { } / \
* • § † ‡ ¶ © ℗ ® ™ ® ¹ ² ³ ½ ¼ ¾   ← ↑ → ↓

TIKSLAS YRA PUOSELĖTI

TIKSLAS YRA PUOSELĖTI

KATArine

Font is one of the most important elements of brand visualization. Suitable font makes it easy to distinguish your corporate identity from rival companies. Custom designed fonts represent a fitted

Font is one of the most important elements of brand visualization. Suitable font makes it easy to distinguish your corporate identity from rival companies. Custom

Font is one of the most important elements of brand visualization. Suitable font makes it easy to distinguish your corporate identity from rival companies. Custom

Font is one of the most important elements of brand visualization. Suitable font makes it easy to distinguish your corporate identity from rival companies. Custom

Font is one of the most important elements of brand visualization. Suitable font makes it easy to distinguish your corporate identity from rival companies. Custom

Font is one of the most important elements of brand visualization. Suitable font makes it easy to distinguish your corporate identity from

Font is one of the most important elements of brand visualization. Suitable font makes it easy to distinguish your corporate identity from rival companies. Custom designed fonts represent a fitted

Font is one of the most important elements of brand visualization. Suitable font makes it easy to distinguish your corporate identity from rival companies. Custom

Font is one of the most important elements of brand visualization. Suitable font makes it easy to distinguish your corporate identity from rival companies. Custom designed fonts represent a fitted

Font is one of the most important elements of brand visualization. Suitable font makes it easy to distinguish your corporate identity from rival companies. Custom

Font is one of the most important elements of brand visualization. Suitable font makes it easy to distinguish your corporate identity from rival companies. Custom

Font is one of the most important elements of brand visualization. Suitable font makes it easy to distinguish your corporate identity from rival companies. Custom

FONT IS ONE OF THE MOST IMPORTANT ELEMENTS OF BRAND VISUALIZATION. SUITABLE FONT MAKES IT EASY TO DISTINGUISH YOUR CORPORATE IDENTITY FROM RIVAL COMPANIES. CUSTOM DESIGNED FONTS REPRESENT

FONT IS ONE OF THE MOST IMPORTANT ELEMENTS OF BRAND VISUALIZATION. SUITABLE FONT MAKES IT EASY TO DISTINGUISH YOUR CORPORATE IDENTITY FROM RIVAL COMPANIES. CUSTOM

FONT IS ONE OF THE MOST IMPORTANT ELEMENTS OF BRAND VISUALIZATION. SUITABLE FONT MAKES IT EASY TO DISTINGUISH YOUR CORPORATE IDENTITY FROM RIVAL COMPANIES. CUSTOM DESIGNED FONTS REPRESENT

FONT IS ONE OF THE MOST IMPORTANT ELEMENTS OF BRAND VISUALIZATION. SUITABLE FONT MAKES IT EASY TO DISTINGUISH YOUR CORPORATE IDENTITY FROM RIVAL COMPANIES. CUSTOM

FONT IS ONE OF THE MOST IMPORTANT ELEMENTS OF BRAND VISUALIZATION. SUITABLE FONT MAKES IT EASY TO DISTINGUISH YOUR CORPORATE IDENTITY FROM

FONT IS ONE OF THE MOST IMPORTANT ELEMENTS OF BRAND VISUALIZATION. SUITABLE FONT MAKES IT EASY TO DISTINGUISH YOUR CORPORATE IDENTITY FROM

FONT IS ONE OF THE MOST IMPORTANT ELEMENTS OF BRAND VISUALIZATION. SUITABLE FONT MAKES IT EASY TO DISTINGUISH YOUR CORPORATE IDENTITY FROM RIVAL COMPANIES. CUSTOM

FONT IS ONE OF THE MOST IMPORTANT ELEMENTS OF BRAND VISUALIZATION. SUITABLE FONT MAKES IT EASY TO DISTINGUISH YOUR CORPORATE IDENTITY FROM

FONT IS ONE OF THE MOST IMPORTANT ELEMENTS OF BRAND VISUALIZATION. SUITABLE FONT MAKES IT EASY TO DISTINGUISH YOUR CORPORATE IDENTITY FROM

FONT IS ONE OF THE MOST IMPORTANT ELEMENTS OF BRAND VISUALIZATION. SUITABLE FONT MAKES IT EASY TO DISTINGUISH YOUR CORPORATE IDENTITY FROM

Katarine Family

Tomáš Brousil
2003

The Katarine family is ideal for book covers, posters, jobbing prints, programs, monographic prints, catalogs, and journal compositions. When the cold austerity of the grotesque is not appropriate but its simplicity and readability are called for, Katarine is the answer.

Entire family consists of 24 fonts. Shown here are Light, Light Bold, Light Italic, Light Bold Italic, PC Light, PC Light Bold, SC Light, SC Light Bold, Medium, Medium Bold, Medium Italic, Medium Bold Italic, PC Medium, PC Medium Bold, SC Medium, SC Medium Bold, Bold, Bold Bold, Bold Italic, Bold Bold Italic, PC Bold, PC Bold Bold, SC Bold, and SC Bold Bold.

Suitcase

Tomáš Brousil
2004

The idea for the Botanika font family came from the thought of a text version of the Magion font. Characters were originally designed according to the same proportional principles but were later modified for better readability. Certain identical attributes of the pattern were retained: for example, the one-sided upper serif in the i and the one-sided lower serif in the l. By lowering middle height, a new original nature of the font was boosted.

The italics, as compared to the roman, are slightly compressed. Although they have the same austere elegance, they are reasonably distinctive for highlighting text.

The alternative faces allow for interesting diversification of typesetting with uncommon variations of the basic font characters. On the other hand, more traditional proportions give more emphasis to lettering. Botanika also contains proportional old style figures.

Such a complex family design includes small capitals as standard. The height of the small caps is slightly bigger than the middle height of the basic roman font characters. Therefore, it does not look smaller in mixed typesetting. Numbers and math and currency cahracters were also designed with the same middle height.

A nonproportional (monospaced) version was designed as a 10 pitch font, which means that 10 characters with a 10-point height fit into a one-inch width. The drawing of individual characters then fits into 60% of an em square. Italics were then designed in the same style.

Botanika Lite Regular

The idea for creating Botanika font family came from the thought of text version of Magion font. Characters were originally designed according to the same proportional principles but later of course modified for better readability. Certain identical attributes of

Botanika Lite Italic

The idea for creating Botanika font family came from the thought of text version of Magion font. Characters were originally designed according to the same proportional principles but later of course modified for better readability. Certain identical attributes of the pattern are

Botanika Altenate Lite Regular

The idea for creating Botanika font family came from the thought of text version of Magion font. Characters were originally designed according to the same proportional principles but later of course modified for better readability. Certain identical attributes of

Botanika Small Caps Lite Regular

THE IDEA FOR CREATING BOTANIKA FONT FAMILY CAME FROM THE THOUGHT OF TEXT VERSION OF MAGION FONT. CHARACTERS WERE ORIGINALLY DESIGNED ACCORDING TO THE SAME PROPORTIONAL PRINCIPLES BUT LATER OF COURSE MODIFIED FOR BETTER READABILITY. CERTAIN IDENTICAL ATTRIBUTES OF

Botanika Demi Regular

The idea for creating Botanika font family came from the thought of text version of Magion font. Characters were originally designed according to the same proportional principles but later of course modified for better readability. Certain identical attributes of

Botanika Demi Italic

The idea for creating Botanika font family came from the thought of text version of Magion font. Characters were originally designed according to the same proportional principles but later of course modified for better readability. Certain identical attributes of

Botanika Altenate Demi Regular

The idea for creating Botanika font family came from the thought of text version of Magion font. Characters were originally designed according to the same proportional principles but later of course modified for better readability. Certain identical attributes of

Botanika Small Caps Demi

THE IDEA FOR CREATING BOTANIKA FONT FAMILY CAME FROM THE THOUGHT OF TEXT VERSION OF MAGION FONT. CHARACTERS WERE ORIGINALLY DESIGNED ACCORDING TO THE SAME PROPORTIONAL PRINCIPLES BUT LATER OF COURSE MODIFIED FOR BETTER READABILITY.

Botanika Lite Bold

The idea for creating Botanika font family came from the thought of text version of Magion font. Characters were originally designed according to the same proportional principles but later of course modified for better readability.

Botanika Lite Bold Italic

The idea for creating Botanika font family came from the thought of text version of Magion font. Characters were originally designed according to the same proportional principles but later of course modified for better readability. Certain

Botanika Altenate Lite Bold

The idea for creating Botanika font family came from the thought of text version of Magion font. Characters were originally designed according to the same proportional principles but later of course modified for better readability.

Botanika Small Caps Lite Bold

THE IDEA FOR CREATING BOTANIKA FONT FAMILY CAME FROM THE THOUGHT OF TEXT VERSION OF MAGION FONT. CHARACTERS WERE ORIGINALLY DESIGNED ACCORDING TO THE SAME PROPORTIONAL PRINCIPLES BUT LATER OF COURSE MODIFIED FOR

Botanika Demi Bold

The idea for creating Botanika font family came from the thought of text version of Magion font. Characters were originally designed according to the same proportional principles but later of course modified for better

Botanika Demi Bold Italic

The idea for creating Botanika font family came from the thought of text version of Magion font. Characters were originally designed according to the same proportional principles but later of course modified for better

Botanika Altenate Demi Bold

The idea for creating Botanika font family came from the thought of text version of Magion font. Characters were originally designed according to the same proportional principles but later of course modified for better

Botanika Small Caps Demi Bold

THE IDEA FOR CREATING BOTANIKA FONT FAMILY CAME FROM THE THOUGHT OF TEXT VERSION OF MAGION FONT. CHARACTERS WERE ORIGINALLY DESIGNED ACCORDING TO THE SAME PROPORTIONAL PRINCIPLES BUT LATER OF COURSE

mail@suitcasetype.com

Botanika Mono Lite Regular

The idea for creating Botanika font family came from the thought of text version of Magion font. Characters were originally designed according to the

Botanika Mono Lite Italic

The idea for creating Botanika font family came from the thought of text version of Magion font. Characters were originally designed according to the

Bo

Botanika Lite

Tomáš Brousil
2004

Entire family consists of 24 fonts. Shown here are Lite, Lite Italic, Lite Alt, Lite SC, Lite Mono, and Lite Mono Italic.

Botanika Mono Demi Regular

The idea for creating Botanika font family came from the thought of text version of Magion font. Characters were originally designed according to the

Botanika Mono Demi Italic

The idea for creating Botanika font family came from the thought of text version of Magion font. Characters were originally designed according to the

ta

Botanika Demi

Tomáš Brousil
2004

Entire family consists of 24 fonts. Shown here are Demi, Demi Italic, Demi Alt, Demi SC, Demi Mono, and Demi Mono Italic.

Botanika Mono Lite Bold

The idea for creating Botanika font family came from the thought of text version of Magion font. Characters were originally designed according to the

Botanika Mono Lite Bold Italic

The idea for creating Botanika font family came from the thought of text version of Magion font. Characters were originally designed according to the

ni

Botanika Lite Bold

Tomáš Brousil
2004

Entire family consists of 24 fonts. Shown here are Lite Bold, Lite Bold Italic, Lite Alt Bold, Lite SC Bold, Lite Mono Bold, and Lite Mono Bold Italic.

Botanika Mono Demi Bold

The idea for creating Botanika font family came from the thought of text version of Magion font. Characters were originally designed according to the

Botanika Mono Demi Bold Italic

The idea for creating Botanika font family came from the thought of text version of Magion font. Characters were originally designed according to the

ka

Botanika Demi Bold

Tomáš Brousil
2004

Entire family consists of 24 fonts. Shown here are Botanika Demi Bold, Demi Bold Italic, Demi Alt Bold, Demi SC Bold, Demi Mono Bold, and Demi Mono Bold Italic.

Suitcase

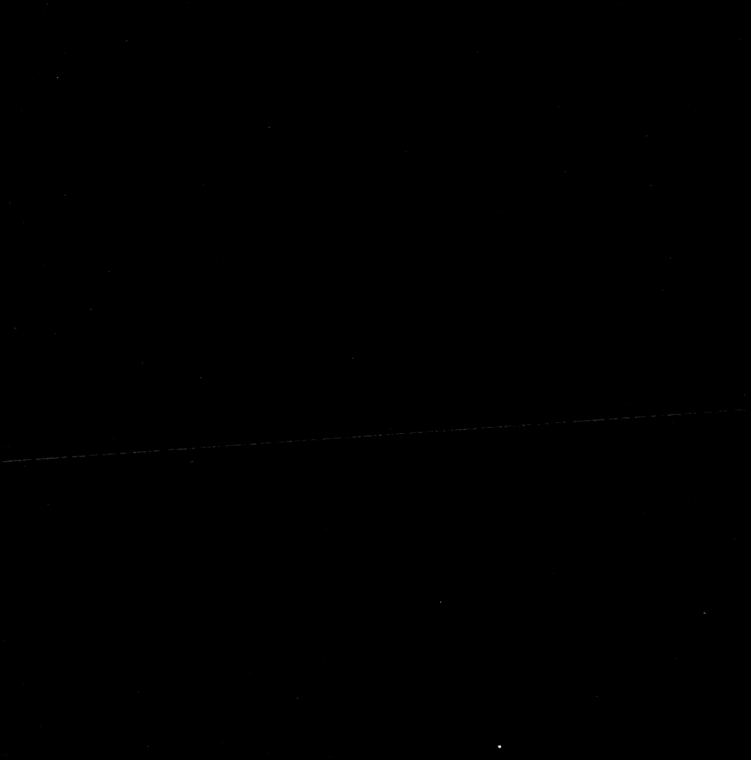

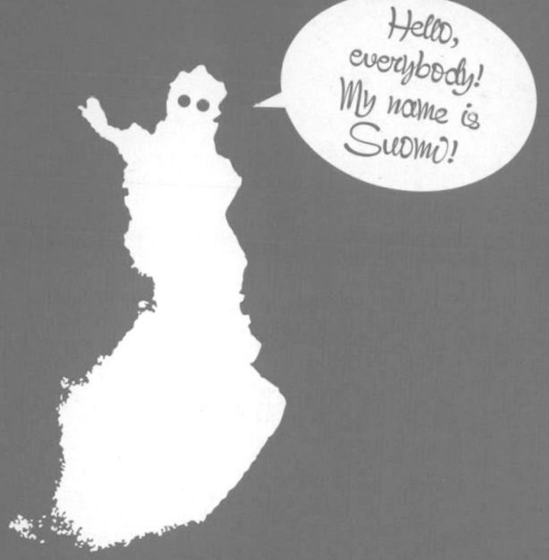
Hello, everybody! My name is Suomi!

www.type.fi
www.type.fi
www.type.fi
www.type.fi
www.type.fi
www.type.fi
www.type.fi
www.type.fi

Type Foundry

THE PARABOLIC CURVE of the set type above shows well the formula this typeface family was made with. This way, the weights are set optically in between each other, unlike the outdated 50% weight ratio. If you set the weights of Helvetica this way, instead of a parabolic curve, you produce a straight line.

This optical weight formula was created by Luc(as) de Groot when he made his extensive Thesis family. In his brilliant formula, the weight of the variant in the middle is the square root of the heavier and lighter weight squared:

$$a \qquad b \qquad c$$
$$a=b^2/c \quad b=\sqrt{ac} \quad c=b^2/a$$

SUOMI TYPE FOUNDRY is a company dedicated to creating high-quality typefaces. The company was founded by Tomi Haaparanta, who has been designing typefaces since 1990. Fonts by Haaparanta are already distributed by Linotype, Monotype, ITC, T-26, and Psy/Ops, and, in 2004, he decided to set up his own font foundry.

THE PHILOSOPHY of Suomi Type Foundry is to make extensive type families so the user has more to choose from. Too often, a designer finds a great typeface, but the weight is just not right. Most Suomi fonts come with an average of seven weights, so it is likely that a user will find the right weight. Also, Suomi does not wish to exclude any users, and strives to keep its range as versatile as possible, from comfortable types for text setting and signage type families to evocative headline fonts for advertising.

Suomi Script

Suomi Script

Tomi Haaparanta
2006

This OpenType font includes more than 1,600 ligatures.

An all new type design from Suomi Type Foundry!

Filled with Open Type stuff for those savvy programs.
(did you notice these ligatures?)

Basic character set

ðŁŽ̌!"№$%&'*()+,-/0123456789¹²³½¼¾:;<=>?@ABCDEFGHIJKL
MNOPQRSTUVWXYZ[\]^_`abcdefghijklmnopqrstuvwxyz{|}~ÄÅÇÉ
ÑÖÜáàâäãåçéèêëûîñôóòõúùûü†°¢£§•¶ß®©™´¨ÆØ±¼µº∞œø¿¡¬ƒ«»…
ÀÃÕŒœ–—""''÷ÿŸ/<>fifl‡·‚„‰ÂÊÁËÈÍÎÏÌÓÔÒÙÚÛÌˆ˜¯˘˙˚¸˝˛ˇ

Some of the ligatures

Ha Hb Hc Hd He Hf Hg Hh Hi Hj Hk Hl Hll Hm Hn Ho Hp Hq Hr Hs Ht Hu Hv Hw Hx Hy Hz Ca Cg Ch Ci Cl Co Cu Cy Ha Hb Hc Hd He
Hf Hg Hh Hi Hj Hk Hl Hm Hn Ho Hp Hq Hr Hs Ht Hu Hv Hw Hx Hy Hz Hä Hö Ka Kb Kc Kd Ke Kf Kg Kh Ki Kj Kk Kl Km Kn Ko Kp Kq
Kr Ks Kt Ku Kv Kw Kx Ky Kz Kä Kö Oa Ob Oc Od Odd Oe Of Og Oh Oi Oj Ok Ol Oll Om On Oo Op Oq Or Os Ot Ou Ov Ow Ox
Oy Oz Ra Rb Rc Rd Re Rf Rg Rh Ri Rj Rk Rl Rm Ru Ro Rp Rq Rr Rs Rt Ru Rv Rw Rx Ry Rz Rä Rö Qu aa ab ac ad ae af ag ah ai aj ak al all
am an ao ap aq ar as at au av aw ax ay az by ca cb cc cd ce cf cg ch ci cj ck cl cm cn co cp cq cr cs ct cu cv cw cx cy cz da db dc dd de
df dg dh di dj dk dl dm dn do dp dq dr ds dt du dv dw dx dy dz ea eb ec ed ee ef eg eh ei ej ek el ell em en eo ep eq er es et eu ev ew ex ey
ez fa fb fc fd fe ff fg fh fi fj fk fl fm fn fo fp fq fr fs ft fu fv fw fx fy fz ha hb hc hd he hf hg hh hi hj hk hl hm hn ho hp hq hr hs ht hu hv hw
hx hy hz ia ib ic id ie if iff ig ih ii ij ik il ill im in io ip iq ir is it iu iv iw ix iy iz ja jb jc jd je jf jg jh ji jj jk jl jm jn jo jp jq jr js jt ju jv jw jx
jy jz ka kb kc kd ke kf kg kh ki kj kk kl km kn ko kp kq kr ks kt ku kv kw kx ky kz la lb lc ld le lf lg lh li lj lk ll lm ln lo lp lq lr ls lt lu lv lw lx ly
lz ma mb mc md me mf mg mh mi mj mk ml mm mn mo mp mq mr ms mt mu mv mw mx my mz na nb nc nd ne nf nh ni nj nm nn nm nn no np nq nr
ns nt nu nv nw nx ny nz oa ob oc od oe of off og oh oi oj ok ol om on oo op oq or os ot ou ov ow ox oy oz sa sb sc sd se sf sg sh si sj sk
sl sm sn so sp sq sr ss st su sv sw sx sy sz sö sä ta tb tc td te tf tg th ti tj tk tl tm tn to tp tq tr ts tt tu tv tw tx ty tz ua ub uc ud ue uf ug
uh ui uj uk ul ull um un uo up uq ur us ut uu uv uw ux uy uz va vb vc vd ve vf vg vh vi vj vk vl vm vn vo vp vq vr vs vt vu vv vw vx vy
vz wa wb wc wd we wf wg wh wi wj wk wl wm wn wo wp wq wr ws wt wu ww www wx wy wz xa xb xc xd xe xf xg xh xi xj xk xl xm xn
xo xp xq xr xs xt xu xv xw xx xy xz ya yb yc yd ye yf yg yh yi yj yk yl yll ym yn yo yp yq yr ys yt yu yv yw yx yy yz yö yä za zb zc zd ze
zf zg zh zi zj zk zl zll zm zn zo zp zq zr zs zt zu zv zw zx zy zä zö äa äb äc äd äe äf äg äh äi äj äk äl äll äm än äo äp äq är äs
ät äu äv äw äx äy äz öa öb öc öd öe öf ög öh öi öj ök öl öll öm ön öö öp öq ör ös öt öu öv öw öx öy öz arr err irr orr wrr yrr ärr örr
for The the art day ing qu why well yell oo 000 01 02 03 04 05 06 07 08 09 10 11 12 13 14 15 16 17 18 19 50 51 52 35 45 55 56 57 58 59

Tang

Nobody has satisfactorily determined the origin of the word 'Suomi', which means Finland in the Finnish language. Some think that the word comes from the word 'suo' (swamp), since Finland is riddled with lakes and marsh lands. Others claim that it is derived from the Old Finnish word 'sauomi', which means 'a man', or 'people', and this theory is much more plausable than the first one. The word 'Finland' comes from the word 'Phoinikee' (pronounced 'Finikee'). The Phoenicans had a colony in the South-West parts of Finland some 3 000 years ago. The

Tang

Nobody has satisfactorily determined the origin of the word 'Suomi', which means Finland in the Finnish language. Some think that the word comes from the word 'suo' (swamp), since Finland is riddled with lakes and marsh lands. Others claim that it is derived from the Old Finnish word 'sauomi', which means 'a man', or 'people', and this theory is much more plausable than the first one. The word 'Finland' comes from the word 'Phoinikee' (pronounced 'Finikee'). The Phoenicans had a colony in the South-West parts of

Tang

Nobody has satisfactorily determined the origin of the word 'Suomi', which means Finland in the Finnish language. Some think that the word comes from the word 'suo' (swamp), since Finland is riddled with lakes and marsh lands. Others claim that it is derived from the Old Finnish word 'sauomi', which means 'a man', or 'people', and this theory is much more plausable than the first one. The word 'Finland' comes from the word 'Phoinikee' (pronounced 'Finikee'). The Phoenicans had a colony in the South-West parts of

Tang

Nobody has satisfactorily determined the origin of the word 'Suomi', which means Finland in the Finnish language. Some think that the word comes from the word 'suo' (swamp), since Finland is riddled with lakes and marsh lands. Others claim that it is de-rived from the Old Finnish word 'sauomi', which means 'a man', or 'people', and this theory is much more plausable than the first one. The word 'Finland' comes from the word 'Phoinikee' (pronounced 'Finikee'). The Phoenicans had a colony in the South-West

Tang

Nobody has satisfactorily determined the origin of the word 'Suomi', which means Finland in the Finnish language. Some think that the word comes from the word 'suo' (swamp), since Finland is rid-dled with lakes and marsh lands. Others claim that it is derived from the Old Finn-ish word 'sauomi', which means 'a man', or 'people', and this theory is much more plausable than the first one. The word 'Finland' comes from the word 'Phoinikee' (pronounced 'Finikee'). The Phoenicans

Tang

Nobody has satisfactorily determined the origin of the word 'Suomi', which means Finland in the Finnish language. Some think that the word comes from the word 'suo' (swamp), since Fin-land is riddled with lakes and marsh lands. Others claim that it is derived from the Old Finnish word 'sauomi', which means 'a man', or 'people', and this theory is much more plausable than the first one. The word 'Finland' comes from the word 'Phoinikee' (pro-

Tang

Nobody has satisfactorily de-termined the origin of the word 'Suomi', which means Finland in the Finnish language. Some think that the word comes from the word 'suo' (swamp), since Finland is riddled with lakes and marsh lands. Others claim that it is derived from the Old Finnish word 'sauomi', which means 'a man', or 'people', and this theory is much more plausable than the first one. The word 'Finland' comes from

Tang

Nobody has satisfactorily de-termined the origin of the word 'Suomi', which means Finland in the Finnish language. Some think that the word comes from the word 'suo' (swamp), since Finland is riddled with lakes and marsh lands. Others claim that it is derived from the Old Finnish word 'sauomi', which means 'a man', or 'people', and this theory is much more plausa-

Tang Type Family

Tang

Tomi Haaparanta
2003

The 7-weight Tang features roman, italic, and small-caps variants. An ultra-black version rounds out the family.

Suomi

Tang *Tang*

Nobody has satisfactorily determined the origin of the word 'Suomi', which means Finland in the Finnish language. Some think that the word comes from the word 'suo' (swamp), since Finland is riddled with lakes and marsh lands. Others claim that it is derived from the Old Finnish

word 'sauomi', which means 'a man', or 'people', and this theory is much more plausable than the first one. The word 'Finland' comes from the word 'Phoinikee' (pronounced 'Finikee'). The Phoenicans had a colony in the South-West parts of Finland some 3000 years ago. The

Tang

Nobody has satisfactorily determined the origin of the word 'Suomi', which means Finland in the Finnish language. Some think that the word comes from the word 'suo' (swamp), since Finland is riddled with lakes and marsh lands. Others claim that it is derived from

the Old Finnish word 'sauomi', which means 'a man', or 'people', and this theory is much more plausable than the first one. The word 'Finland' comes from the word 'Phoinikee' (pronounced 'Finikee'). The Phoenicans had a colony in the South-West parts of

Tang

Nobody has satisfactorily determined the origin of the word 'Suomi', which means Finland in the Finnish language. Some think that the word comes from the word 'suo' (swamp), since Finland is riddled with lakes and marsh lands. Others claim that it is

derived from the Old Finnish word 'sauomi', which means 'a man', or 'people', and this theory is much more plausable than the first one. The word 'Finland' comes from the word 'Phoinikee' (pronounced 'Finikee'). The Phoenicans had a colony in the South-West

Tang

Nobody has satisfactorily determined the origin of the word 'Suomi', which means Finland in the Finnish language. Some think that the word comes from the word 'suo' (swamp), since Finland is riddled with lakes and marsh lands. Others claim that it is

derived from the Old Finnish word 'sauomi', which means 'a man', or 'people', and this theory is much more plausable than the first one. The word 'Finland' comes from the word 'Phoinikee' (pronounced 'Finikee'). The Phoenicans had a colony in the South-

Tang

Nobody has satisfactorily determined the origin of the word 'Suomi', which means Finland in the Finnish language. Some think that the word comes from the word 'suo' (swamp), since Finland is riddled with lakes and marsh lands. Others

claim that it is derived from the Old Finnish word 'sauomi', which means 'a man', or 'people', and this theory is much more plausable than the first one. The word 'Finland' comes from the word 'Phoinikee' (pronounced 'Finikee'). The Phoenicans

Tang

Nobody has satisfactorily determined the origin of the word 'Suomi', which means Finland in the Finnish language. Some think that the word comes from the word 'suo' (swamp), since Finland is riddled with lakes and marsh

lands. Others claim that it is derived from the Old Finnish word 'sauomi', which means 'a man', or 'people', and this theory is much more plausable than the first one. The word 'Finland' comes from the word 'Phoinikee' (pro-

Tang

Nobody has satisfactorily determined the origin of the word 'Suomi', which means Finland in the Finnish language. Some think that the word comes from the word 'suo' (swamp), since Finland is riddled

with lakes and marsh lands. Others claim that it is derived from the Old Finnish word 'sauomi', which means 'a man', or 'people', and this theory is much more plausable than the first one. The word 'Finland' comes from

Tang *noun*

1 a strong taste, flavour, or smell; *a strong, characteristic tang of lemon.*

Tang *verb*

2 to make a loud ringing or clanging sound; *the brass bells are tanging.*

Tang *noun*

3 An algae eating surgeonfish commonly sited on reefs *(Acanthurus Coeruleus).*

Tang SCOSF Ultra Light

TANG

NOBODY HAS SATISFACTORILY DETERMINED THE ORIGIN OF THE WORD 'SUOMI', WHICH MEANS FINLAND IN THE FINNISH LANGUAGE. SOME THINK THAT THE WORD COMES FROM THE WORD 'SUO' (SWAMP), SINCE FINLAND IS RIDDLED WITH LAKES AND MARSH LANDS. OTHERS CLAIM THAT IT IS DERIVED FROM THE OLD FINNISH

WORD 'SAUOMI', WHICH MEANS 'A MAN', OR 'PEOPLE', AND THIS THEORY IS MUCH MORE PLAUSABLE THAN THE FIRST ONE. THE WORD 'FINLAND' COMES FROM THE WORD 'PHOINIKEE' (PRONOUNCED 'FINIKEE'). THE PHOENICANS HAD A COLONY IN THE SOUTH-WEST PARTS OF FINLAND SOME 3 000 YEARS AGO. THE PHOENICANS

Tang SCOSF Thin

TANG

NOBODY HAS SATISFACTORILY DETERMINED THE ORIGIN OF THE WORD 'SUOMI', WHICH MEANS FINLAND IN THE FINNISH LANGUAGE. SOME THINK THAT THE WORD COMES FROM THE WORD 'SUO' (SWAMP), SINCE FINLAND IS RIDDLED WITH LAKES AND MARSH LANDS. OTHERS CLAIM THAT IT IS DERIVED FROM THE OLD

FINNISH WORD 'SAUOMI', WHICH MEANS 'A MAN', OR 'PEOPLE', AND THIS THEORY IS MUCH MORE PLAUSABLE THAN THE FIRST ONE. THE WORD 'FINLAND' COMES FROM THE WORD 'PHOINIKEE' (PRONOUNCED 'FINIKEE'). THE PHOENICANS HAD A COLONY IN THE SOUTH-WEST PARTS OF FINLAND SOME 3 000 YEARS AGO.

Tang SCOSF Light

TANG

NOBODY HAS SATISFACTORILY DETERMINED THE ORIGIN OF THE WORD 'SUOMI', WHICH MEANS FINLAND IN THE FINNISH LANGUAGE. SOME THINK THAT THE WORD COMES FROM THE WORD 'SUO' (SWAMP), SINCE FINLAND IS RIDDLED WITH LAKES AND MARSH LANDS. OTHERS CLAIM THAT IT IS DERIVED FROM THE OLD

FINNISH WORD 'SAUOMI', WHICH MEANS 'A MAN', OR 'PEOPLE', AND THIS THEORY IS MUCH MORE PLAUSABLE THAN THE FIRST ONE. THE WORD 'FINLAND' COMES FROM THE WORD 'PHOINIKEE' (PRONOUNCED 'FINIKEE'). THE PHOENICANS HAD A COLONY IN THE SOUTH-WEST PARTS OF FINLAND SOME 3 000 YEARS AGO.

Tang SCOSF Book

TANG

NOBODY HAS SATISFACTORILY DETERMINED THE ORIGIN OF THE WORD 'SUOMI', WHICH MEANS FINLAND IN THE FINNISH LANGUAGE. SOME THINK THAT THE WORD COMES FROM THE WORD 'SUO' (SWAMP), SINCE FINLAND IS RIDDLED WITH LAKES AND MARSH LANDS. OTHERS CLAIM THAT IT IS DERIVED FROM THE OLD

FINNISH WORD 'SAUOMI', WHICH MEANS 'A MAN', OR 'PEOPLE', AND THIS THEORY IS MUCH MORE PLAUSABLE THAN THE FIRST ONE. THE WORD 'FINLAND' COMES FROM THE WORD 'PHOINIKEE' (PRONOUNCED 'FINIKEE'). THE PHOENICANS HAD A COLONY IN THE SOUTH-WEST PARTS OF FINLAND SOME 3 000 YEARS AGO.

Tang SCOSF Medium

TANG

NOBODY HAS SATISFACTORILY DETERMINED THE ORIGIN OF THE WORD 'SUOMI', WHICH MEANS FINLAND IN THE FINNISH LANGUAGE. SOME THINK THAT THE WORD COMES FROM THE WORD 'SUO' (SWAMP), SINCE FINLAND IS RIDDLED WITH LAKES AND MARSH LANDS. OTHERS CLAIM THAT

IT IS DERIVED FROM THE OLD FINNISH WORD 'SAUOMI', WHICH MEANS 'A MAN', OR 'PEOPLE', AND THIS THEORY IS MUCH MORE PLAUSABLE THAN THE FIRST ONE. THE WORD 'FINLAND' COMES FROM THE WORD 'PHOINIKEE' (PRONOUNCED 'FINIKEE'). THE PHOENICANS

Tang SCOSF Bold

TANG

NOBODY HAS SATISFACTORILY DETERMINED THE ORIGIN OF THE WORD 'SUOMI', WHICH MEANS FINLAND IN THE FINNISH LANGUAGE. SOME THINK THAT THE WORD COMES FROM THE WORD 'SUO' (SWAMP), SINCE FINLAND IS RIDDLED WITH LAKES AND MARSH

LANDS. OTHERS CLAIM THAT IT IS DERIVED FROM THE OLD FINNISH WORD 'SAUOMI', WHICH MEANS 'A MAN', OR 'PEOPLE', AND THIS THEORY IS MUCH MORE PLAUSABLE THAN THE FIRST ONE. THE WORD 'FINLAND' COMES FROM THE WORD 'PHOINIKEE' (PRO-

---

Tang SCOSF Black

TANG

NOBODY HAS SATISFACTORILY DETERMINED THE ORIGIN OF THE WORD 'SUOMI', WHICH MEANS FINLAND IN THE FINNISH LANGUAGE. SOME THINK THAT THE WORD COMES FROM THE WORD 'SUO' (SWAMP), SINCE FINLAND

IS RIDDLED WITH LAKES AND MARSH LANDS. OTHERS CLAIM THAT IT IS DERIVED FROM THE OLD FINNISH WORD 'SAUOMI', WHICH MEANS 'A MAN', OR 'PEOPLE', AND THIS THEORY IS MUCH MORE PLAUSABLE THAN THE FIRST ONE.

info@type.fi

There are many broken-faced typefaces around, **but this is** the first with 6 (SIX) weights!!

First with Weights!

First with Weights!

First with Weights!

First with Weights!

First with Weights!

First with Weights!

First with Weights!

Thaw

Tomi Haaparanta
2004

This broken-faced font family has 6 weights, with rough alternate styles to follow.

Thaw Thin

Thaw Light

Thaw Book

Thaw Medium

Thaw Bold

Thaw Black

Thaw Medium Rough

Suomi

Tomi Haaparanta
2005

This super-fat display typeface has 3 variants.

"Quality

of this pictoresque,

Stylish

new typeface

can be described as

finely tuned."

Tubby is a family of three variants with full character sets: Book, Italic and Swash Italic. It has even more character than good old Cooper Black.

DARE TO BE FAT!

Tubby Book

ðŁŽ!"№$‰&'*()+,-./0123456789¹²³½¼¾:;<=>?@ABCDEFGHIJKLMNOPQRSTUVWXYZ[\]^_` abcde
fghijklmnopqrstuvwxyz{|}~ÄÅÇÉÑÖÜáàâäãåçéèêëíìîïñóòôöõúùûü†°¢£§•¶ß®©™´¨ÆØ±
¥µₐₑæ¿¡¬ƒ«»…ÀÃÕŒœ––""''÷ÿŸ⁄€fiflßţ¢ł‡·‚„‰ÂÊÁËÈÍÎÏÌÓÔ€ÒÚÛÙ¹ˆ˜¯˘˙˚¸˝˛ˇ

Tubby Italic

ðŁŽ!"№$‰&'()+,-./0123456789¹²³½¼¾:;<=>?@ABCDEFGHIJKLMNOPQRSTUVWXYZ[\]^_` abcde
fghijklmnopqrstuvwxyz{|}~ÄÅÇÉÑÖÜáàâäãåçéèêëíìîïñóòôöõúùûü†°¢£§•¶ß®©™´¨ÆØ±¥
µₐₑæ¿¡¬ƒ«»…ÀÃÕŒœ––""''÷ÿŸ⁄€fiflßţ¢ł‡·‚„‰ÂÊÁËÈÍÎÏÌÓÔ€ÒÚÛÙ¹ˆ˜¯˘˙˚¸˝˛ˇ*

Tubby Swash Italic

ðŁŽ!"№$‰&'()+,-./0123456789¹²³½¼¾:;<=>?@ABCDEFGHIJKLMNOPQRSTUVWXYZ[\]^_` ab
cdefghijklmnopqrstuvwxyz{|}~ÄÅÇÉÑÖÜáàâäãåçéèêëíìîïñóòôöõúùûü†°¢£§•¶ß®©™´¨
ÆØ±¥µₐₑæ¿¡¬ƒ«»…ÀÃÕŒœ––""''÷ÿŸ⁄€fiflßţ¢ł‡·‚„‰ÂÊÁËÈÍÎÏÌÓÔ€ÒÚÛÙ¹ˆ˜¯˘˙˚¸˝˛ˇ*

Tee Franklin

Tee Franklin

Tomi Haaparanta
2001

Tee Franklin features roman and oblique styles in 7 weights.

Ultra

Tee Franklin Ultra Light

THE BRITISH VOGUE commissioned this typeface for their magazine re-design in 2001. After studying the originals of Morris Fuller Benton and the existing versions, this font was designed with all new thin weights. Just when the family was finished, Vogue informed that they had decided to use American Typewriter instead. Bastards. But here is a true classic typeface with a facelift. The

Thin

Tee Franklin Thin

THE BRITISH VOGUE commissioned this typeface for their magazine re-design in 2001. After studying the originals of Morris Fuller Benton and the existing versions, this font was designed with all new thin weights. Just when the family was finished, Vogue informed that they had decided to use American Typewriter instead. Bastards. But here is a true classic typeface with a

Light

Tee Franklin Light

THE BRITISH VOGUE commissioned this typeface for their magazine re-design in 2001. After studying the originals of Morris Fuller Benton and the existing versions, this font was designed with all new thin weights. Just when the family was finished, Vogue informed that they had decided to use American Typewriter instead. Bastards. But here is a true classic typeface

Book

Tee Franklin Book

THE BRITISH VOGUE commissioned this typeface for their magazine re-design in 2001. After studying the originals of Morris Fuller Benton and the existing versions, this font was designed with all new thin weights. Just when the family was finished, Vogue informed that they had decided to use American Typewriter instead. Bastards. But here is a true classic

Medium

Tee Franklin Medium

THE BRITISH VOGUE commissioned this typeface for their magazine re-design in 2001. After studying the originals of Morris Fuller Benton and the existing versions, this font was designed with all new thin weights. Just when the family was finished, Vogue informed that they had decided to use American Typewriter instead. Bastards. But here is

Bold

Tee Franklin Bold

THE BRITISH VOGUE commissioned this typeface for their magazine re-design in 2001. After studying the originals of Morris Fuller Benton and the existing versions, this font was designed with all new thin weights. Just when the family was finished, Vogue informed that they had decided to use American Typewriter instead. Bas-

Heavy

Tee Franklin Heavy

THE BRITISH VOGUE commissioned this typeface for their magazine re-design in 2001. After studying the originals of Morris Fuller Benton and the existing versions, this font was designed with all new thin weights. Just when the family was finished, Vogue informed that they had decided to use American Type-

Full character set

ðŁŽ!"#$%&'*()+,-/0123456789¹²³½¼¾:;<=>?@ABCDEFGHIJKLMNOPQRSTUVWXYZ[\
]^_`abcdefghijklmnopqrstuvwxyz{|}~ÄÅÇÉÑÖÜáàâäãåçéèêëíììñóòôöõúùûü†°¢£§•¶ß®
©™´¨ÆØ±¥µªºæø¿¡¬ƒ«»…ÀÃÕŒœ——""''÷ÿŸ⁄fifl‡·‚„‰ÂÊÁËÈÍÎÏÌÓÔⱤÒÚÛÙı^˜¯˘˙˚¸˝˛ˇ

Tee Franklin Ult. Li. Obl.

Ultra

TEE FRANKLIN has seven weights with obliques, the Heavy being just slightly heavier than the existing versions from Adobe and ITC, and moving down to totally new Ultra Light, using Luc(as) de Groots formula to keep the weights optically correct. The glyphs are the same as the Morris Fuller Benton's original from 1902, except for the upper case Q, which was re-designed with a loop in

Tee Franklin Thin Obl.

Thin

TEE FRANKLIN has seven weights with obliques, the Heavy being just slightly heavier than the existing versions from Adobe and ITC, and moving down to totally new Ultra Light, using Luc(as) de Groots formula to keep the weights optically correct. The glyphs are the same as the Morris Fuller Benton's original from 1902, except for the upper case Q, which was re-designed with a

Tee Franklin Light Obl.

Light

TEE FRANKLIN has seven weights with obliques, the Heavy being just slightly heavier than the existing versions from Adobe and ITC, and moving down to totally new Ultra Light, using Luc(as) de Groots formula to keep the weights optically correct. The glyphs are the same as the Morris Fuller Benton's original from 1902, except for the upper case Q, which was re-designed

Tee Franklin Book Obl.

Book

TEE FRANKLIN has seven weights with obliques, the Heavy being just slightly heavier than the existing versions from Adobe and ITC, and moving down to totally new Ultra Light, using Luc(as) de Groots formula to keep the weights optically correct. The glyphs are the same as the Morris Fuller Benton's original from 1902, except for the upper case Q, which

Tee Franklin Medium Obl.

Medium

TEE FRANKLIN has seven weights with obliques, the Heavy being just slightly heavier than the existing versions from Adobe and ITC, and moving down to totally new Ultra Light, using Luc(as) de Groots formula to keep the weights optically correct. The glyphs are the same as the Morris Fuller Benton's original from 1902, except for the upper case Q,

Tee Franklin Bold Obl.

Bold

TEE FRANKLIN has seven weights with obliques, the Heavy being just slightly heavier than the existing versions from Adobe and ITC, and moving down to totally new Ultra Light, using Luc(as) de Groots formula to keep the weights optically correct. The glyphs are the same as the Morris Fuller Benton's original from 1902, except for

Tee Franklin Heavy Obl.

Heavy

TEE FRANKLIN has seven weights with obliques, the Heavy being just slightly heavier than the existing versions from Adobe and ITC, and moving down to totally new Ultra Light, using Luc(as) de Groots formula to keep the weights optically correct. The glyphs are the same as the Morris Fuller Benton's original from 1902,

info@type.fi

TicTac

Tomi Haaparanta
1999

An axiometric typeface designed
for display uses, TicTac features
2 variants designed to be layered for two-tone effects. TicTac
is an all-cap font, with alternates
on upper- and lowercase glyphs.

Suomi

Full character set

BCDEFGHIJKLMNOPQRSTUVWXYZ[\]

TicTac Toe

Full character set

BCDEFGHIJKLMNOPQRSTUVWXYZ[\]

TicTac Back

Tomi Haaparanta
2002

This old style serif family includes 19 variants: 4 weights with lining and old style figures, and small caps, irregular, and handtooled styles.

This is That.

And That.

And That.

AND THAT.

AND THAT.

And That.

And That.

And That.

And That.

And That.

And That's that.

info@type.fi

That Light

ðŁŽ!"#$%&'°()+,-/0123456789¹²³½¼¾:;<=>¿@ABCDEFGHIJKLMNOPQRSTUVWXYZ[\]^_`abcdefghijklmnopqr stuvwxyz{|}~ÄÅÇÉÑÖÜáàâäãåçéèêëíìîïñóòôöõúùûü†°¢£§•¶ß®©™´¨ÆØ±¥µªºæøï¬ƒ«»…ÀÃÕŒœ—""''÷ÿŸ/◊fifl ‡·'‚„‰ÂÊÁËÈÍÎÏÌÓÔ◊ÒÚÛÙı^˜¯˘˙°¸˚˛ˇ

0123456789¹²³½¼¾

That Light Italic

ðŁŽ!"#$%&'°()+,-/0123456789¹²³½¼¾:;<=>¿@ABCDEFGHIJKLMNOPQRSTUVWXYZ[\]^_`abcdefghijklmnopqrst uvwxyz{|}~ÄÅÇÉÑÖÜáàâäãåçéèêëíìîïñóòôöõúùûü†°¢£§•¶ß®©™´¨ÆØ±¥µªºæøï¬ƒ«»…ÀÃÕŒœ—""''÷ÿŸ/◊fifl‡·'‚„‰ ÂÊÁËÈÍÎÏÌÓÔ◊ÒÚÛÙı^˜¯˘˙°¸˚˛ˇ

0123456789¹²³½¼¾

That Book

ðŁŽ!"#$%&'°()+,-/0123456789¹²³½¼¾:;<=>¿@ABCDEFGHIJKLMNOPQRSTUVWXYZ[\]^_`abcdefghijklmno pqrstuvwxyz{|}~ÄÅÇÉÑÖÜáàâäãåçéèêëíìîïñóòôöõúùûü†°¢£§•¶ß®©™´¨ÆØ±¥µªºæøï¬ƒ«»…ÀÃÕŒœ—""''÷ÿ Ÿ/◊fifl‡·'‚„‰ÂÊÁËÈÍÎÏÌÓÔ◊ÒÚÛÙı^˜¯˘˙°¸˚˛ˇ

0123456789¹²³½¼¾

That Book Italic

ðŁŽ!"#$%&'°()+,-/0123456789¹²³½¼¾:;<=>¿@ABCDEFGHIJKLMNOPQRSTUVWXYZ[\]^_`abcdefghijklmnopq rstuvwxyz{|}~ÄÅÇÉÑÖÜáàâäãåçéèêëíìîïñóòôöõúùûü†°¢£§•¶ß®©™´¨ÆØ±¥µªºæøï¬ƒ«»…ÀÃÕŒœ—""''÷ÿŸ/◊fi fl‡·'‚„‰ÂÊÁËÈÍÎÏÌÓÔ◊ÒÚÛÙı^˜¯˘˙°¸˚˛ˇ

0123456789¹²³½¼¾

That Medium

ðŁŽ!"#$%&'°()+,-/0123456789¹²³½¼¾:;<=>?@ABCDEFGHIJKLMNOPQRSTUVWXYZ[\]^_`abcdefgh
ijklmnopqrstuvwxyz{|}~ÄÅÇÉÑÖÜáàâãäåçéèêëíìîïñóòôõöúùûü†°¢£§•¶ß®©™´¨ÆØ±¥µªºæø¿¡¬ƒ«»…
ÀÃÕŒœ—""''÷ÿŸ/◊fifl‡·‚„‰ÂÊÁËÈÍÎÏÌÓÔ�ÒÚÛÙ¹ˆ˜¯˘˙˚¸˝˛ˇ`

0123456789¹²³½¼¾

That Medium Italic

*ðŁŽ!"#$%&'°()+,-/0123456789¹²³½¼¾:;<=>?@ABCDEFGHIJKLMNOPQRSTUVWXYZ[\]^_`abcdefghijklm
nopqrstuvwxyz{|}~ÄÅÇÉÑÖÜáàâãäåçéèêëíìîïñóòôõöúùûü†°¢£§•¶ß®©™´¨ÆØ±¥µªºæø¿¡¬ƒ«»…ÀÃÕŒœ—""
''÷ÿŸ/◊fifl‡·‚„‰ÂÊÁËÈÍÎÏÌÓÔ�ÒÚÛÙ¹ˆ˜¯˘˙˚¸˝˛ˇ`*

0123456789¹²³½¼¾

That Bold

**ðŁŽ!"#$%&'°()+,-/0123456789¹²³½¼¾:;<=>?@ABCDEFGHIJKLMNOPQRSTUVWXYZ[\]^_`abcde
fghijklmnopqrstuvwxyz{|}~ÄÅÇÉÑÖÜáàâãäåçéèêëíìîïñóòôõöúùûü†°¢£§•¶ß®©™´¨ÆØ±¥µªºæø
¿¡¬ƒ«»…ÀÃÕŒœ—""''÷ÿŸ/◊fifl‡·‚„‰ÂÊÁËÈÍÎÏÌÓÔ�ÒÚÛÙ¹ˆ˜¯˘˙˚¸˝˛ˇ`**

0123456789¹²³½¼¾

That Bold Italic

***ðŁŽ!"#$%&'°()+,-/0123456789¹²³½¼¾:;<=>?@ABCDEFGHIJKLMNOPQRSTUVWXYZ[\]^_`abcdef
ghijklmnopqrstuvwxyz{|}~ÄÅÇÉÑÖÜáàâãäåçéèêëíìîïñóòôõöúùûü†°¢£§•¶ß®©™´¨ÆØ±¥µªºæø¿¡¬ƒ«
»…ÀÃÕŒœ—""''÷ÿŸ/◊fifl‡·‚„‰ÂÊÁËÈÍÎÏÌÓÔ�ÒÚÛÙ¹ˆ˜¯˘˙˚¸˝˛ˇ`***

0123456789¹²³½¼¾

info@type.fi

That Open

ðŁŽ!"#$%&'°()+,-/0123456789¹²³¹⁄₂¼¾:;<=>¿@ABCDEFGHIJKLMNOPQRSTUVWXYZ[\]^_`abcdefgh
ijklmnopqrstuvwxyz{|}~ÄÅÇÉÑÖÜáàâäãåçéèêëíìîïñóòôöõúùûü†°¢£§•¶ß®©™´¨ÆØ±¥µªºæø¿i¬ƒ«»…
ÀÃÕŒœ—–""''÷ÿŸ/◊fifl‡·‚„‰ÂÊÁËÈÍÎÏÌÓÔ®ÒÚÛÙı ˆ˜¯˘˙°¸˛ˇ`
0123456789¹²³¹⁄₂¼¾

THAT SMALL CAPS

ðŁŽ!"#$%&'°()+,-/0123456789¹²³¹⁄₂¼¾:;<=>¿@ABCDEFGHIJKLMNOPQRSTUVWXYZ[\]^_`ABCDEFGHIJKLMNOPQRS
TUVWXYZ{|}~ÄÅÇÉÑÖÜÁÀÂÄÃÅÇÉÈÊËÍÌÎÏÑÓÒÔÖÕÚÙÛÜ†°¢£§•¶SS®©™´¨ÆØ±¥UªºÆØ¿I¬ƒ«»…ÀÃÕŒœ—–""''÷ŸŸ/◊FI
FL‡·‚„‰ÂÊÁËÈÍÎÏÌÓÔ®ÒÚÛÙı ˆ˜¯˘˙°¸˛ˇ`

THAT IRREGULAR

ðŁŽ!"#$%&'°()+,-/0123456789¹²³¹⁄₂¼¾:;<=>¿@ABCDEFGHIJKLMNOPQRSTUVWXYZ[\]^_`ABCDEFGHIJKLMNOPQRS
TUVWXYZ{|}~ÄÅÇÉÑÖÜÁÀÂÄÃÅÇÉÈÊËÍÌÎÏÑÓÒÔÖÕÚÙÛÜ†°¢£§•¶SS®©™´¨ÆØ±¥UªºÆØ¿I¬ƒ«»…ÀÃÕŒœ—–""''÷ŸŸ/◊
FIFL‡·‚„‰ÂÊÁËÈÍÎÏÌÓÔ®ÒÚÛÙı ˆ˜¯˘˙°¸˛ˇ`

NOBODY has satisfactorily determined the origin of the word 'Suomi', which means Finland in the Finnish language. Some think that the word comes from the word 'suo' (swamp), since Finland is riddled with lakes and marsh lands. Others claim that it is derived from the Old Finnish word 'sauomi', which means 'a man', or 'people', and this theory is much more plausable than the first one. The word 'Finland' comes from the word 'Phoinikee' (pronounced 'Finikee'). The Phoenicans had a colony in the South-West parts of Finland some 3000 years ago. The Phoenicans brought the varjag genes to the Finns.

Q Q Q Q

Q Q Q Q

Q Q Q Q

0 1 2 3 4 5 6 7 8 9

0 1 2 3 4 5 6 7 8 9

info@type.fi

Pannartz Book

from

❦ Suomi Type Foundry ❧

Pannartz Book is based on a type sample from Sweynheim & Pannartz from 1467. Even though Adolf Rusch had made a typeface in Antiqua style earlier, it still had such a heavy Gothic influence, that this typeface is considered to be the first actual Antiqua style font.

Each glyph of this font is first scanned to computer, then auto-traced and brought to font program, and then hand drawn on top of the auto-traced image to make the result to appear as though it's been printed in 14-16 points on a fairly rough paper.

Ðð Þþ Šš ¤ ! " № $ % & ' * ( ) + , - / 0 1 2 3 4 5 6 7 8 9 ¹ ² ³ ½ ¼ ¾ : ; < = > ? @
A B C D E F G H I J K L M N O P Q R S T U V W X Y Z [\ ] ^ _ `
a b c d e f g h i j k l m n o p q r s t u v w x y z { | } - Ä Å Ç É Ñ Ö Ü á à â ä ã å
é è ê ë í ì î ï ñ ó ò ô ö õ ú ù û ü ƒ ° ¢ £ § • ¶ ß ® © ™ ´ ¨ Æ Ø ± ¥ ∫ ª º æ ø ¿ ¡ ¬ ƒ « » …
À Á Õ Œ œ – — " " ' ' ÷ ÿ Ÿ / € ‹ › fi fl ffl ffi & st ♮ · ‚ „ ‰ Â Ê Á Ë È Í
Î Ï Ì Ó Ô Ò Ù Ú Û Ù ı ˆ ˜ ¯ ˘ ˙ ˚ ¸ ˝ ˛ ˇ

village

vllg.com

Hi!

Chester & Tracy Jenkins
2005

Galaxie
Polaris

646-654-1506

ABCDEFGHIJKLMNOPQRSTUVWXYZ
abcdefghijklmnopqrstuvwxyz
0123456789&0123456789

AÁÀÂÄÃÅĂĀĂÂÀÅĄΛÆÆÆBCĆĈČĊÇDĎĐEÉÈ
ÊËĚĒĔÊĖĚĘFGĠĜĜGĞĠGHÂĦḤHHIÍÌÎÏĨĬĪĬ ÎÌ ịJ
ĴKĶĶĶKLĹĽĻĻĻĻĿMMŅNŃÑÑŇŇŅŅŅŅOÓÒÔÖÕŎ
ŌŎŌŐÒǪǬǪØǾŒPQRŔŘ ̂RÞŖŖṚŘSŚŜŠ ̧SŞTŤŢ
Ţ ̧TŦUÚÙÛÜŨŮŬŪŬÛŰÙŲ ŒVWẂẀŴẄXYÝ ̀Y ̈Y ̂Y
ȲIJZŹŽŻÐŊÞƷǮ aáàâäãåăāăâàåąa áàâäãåăāăâ
àåqæǽæbcćĉčċçdďđeéèêëěēĕêèėěęfgǵĝğ ̃ǧġ
ġghĥħḥhҺɦιíìî ïĩĬī ̂î ̀ ijjĵkǩ ̧ķ ̧ĸkllĺľ ̧lׅׅ ׅl·łmṃnńǹ ñň ̀n ̣n
ŋoóòôöõŏōŏ ̂őòǫǭǫøǿœpqrŕř ̂r ̀rŗ ̣rῑsśŝšṣ ̧ṣßtťţ
ṭṭŧuúùûüũůŭūŭûűùųuŒvwẃẁŵ ̈xyýỳ ̈ÿ ̂y ̄yijzźžżðŋ
þʒ ̌ᵃᶜᵒᵃᵇᶜᵈᵉᶠᵍʰ ijklmnopqrstuvwxyz fi fi fl & ' ` ^ ¨ ~ ° ˇ ˉ -
˘ ˙ ˝ ˛ ' ` ^ ¨ ~ ° ˇ ˉ - ˘ ˙ ˝ ˛ . , ; .
. , : ; … ! ¡ ¡ ? ¿ ¿ ? ¡ ¡ * † ‡
§ ¶ ^ ~ _ _ _ ' " " " @ @ © ® ® Ⓟ ™ ℠ € $ ¢ £ ƒ ¥ ₡ ₢ ₣ £ ₦ Pts Rs ₩ ₪ ₮ ₱
#01234567890 0123456789 € $ ¢ £ ƒ ¥ ₡ ₢ ₣ £ ₦ pts
RS ₩ ₪ ₮ ₱ # 0 1 2 3 4 5 6 7 8 9 0 1 2 3 4 5 6 7 8 9 ⁰¹²³⁴⁵⁶⁷⁸⁹ + − =
⁽¹ ₀₁₂₃₄₅₆₇₈₉ + − = ₍₎ ₀₁₂₃₄₅₆₇₈₉ + − = ( ) / ¼ ½ ¾ % ‰ % ‰ № ¤
ℓ e ♭ ♮ ♯ ← → ↑ ↓ ↖ ↗ ↘ ↙ ● ○ • ■ □ ⊠ ▪ □ ⊠ ◀ ▶ ▲ ▽ ▼ ◀ ▲
☉ ★ ☀ ☽ ♲ ✿ ♻ ♠ ♣ ♥ ♦ ☀ ☁ ☁ ☂ ☂ ☔ ☇ ❄ + − ± × ÷ = ≠ ≈ < >
≤ ≥ + − × ÷ = < > μ π ¬ ∞ ∂ ∫ √ Δ Ω Π Σ ◇ ° ' ' " " ‚ ' " ‹ › « » ‹ › « » / \ |
‖ | ▪ · · - - - - – — ( ) [ ] { } ( ) ( ) [ ] { } ( )

Light

Light Italic

Book

Book Italic

Medium

Medium Italic

Bold

Bold Italic

Heavy

Heavy Itali-

646-654-1506

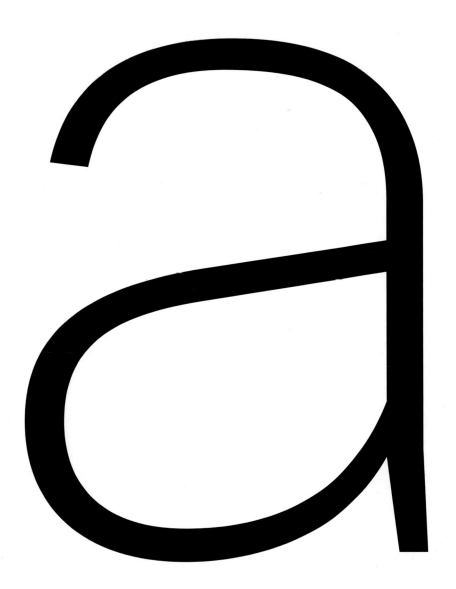

Village

Chester & Tracy Jenkins
2006

Galaxie Cassiopeia

646-654-1506

ABCDEFGHIJKLMNOPQRSTUVWXYZ
abcdefghijklmnopqrstuvwxyz
&0123456789

AÁÀÂÄÃÅĀĂĄÆBCĆĈČĊÇDĎÐEÉÈÊËĚĒĖ
ĘFĜ Ğ Ġ Ġ H Ĥ Ħ IÍÌÎÏĨĪİ ĮJĴ K Ķ Ł Ĺ Ľ Ļ Ŀ MNŃ
Ñ Ň Ņ O ÓÒÔ ÖÕ Ō Ŏ Ő Ø Œ P Q R Ŕ Ř Ŗ S ŚŜŠ Ş Ş T ŤŢ
Ŧ U ÚÙ Û Ü Ũ Ū Ů Ū Ŭ Ű Ų V W X Y Ý Ÿ Z Ź Ž Ż Ð Ŋ Þ a á à â
ã å ā ă ą a á à â ä ã å ā ă ą æ b c ć ĉ č ċ ç d ď đ e é è ê ë ě ē ė ę f
g ĝ ğ ġ ġ h ĥ ħ ı i í ì î ï ĩ ī i į j ĵ k ķ ĸ l ĺ ľ ļ ŀ ł m n ń ñ ň ņ o ó ò ô ö õ ō
ő ø œ p q r ŕ ř ŗ s ś ŝ š ş ş t ť ţ ŧ u ú ù û ü ũ ū ů ū ŭ ű ų v w x y ý ÿ z ź
ž ż ð ŋ þ & ´ ` ^ ~ ¯ ˘ ˙ ¨ ˚ ˝ ' ' ` , . . ˛ ´ ` ^ ~ ¯ ˘ ˙ ¨ ˚ ˝ ' ' ` ., :;
… ! ¡ ? ¿ ¿ ‽ ¡ ⸘ * † ‡ § ¶ ^ ~ _ ' " " ‴ @ © ® ℗ € $ ¢ £ ƒ ¥ # 0 1 2 3 4
5 6 7 8 9 % ‰ + − ± × ÷ = ≠ ≈ ‹ › ∂ ° ' ' " " , „ ' " ‹ › « » / \ | • - - - — —
— ( ) [ ] { } ⟨ ⟩

Aardvark Buzz Commonality Dervish Elegiac Fortifications
Guerilla Hiking Innocently Juveniles Keeling Laxity Millions
Neverending Occultations Phenomenally Quietly Rheostatic
Swedish Truncate Undulating Variety Whichever Xenophile
Yorubans Zarzuela aarappel buzzards commons devilishly
elegies fortitude guerilla hiking innocent juvenile keepsake
laxity millions never occult phenomenon quietly rheostatics
sweetish truncates undulation varietal whichever xenophile
yoruban zarzuela

Bold
Basic Bold

646-654-1506

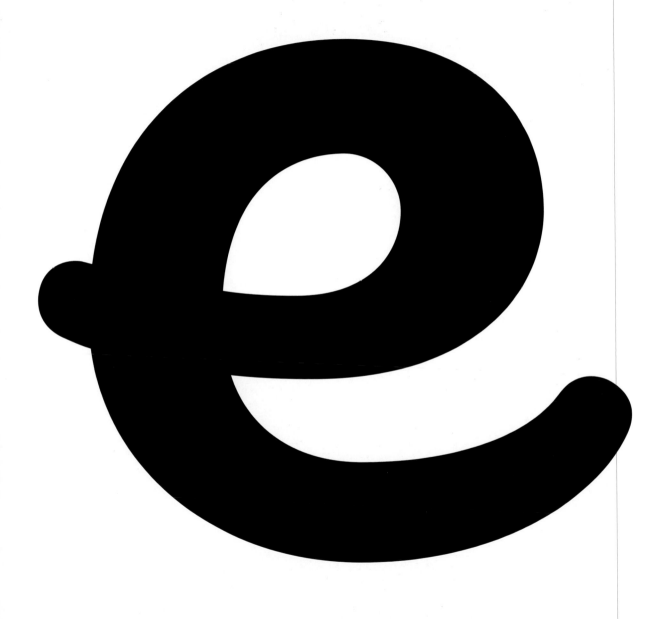

Village

Chester & Tracy Jenkins
2005

Mavis

646-654-1506

ABCDEFGHIJKLMNOPQRSTUVWXYZ
abcdefghijklmnopqrstuvwxyz
&0123456789

AÁÀÂÄÃÅĂĀĂÂÅĄΛÆǼÆBBCĆĈČĊÇCĆĈČĊÇDĎ
ÐEÉÈÊËĔĒĚÊĖĘFGĜĜĞĞĠĢGGĢĜĜĞĞĠĢGHĤḦHHIÍÌ
ÎÏĨǏĪİÎIĮJĴĴJĴĴ KKĶ KKLĹĽĻḶĿ ŁMMṂNŃÑŇṄŅṆ NOÓ
ÒÔÖÕŎŌŎÔŐǪŌǫ ØǾƏŒPQRŔŘR̂ŖṚ R̄SŚŜŠŞŞ SŚ
ŜŠŞŞŞTŤŢṬŦUÚÙÛÜŨŮǓŪŬÛŐ Ű ɥVWẂẀŴ ẄXYÝ
ỲŸŶ ỲIJZŹŽŻ ÐŊÞ ʒƷ ƏƏaáàâäãåăāăâåąɑáàâä
åăāăâåąæǽæææǽæbćĉčċçcĉĉčċçdďđeéèêë
ēĕēėěęeéèêëēĕēėěęfgǵĝğǧġģggǵĝğǧġģgh
ĥḧ ħıíìîïĩǐīíîıįjĵ jj ǩ ķ ķ kklĺľ ļ ḷ ŀ ł mmṃ nńñ ň ṅ ņṇ ŋoóò
ôöõŏōŏôőǫ ōǫ ø ǿ əœœpqrŕř r̂ ŗṛ r̄sśŝ š ş ş s śŝš ş ş
şßtťţṭŧuúùûüũůǔūŭ û űɥvwẃẁŵ ẅxy ý ỳ ÿ ŷ ỹ ij
zźžż ð ŋþ ʒ ʒ ə ə ᵃᵃᶜᶜᵒfb ffb ff fh ffh fi ffi fı ffı fj ffj fk
ffk fl ffl ft fft ftt tt &´ ` ^ ¨ ˜ ¯ ˘ ˙ ˚ ¸ ˝ ˛ ˇ ´ ` ^ ¨ ˜ ˙ ˇ ¸ ˝
˝ ˙ .,:;…!¡?¿¿?¿¿¡*†‡§¶•₧€¢£ƒ¥₺₢₣₤
₦₧₨₩₪₮₱฿#0122334556789/%‰№₶ªℓ←→↑
↓↖↗↙↘●○●■□⊠■□+−±×÷=≠≈<>≤≥µπ¬∞∂∫√∆ΩΠΣ◊
°''‚""„‹›«»/\|¦·■·‐–—()[]{}⟨⟩

Allah Bible Cocoa Dad Eccentric Fluffer Gaggle Highhats Illicit Jamjar Khaki Lull Mama Nine Onomatopeia Papal Quaque Roar Star Tots Uvula Valve Wow Xerox Yay Zizzy

Regular Counterpunch

646-654-1506

646-654-1506

ABCDEFGHIJKLMNOPQRSTUVWXYZ
abcdefghijklmnopqrstuvwxyz
&0123456789

ABCDEFGHIJKLMNOPQRSTUVWXYZabc
defghijklmnopqrstuvwxyz&.,;!?¿012345
56789+=/|\\()[]
(This font is on the CD.)

Chester & Tracy Jenkins
2003

Village

VIRUS

HERE BEGINS
YOUR SEARCH FOR *enlightenment*
CHOOSE WISELY
FROM THE FOLLOWING
DESIGNS & *Paradise*
WILL BE YOURS WITH
MATERIAL RICHES
GREATER
than you can POSSIBLY
IMAGINE

The now infamous team of Jonathan Barnbrook and Marcus McCallion
has produced an extraordinary range of typefaces. Elegant and beautifully presented, the Virus collection
brings many of these unusual, sometimes disturbing, typefaces together for the first time.
The Virus Foundry has been producing innovative typographic work since 1990.

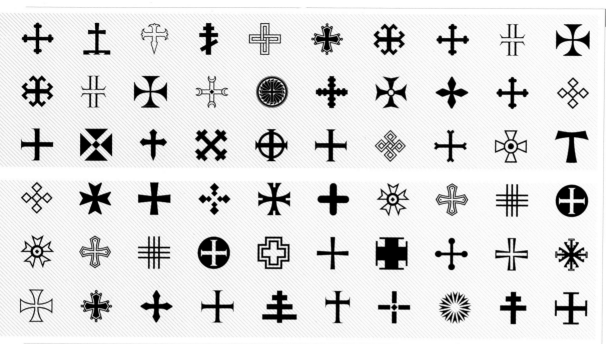

Apocalypso Crosses

Jonathan Barnbrook
1997

Apocalypso Crosses is a font of 75 different designs that may or may not be useful when the world ends. The name is a combination of two words: apocalypse (the end of the world) + calypso (joyful West Indian improvised music) = fiddling while Rome burns.

Apocalypso Pictograms

Jonathan Barnbrook
1997

Apocalypso Pictograms is a font containing more than 50 designs expressing very different problems and ideologies to be used when the end of the world happens. Apocalypso wittily satirizes many of the problems facing the world today.

Virus

Bastard Spindly

Jonathan Barnbrook
1990

Bastard is a blackletter font drawn with a contemporary eye. When constructing this typeface, Barnbrook thought it should acknowledge that the letterforms were drawn on a computer. Therefore a set of modular parts was devised to create a font that is a modern interpretation of historic forms.

Bastard Spindly 16 on 16 pt.

Aliquam elementum kravida est. Donec commodo gravida massa. Cras a felis vestibulum orci convallis facilisis. Enteger tincidun kops scelerisque lacus. Sed lacinia elit a duiner. Aliquam elementum gravida est. Donec commodo gravida massa. Cras a felis vestibulum orci convallis facilisis. Enteger tincidun kops

Bastard Spindly 30 on 24 pt.

Aliquam elapin kaida mestix. Donec commodo massa. Cras a felis vestibulum orci convallis facilisis. Enteger

Bastard Fat

Jonathan Barnbrook
1990

Bastard Fat 16 on 16 pt.

Aliquam elementum kravida nest. Donec commodo gravida fasaras felis vestibulum orci convallis foncault. Enteger tincidun kops puscell erisque lacus. Sed lacinia elit a duiner. Nam gravida porta thrisus.

Bastard Fat 30 on 24 pt.

Aliquam elapin hai mestix. Ronec Ferash gesling vesty muilder porcine

Bastard Even Fatter

Jonathan Barnbrook
1990

Bastard Even Fatter 16 on 16 pt.

Aliquam elementum kravida est. Runec ne mmmln gravida massa. Cras a felis vesting fulum ruci cunvallis facilisis. Tintum puze

Bastard Even Fatter 30 on 24 pt.

Aliquam elapin hamid mestix. Runec Gesting

virus@virusfonts.com

ABCDEFGHJKLMNOPQRSTUVWXYZ
abcdefghjklmnopqrstuvwxyz123

Bourgeois Light

Jonathan Barnbrook &
Marcus McCallion
2005

This usable and well-crafted
font echoes early twentieth-
century letterforms drawn
in a contemporary style. The
extensive Bourgeois family is
available in 32 different styles.

Bourgeois Light and Bourgeois Light Italic 9 on 11 pt.

Aliquam elementum gravida est. Donech commodo gravida maslaw
braye felis vestibulum orcie convallis laffis manigraze elitik Enteger.
Aliquam elementum gravida est. Donech commodo gravida maslaw
braye felis vestibulum orcie convallis laffis manigraze elitik Enteger.

Bourgeois Light Condensed and Bourgeois Light Condensed Italic 9 on 11 pt.

Aliquam elementum gravida est. Donec commodo gravida masa. Wrase velit ontiger neap
cidunting weras. Sed lacina elit a dui scelique lacus. Nulla pellentesque condimentum.
Aliquam elementum gravida est. Donec commodo gravida masa. Wrase velit ontiger neap
cidunting weras. Sed lacina elit a dui scelique lacus. Nulla pellentesque condimentum.

ABCDEFGHJKLMNOPQRSTUVWXYZ
abcdefghjklmnopqrstuvwxyz123

Bourgeois Book

Jonathan Barnbrook &
Marcus McCallion
2005

Bourgeois Book and Bourgeois Book Italic 9 on 11 pt.

Aliquam elementum gravida est. Dinech comodo gravida braye
felis vestiblum. Enteger convallis porcie laffis manigraze elitik.
Aliquam elementum gravida est. Dinech comodo gravida braye
felis vestiblum. Enteger convallis porcie laffis manigraze elitik.

Bourgeois Book Condensed and Bourgeois Book Condensed Italic 9 on 11 pt.

Aliquam elemintum gravida est. Donec comodo gravida. Wrase veliter poonting
neap cidunting weras. Sed gacina efit a dui. Nua scelique lacus pellen tesque.
Aliquam elemintum gravida est. Donec comodo gravida. Wrase veliter poonting
neap cidunting weras. Sed gacina efit a dui. Nua scelique lacus pellen tesque.

ABCDEFGHJKLMNOPQRSTUVWXYZ
abcdefghjklmnopqrstuvwxyz123

Bourgeois Bold

Jonathan Barnbrook &
Marcus McCallion
2005

Bourgeois Bold and Bourgeois Bold Italic 9 on 11 pt.

Aliquam elementum gravida est. Donech commodo gravida
maslaw braye gelis Estibe fum orcie convalis laffis grazem.
Aliquam elementum gravida est. Donech commodo gravida
maslaw braye gelis Estibe fum orcie convalis laffis grazem.

Bourgeois Bold Condensed and Bourgeois Bold Condensed Italic 9 on 11 pt.

Aliquam elemint gravda kesty. Donec comdo wrase veliter ponting neap
cidunting weras. Sed pacina efit a dua scelique lacus gellen noxtesque.
Aliquam elemint gravda kesty. Donec comdo wrase veliter ponting neap
cidunting weras. Sed pacina efit a dua scelique lacus gellen noxtesque.

ABCDEFGHJKLMNOPQRSTUVWXYZ
abcdefghjklmnopqrstuvwxyz123

Bourgeois Ultra

Jonathan Barnbrook &
Marcus McCallion
2005

Bourgeois Ultra and Bourgeois Ultra Italic 9 on 11 pt.

Aliquam elementum gravida est. Donech commodo gor
vaye gelish Estiben fum porcine convalis laffis grazem.
Aliquam elementum gravida est. Donech commodo gor
vaye gelish Estiben fum porcine convalis laffis grazem.

Bourgeois Ultra Condensed and Bourgeois Ultra Condensed Italic 9 on 11 pt.

Aliquam elemint gravda kesty. Donec comdo wrase veliter ponting
neap dunting wis. Sed pacina efit scelique lacus gele noxtesque.
Aliquam elemint gravda kesty. Donec comdo wrase veliter ponting
neap dunting wis. Sed pacina efit scelique lacus gele noxtesque.

Virus

This usable and well-crafted font echoes early twentieth-century letterforms drawn in a contemporary style. The extensive Bourgeois family is available in 32 different styles.

ABCDEFGH|KLMNOPQRS+UVWXYZ
123abcdefghjklmnopqrstuvwxyz

Bourgeois Light Alternate and Bourgeois Light Italic Alternate 9 on 11 pt.

Aliquam elementum gravida est. Donec commodo gravida massa.
Cras a felis vestibulum orci convallis facilisis. Enteger tincidun kops.
Aliquam elementum gravida est. Donec commodo gravida massa.
Cras a felis vestibulum orci convallis facilisis. Enteger tincidun kops.

Bourgeois Light Condensed Alternate and Bourgeois Light Condensed Italic Alternate 9 on 11 pt.

Aliquam elementum gravida est. Donec commodo gravida massa. Cras a felis vestibulum
orci convallis facilisis. Enteger tincidun kops scelerisque lacus. Sed lacinia elit a duiner.
Aliquam elementum gravida est. Donec commodo gravida massa. Cras a felis vestibulum
orci convallis facilisis. Enteger tincidun kops scelerisque lacus. Sed lacinia elit a duiner.

Bourgeois Book Alternate

*Jonathan Barnbrook &
Marcus McCallion*
2005

ABCDEFGH|KLMNOPQRS+UVWXYZ
123abcdefghjklmnopqrstuvwxyz

Bourgeois Book Alternate and Bourgeois Book Italic Alternate 9 on 11 pt.

Aliquam elementum gravida est. Donec commodo gravid mas
pellon vesting bulum. Eras a felish porcine convallis facilis velit.
Aliquam elementum gravida est. Donec commodo gravid mas
pellon vesting bulum. Eras a felish porcine convallis facilis velit.

Bourgeois Book Condensed Alternate and Bourgeois Book Condensed Italic Alternate 9 on 11 pt.

Aliquam elemintum gravida est. Danek commodo gravider masa wraze felish vet
oul orci convallis facilisis. Enteger tindom kops sceler Sed plinth oplite nisque.
Aliquam elemintum gravida est. Donek commodo gravider masa wraze felish vet
oul orci convallis facilisis. Enteger tindom kops sceler Sed plinth oplite nisque.

Bourgeois Bold Alternate

*Jonathan Barnbrook &
Marcus McCallion*
2005

ABCDEFGH|KLMNOPQRS+UVWXYZ
123abcdefghjklmnopqrstuvwxyz

Bourgeois Bold Alternate and Bourgeois Bold Italic Alternate 9 on 11 pt.

**Aliquam elementum gravida est. Donech commodo gravid
mas pellon vesting bulum. Eras un felish porcine convallis.**
***Aliquam elementum gravida est. Donech commodo gravid
mas pellon vesting bulum. Eras un felish porcine convallis.***

Bourgeois Bold Condensed Alternate and Bourgeois Bold Condensed Italic Alternate 9 on 11 pt.

**Aliquam elementum gravida est. Donec commodo gravida miras ath felis
vestibulum orci convallis facilisis. Wrase veliper incidunt erisque lacus.**
***Aliquam elementum gravida est. Donec commodo gravida miras ath felis
vestibulum orci convallis facilisis. Wrase veliper incidunt erisque lacus.***

Bourgeois Ultra Alternate

*Jonathan Barnbrook &
Marcus McCallion*
2005

ABCDEFGH|KLMNOPQRS+UVWXYZ
123abcdefghjklmnopqrstuvwxyz

Bourgeois Ultra Alternate and Bourgeois Ultra Italic Alternate 9 on 11 pt.

**Aliquam elementum est. Donech commodo gravid mazy
pellon vesting. Erash bulum un felish porcine cinvales.**
***Aliquam elementum est. Donech commodo gravid mazy
pellon vesting. Erash bulum un felish porcine cinvales.***

Bourgeois Ultra Condensed Alternate and Bourgeois Ultra Condensed Italic Alternate 9 on 11 pt.

**Aliquam elementum gravida est. Donec commodo gravida mirash
felis vest bulum. Wrase liper porcine facilis incidunt quet lacing.**
***Aliquam elementum gravida est. Donec commodo gravida mirash
felis vest bulum. Wrase liper porcine facilis incidunt quet lacing.***

ABCDEFGHJKLMNOPQRST+UVWXYZ
ABCDEFGHJKLMN&1234567890!

Coma Regular

Jonathan Barnbrook and Marcus McCallion
2001

Coma was originally designed to be used with Japanese text (which is based on a square) both horizontally and vertically in layouts. However, with its sleek modern feel it stands up very well to a number of different uses.

Coma Regular 9 on 11 pt.

ALIQUAM ELEMEN+UM GRAVIDO ES+ONE COMMODO GRAVIDO MASSO. CRAS LORP FELIS VES+IBULUM ORCI CONVOL BLISH FACILISIS. CRAS VELI+. IN+E GERVONIC

Coma Regular 13 on 15.5 pt.

ALIQUAM ELEMEN+ GRIVEN IDOR ES+. DONEC COMMODO GRAVIDO MASSO. CRAS OUP

ABCDEFGHJKLMNOPQRST+UVWXYZ
ABCDEFGHJKLMN&1234567890!

Coma Black

Jonathan Barnbrook and Marcus McCallion
2001

Coma Black 9 on 11 pt.

ALIQUAM ELEMEN+UM GRAVIDO ESY MON COMMODO GRAVIDO MASSO. CRAS BIPEL FELIS VES+IBULUM ORCI CONVOL GLIS+ BOLISINE. CRAS VELI+. IN +EGOR KINCE

Coma Black 13 on 15.5 pt.

ALIQUAM ELIMON+ OGRIME IDO ES+. DONEWY COMMODO GRAVIDO MASSO. CRAS YON

A B C D E F G H J K L M N O P Q R S T U V W X Y Z
A B C D E F G H J K L M N & 1 2 3 4 5 6 7 8 9 0 ! ?

Delux

Jonathan Barnbrook
1997

Retro-futuristic, life-enhancing, resource-guzzling, environment-destroying, ozone-depleting, labour-exploiting, ghetto-creating, state-corrupting, beautiful and wonderful designer label Delux. Satisfy your every desire.

Delux 7 on 11 pt.

ALIQUAM ELEMENTUM GRAVIDA EST. DONEC COMMODO GRAVIDA MASTINE CRAS A FELIS VESTIBULUM ORCI CONVALLIS FACILISIS. CRAS BUNE VELIT. INTEGER TINCIDUNT EROS SCELERISQUE LACUS. SED LACINIA WELIT NAW DUI. NULLA PELLENTESQUE CONDIMENTUM EROS. INTEGER EU LIGULA VEL

Delux 11 on 15.5 pt.

ALIQUAM ELEMENTUM GRAVIDA EST. RONECH COMMODO GRAVIDA MASSA. CRAS A FELIS STIB GLEM ORCI CONVALLIS FACILISIS. CRAS VELIT.

A B C D E F G H J K L M N O P Q R S T U V W X Y Z
A B C D E F G H J K L M N & 1 2 3 4 5 6 7 8 9 0 ! ?

Delux Delux

Jonathan Barnbrook
1997

Delux Delux 7 on 11 pt.

ALIQUAM ELEMENTUM GRAVIDA EST. DONEC COMMODO GRAVIDA MASTE CRAS A FELIS VESTIBULUM ORCI CONVALLIS FACILISIS. CRAS VELITH. INTEGER TINCIDUNT EROS SCELERISQUE LACUS. SED LACINIA ELIT ATH DUI NULLA PELLENTESQUE. CONDIMENTUM EROS. INTEGER EU LIGULA

Delux Delux 11 on 15.5 pt.

ALIQUAM ELEMENTUM GRAVIDA EST. DONEC COMMODO GRAVIDA MASSA. CRAS A FEO LISM VESTIBULUM ORCI CONVALLIS FACIAS VELIT.

Virus

Jonathan Barnbrook
1995

Drone is something you just don't want to hear. Drone is a religious dogma spoken at you for hours on end. Drone is the sound of impending disaster. Drone is a badly proportioned font based on primitive serif lettering seen in Hispanic Catholic churches.

ABCDEFGHJKLMNOPQRSTUVWXYZ
ABCDEFGHJKLMM&£$€¥1234567890%!?

Drone No. 90210 9 on 11 pt.

ALIQUAM ELEMENTUM GRAVIDA EST. DONEC WOM MODO GRAVIDA MASSA. CRAS A FELIS VESTIBULUM ORCI CONVALLIS FACILISIS. CRAS VELIT. INTEGER ASTIN CIDUNT EROS SCELERISQUE VOCUS. SEID LACINIA ELITA

Drone No. 90210 15 on 15 pt.

ALIQUAM ELIBENT GRAWE KUDE EST. DONEC COMMODO GRAWE IDA MASSA. CRAS OU FELIS GEIST

Drone No. 666

Jonathan Barnbrook
1995

ABCDEFGHJKLMNOPQRSTUVWXYZ
ABCDEFGHJKLMM&£$€¥1234567890!?

Drone No. 666 9 on 11 pt.

ALIQUAM ELEMENTUM GRAVIDA EST. DONEC COLM HOMITH GRAVIDA MASSA. CRAS A FOLIS VESBULUM ORCI CINVALLOS FACILISIS. VELITOGER TIN CODUNT EROCELERIS LACUS. SED QUE LACINIA ELITA DUI. NULLA

Drone No. 666 15 on 15 pt.

ALIQUAM ELEMENT GRAWE IDA EST. DONEC NOOPER FACILIRAS ELIT. INTEGER TINCIDUNT EROS SCELER-

Echelon

Jonathan Barnbrook & Marcus McCallion
2001

Named after the massive government surveillance system, Echelon is a font based on 1970s Eastern European pipe-style typefaces.

http://en.wikipedia.org/wiki/ECHELON

ABCDEFGHJKLMNOPQRSTUVWXYZ
abcdefghjklmn&£$?¥1234567890

Echelon 9 on 11 pt.

Sed lacinia elit a dui. Nulla pellentesque con dimentum eros. Integer eu ligula vel felis ull amcorper aliquet. Donec ut libera. Arcu tellu sorrare sodales, facilisis in, interdum ut, leo.

Echelon 14 on 16 pt.

ALIQUAM WAN ELEMENTIUM gravida est. Donec commodos a felis vestibulum vallish we

Echelon Alternate

Jonathan Barnbrook & Marcus McCallion
2001

ABCDEFGHJKLMNOPQRSTUVWXYZ
abcdefghjklm&£$?¥1234567890

Echelon Alternate 9 on 11 pt.

Sed lacinia elit a dui. Nulla pellentesque con dimentum eros. Integer eu ligula vel felisull amcorper aliquet. Donec ut libera. Arcu teila us, orrare sodales, facilisis in, interdum ut,

Echelon Alternate 14 on 16 pt.

ALIQUAM WAN ELEMENTUUM Gravida Est. Donec Commodor Gravida Massa. Cras a Felish

ABCDEFGHJKLMNOPQRSTUUWXYZ

abcdefghjklmnopqrstuuuxyz1234567890

*Jonathan Barnbrook &
Marcus McCallion*
2001

Expletive Script is a delightful
modular script font based on
a circular form. The characters
can go above and below the
baseline to create interesting
display typography and
complex background patterns.

Expletive Script Light 10 on 16 pt.

Agiquan emax nent min gravida est Darecly
cannada gravida massa Uras a felish marb
vestibulum arci carvallis facilisis Crasling

Expletive Script Light Caps 10 on 16 pt

AGIQUAM EMAX MENT MIN GRAUIDA EST
DANECLY CANNADA GRAUIDA MASSA
URAS A FELISH MORB MESTIBULUM ORCI

ABCDEFGHJKLMNOPQRSTUUWXYZ

abcdefghjklmnopqrst uvwx1234567890

Expletive Script Light Alt

*Jonathan Barnbrook &
Marcus McCallion*
2001

Expletive Script Light Alternate 10 on 16 pt.

Agiquan emax nent min gra ifa est woneh
coeno ny gra ifa massa Cras a felisn werk
vestibuln ori corvallis facilisis Cras velit

Expletive Script Light Alternate Caps 10 on 16 pt

AGIQUAM EMAX MENT MIN GRAUIDA EST
MANECH CAENAMA GRAUIDA MASSA
CRAS A FELISN MERK MESTIBULUM ORCI

ABCDEFGHJKLMNOPQRSTUUWXYZ

abcdefghjklmnopqrstuuuxyz1234567890

Expletive Script Regular

*Jonathan Barnbrook &
Marcus McCallion*
2001

Expletive Script Regular 10 on 16 pt.

Agiquan emax nert min gravida est Darechi
cannada gravida massa Cras a felisk walner
vestibulum arci carvallis facilisis Cras velit

Expletive Script Regular Caps 10 on 16 pt

AGIQUAM EMAX MENT MIN GRAUIDA EST
DANECHI CANNADA GRAUIDA MASSA
CRAS A FELISK MALNER MESTIBULUM ORCI

ABCDEFGHJKLMNOPQRSTUUWXYZ

abcdefghjklmnopqrst uvwx z1234567890

Expletive Script Alternate

*Jonathan Barnbrook &
Marcus McCallion*
2001

Expletive Script Alternate 10 on 16 pt.

Agiqu an emax nert min gra ifa est Darecher
connodo gra ifa massa Cras a felis welnert
vestibuln ori corvallis facilisis Cras velit

Expletive Script Alternate Caps 10 on 16 pt

AGIQUAM EMAX MENT MIN GRAUIDA EST
DANECHER CANNADA GRAUIDA MASSA
CRAS A FELIS WELNERT MESTIBULUM ORCI

Virus

Jonathan Barnbrook
1995

False Idol is based on distorted rubdown lettering taken from 1970s pornographic magazines "that, er, I haven't seen," says Barnbrook. The letterforms it was based on were trying to mimic a feeling of glamour but succeeded only in looking seedy.

ABCDEFGHJKLMNOPQRSTUVWXYZ
abcdefghjklmnopqrstuvwxyz&123

False Idol Regular 8 on 11 pt.

Aliquam elementum gravida est. Donec commodo wun gravida massa. Cras arn felis vestibulum orci convallis facilisis. Braip velit. Integer tincidunt erios sceleisque lacus. Sed lacinia elit a dui. Nulla pellentesque bluxed

False Idol Regular 12 on 15 pt.

Aliquam element grave idalest. Dao nec lomody grae ida massa. Cras ou felis vest tibulum orci conjal wakler

Jonathan Barnbrook
1995

ABCDEFGHJKLMNOPQRSTU
abcdefghjklmnopqrstuvwxyz123456789

False Idol Italic 9 on 11 pt.

Aliquam elementum gravida est. Donec commodo gravida wey massa. Cras a felis vestibulum orci convallis facilisis. Bris velit. integer tidunt eros lerisque lacus. Sed linia elit a dui. Nulla pell entesque condimentum eros. Integer eu ligula vel felis wolner ujo

False Idol Italic 12 on 15 pt.

Aliquam element grave daw est. Donex comodo grave ida massa. Gras ou felis vest tibulum orci convallis facilis is. Velinte gerlowi edunt Erip uje

*Jonathan Barnbrook &
Marcus McCallion*
2003

Infidel is a typeface based on letterforms found in Christian illuminated manuscripts and Bibles from the Middle Ages. These wonderfully idiosyncratic forms have been redrawn in an interesting and innovative yet contemporary way.

ABCDEFGHJKLMNOPQRSTUVWXYZ
ABCDEFGHJKLME 1234567890%!?

Infidel A 8 on 11.5 pt.

aliquam elementum gravida est. donec commodo giry avida massa. cras a felis vestibulum orci con val lism facilisis. cras velit. integer tinciount niros sceleori sque lacus. seo lacinia elit a dui. nulla pellentesque

Infidel A 11 on 16 pt.

aliquam wan elementum gravida vost. donec commodo gravida massa. crawa felis vestibulum orci convallis falish.

*Jonathan Barnbrook &
Marcus McCallion*
2003

ABCDEFGHJKLMNOPQRSTUVWXYZ
ABCDEFGHJKLME 1234567890%!?

Infidel B 8 on 11.5 pt.

aliquam elementum gravida ext. donec commodo ciay ida maxxa. crax a felis yextibulum orci con yal flixh acilixix. crax yelit. integ boen ir tincidunt erox xcele rixque lacus. xed lacinia elita dui. nuw pellentexque

Infidel B 11 on 16 pt.

aliquam wane elementum gravida bixty donec commodo gravida hexxa. craxa felix yextibulum orci conyallix junfe

ABCDEFGHIJKLMNOPQRSTUVWXYZ
ABCDEFGHIJKLMFO1234567890%?

Infidel C

Jonathan Barnbrook &
Marcus McCallion
2003

Infidel C 8 on 11.5 pt.

Aliquam elementum gravida est. Donec commodo gravu ida massa. Cras a felis vestipulum orci con val lis xacy lisis. Cras velit. Integer tincidunt eros sceleri sque lacus. Sed lacinia elit a dui. Nulla pellen omni tesgue

Infidel C 11 on 16 pt.

Aliquam wan elementum gravida estin. Donec commodo gravida massa. Crasow felis vestipuwum orci convalis lacios.

ABCDEFGHIJKLMNOPQRS*UVWXYZ
ABCDEFGHIJKLMF1234567890%?

Infidel D

Jonathan Barnbrook &
Marcus McCallion
2003

Infidel D 8 on 11.5 pt.

Aliquam elemen*um gravida es*. Donec commodo gio ravida massa. Cras a felis ves*ibulum orci con val lis facilisis. Cras veli*. In*eger *incidun* eros scele ris que lacus. Sed lacinia eli* abo dui. Hul pollew *esgue

Infidel D 11 on 16 pt.

Aliquam wah elemen*um gravida kis*e. Donec commodo gravida massa. Crasa felis ves*ibulum orci convallis lacios.

ABCDEFGHIJKLMNOPQRSTUVWXYZ
abcdefghijklmnopqrstuvwxyz 1 2 3

Melancholia

Jonathan Barnbrook &
Marcus McCallion
2001

Melancholia is a delicate and usable sans serif font featuring the swash style characters normally used in calligraphy. The italic is based on original historical italics such as Garamond. Altogether, it makes up a subtle and elegant type family.

Melancholia 9 on 11 pt.

Sed lacinia elit a dui. Nulla pellentesque condimentum eropy. Integer eu ligula vel felis ullamcorper aliquet. Donec unt libero. Aliquam arcu tellus, ornare sodales, facilisis in, interdum kute leo. Fusce et sapien. Aliquam erat volutpat. Proin mattis erati

Melancholia Italic 9 on 11 pt.

Aliquam elementum gravida est. Donech commodo twelnner gravida. Cras a felis vestibulum asnorci iconvallis facilisis. Cras luon velit. Inge tincidunt scelerisque lacus. Sed lacinia elit a dui. Nulla pellentesque condimentum eros. Integer eu

ABCDEFGHIJKLMNOPQRSTUVWXYZ
abcdefghijklmnopqrstuvwxyz 1 2 3

Melancholia Alternate

Jonathan Barnbrook &
Marcus McCallion
2001

Melancholia Alternate 8 on 16 pt.

Sed lacinia elit a dui. Nulla pellentesque condimentum eros. Integer eiu ligula vel felis ullamcorper aliquet. Donec ut libero. Eliquam arcu tellus, ornare sodales, facilisis in, interdum ut. Fusce et sapien. Volutpat kroine

Melancholia Alternate 16 on 26 pt.

Aliquam elementum rifan hest. Ripo nejox comady gravida quissa weza il

Virus

Moron is a cute/nasty, old/new drawing of Victorian sans serif letterforms with a bit of the 1970s sausage fonts thrown in. This odd-sounding combination makes for a font that has a fresh and original feel.

ABCDEFGHIJKLMNOPQRSTUVWXYZ
ABCDEFGHIJKLMNOPQRSTUVWXYZ

Moron Regular 9 on 11 pt.

ALIQUAM ELEMENTUM GRAVLDA EST. DONEC COM MODO GRAVIDA MASSA. CRAS A FELIS VEST LIBUM ORCI CONVALLIS FACILISIS. CRAY VELM. INTEGER TINCIDUNT EROS SCELERISQUE LACUS. KILNE SEOD

Moron Regular 14 on 15 pt.

ALIQUAM ELEMENTUM HERUVIO IDA EST. DONEC COMYODOS ILN GRAVIDA MASSA. JURAS A FELIS

ABCDEFGHIJKLMNOPQRSTUVWXYZ
ABCDEFGHIJKLMNOPQRSTUVWXYZ

Moron Thick 9 on 11 pt.

ALIQUAM ELEMENTUM GRAVILDA EST. DONE COM MODO GRAVID MASA. CRAS A FELS VESO LIBUM ORCI CONVALIS FACILISIS. CRAW VELIT. INTEGER TINCIDUNT EROS SCELESQUE LACUS. KILNE SEOD

Moron Thick 14 on 15 pt.

ALIQUAM ELEMENTUM HERUVIO IDA EST. DONEC COMYODO ILN GRAVIDA MASSA. JURAS AFELS

Stalinist Russian architectural forms greatly influenced the design of Newspeak. The name comes from George Orwell's novel *1984*, in which a language is invented so that people cannot express themselves outside the politics of the dictatorship in power.

ABCDEFGHIJKLMNOPQRSTUVWXYZ
ABCDEFGHIJKLMNOPQRSTUVWXYZ

Newspeak Light 7 on 11 pt.

ALIQUAM ELEMENTUM GRAVIDA EST OD ONECHY CUMMUDU GRAVIDA MASSA CRAS ENTH FELIZE VESTIBULUM ORCI CUNVALLIS FACILISIS GRISAND VELIT INTH EGER TINCIDUNT ERUS SCEL ERISQUE

Newspeak Light 10 on 16 pt.

ALIQUAM ELEMENTUM RHEM NIV DALLEST BUNIC MULLNER FULVING SILN GRAVIDA TUSSUR KLACK HITE

ABCDEFGHIJKLMNOPQRST
ABCDEFGHIJKLMNOPQRST

Newspeak Heavy 7 on 11 pt.

ALIQUAM ELEMENTUM GRAV IDEST. OD ONECHY CUMMUDITY SACRAS ENF ELIZE VESTIBULUM ORCI CYNVALUS FACILISIS. GRISAVLY VELIT. FLUTH

Newspeak Heavy 10 on 16 pt.

ALIQUAM ELUTIVE FUM RUXLY FRIST. KLIDS ZUM MULLING NIFE FULVER

NixonScript Medium

A B C D E F G H J K L M N O P Q R S T U V W X Y Z
a b c d e f g h j k l m n o p q r s t u v w x y z 1 2 3 4 5

NixonScript Medium 14 on 15 pt.

Aliquam elementum gravida est. Donec commoding gravida massa. Cras a felis vestibulum orci convaluat facilicer tincidunt eros scelerisque lacus. Sead

NixonScript Medium Caps 14 on 15 pt.

ALIQUAM ELAMONT JIB GRAFE UMBY TEMUS DONACH COLLEDIO RAIV DAG MESTA RAJOS A FELLISH VESTIBULE.

NixonScript Medium

Jonathan Barnbrook
1997

NixonScript was based loosely on a piece of lettering found on the front of a 1960s camera. It quickly developed from the retro script to something that had the spirit of the American Dream and a pious religious feel.

NixonScript Bold Italic

A B C D E F G H J K L M N O P Q R S T U V W X Y Z
a b c d e f g h j k l m n o p q r s t u v w x y z 1 2 3 4 5

NixonScript Medium 14 on 15 pt.

Aliquam elementum gravida est. Foner comey modo gravida massa. Eras a felis vestibulum orci convallis facilisis. Rraa velit unforging

NixonScript Bold Italic Caps 14 on 15 pt.

ALIQUAM ELAMONT JIB GRAFE UMBY BIDDA TEMUS DONACH COLEDO RAIVE DAG MESTA RAJOS FELISH VETIBULE.

NixonScript Bold Italic

Jonathan Barnbrook
1997

Draylon

A B C D E F G H J K L M N O P Q R S T U V W X Y Z
A B C D E F G H J K L M N & $ £ ¥ 1 2 3 4 5 6 7 8 9 0 !

Draylon 10 on 12 pt.

ALIQUAM ELEMENTUM GRAVIDA EST. DONCH COMMODO GRAVIDA MASSA. RAJS A FESKIOL VESTIBULUM ORCI CONWALIS FACILISIS. IZRA RELIT. INTEGER TINCIDUNT EUROPALE RISQUE

Draylon 14 on 16 pt.

ALIQUAM ELAMONT JIB GRAFFUM BIDDA TEMUS DONACH COLLEDIO VRAIDAG MESTA. RAJOS A FELLISH

Draylon

Jonathan Barnbrook
1995

Forming part of the Nylon package, Draylon is based on naïve seventeenth- to eighteenth-century versions of serif letterforms. Both were drawn to reflect the fact that they were produced on a computer and constructed to be mixed to suit individual tastes.

Nylon

A B C D E F G H J K L M N O P Q R S T U V W X Y Z
A B C D E F G H J K L M N † $ £ ¥ 1 2 3 4 5 6 7 8 9 0 !?

Nylon 10 on 12 pt.

ALIQUAM ELEMENTUM GRAVIDA EST DOCH COMMODO GRAVIDA MASSA. RAJS A FELISKY LOID VESTIBULUM RO CONWALLIS FACILISIS. CRAIZ RELIT. AGERT INCEROP PISCEL RISQUE

Nylon 14 on 16 pt.

ALIQUAM ELAMONT BI GRAFFUM BIDDA TEMUS DONACH COLLEDO VRAIDAG MEAST RAJOS A FELLIS

Nylon

Jonathan Barnbrook
1995

Nylon is based on letterforms from thirteenth- to sixteenth-century European paintings. The original source material had many delightfully unusual manic shapes which Barnbrook wanted to put into the font. As with Draylon, Nylon was drawn to reflect the fact that both types were produced on a computer and constructed to be mixed to suit individual tastes.

Olympukes

*Jonathan Barnbrook &
Marcus McCallion*
2004

Olympics + Puke = Olympukes.
This typeface was born out of the
frustration Barnbrook had felt
about the pictograms that had
been designed for the past few
Olympic games. They simply
did not reflect the true nature
of the event, portraying instead
some wooly idea of the ultimate
in human endeavor with
no acknowledgement of the
bribery, political manipulation,
drug-taking, and greed behind
the event.

Enter Olympukes–real
pictograms which wittily take the
ultimate designer's commission
and accurately reflect the
complexity, contradictions, and
skullduggery inherent in the
modern Olympics.

Patriot Light

Jonathan Barnbrook
1997

Patriot is the sans version of
Barnbrook's popular Exocet
(released through Emigre).
This font is similarly based on
early Greek and Roman stone
carving. Removing the serifs
generates a modern and
mechanical-looking design.

ABCDEFGHJKLMN⊙OPQRSTUVWXYZ

ABCDEFGHJKLMN⊕PQRS+UVWXYZ

Patriot Light 9 on 11 pt.

ALIQUAM ELEMEN+UM GRIB VIDA PRUSD⊕
NEC COMM⊕D⊕ GRAVIDA MASSA. CRASLIS
VES+I BULUM ⊕RCI CON VALLIS FACILIBIR
WELI+EGER RISQUE WINYING UN+ ERSSCE

Patriot Light 12 on 16 pt.

ALIQUAM ELEM ON+UM GRAWE
PIDES+. AX D⊕NEC MASWA CRAS
FELIS VES+IBULUM SCRI NALLIT

Patriot Heavy

Jonathan Barnbrook
1997

ABCDEFGHJKLMN⊙OPQRSTUVWXYZ

ABCDEFGHJKLMN⊕PQRS+UVWXYZ

Patriot Heavy 9 on 11 pt.

**ALIQUAM ELEMEN+UM GRIB VIDA PRUSP
NEC COMM⊕D⊕ GRAVIDA MASSA. CRASIS
VES+I BULUM ⊕RCI CON VALLIS FACCILY
BIR WELI+EGER RISQUE WINYING UN+**

Patriot Heavy 12 on 16 pt.

**ALIQUAM ELEM ON+UM GRAW
EPIDE S+AX D⊕NEC MASTRAS
FELIS VES+IBULUM SCRI NALL**

ABCDEFGHJKLMNOPQRSTUVWXYZ
ABCDEFGHJKLM&£$¥1234567890!?

Prototype Plain

Jonathan Barnbrook
1994

Prototype is a universal alphabet with a contemporary identity crisis. Is it new or old? Serif or sans serif? Uppercase or lowercase? The letterforms are experimental but retain the irritating familiarity of a cover version of a played-to-death pop song. Prototype tries to be all things to all people.

Prototype Plain 9 on 11 pt.

ALIQUAM ELEMENTUM GRAVIDA EST. DONEC COMMODO GRAVIDA MASSA. CRAS A FELIS VESTIBULUM ORCONVALLIS FACILISIS. MELCHING VELIT. INTEGER TINCI DUNT ERSCELE RISQUE LACUS. SED LACINIA ELIT A DUI. NULLA PENTESLUE

Prototype Plain 14 on 16 pt.

ALIQUAM ELEMENTUM GRAVIDA JEST DONEC COMMODO. PRAS A FELISSA VESTIBULUM RASTIN DUNT LACHUS.

ABCDEFGHJKLMNOPQRSTUVWXYZ
ABCDEFGHJKLM&£$¥1234567890!?

Prototype Bold

Jonathan Barnbrook
1994

Prototype Bold 9 on 11 pt.

ALIQUAM ELEMENTUM GRAVIDA EST. DONEC COMMODO GRAVIDA MASSA. CRAS A FELIS VESTIBULUM ORCONVALLIS FACILISIS. MELCHING VELIT. INTEGER TINCI DUNT ERSCELE RISQUE LACUS. SED LACINIA ELIT A DUI. NULLA PENTESLUE

Prototype Bold 14 on 16 pt.

ALIQUAM ELEMENTUM GRAVIDA JEST DONEC COMMODO. PRAS A FELISSA VESTIBULUM RASTIN DUNT LACHUS.

ABCDEFGHJKLMNOPQRSTUVWXYZ
ABCDEFGHJKLM&$£¥1234567890!?

Prozac Lite

Jonathan Barnbrook
1997

Prozac was an experiment in making a universal alphabet with just six shapes, flipped or rotated. The name Prozac comes from the aesthetic of the font–it looks like it was designed by scientists in a utopian, genetically engineered society.

Prozac Lite 9 on 11 pt.

ALIQUAM ELEMENTUM GRAVIDA EST. DONEC COMMODO GRAVIDA MASSA. CRAS A FELIS VESTIBULUM ORCI CONVALLIS FACILISIS. CRAS VELIT. INTEGER TINCIDUNT EROS SCELERISQUE LACUS. SED LACINIA

Prozac Lite 14 on 16 pt.

ALIQUAM ELEMENTUM GRAVI DA EST. DONEC COMMODO MIG AVIDA MASSA. CRAS A FELIS VESTIBULUM

ABCDEFGHJKLMNOPQRSTUVWXYZ
ABCDEFGHJKLM&$£¥1234567890!?

Prozac Max

Jonathan Barnbrook
1997

Prozac Max 9 on 11 pt.

ALIQUAM ELEMENTUM GRAVIDA EST. DONEC COMMODO GRAVIDA MASSA. CRAS A FELIS VESTIBULUM ORCI CONVALLIS FACILISIS. CRAS VELIT. INTEGER TINCIDUNT EROS SCELERISQUE LACUS. SED LACINIA

Prozac Max 14 on 16 pt.

ALIQUAM ELEMENTUM GRAVI DA EST. DONEC COMMODO MIG AVID MASSA. CRAS A FELIS VESTIBULUM

Virus

Shock and Awe Enola Gay

Jonathan Barnbrook &
Marcus McCallion
2004

The design is based on the nose cone lettering of *Enola Gay*, the name given to the B-29 airplane that dropped the first atomic bomb on Hiroshima in 1945. The Shock and Awe series was created to release fonts of special political significance.

ABCDEFGHJKLMNOPQRSTUVWXYZ
ABCDEFGHJKLM&£$¥1234567890

Shock and Awe Enola Gay 9 on 11 pt.

ALIQUAM ELEMENTUM GRAVIDA ES DONEC COMOD GRAVIDA MASSA. CRAS A FELIS VESTIBULUM ORCI CONVLIS FACILISIST CRAS VELIT. INTEGER TINCIDUNT EROS SCELERISQUE LACUS. SED LACINIA ELIT A DUI. NULLA PELLEN OTESQUE DIMENTUM

Shock and Awe Enola Gay 13 on 16 pt.

ALIQUAM ELEM ONTUM GRAWE PIDES TEU DAXO STAMACE IB TASY FELIS VESTIBULE ECRINA MOLLIT FACLIT GERTINC DUNTER

Shock and Awe Tomahawk

Jonathan Barnbrook &
Marcus McCallion
2004

This design extrapolates the lettering used on the Tomahawk cruise missile. The Shock and Awe series was created to release fonts of special political significance.

ABCDEFGHJKLMNOPQRSTUV
ABCDEFGHJ&£$¥123456789

Shock and Awe Tomahawk 7 on 11 pt.

ALIQUAM ELEMENTUM GRAVIDA SIBBELA DONEC COMMODO GRAVIDA MASSA. CRAS A FELIS VES+IBULUM ORCI CONVALLIS UN FACILISIS. CRAS VELI+. IN+EGER +INCID-

Shock and Awe Tomahawk 11 on 16 pt.

ALIQUAM ELIMA NI BUXOR GRAWE PIS+ DAXO S+AME +ASEY FELIS WES+IBULE

State Machine Light

Jonathan Barnbrook &
Marcus McCallion
2004

State Machine is based on lettering used on both Russian and American military vehicles during the Cold War. Additionally, in the lowercase, some more naïve characters have been included that were inspired by handmade political banners from the 1970s.

ABCDEFGHJKLMNOPQRSTUVWXYZ
ΛbCDEFGHJKLMNO&1234567890

State Machine Light 9 on 11 pt.

ALIQUAM ELEMENTUM GRAVIDA EST. DONEC COMMODO GRAVIDA MASSA. CRAS A FELIS VESTIBULUM ORCI CONVALLIS MIN FACILISIS. CrΛ$ VELI+. IN+EGER +INCIDUN+ ErO$ $CELErI$QUE LΛCU$. $ED LΛCINIΛ ELI+ Λ DUI. NULLΛ PELLEN+E$QUE CONDIMEN+UM ErO$.

State Machine Light 13 on 16 pt.

ALIQUAM ELEM ONTUM GRAWE PIDEST DAXO S+ΛMΛCE TΛ$EY FELI$ VE$+IBULE ECrINΛ LI+ FΛCLI+ GEr+INC DUN+Er O$CELE rI$QUE

State Machine Medium

Jonathan Barnbrook &
Marcus McCallion
2004

ABCDEFGHJKLMNOPQRSTUVWXYZ
ΛbCDEFGHJKLMNO&1234567890

State Machine Medium 9 on 11 pt.

ALIQUAM ELEMENTUM GRAVIDA EST. DONEC COMMODO GRAVID MASSA. CRAS A FELIS VESTIBULUM ORCI CONVALLIS FACILISIS. CrΛ$ VELI+. IN+EGER +INCIDUN+ ErO$ $CELErI$QUE LΛCU$. $EΛD LΛCINOLE+ Λ DUI. NULLΛ PELLEN +E$QUE ECrODIMEN+

State Machine Medium 9 on 11 pt.

ALIQUAM ELEM ONTIM GRAWE PIDEST DAXO S+ΛMΛCE TΛ$EY FELI$ VE$+IBULE ECrINΛ LI+ FΛCLI+ GEr+INC DUN+Er O$CEL rI$QUE

virus@virusfonts.com

ABCDEFGHJKLMNOPQRSTUVWXYZ
ʌьcdEFGh|KLMNOG1234567890

State Machine Demi Bold

Jonathan Barnbrook & Marcus McCallion
2004

State Machine Demi Bold 9 on 11 pt.

ALIQUAM ELEMENTUM GRAVIDA EST. DONEC COMMODO GRAVIDA MASSA. CRAS A FELIS VESTIBULUM ORCI CONVALLIS MIN FACILISIS. CrA$ vELi+. IN+EGER +iNCidUN+ ErO$ $cELEri$QUE LACU$. $Ed LACINiA ELi+ A dui. NULLA

State Machine Demi Bold 14 on 16 pt.

ALIQUAM ELEM ONTUM GRAWE PIDEST DAXO S+ʌMACE TA$EY FELi$ vE$+ibULE ECrINA LI+ FACLI+ GEr+INC dUN+Er

ABCDEFGHJKLMNOPQRSTUVWXYZ
ʌьcdEFGh|KLMNOG1234567890

State Machine Bold

Jonathan Barnbrook & Marcus McCallion
2004

State Machine Bold 9 on 11 pt.

ALIQUAM ELEMENTUM GRAVIDA EST. DONEC COMMODO GRAVID MASSA. CRAS A FELIS VESTIBULUM ORCI CONVALLIS FACILISIS. CrA$ vELi+. iN+EGEr +iNCidUN+ ErO$ $cELEri$QUE LACU$. $EʌD LACINOLE+ ʌ dui. NULLA

State Machine Bold 14 on 16 pt.

ALIQUAM ELEM ONTIM GRAWE PIDEST DAXO S+ʌMACE TA$EY FELi$ vE$+i-bULE ECrINA LI+ FACLI+ GEr+INC

Tourette Extreme

Jonathan Barnbrook & Marcus McCallion
2005

This whimsical and delicate font was based on light slab letterforms of the eighteenth and nineteenth centuries. Tourette is available in two versions, Normal and Extreme.

Tourette Extreme 9 on 11 pt.

Aquam vermontum gravidy est. Donec commodo gravida massa. Cras a felis vestibulum orci convallis facilisis. Cras velit. Integer tincidunt eros scelerisque lacus. Sed lacinia elit a duteur. Nulla pepen tesque. Inteuligula vekat helies

Tourette Extreme 13 on 16 pt.

Aquamont umawe yelk hedge pibest dax stamalle tasye felis bestip abu rina Mit maggit. Wekrin zuntre. Geist erin risque

Tourette Normal

Jonathan Barnbrook & Marcus McCallion
2005

Tourette Normal 9 on 11 pt.

Aquam vermontum gravida est. Donec commodo gravida massa. Cras a felis vestibulum orci convallis facilisis. Cras velit. Imp tejer tincidunt eros scelerisque lacus. Sed lacinia elit a dui. Nulla pemi entesque condimentum eros. Integer eu ligula vel iffelis ucoper

Tourette Normal 13 on 16 pt.

Aquamont vin umawe yelk wrage pidest daxo stamace tasey felis vestibule ecrina lit jaclith gertinc dunter oscel. Sed lacinia effit a duip.

Virus

WILTON FOUNDRY was created by Robbie de Villiers in 2003. Years ago, Robbie read an article in *U&lc* magazine about a reading and comprehension test using Times New Roman, Gill Sans, and Helvetica. This article, combined with extensive training in calligraphy, fueled him to focus on typography and its role in design communications. His fascination and love lie with the challenge of designing fonts that are beautiful not just as individual letters, but in the combinations that form words. He considers it a huge privilege to design fonts that become messengers of both small and large thinking.

Wilton Foundry's other proud member is Robbie's oldest daughter, Michelle Newton. She has a degree in packaging design and is an integral part of the business, sharing his vision and love of typography. Michelle brings along her Maltese, Pippin, to the studio to make sure they all stay a little crazy. Wilton Foundry's other mascots include two Labradors, three cats, two African gray parrots, one sassy cockatiel, and a gigantic goldfish.

Robbie de Villiers Design—International Recognition: two Clio Awards and nineteen International Clio Award Nominations; Communication Arts Awards, USA; London Institute for Packaging, United Kingdom; Novum Gebrausgraphik, Germany; Office de la Vigne et du Vin, France; NOAH, Japan; Loerie, South Africa; Graphis, Switzerland; Graphis Packaging, Switzerland; Print, USA.

info@wiltonfoundry.com   ●   www.wiltonfoundry.com

Fred specialized in the job of making very quaint wax toys. He'd planned to be a dentist, but that suddenly changed on a fateful visit to a curio shop at Niagara Falls. As soon as he saw the tiny wax car in the shop he knew there would be no teeth pulling in his future. It was true love at first sight! All day and night he studied the fine intricacies of wax.

BENJAMIN

FRED SPECIALIZED IN THE JOB OF MAKING VERY QUAINT WAX TOYS. HE'D PLANNED TO BE A DENTIST, BUT THAT SUDDENLY CHANGED ON A FATEFUL VISIT TO A CURIO SHOP AT NIAGARA FALLS. AS SOON AS HE SAW THE TINY WAX CAR IN THE SHOP, HE KNEW THERE'D BE NO TEETH PULLING IN HIS FUTURE. IT WAS TRUE LOVE AT

Fred specialized in the job of making very quaint wax toys. He'd planned to be a dentist, but that suddenly changed...

AaBbCcDdEeFf
GgHhIiJjKkLlMm
NnOoPpQqRrSs
TtUuVvWwXxYy
Zz!?&@#$%*)(=
[01234567890]

AaBbCcDdEeFf
GgHhIiJjKkLlMm
NnOoPpQqRrSs
TtUuVvWwXxYy
Zz!?&@#$%*)(=
[01234567890]

AaBbCcDdEeFf
GgHhIiJjKkLlMm
NnOoPpQqRrSs
TtUuVvWwXxYy
Zz!?&@#$%*)(=
[01234567890]

Wilton

Originally the term was boon doggle referring to a bone or metal ring used to secure the scarf of a Boy Scout (also called a woggle). American Scoutmaster Robert H. Link (died 1959) is credited with coining the term. From this, the term came to refer to the lanyards worn on the uniform of a scout, or to similar small decorative objects. Boondoggle has also come to refer in the USA for the plaiting craft known elsewhere as Scoubidou, since many such objects are made by this craft. For examples of "boondoggle" in this sense, refer to the Napoleon Dynamite. Originally the term was boon doggle referring to a bone or metal ring used to secure the scarf of a Boy Scout (also called a woggle). Scoutmaster Robert H. Link (died 1959) is credited with coining the term. From this, the term came to refer to the lanyards worn on the uniform of a scout, or to similar small decorative objects. Boondoggle has also come to refer in the USA for the plaiting craft known elsewhere as Scoubidou, since

But anyways, like a wise man once said, explaining camp to people who have never been is like trying to explain basketball to a jelly fish. Life isn't camp...sometimes I wish it were!

Boondoggle

AaBbCcDdEeFfGgHhIiJjKKLlM mNnOoPpQqRrSsTtUuVvWwXxY yZz0123456789 0123456789

★ ★ ★ ★ ★ ★ ★ ★

Brown Fox

THE QUICK BROWN FOX JUMPS OVER THE LAZY DOG...BUT THAT WAS NOT THE END OF THE STORY!!

The quick brown fox jumps over the lazy dog. But that was not the end of the story...what the fox did not realize was that the lazy dog was not truly lazy. Instead, he was merely taking a breather between training sessions for the doggie olympics! The "lazy" dog knew that the quick, but egotistical fox had grossly underestimated him and needed to be taught a major lesson in how to treat his fellow animals. His ongoing flaunting of fastness was highly offensive and many other animals were now in therapy due to the

AaBbCcDdEeFfGgHhIiJjK kLlMmNnOoPpQqRrSsTtU uVvWwXxYyZz0123456789

The quick brown fox jumps over the lazy dog. But that was not the end of the story...what the fox did not realize was that the lazy dog was not truly lazy. Instead, he was merely taking a breather between training sessions for the doggie olympics! The "lazy" dog knew that the quick, but egotistical fox had grossly underestimated him and needed to be taught a major lesson in how to treat his fellow mammals. His ongoing flaunting of

MANY ANIMALS WERE IN THERAPY DUE TO THE COMPLEXES THAT HE HAD GIVEN THEM. IT WOULD NEVER TRULY END UNTIL THE FOX LEARNED HIS LESSON AND CAME TO UNDERSTAND THAT HE IS NOT THE ONLY QUICK ANIMAL ON THIS EARTH. SO THE "LAZY" DOG CHALLENGED THE "QUICK" FOX TO A RACE. NOTHING FANCY, JUST A GOOD OL' ROAD RACE. ON RACE DAY, ALL OF THE ANIMALS CHEERED FOR THE DOG AND THE FOX LAUGHED AT THEM. BUT GUESS WHO WON...

THE LAZY DOG

Robbie de Villiers
2006

Alfredo just must bring very exciting news to the plaza quickly. He ran through the narrow alleys and jumped over the canal until he finally reached the glorious plaza. A few minutes earlier, the grand bishop proclaimed a new day of festival and Alfredo was now his hardy messenger. Since everyone knows that in this day and age a festival in Venice is nothing to sneeze at, Alfredo was feeling greatly honored to make the announcement. The most exciting part of this particular festival was that it would celebrate something that is both near and dear to all Venetians - vermillion red. It will be named the "Day of the Red" and all citizens will be ordered to wear red, think red and ultimately become red. Every other hues will be outlawed (not permanently, don't get flustered) and in the evening the festivities will commence with a large feast of purely red colored foods. As Alfredo took a breather in is now long-winded message, the crowd in the plaza let out a giant roar. Men were yelling with joy, women cried with pleasure, children laughed with happiness and the poor little babies were absolutely and completely overwhelmed. Everyone in the plaza was so excited that they dispersed to prepare immediately. Poor old Alfredo was left standing in the middle of the empty plaza with absolutely no one in sight. He felt totally dejected and at a complete loss. How would he explain to the grand bishop that he had failed in his sole mission? You see, the newly named "Day of the Red" was but a new festival and, since these things take lots of planning, it would be held on May 2. Being that today is May 3...

Cannette Script

Alfredo just must bring very exciting news to the plaza quickly. He ran through the narrow alleys and jumped over the canal

Cannette Alternatives

Wilton

– Carnegie with Flourishes –

An inspired calligrapher can create pages of beauty using stick ink, quill, brush, pick-axe, buzz saw, or even strawberry jam. In fact, it doesn't even need to be strawberry jam. It could be grape, apple, fig,

An inspired calligrapher can create pages of beauty using stick ink, quill, brush, pick-axe, buzz saw, or even strawberry jam. In fact, it doesn't even need to be strawberry jam. It can be grape, apple, fig, raspberry or even marmalade. Imagine that –a page of real beauty straight from a little bottle of jam. An inspired calligrapher can create pages of beauty using stick ink, quill, brush, pick-axe, buzz saw, or

An inspired calligrapher can create pages of beauty using stick ink, quill, brush, pick-axe, buzz saw, or even

AaBbCcDdEeFfGgHhIiJjKkLlMmNnOoPpQg RrSsTt Uu V Ww XxYyZzf ffe-Flft Ggfh Lfigh L Fl0Fr Srt Thstt !? & ~ $ € 0123456789 0

Nere ntin venico onge f lest l lissited to oral elana no vi detat w hea oun mari wa yl usec ro ca tryphiolys t ia ymemid ilomo ullurtho op osha ltychy givac ga. Grm tump ruttl dimbl to asub upepr ceotsci abipoctw amu tmyn ogl pap tnb

Aa Bb Cc Dd Ee Ff Gg Hh Ii Jj Kk Ll Mm Nn Oo Pp Qg Rr Ss Tt Uu Vv Ww Xx Yy Zz ( ) ?! € & %

Diplomat

Tryphiolyia ymemid ilomo ope givac ga grm tump ruttl osha cas

Aa Bb Cc Dd Ee Ff Gg Hh Ii Jj Kk Ll Mm Nn Oo Pp Qq Rr Ss Tt Uu Vv Ww Xx Yy Zz & ()0123456789

Duet 2 with Flourishes

The juke box music puzzled a gentle visitor from a quaint valley town. My help squeezed back in again and joined the weavers after six. Verbatim reports were quickly given by Jim Fox to his amazed audience. William said that everything about his jacket was in quite good condition except for the zippers that were there. Lemon curry? The juke box music puzzled a gentle visitor from a quaint valley town. My help squeezed back in again and joined the

a b c d e f g h i j k l m n o p q r s t u v w x y f z

The juke box music puzzled a gentle visitor from a quaint valley town. My help squeezed back in again and joined the weavers after six. Verbatim reports were quickly given by Jim Fox to his amazed audience. William said that everything about his jacket was in quite good condition except for the zippers that were

0123456789 0123456789

· Bold ·

Bold for the most elegant of folks

Aa Bb Cc Dd Ee Ff Gg Hh Ii Jj Kk Ll Mm Nn Oo Pp Qq Rr Ss Tt Uu Vv Ww Xx Yy Zz

Wilton

Granola

The names Granula, Granola and Ganolietta were trademarks in the late nineteenth century United States for foods consisting of whole grain products crumbled and baked until crispy; compare the contemporary Swiss invention, Muesli. The food and name were revived in the 1960s, and fruits and nuts were added to it to make it a

AaBbCcDdEeFfGgHhIiJjKk
LlMmNnOoPpQqRrSsTtU
uVvWwXxYyZz123456789

The names Granula, Granola and Ganolietta were trademarks in the late nineteenth century United States for foods consisting of whole grain products crumbled and baked until crispy; compare the contemporary Swiss invention, Muesli. The food and name were revived in the 1960s, and fruits and nuts were added to it to make it a health food popular with the hippie movement. Granola made a major appearance at the 1969 Woodstock Music and Art Festival. The names Granula,

THE NAMES GRANULA, GRANOLA AND GANOLIETTA WERE TRADE-MARKS IN THE LATE NINETEENTH CENTURY UNITED STATES FOR FOODS CONSISTING OF WHOLE GRAIN PRODUCTS CRUMBLED AND BAKED UNTIL CRISPY; COMPARE THE CONTEMPORARY SWISS INVENTION, MUESLI. THE FOOD AND NAME WERE REVIVED IN THE 1960S, AND FRUITS AND NUTS WERE ADDED TO IT TO MAKE IT A HEALTH FOOD POPU-

1969 WOODSTOCK MUSIC & ART FESTIVAL

Sixty zippers were quickly picked from the woven jute bag. Seriously, what type of girl would possibly be seen with a zippered purse this season? Anyone can tell you that zippers went out with tiaras and facial glitter... let's not even mention chunky heels, ew! I would be totally embarrassed to be seen within a boutique's length of any of them. Now, if you want something absolutely fabulous, you must visit Mimi at her new boutique. She has fab finds that are "oh so hot" and, thankfully, no zippered purses.

AaBbCcDdEeFfGg
HhIiJjKkLlMmN
nOoPpQqRrSsTt
UuVvWwXxYyZz
0 1 2 3 4 5 6 7 8 9 0

SIXTY ZIPPERS WERE QUICKLY PICKED FROM THE WOVEN JUTE BAG. SERIOUSLY, WHAT TYPE OF GIRL WOULD POSSIBLY BE SEEN WITH A ZIPPERED PURSE THIS SEASON? ANYONE CAN TELL YOU THAT ZIPPERS WENT OUT WITH TIARAS & GLITTER...

* Miss Pink

The juke box music puzzled a gentle visitor from a quaint valley town. My help squeezed back in again and joined the weavers after six. Verbatim reports were quickly given by Jim Fox to his amazed audience. William said that everything about his jacket was in quite good condition except for the zippers that were there. Lemon curry?

Modus Regular

Robbie de Villiers
2005

AaBbCcDdEeFfGgHhIiJjKkLlMmNnOoPpQqRrSsTtUuVvWwXxYyZz

Fretabladidenga

The juke box music puzzled a gentle visitor from a quaint valley town. My help squeezed back in again and joined the weavers after six. Verbatim reports were quickly given by Jim Fox to his guy

The juke box music puzzled a gentle visitor from a quaint valley town. My help squeezed back in again and joined the weavers after six. Verbatim reports were quickly given by Jim Fox to his guy

---

The juke box music puzzled a gentle visitor from a quaint valley town. My help squeezed back in again and joined the weavers after six. Verbatim reports were quickly given by Jim Fox to his amazed audience. William said that everything about his jacket was in quite good condition except for the zippers that were there. Lemon curry?

Modus Italic

Robbie de Villiers
2005

AaBbCcDdEeFfGgHhIiJjKkLlMmNnOoPpQqRrSsTtUuVvWwXxYyZz

Fretabladidenga

The juke box music puzzled a gentle visitor from a quaint valley town. My help squeezed back in again and joined the weavers after six. Verbatim reports were quickly given by Jim Fox to his guy

The juke box music puzzled a gentle visitor from a quaint valley town. My help squeezed back in again and joined the weavers after six. Verbatim reports were quickly given by Jim Fox to his guy

---

The juke box music puzzled a gentle visitor from a quaint valley town. My help squeezed back in again and joined the weavers after six. Verbatim reports were quickly given by Jim Fox to his amazed audience. William said that everything about his jacket was in quite good condition except for the zippers that were there. Lemon curry?

Modus Bold

Robbie de Villiers
2005

AaBbCcDdEeFfGgHhIiJjKkLlMmNnOoPpQqRrSsTtUuVvWwXxYyZz

Fretabladidenga

The juke box music puzzled a gentle visitor from a quaint valley town. My help squeezed back in again and joined the weavers after six. Verbatim reports were quickly given by Jim Fox to his guy

The juke box music puzzled a gentle visitor from a quaint valley town. My help squeezed back in again and joined the weavers after six. Verbatim reports were quickly given by Jim Fox to his guy

---

The juke box music puzzled a gentle visitor from a quaint valley town. My help squeezed back in again and joined the weavers after six. Verbatim reports were quickly given by Jim Fox to his amazed audience. William said that everything about his jacket was in quite good condition except for the zippers that were there. Would you like a plate of yummy lemon curry?

Modus Bold Italic

Robbie de Villiers
2005

AaBbCcDdEeFfGgHhIiJjKkLlMmNnOoPpQqRrSsTtUuVvWwXxYyZz

Fretabladidenga

The juke box music puzzled a gentle visitor from a quaint valley town. My help squeezed back in again and joined the weavers after six. Verbatim reports were quickly given by Jim Fox to his guy amazed audience. William said that everything

The juke box music puzzled a gentle visitor from a quaint valley town. My help squeezed back in again and joined the weavers after six. Verbatim reports were quickly given by Jim Fox to his guy amazed audience. William said that everything

Wilton

Nobodi Roman

Robbie de Villiers
2005

nobodi
bodoni

AaBbCcDdEeFfGgHhIiJjKkLlMmNnOoPpQqRrSsTtUuVvWwXxYyZz123456789

North Condensed Light

Robbie de Villiers
2005

Jaded zombies acted quaintly but kept driving their oxen forward. Six big juicy steaks sizzled in a pan as five workmen left the quarry. West quickly gave Bert handsome prizes for six juicy plums. Watch all five questions asked by experts amaze the judge. Back in June we delivered oxygen equipment of the same size. An inspired calligrapher can create pages of beauty using stick ink, quill, brush, pick-axe, buzz saw, or even strawberry jam for that matter.

Jaded zombies acted quaintly but kept driving their oxen forward. Six big juicy steaks sizzled in a pan as five workmen left the quarry. West quickly gave Bert handsome prizes for six juicy plums. Watch all five questions asked by experts amaze the judge. Back in June we delivered oxygen equipment of the same size. An inspired calligrapher can create pages of beauty using stick ink, quill, brush, pick-axe,

JADED ZOMBIES
ACTED QUAINTLY BUT
KEPT DRIVING THEIR
OXEN FORWARD

NORTH

AaBbCcDdEeFfGgHhIiJjKkLlMmNnOo
PpQqRrSsTtUuVvWwXxYyZz12345678

AaBbCcDdEeFfGgHhIiJjKk
LlMmNnOoPpQqRrSsTtUu
VvWwXxYyZz(123456789)

abcdefghjklmn

This derives from the legend of young Hallvard, of royal lineage, who sacrificed his life in a deed of valour some nine hundred years ago. According to legend, a pregnant woman was fleeing from assailants who had accused her of theft and were therefore trying to kill her. Hallvard was present and wanted to help the woman escape. He rowed her out on the fjord in a boat but was unable to escape the pursuers.

Hallvard and the woman were both killed. They put a millstone around Hallvard's neck and sank his body in the cold water. Shortly after a strange thing happened: his body floated to the surface with the millstone still round his neck. This event led to the canonization of Hallvard, making him a saint. Today, St. Hallvard adorns the Oslo city arms and is known as its patron saint.

Oslo Light

Robbie de Villiers
2005

AaBbCcDdEeFfGgHhIiJjKkLlMmNnOoPpQqRrSsTtUuVvWwXxYyZz123456789

St. Hallvard is Oslo's patron saint

AaBbCcDdEeFfGgHhIiJjKkLlMmNnOoPpQqRrSsTtUuVvWwXxYyZz

Password

Robbie de Villiers
2005

AABBCCDDEEFFGGHHIIJJKKLLMMNNO
PQQRRSSTTUUVVWXXVVZZØ123456789!

WHAT IS YOUR PASSWORD?

Peekaboo

Robbie de Villiers
2005

PEEKABOO

AaBbCcDdEeFfGgHhIiJj KkLlMmNnOoPpQqRrSsTt UuVvWwXxYyZz!?$@ #%*)(=0123456789 0

I SEE YOU!

About sixty codfish eggs will make a quarter pound of very fizzy jelly. Good deal, but who truly enjoys codfish jelly? It's not like it's caviar or anything!

Wilton

Petronella

Sexy qua lijf, doch bang voor het zwempak. Fripon, mixez l'abject whisky qui vidange. Franz jagt im komplett verwahrlosten taxi quer durch Bayern. We have just quoted on nine dozen boxes of gray lamp wicks. We promptly judged antique ivory buckles for the next prize.

Aa Bb Cc Dd Ee Ff Gg Hh Ii Jj Kk Ll Mm Nn Oo Pp Qq Rr Ss Tt Uu Vv Ww Xx Yy Zz

Pippin is a very little dog, a very little dog indeed. He loves to bark & strut his stuff while ruling over all other beings. Every day he goes

AaBbCcDdEeFfGgHhIiJjKkLlMmNnOoPpQq
RrSsTtUuVvWwXxYyZz?!&@0123456789 0

Pippin is a very little dog, a very little dog indeed. He loves to bark & strut his stuff while ruling over all the other creatures. Every day he goes to work and designs many great things. Because of this, his office pals ignore his shortcomings. Even when he barks out loud while they're on the phone with clients, they look at Pippin & have to laugh

Pippin Regular?

info@wiltonfoundry.com

Pippin Italic

Robbie de Villiers
2005

AaBbCcDdEeFfGgHhIiJj
KkLlMmNnOoPpQqRrS
sTtUuVvWwXxYyZz&€
01234567890

Pippin Italic &

Pippin is a very little dog, a very little dog indeed. He loves to bark & strut his stuff

Pippin is a very little dog, a very little dog indeed. He loves to bark & strut his stuff while ruling over all other creatures. Every day he goes to work and designs lots of great things. Because of this, his office pals ignore his many shortcomings. Even when he barks out loud while they are on the phone with clients, they look at Pippin and have to laugh

Pippin Bold

Robbie de Villiers
2005

[AaBbCcDdEeFfGgHhIi
JjKkLlMmNnOoPpQqR
rSsTtUuVvWwXxYyZz]

PiPPIN BOLD!

PIPPIN IS A VERY LITTLE DOG, A VERY LITTLE DOG IN-
DEED. HE LOVES TO BARK & STRUT HIS STUFF WHILE
RULING OVER ALL OTHER BEINGS. EVERY DAY HE GOES

Pippin Bold Italic

Robbie de Villiers
2005

AaBbCcDdEeFfGgHhIiJjKkLl
MmNnOoPpQqRrSsTtUuVv
WwXxYyZz!?&@()0123456789

Pippin is a very little dog, a very little dog indeed. He loves to bark & strut his stuff while ruling over all the other creatures. Every day he goes to work and designs many great things. Because of this, his office pals ignore his shortcomings. Even when he barks really loud...

Pippin is a very little dog, a very little dog indeed. He loves to bark & strut his stuff while ruling over all other creatures. Every day he goes to work and designs lots of great things. Because of this, his office pals ignore his many shortcomings. Even when he barks

Pippin Bold Italic

AaBbCcDdEeFfGgHhIiJjKkLlMmNnOoPpQqRrSsTtUuVvWwXxYyZz

Grumpy wizards make toxic brew for the evil Queen and Jack. It was the end of the month and their paychecks were late again. Again! There's only so much time that a wizard will work for free. Making magic potions and casting spells on unfavorable squires is no piece of cake. Besides, the castle dungeon is not the safest of work environments. So the grumpy wizards banded together to teach the evil Queen a lesson. Their toxic brew would attack where it hurt most...her vanity. It was excellent in design & would accomplish a perfect amount of "ugly" after being

SPARK

Grumpy wizards make toxic brew for the evil Queen and Jack. It was the end of the month and their paychecks were late again. Again! There's only so much time that a wizard will work for free. Making magic potions and casting spells

0123456789 0

Sepia

Sepia Regular & Italic

Robbie de Villiers
2005

AaBbCcDdEeFfGgHhIiJjKkLlMm
NnOoPpQqRrSsTtUuVvWwXxYy
Zz)(?!01234567890@#$%^&*§¢£¥¤

Sepia tone is a type of monochrome photographic image in which the picture appears in shades of brown as opposed to greyscale as in a black & white image. It was originally produced by adding a pigment made from the Sepia cuttlefish to the positive print of a photograph taken with any number of negative pro

THE CHEMICAL PROCESS INVOLVED CONVERTS ANY OF THE REMAINING METALLIC SILVER TO A SULPHIDE WHICH IS MUCH MORE RESISTANT TO BREAKDOWN OVER TIME. THIS IS WHY MANY "OLD TIME" PHOTOGRAPHS ARE SEPIA TONED—THOSE ARE THE ONES THAT HAVE SURVIVED UNTIL TODAY. CUTTLEFISH HAVE INK, LIKE SQUID AND OCTOPUSES. THIS INK WAS FORMERLY AN IMPORTANT DYE, CALLED SEPIA. TODAY ARTIFICIAL DYES HAVE REPLACED NATURAL SEPIA. CUTTLEFISH ARE CAUGHT FOR FOOD, THOUGH SQUID IS MORE POPULAR. CUTTLEFISH EYES ARE AMONG THE MOST DEVELOPED IN THE ANIMAL KINGDOM. THEY'VE GOT SIMILAR EYES TO HUMANS, BUT THE PUPIL IS A SMOOTHLY-CURVING

Cuttlefish have ink, like squid and octopuses. This ink was formerly an important dye, called sepia. Today artificial dyes have replaced natural sepia. Cuttlefish are caught for food, though squid is more popular. Cuttle fish eyes are among the most developed in the animal kingdom. They have similar eyes to humans, but the pupil is a smoothly-curving "w" shape. Although they can't see color, they can perceive the polarity of light, which essentially enhances their perception of contrast. They have two spots of concentrated sensor cells on their retina (known as fovea), one to look more forward, and one to look more backwards. The lenses, instead

ABCDEFGHIJKLMNOPQRSTUVWXYZabcdefghijklmnopqrstuvw
xyz1234567890-=[]\;',./~!@#$%^&*()+{}|'":<>?-~¢£¥¤¦§¨©ª«®¯°±=µ¶=»
¼½¾¿ÀÁÂÃÄÅÆÇÈÉÊËÌÍÎÏÐÑØÒÓÔÕ×ØÙÚÛÜÝÞßàáâãäåæçè
éêëìíîïðñòóôõö÷øùúûüýþÿæçß=™

Sepia Italic

{ *Sepia tone is a type of monochrome photographic image in which the picture appears in shades of brown as opposed to greyscale as in a black-and-white image. It was originally produced by adding a pigment made from the Sepia cuttlefish to the positive print of a photograph taken with any number of negative processes. The chemical process involved converts remaining metallic silver to a sulphide which is* }

*AaBbCcDdEeFfGgHhIiJjKkLlMmNn
OoPpQqRrSsTtUuVvWwXxYyZz*

Robbie de Villiers
2005

Entire family consists of Light, Regular, Italic, Small Caps, Bold, Bold Italic, Outline, and Serif.

Listen. Ask. Listen. There are many wonderful things that will never be done if you don't do them. It's not what you say, it's what you do. The difficulty lies not so much in developing new ideas as in escaping from the old ones. Things do not remain, but their effects do. It seems that when the back of greed is broken, the human spirit soars into regions of unselfishness. We are rich only through what we give, and poor only through what we refuse & keep.

Listen. Ask. Listen. There are many wonderful things that will never be done if you don't do them. It's not what you say, it's what you do. The difficulty lies not so much in developing new ideas as in escaping from the old ones. Things do not remain, but their effects do. It seems that when the back of greed is broken, the human spirit soars into regions of unselfishness. We are rich only through what we give, and poor only through what we refuse & keep.

Listen. Ask. Listen. There are many wonderful things that will never be done if you don't do them. It's not what you say, it's what you do. The difficulty lies not so much in developing new ideas as in escaping from the old ones. Things do not remain, but their effects do. It seems that when the back of greed is broken, the human spirit soars into regions of unselfishness. We are rich only through what we give, and poor only through what we refuse & keep.

LISTEN. ASK. LISTEN. THERE ARE MANY WONDERFUL THINGS THAT WILL NEVER BE DONE IF YOU DON'T DO THEM. IT'S NOT WHAT YOU SAY, IT'S WHAT YOU DO. THE DIFFICULTY LIES NOT SO MUCH IN DEVELOPING NEW IDEAS AS IN ESCAPING FROM THE OLD ONES. THINGS DO NOT REMAIN, BUT THEIR EFFECTS DO. IT SEEMS THAT WHEN THE BACK OF GREED IS BROKEN, THE HUMAN SPIRIT SOARS INTO REGIONS OF UNSELFISHNESS. WE ARE RICH ONLY THROUGH WHAT WE GIVE, AND POOR ONLY THROUGH WHAT WE REFUSE AND KEEP. LISTEN. ASK...

The difficulty lies not so much in developing new ideas as in escaping from the old ones...

vecta

AaBbCcDdEeFfGg
HhIiJjKkLlMmNnO
oPpQqRrSsTtUuVv
WwXxYyZz!o12345
67890")(@#$%&
*(){}~¢£¥€§<>!?"

There are many wonderful things that'll never be done if you don't do them. It is not what you say, it is what you do. Listen. Ask. Listen.

Listen. Ask. Listen. There are many wonderful things that will never be done if you don't do them. It's not what you say, it's what you do. The difficulty lies not so much in developing new ideas as in escaping from the old ones. Things do not remain, but their effects do. It seems that when the back of greed is broken, the human spirit soars into regions of unselfishness.

AaBbCcDdEeFfGgHhI
IJjKkLlMmNnOoPpQq
RrSsTtUuVvWwXxYyZ
z@$^&*()+{}~¢£¥€

LISTEN. ASK. LISTEN.

Listen.Ask

AaBbCcDdEeFfGgHhIi JjKkLlMmNnOoPpQqR rSsTtUuVvWwXxYyZz!

(?!01234567890@# $%^&*()+{}~¢£¥€¦ §01234567890!<>)

0123456789

Listen. Ask. Listen. There are many wonderful things that will never be done if you don't do them. It's not what you say, it's what you do. The difficulty lies not so much in developing new ideas as in escaping from the old ones. Things do not remain, but their effects

It seems that when the back of greed is broken, the human spirit soars into regions of unselfishness. We are rich only through what we give, and poor only through what we refuse to keep. Regardless of everything else, remember to... "Listen. Ask. Listen."

Listen. Ask. Listen. There are many wonderful things that will never be done if you don't do them. It's not what you say, it's what you do. The difficulty lies not so much in developing new ideas as in escaping from the old ones. Things don't remain, but their effects do. When the back of greed is broken, the human spirit soars into new regions of unselfishness. Listen. Ask.

Listen. Ask. Listen. There are many wonderful things that will never be done if you don't do them. It's not what you say, it's what you do. The difficulty lies not so much in developing new ideas as in escaping from the old ones. Things do not remain, but their effects do. It seems that when the back of greed is broken, the human spirit soars into regions of unselfishness. We are rich only through what we give, and poor only through what we refuse & keep.

Listen. Ask. Listen. There are many wonderful things that will never be done if you don't do them. It's not what you say, it's what you do. The difficulty lies not so much in developing new ideas as in escaping from the old ones. Things do not remain, but their effects do. It seems that when the back of greed is broken, the human spirit soars into regions of unselfishness. We are rich only through what we give, and poor only through what we refuse & keep.

Listen. Ask. Listen. There are many wonderful things that will never be done if you don't do them. It's not what you say, it's what you do. The difficulty lies not so much in developing new ideas as in escaping from the old ones. Things do not remain, but their effects do. It seems that when the back of greed is broken, the human spirit soars into regions of unselfishness. We are rich only through what we give, and poor only through what we refuse & keep.

Listen. Ask. Listen. There are many wonderful things that will never be done if you don't do them. It's not what you say, it's what you do. The difficulty lies not so much in developing new ideas as in escaping from the old ones. Things do not remain, but their effects do. It seems that when the back of greed is broken, the human spirit soars into regions of unselfishness. We are rich only through what we give, and poor only through what we refuse & keep.

FTF Vecta

Robbie de Villiers
2005

Entire family consists of Light, Regular, Italic, Small Caps, Bold, Bold Italic, Outline, and Serif.

Wilton

Appendix A:
Character Reference Chart

The chart shown opposite corresponds to the U.S. ASCII (American Standard Code for Information Interchange) keyboard layout. This chart is intended for general reference only. Individual keyboard and font layouts may vary.

A	B	C	D	E	F	G	H	I	J	K	L	M	N	O	P	Q	R	S
a A	b B	c C	d D	e E	f F	g G	h H	i I	j J	k K	l L	m M	n N	o O	p P	q Q	r R	s S
t T	u U	v V	w W	x X	y Y	z Z	A Sh-A	B Sh-B	C Sh-C	D Sh-D	E Sh-E	F Sh-F	G Sh-G	H Sh-H	I Sh-I	J Sh-J	K Sh-K	L Sh-L
M Sh-M	N Sh-N	O Sh-O	P Sh-P	Q Sh-Q	R Sh-R	S Sh-S	T Sh-T	U Sh-U	V Sh-V	W Sh-W	X Sh-X	Y Sh-Y	Z Sh-Z	1 1	2 2	3 3	4 4	5 5
6 6	7 7	8 8	9 9	0 0	! Sh-1	@ Sh-2	# Sh-3	$ Sh-4	% Sh-5	^ Sh-6	& Sh-7	* Sh-8	(Sh-9	) Sh-0	, ,	. .	; ;	: Sh-;
- -	/ /	? Sh-/	' '	" Sh-'	¡ Op-1 Alt-0161	¿ Sh-Op-/ Alt-0191	– Op-- Alt-0173	+ Sh-=	≈ Op-x Alt-0215	÷ Op-/ Alt-0247	= =	± Sh-Op-= Alt-0177	< Sh-,	> Sh-.	[[	]]	{ Sh-[	} Sh-]
' Op-] Alt-0145	' Sh-Op-] Alt-0146	" Op-[Alt-0147	" Sh-Op-[Alt-0148	‹ Sh-Op-3 Alt-0139	› Sh-Op-4 Alt-0155	« Op-\ Alt-0171	» Sh-Op-\ Alt-0187	‚ Sh-Op-0 Alt-0130	„ Sh-Op-W Alt-0132	— Sh-Op-- Alt-0151	~ Sh-`	\ \	¦ Sh-\	_ Sh--	… Op-; Alt-0133	° Sh-Op-8 Alt-0176	• Sh-Op-9 Alt-0183	● Op-8 Alt-0149
ä Op-U A Alt-0228	â Op-I A Alt-0226	á Op-E A Alt-0225	à Op-` A Alt-0224	ã Op-N A Alt-0227	å Op-A Alt-0229	ë Op-U E Alt-0235	ê Op-I E Alt-0234	é Op-E E Alt-0233	è Op-` E Alt-0232	ï Op-U I Alt-0239	î Op-I I Alt-0238	í Op-E I Alt-0237	ì Op-` I Alt-0236	ö Op-U O Alt-0246	ô Op-I O Alt-0244	ó Op-E O Alt-0243	ò Op-` O Alt-0242	õ Op-N O Alt-0245
ü Op-U U Alt-0252	û Op-I U Alt-0251	ú Op-E U Alt-0250	ù Op-` U Alt-0249	Ä Op-U Sh-A Alt-0196	Â Op-I Sh-A Alt-0194	Á Op-E Sh-A Alt-0193	À Op-` Sh-A Alt-0192	Ã Op-N Sh-A Alt-0195	Å Sh-Op-A Alt-0197	Ë Op-U Sh-E Alt-0203	Ê Op-I Sh-E Alt-0202	É Op-E Sh-E Alt-0201	È Op-` Sh-E Alt-0200	Ï Sh-Op-F Alt-0207	Î Sh-Op-D Alt-0206	Í Sh-Op-S Alt-0205	Ì Op-` Sh-I Alt-0204	Ö Op-U Sh-O Alt-0214
Ô Op-I Sh-O Alt-0212	Ó Op-E Sh-O Alt-0211	Ò Op-` Sh-O Alt-0210	Õ Op-N Sh-O Alt-0213	Ü Op-U Sh-U Alt-0220	Û Op-I Sh-U Alt-0219	Ú Op-E Sh-U Alt-0218	Ù Op-` Sh-U Alt-0217	ç Op-C Alt-0231	Ç Sh-Op-C Alt-0199	ñ Op-N N Alt-0241	Ñ Op-N Sh-N Alt-0209	ø Op-O Alt-0248	Ø Sh-Op-O Alt-0216	ß Op-S Alt-0223	æ Op-' Alt-0230	Æ Sh-Op-' Alt-0198	œ Op-Q Alt-0156	Œ Sh-Op-Q Alt-0140
ð Ctrl-B Alt-0240	Đ Ctrl-A Alt-0208	ł Ctrl-D	Ł Ctrl-C	š Ctrl-F Alt-0154	Š Ctrl-E Alt-0138	ÿ Op-U Y Alt-0255	ý Ctrl-H Alt-0253	Ÿ Op-U Sh-Y Alt-0159	Ý Ctrl-G Alt-0221	ž Ctrl-O	Ž Ctrl-N	þ Ctrl-L Alt-0254	Þ Ctrl-K Alt-0222	ı Sh-Op-B	a Op-9 Alt-0170	o Op-0 Alt-0186		
¨ Sh-Op-U Alt-0168	ˆ Sh-Op-I Alt-0136	´ Sh-Op-E Alt-0180	` `	˜ Sh-Op-N Alt-0152	˚ Op-K	¯ Sh-Op-, Alt-0175	˘ Sh-Op-.	˙ Op-H	˝ Sh-Op-G	ˇ Sh-Op-T	¸ Sh-Op-Z Alt-0184	˛ Sh-Op-X	£ Op-3 Alt-0163	¥ Op Y Alt-0165	ƒ Op-F Alt-0131	¢ Op-4 Alt-0162	€ Sh-Op-2 Alt-0164	
© Op-G Alt-0169	® Op-R Alt-0174	π Op-P	™ Op-2 Alt-0153	⁄ Sh-Op-1	‰ Sh-Op-R Alt-0137	µ Op-M Alt-0181	§ Op-6 Alt-0167	† Op-T Alt-0134	‡ Sh-Op-7 Alt-0135	¶ Op-7 Alt-0182	¦ Ctrl-[Alt-0166	¹ Ctrl-W Alt-0185	² Ctrl-Z Alt-0178	³ Ctrl-Y Alt-0179	¼ Ctrl-V Alt-0188	½ Ctrl-U Alt-0189	¾ Ctrl-X Alt-0190	

U.S. ACSII keyboard layout; others may vary. This chart is intended for general reference. Individual font layouts may vary.

[gray box] Characters generally not available in Windows.

[half-gray box] Characters generally not available in Macintosh OS.

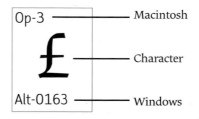

Op-3 ——— Macintosh
£ ——— Character
Alt-0163 ——— Windows

Appendix B:
Foundry Contacts

Baseline Fonts Design & Type Co.
4421 N. Rushwood Court
Bel Aire, KS 67226 USA
TEL 316-260-5294
www.baselinefonts.com
info@baselinefonts.com

Blue Vinyl Fonts
204 Wilson Mountain Road
Falkville, AL 35622 USA
www.bvfonts.com
bluevinylfonts@bvfonts.com

Device Fonts
2 Blake Mews
Kew Gardens
TW9 3GA
United Kingdom
TEL +44 (0)208 896 0626
FAX +44 (0)208 439 9080
www.devicefonts.co.uk
info@devicefonts.co.uk

E-phemera Fonts
489 Mavis Drive
Los Angeles, CA 90065 USA
TEL 323-646-4798
www.ahleman.com
ephemera@ahleman.com

Font Brothers Inc.
5117 38th Avenue S.
Minneapolis, MN 55417 USA
www.fontbros.com
orders@fontbros.com

Handselecta
160 Ainslie Street, #3
Brooklyn, NY 11211 USA
www.handselecta.com
info@handselecta.com

Jeremy Tankard Typography
The Old Fire Station
39 Church Lane
Lincoln, Lincolnshire
LN2 1QJ
United Kingdom
TEL +44 (0)1522 805 654
FAX +44 (0)1522 805 628
www.typography.net
info@typography.net

Kenn Munk
Ingerslevs Boulevard 4, 2.tv
DK-8000 Århus C
Denmark
TEL +45 26 74 02 42
www.kennmunk.com
info@kennmunk.com

Letterhead Fonts
2763 West Avenue L, #249
Lancaster, CA 93536 USA
TEL 661-951-1939
www.letterheadfonts.com
sales@letterheadfonts.com

Pizzadude
Hedebygade 14, 4th
1754 Kbh V
Denmark
TEL +45 30 25 67 57
www.pizzadude.dk
jakob@pizzadude.dk

Positype
PO Box 42
Athens, GA 30603 USA
TEL 706-546-9353
FAX 706-543-7322
www.positype.com
info@positype.com

Process Type Foundry
523 Jackson Street, #307
St. Paul, MN 55101 USA
TEL 651-228-1541
www.processtypefoundry.com
info@processtypefoundry.com

Rimmer Type Foundry
PO Box 770
Buffalo, NY 14213 USA
TEL 800-722-5080
    716-885-4490
FAX 716-885-4482
www.p22.com/rtf
rimmer@p22.com

Shinn Type Foundry Inc.
364 Sunnyside Avenue
Toronto, ON M6R 2R8
Canada
TEL 416-769-1078
www.shinntype.com
nick@shinntype.com

SparkyType
PO Box 9590
Marion Square
Wellington
New Zealand
TEL +64 4 977 0495
www.sparkytype.com
info@sparkytype.com

Suitcase Type Foundry
Soběslavská 27
130 00 Prague 3
Czech Republic
www.suitcasetype.com
mail@suitcasetype.com

Suomi Type Foundry
Tähtitorninkatu 8 D 22
00140 Helsinki
Finland
TEL +358 50 571 9067
www.type.fi
info@type.fi

Village
168 Second Avenue, #253
New York, NY 10003 USA
TEL 646-654-1506
FAX 646-429-8597
www.vllg.com
village@vllg.com

Virus Fonts
Studio 12
10-11 Archer Street
London
W1D 7AZ
United Kingdom
TEL +44 (0)20 7287 3848
FAX +44 (0)20 7287 3601
www.virusfonts.com
virus@virusfonts.com

Wilton Foundry
43 Old Wagon Road
Wilton, CT 06897 USA
TEL 203-762-5923
www. wiltonfoundry.com
info@wiltonfoundry.com

Appendix C:
Bonus Fonts CD

The 53 indie fonts listed on the following pages are included on an unlocked Bonus Fonts CD-ROM located in a sealed package contained in this book. The fonts are licensed from each contributing foundry for use solely by the owner of this book and may be used only in accordance with the terms set forth in the respective End User License Agreements (EULA). Any further redistribution or transfer of the license to use this software is strictly prohibited. Please consult the individual "read me" files and/or EULA files located in each foundry's directory.

By breaking the sealed package containing this CD-ROM, you are agreeing to be bound by the terms of the license agreement and limited warranty set forth by each foundry. If you do not agree to the terms of said agreements, please do not use these fonts.

Font Format Key
PS = PostScript Type 1
TT = TrueType
OT = OpenType (cross-platform)

PostScript Type 1 was developed by Adobe Systems for use with PostScript output devices. In Mac OS, a Type 1 font consists of an outline font (printer font) and a bitmap font (screen font) that also carries the metrics data. In Windows, a Type 1 font also uses two files, one containing the outlines (.PFB), and one containing the printer font metrics (.PFM). Thousands of PostScript fonts have been developed for use with both Mac OS and Windows, although the same font files cannot be used interchangeably on both platforms.

TrueType, developed by Apple and intended for use with Mac OS 7, was also adopted by Microsoft for use with Windows (.TTF). TrueType fonts consist of a single file used for both screen display and printing, eliminating the need for separate outline and bitmap fonts. TrueType font files also cannot be used interchangeably on both platforms.

OpenType, developed jointly by Adobe and Microsoft, is a font format designed to combine the best of TrueType and PostScript into a single format for use on both Macintosh and Windows platforms. OpenType allows for up to 65,000 glyphs and conditional letter combinations, with easier access to full expert set characters, facilitating multilingual and advanced typography. An OpenType font consists of one font file that can be installed on either Mac OS or Windows, eliminating the need for a separate font file for each platform.

Foundry	Mac Fonts	Win Fonts	Font
Baseline Fonts	PS & TT	PS & TT	Tuscan Loose
Baseline Fonts	PS & TT	PS & TT	Tuscan Condensed
Baseline Fonts	OT	OT	Grit Typesorts
Blue Vinyl	PS & TT	PS & TT	Grumble
Blue Vinyl	PS & TT	PS & TT	Gros Marqueur
Device	PS	PS & TT	Paralucent Condensed Light Italic
Device	PS	PS & TT	Dynasty Light
Device	PS	PS & TT	Bocacurrentcameo
E-Phemera	PS & OT	TT & OT	CABLEGRAM
Font Brothers	TT	TT	Lochen AOE
Font Brothers	TT	TT	Chicken Scratch AOE
Font Brothers	TT	TT	Runtron 1988
Font Brothers	TT	TT	Surfin Bird
Handselecta	PS	PS	
Handselecta	PS	PS	
Jeremy Tankard	OT	OT	Arjowiggins Inuit
Kenn Munk	PS	TT	Ascotone
Kenn Munk	PS	TT	Aether
Kenn Munk	PS	TT	Karmaflage
Kenn Munk	PS	TT	Lineman
Kenn Munk	PS	TT	Psychophante
Letterhead	OT	OT	LHF Café Corina
Pizzadude	TT	TT	Ankertill Brewer
Pizzadude	TT	TT	Empty Head
Pizzadude	TT	TT	Empty Head 2
Pizzadude	TT	TT	Mutaints
Pizzadude	TT	TT	Mutaints Xtra
Pizzadude	TT	TT	Sure Shot
Positype	OT	TT & OT	Truss Ultra Light
Positype	OT	TT & OT	Truss Ultra Light Oblique

Foundry	Mac Fonts	Win Fonts	Font
Process	OT	OT	Entovo
Rimmer	OT	OT	ᑕᐊᓈᐃᐊᑎ ᐁᐢᒪᐠᐁ
Shinntype	PS	PS & TT	**Brown Heavy**
Shinntype	OT	OT	Goodchild Regular
Shinntype	OT	OT	*Goodchild Italic*
Shinntype	PS	PS & TT	**Nicholas Bold**
Shinntype	OT	OT	*Handsome Pro Classic*
Shinntype	OT	OT	**Softmachine**
Sparky	OT	OT	**RUBY**
Sparky	OT	OT	**Sundae**
Suitcase	PS	PS	**ORGOVAN ROUNDED**
Suitcase	PS	PS	**ORGOVAN BRUSH**
Suitcase	PS	PS	**ORGOVAN PUNK**
Suitcase	PS	PS	**ORGOVAN HAIRY**
Suitcase	PS	PS	**ORGOVAN FLOWER POWER**
Suitcase	PS	PS	**ORGOVAN FAT CAP**
Suomi	OT	TT & OT	Caxton Script
Village	OT	OT	Daily
Virus	PS	PS & TT	Olympukes Light
Virus	PS	PS & TT	Olympukes Dark
Wilton	PS, TT & OT	PS, TT & OT	**PASSWORD**
Wilton	PS & TT	PS & TT	Spark
Wilton	PS & TT	PS & TT	*Boondoggle*

PostScript, TrueType, and/or OpenType formats are included or available for the Mac OS and/or Windows operating systems. Not all foundries provide fonts in all available formats/platforms on this CD-ROM.

P-Type Publications is not responsible for errors, omissions, or technical problems inherent in the font software or in its accompanying documentation. Please contact the individual foundries for more information on licensing, upgrades, or support.

Index

Legal Information

The Indie Fonts Series

The *Indie Fonts* series of type specimen books showcases the diversity to be found in the international type and design community. Take a look at the foundries that were featured in the first two volumes—together with *Indie Fonts 3*, these books show the bounty of possibilities waiting to be discovered by the typographic explorer.

Indie Fonts

Altered Ego Fonts/USA
Astigmatic One Eye/USA
Carter & Cone Type/USA
The Chank Company/USA
Font Diner/USA
fontBoy/USA
Fountain/Sweden
GarageFonts/USA
International House of Fonts/USA
LettError/The Netherlands
P22 type foundry/USA
Psy-Ops/USA
Synfonts/USA
Test Pilot Collective/USA
Typebox/USA
Typeco/USA
Typodermic/Canada
Typotheque/The Netherlands

Indie Fonts 2

Atomic Media/USA
Feliciano Type Foundry/Portugal
Galápagos/USA
Holland Fonts/USA
The Identikal Foundry/United Kingdom
ingoFonts/Germany
Jukebox/USA
MVB Fonts/USA
Neufville Digital/The Netherlands
Nick's Fonts/USA
No Bodoni Typography/USA
Parkinson Type Design/USA
Mark Simonson Studio/USA
Sherwood Type Collection/USA
Storm Type Foundry/Czech Republic
Terminal Design/USA
Underware/The Netherlands
Union Fonts/United Kingdom
YouWorkForThem/USA

Colophon

This book was designed by
James Grieshaber.

The text face is *Alisal*,
designed by Matthew Carter
from Carter & Cone.

The headlines and labeling are set
in various weights of *Faceplate*,
designed by Rodrigo Xavier
Cavazos from Psy/Ops.